EXPERIMENTS IN PSYCHOLOGY

Experiments in PSYCHOLOGY

S.M. Mohsin
Formerly, Professor and Head of the
Department of Psychology,
Patna University (Patna)

MOTILAL BANARSIDASS
Delhi • Mumbai • Chennai • Kolkata
Bangalore • Varanasi • Pune • Patna

8th Reprint: Delhi, 2016
Second Edition: Delhi, 1982

ISBN: 978-81-208-2975-6 (Cloth)
ISBN: 978-81-208-0875-1 (Paper)

Also available at:

MOTILAL BANARSIDASS

41 U.A. Bungalow Road, Jawahar Nagar, Delhi 110 007
8 Mahalaxmi Chamber, 22 Bhulabhai Desai Road, Mumbai 400 026
203 Royapettah High Road, Mylapore, Chennai 600 004
236, 9th Main III Block, Jayanagar, Bengaluru 560 011
8 Camac Street, Kolkata 700 017
Ashok Rajpath, Patna 800 004
Chowk, Varanasi 221 001

Printed in India

by RP Jain at NAB Printing Unit,
A-44, Naraina Industrial Area, Phase I, New Delhi–110028
and published by JP Jain for Motilal Banarsidass Publishers (P) Ltd,
41 U.A. Bungalow Road, Jawahar Nagar, Delhi-110007

To

My Wife

MAHFOOZA MOHSIN

PREFACE

PSYCHOLOGY is a biosocial science. As a social science, its subject matter overlaps with the other social sciences. As a biological science, its methodology has been modelled after the biological sciences. That is why training in laboratory methods is a desideratum for a course in psychology. Experiments in psychology, however, have not reached the level attained by the biological sciences. Nevertheless, psychologists are seeking to introduce experimental methodology even in such domains of their interest which were at first deemed out-of-bound for the experimental method. Social psychology is an example. The need, therefore, to make the training in experimental psychology more meaningful is being increasingly emphasised, which acted as the main stimulus for writing this book.

During all the years he has been associated with training undergraduate and post-graduate students in the use of laboratory methods, the feeling has been growing in the writer that a mechanical approach to the laboratory exercises cuts no ice. A laboratory manual, of which there are many in existence today, though of great help to the student, falls short of creating in him the desired orientation. The principal object in preparing this volume, which will be evident from the first three chapters, is to make the student realise that any practical work he is called upon to perform poses a challenge to his understanding, insightfulness, initiative, and constructive abilities. Every step that he takes has a rationale of which he should be no less aware than his instructor or the author of a laboratory manual. With this end in view, all basic concepts relevant to a given experiment have been brought home to the student in a simple and straightforward manner.

Every chapter of the book, from the fourth to the last, contains one or more complete reports of experiments, based on purely hypothetical data. Accounts of related problems and, in several cases, description of the ways to answer them, supplement the detailed reports. Appendix II lists all the problems thus indicated, numbering as many as one hundred and sixty-five. These may serve as a guide in planning an undergraduate or post-graduate laboratory course in psychology.

With the increasing use of the method of objective observation and the growing tendency to introduce the quantitative methods in psychological research, group experiments have almost supplanted individual experiments. But the average undergraduate or post-graduate training programme can ill afford to fulfil the requirements of group experiments. To give the student at least a nodding acquaintance with group experiments, a chapter has been appended (Appendix I) which brings to the fore some special features of group experiments, like selection of sample, design of group experiments, and treatment of group data. A way has also been suggested for utilising data pooled from individual experiments by fitting them into a group experiment design.

Appendix III contains drawings of the apparatus mentioned and described in the text. It will, however, be noticed that more than two thirds of the experiments reported or described do not require any sophisticated apparatus so that the book retains its value even for conducting such courses that avoid the use of costly apparatus and have to depend mainly on locally improvised materials.

I express my sincere thanks to those senior teachers of psychology in the different universities of India and my own colleagues to whom I read out a few chapters in the earlier stage of the preparation of this volume, for their appreciation of its value and their encouragement during the progress of this work. I am thankful to the National Book Trust authorities for subsidising its publication. Special acknowledgment is made to my son Dr. M. A. Mohsin, for his meticulously drawn sketches of the apparatus that have been reproduced in Appendix III.

April, 1975 S. M. Mohsin

CONTENTS

CHAPTER I

The Experimental Method

What is an Experiment ?

PSYCHOLOGY is the study of human behaviour. Behaviour like all other facts is caused. To understand human behaviour we have to discover its causes, and when we know them we may try to utilise them to control human behaviour. We know that interest in a task helps in learning the task. In teaching children we, therefore, try to create the child's interest in what he learns. We know that if some one dislikes a person he will not be sincere and just in dealing with that person. If we desire to change his behaviour to that person, we will try to change the dislike into liking, so that behaviour may be changed accordingly.

In order to discover the causes of human behaviour, psychology applies the same methods that are used by other sciences. The scientists observe the conditions under which an event takes place. They find that the same conditions are always present whenever the event occurs. The conditions are absent when the event does not occur. They relate these conditions to the occurrence of the event. In other cases, scientists find that whenever there is some change in the value or extent of an existing condition, there is also a change in a particular fact or event. That condition is supposed to be related to the event. When the scientist discovers the causes of facts and events happening in nature by observing them, he sometimes finds that his observations do not provide him with the correct information. To make sure that his discovery is correct, he also performs an experiment. He brings about the condition in his laboratory to see if the fact or event is produced. The chemist combines two atoms of hydrogen with one atom of oxygen and finds that the result of the combination is the formation of water.

To discover and ascertain the causes of behaviour, the psychologist too uses the methods of observation and experiment. He performs his experiments in much the same way as other scientists do. The objects of his experiment, however, are persons. Some psychologists are interested in the study of animal behaviour also ; the objects of their experiments are animals. The persons on whom experiments are done in psychology are called subjects of the experiment. One who performs the experiment is called the experimenter. Suppose an experiment is done to find out the effect of a sudden loud noise on the breathing of the subject. The experimenter observes the subject's breathing in a quiet condition, that is, when there is no noise. He then bursts a cracker without warning to the subject. He notices that the subject's breathing becomes irregular, sometimes quick and sometimes slow. He comes to the conclusion that sudden noise produces a change in breathing. He has discovered a relation between sudden noise and breathing.

Variables in an Experiment

Breathing or sudden noise is a fact or event. Each fact or event belongs to a class of similar facts or events that vary or change in quantity or quality. A noise may be of different intensities of loudness ; it may be a continuous or discontinuous noise ; it may occur for a single moment or for several minutes or hours. Similarly, the breathing too may vary in all sorts of ways ; it may be regular or irregular, rapid or slow, deep or shallow. The noise as well as the breathing, is, therefore, called a variable. A variable is any fact or event that does not always have the same quality or quantity. Thus height, weight, intelligence, age, shape and size of letters, hours of work, and everything else that you may use in an experiment is a variable.

In an experiment we try to find out relationship between any two or more variables. You may try to find out the relationship between intensity of light and perception of colour, increase in temperature and sensation of heat, amount of difference between any two values of a stimulus and perception of the difference, amount of noise and loss of concentration, amount of learning material and speed of learning, knowledge of how one perfoms a task and improvement in the performance, experience of success or failure and the motivation to perform a task, and so on. In every case you are trying to find out a relation between the variables.

An experiment is done not only to discover a relation. It is also done to ascertain a relation that is already discovered. For example, workers in a factory used to work ceaselessly for eight to ten hours. Some one got interested in discovering the effect on the performance if the work period was broken and a rest was provided in between. An experiment revealed that the amount of production increased and the quality of the production improved with the introduction of the break in work period. Similar experiments were then planned to ascertain the relationship between rest interval and quantity and quality of output.

Exploratory and Confirmatory Experiments

An experiment that is done to discover a relationship is called exploratory experiment. The experimenter explores what would happen if he introduces a variable in a situation, or if he does something to an existing variable. For example, how will the subject's perception of a line be affected if he is required to judge the length of a line after two other persons have already reported their judgment in his presence ? A social variable is introduced in the perceptual situation. It may be found that the subject's judgment is influenced by the judgment of the other persons ; the discovery is made that social factors influence perception. In other experiments, the experimenter starts with the supposition, for example, that frustration produces aggression—obstacle in the on-going activity of a person leads the person to attack or destroy what causes the obstacle. Such a supposition is called a hypothesis. The experimenter plans an experiment to test the hypothesis, to ascertain the relationship between frustration and aggression. Such experiments are called confirmatory experiments. Their purpose is to confirm, or make sure about, an expected relationship.

Dependent and Independent Variables

An experiment is done to explore or confirm a relationship. The relationship is that of dependance. One variable depends upon the other. Suppose you find a relationship between meaningfulness of the learning material and speed of learning. Speed of learning then depends upon meaningfulness ; the greater the meaningfulness, the faster the learning. The speed of learning is, therefore, called dependent variable ; meaningfulness is independent variable. Similarly, rest between work periods is independent variable ; output of work is dependent variable. Sudden noise is independent variable ; change in breathing is dependent variable. In an experiment one discovers and confirms a relationship between an independent variable and a dependent variable.

Kinds of Independent and Dependent Variables

The independent variable may be an object of the environment, for example, light or sound of a given intensity, continuous or discontinuous noise, a heavy or a light weight, kind of the learning material—meaningful or nonsense, duration of rest, etc. Each one is called a stimulus variable It is so called because each one is a quality of an external object or event and we become aware of an external object or event only when it stimulates the sense organs.

The independent variable may also be a characteristic of the organism, for example, your subject's rich or poor home, his race or caste, his age, his intelligence, his sex, his being married or unmarried, his learning capacity, his skills and habits, his level of education, and so on. These are called organismic variables. These are more or less permanent characteristics of persons. There may be other temporary characteristics or states of the organism, for example, your subject's level of motivation, his interest in performing the given task, his freshness or tiredness, his feelings of ease or discomfort, of success or failure, his emotion of anger or fear, love or hate, hope or despair, and so on. These temporary or transient organismic variables may be dependent or independent according to the situation of the experiment. For example, anger is an independent variable in relation to the attack that it evokes ; motivation, freshness or fatigue, is an independent variable in relation to the quantity or quality of the subject's performance—a highly motivated subject performs better as compared to a subject working with poor motivation, or, output is higher when a worker is fresh than when he is fatigued. Anger, motivation, fatigue, or other temporary states of the organism may also be a dependent variable. Obstruction in a person's activity produces anger, offer of reward increases motivation, continuous work produces fatigue.

Besides the temporary organismic variable which, as noted above, may also be a dependent variable in an experiment, your subject's speed of performance or learning, his errors of perception, the amount or quality of work done by him, and so on, are other dependent variables. These variables are called response variables.

Ways of Manipulating the Independent Variable

You know the difference between naturalistic observation and experiment. In naturalistic observation, you observe the relationship between the independent and the dependent variables. In an experiment you first do something with the independent variable and then observe what happens to the dependent variable. Doing something with the independent variable is called manipulation. There are two ways of manipulating the independent variable. One way is to make it appear in one situation and disappear in another situation and observe how this affects the dependent variable. Suppose you are trying to find the effect of noise on the solving of complex arithmetical problems. You let your subject work on the problems in the absence of noise and you note the time taken in solving them. You then let him work on similar problems under noise and you again note the time taken. If you find that your subject has taken longer time in the second case, you explain this as due to the distraction from the noise. The situation in which you introduce the independent variable is called the experimental condition. The situation from which it is withdrawn is called the control condition.

The other way to manipulate the independent variable is to change its value, increase or decrease its amount. If the change in the value of the independent variable is followed by a change in the value of the dependent variable, you presume that the two are related. Suppose you want to determine the relationship between the number of items in a list of words and the speed of learning the list. The independent variable here is the number of items or the amount of learning material. You cannot remove the independent variable altogether in this case, in order to bring about the control condition. Its complete disappearance would mean zero or no amount of learning material ; there will be nothing to learn. All that you can do, therefore, is to change the value or amount of the material, i.e., increase or decrease it, by having lists containing different numbers of items. If you find that a shorter list is learned more quickly than a longer list, you come to the conclusion that the speed of learning depends upon the amount of the learning material. When you manipulate the independent variable by changing its value, you cannot have a separate control condition, besides the experimental condition. You have two or more experimental conditions. Each experimental condition functions as a control for the other experimental condition. If a list containing, say, 12 items takes a longer time to learn than a list containing 8 items, learning of the second list becomes control condition for the learning of the first list.

Extraneous Variables

When you perform an experiment, you come across not only a single independent variable which you manipulate in the experiment in one of the two ways, in order to find what happens to the dependent variable. There will be other independent variables also that you do not manipulate in the experiment. These also influence the dependent variable. For example, in the experiment on the relation between amount of learning material and speed of learning, there will be other independent variables too. These are : the kind of the material—whether it is meaningful or nonsense, the manner of presentation of the material—visual or auditory, size of the print—whether the letters composing the words are large or small, the time for which each item is presented, and so on. Each one will have its own influence on the time taken in learning the list. At the moment, however, you are not interested in finding their effects on the dependent variable. Such independent variables are called extraneous or additional variables that affect the dependent variable. The independent variable which you manipulate in the experiment is called the experimental variable.

The experimenter exercises his control over this variable by manipulating it. He has also to exercise his control over the extraneous independent variables by keeping them constant or the same in all conditions of the experiment. If he does not do this, the result of the experiment will be uncertain. Suppose, he presents the longer list by **showing** the items and the shorter list by **reading** out the items, or, he presents both lists visually, but the items of the longer list are shown at the rate of one second each, while those of the shorter list at the rate of two seconds each. In such a case if he finds a difference between the two lists in the speed of learning, it may be due to the difference in the mode of presentation of the lists, or to the difference in the exposure time of the items. One cannot arrive at a definite conclusion from the result of the experiment. But if the two conditions of the experiment differ only in the length of the learning lists, one can be sure about the result. One can say with confidence that the observed difference in the speed of learning is due to the difference in the amount of the learning material. One can do this because the extraneous independent variables have been controlled or kept constant.

Experimental Control

It will be clear from the above that when you plan or design an experiment, you have two considerations. The first one is how to manipulate the experimental variable ; whether the design of your experiment will involve one control condition and one or more experimental conditions, or it would involve two or more experimental conditions. The second consideration is how to control the extraneous variables ; how to keep them constant. The design of an experiment thus fulfils these two requirements : (1) controlling the experimental variable and (2) controlling the extraneous variables. When the extraneous independent variables are stimulus variables, the matter of controlling them is simple. You can arrange to have the values of all these variables the same or constant in the two or more conditions of the experiment. You will use in the different conditions, for example, the same kind of task, to be performed in the same situation and in the same manner, at the same time of the day, under the same conditions of temperature, lighting and atmosphere, at the same place, in the same surroundings and so on. When you are using the same subject in the two or more conditions of the experiment, you have no problem about controlling the more or less permanent organismic variables also. All the permanent characteristics of your subject will be identical in whatever conditions of experiment you use that subject. The main difficulty will arise in controlling the transient organismic independent variables. To solve this you will have to use special designs of experiment.

In an experiment you have to use more than one condition. When you use the same subject in all the conditions, the conditions have to be arranged in a certain order ; one condition should come before or after another condition. The fact of coming before or after will have its own effect ; this effect is called, therefore, effect of sequence. The sequence effect may be of different kinds. Having performed the same task in one condition, the subject's interest in performing it may decline in the condition that follows. The performance in the preceding condition may also produce fatigue which will influence the subject's performance in the next condition. No doubt sufficient rest between the conditions may clear out the fatigue effect. Rest cannot, however, kill the feeling of monotony or boredom, which requires change of task. Sometimes repeated performance of a task may produce progressive improvement ; the improvement will be greater in the condition that follows. The subject's performance in this condition will be better on this account. In short, the subject's performance in the next condition will improve on account of practice, or it will deteriorate—become poorer, on account of fatigue. Suppose an experiment is done for finding the difference in the reaction time to a visual and to an auditory stimulus. In a reaction time experiment, the experimenter exposes a stimulus—a light, a sound or any other stimulus. The subject is instructed to press a key immediately after the presentation of the stimulus. The time between the presentation of the stimulus and the occurrence of the response, i.e., pressing the key, is measured. This time is the reaction time of the subject. If you take a single trial of the reaction time of the subject to each of the light and sound stimuli, you can come to no conclusion. The reaction time to one or the other stimulus may be small or large as a result of chance only. In order to make a reliable estimate of your subject's reaction time to each kind of stimulus, you have to take several trials of each and then calculate the Mean or Average for each. If you obtain different Means in the two conditions of the experiment, you will come to the conclusion that your subject's reaction time, say, to a visual stimulus is longer than to an auditory stimulus. But may be the condition in which you used the visual stimulus as your experimental variable came after the condition in which you used the auditory stimulus as the experimental variable. Performance of the same task, namely, pressing the key with the same finger over and over again, is likely to produce fatigue in the finger muscles. The response to the visual stimulus was slow on this account. Rest between the two conditions will not solve the problem. Repetition of the same task produces feeling of monotony or boredom in a subject, which may also affect his performance in the task. Suppose you designed your experiment the other way round, namely, the condition in which the auditory stimulus was introduced came next. If the Mean for this condition is smaller than the Mean for the condition in which visual stimulus was used, you may think that fatigue had no effect on the subject's performance. Still the result obtained in the experiment will remain uncertain; the difference between the Means may be due to practice effect. After all, the subject is performing the same task, i.e., pressing the key in both conditions. Practice in the task may have produced faster pressing of the key in the second condition.

The Design of Experiments

You can solve the above difficulty by using the so-called counterbalancing design. In this design it is possible to counteract and thus neutralise practice or fatigue effect. You have to assign separate symbols to the two conditions, A to condition I and B to condition II. Suppose you decide to take 20 trials under each condition. First take 10 trials under condition I, after this, 10 plus 10 or 20 trials under condition II, and then the remaining 10 trials under condition I. Symbolically the design will be called ABBA design. The advantages and disadvantages that result from a certain ordering of the conditions are neutralised in both conditions. The first 10 trials under condition I have the maximum advantage of freshness in your subject. This is counterbalanced by the maximum disadvantage from fatigue in the last 10 trials ûnder that condition. Similarly, if there is a practice effect, the advantage in the last 10 trials is counterbalanced by the disadvantage in the first 10 trials. Same thing happens with condition II. The moderate advantage from practice and moderate disadvantage from fatigue counterbalance and neutralise each other. When you find the difference between the Mean of the 20 trials of condition I and the Mean of the 20 trials of condition II, your result becomes more sound. You can come definitely to the conclusion that your subject responds more quickly to an auditory stimulus than to a visual stimulus. If you use more than two conditions, say one control and two experimental conditions in an experiment, the order of trials in each condition, or the design of the experiment will be : ABCCBA.

We use the counterbalancing design to control the effect of an extraneous organismic variable, namely, practice or fatigue. Suppose practice or fatigue is itself your experimental variable. In other words, you are interested in finding out the effect of practice or fatigue. If the problem is to find the effect of practice or fatigue in the same task, the matter is simple. You will just divide the work period into halves or quarters. You will then compare the performance in the first half or the first quarter with that in the second half or the last quarter. If the second half or last quarter shows better Mean performance than the first half or first quarter, practice effect is indicated. Fatigue effect will be shown when the first half or first quarter is better than the second half or the last quarter. You arrive at this conclusion because practice shows progressive gain, while fatigue shows progressive loss, in the quantity and quality of performance.

Suppose you wish to determine whether practice or fatigue in **one** task influences the performance of **another** task. In this case, fatigue or practice being your independent variable, the first task has to be performed for some time in order to build up practice or fatigue effect. The second task, however, is only to be tested in one or two trials. The very common design of having an experimental and a control condition will require the presence of the independent variable in one condition, and its absence from the other condition. All other variables will have to be kept constant, including the second task whose performance will be tested ; it should be identical in the two conditions, otherwise, the difference between the two conditions in the performance of this task may also be due to the difference in the task itself. Having, thus, provided for the experimental and the control conditions, the next question will be about their order ; which condition should be used first, experimental or control ? Suppose you decide for the experimental condition to come first and the control condition to follow it. You will then let your subject perform the first task for a fairly long time so that you get clear indication of progressive improvement or progressive deterioration in the performance. After this, you will test his performance in the second task. This will complete the experimental condition. You will then again test his performance in the second task for your control condition. But then the control condition will become a part of the experimental condition ; it would really be a continuation of the second task for one or two extra trials. In order to obtain two separate conditions for your experiment, you may decide to introduce a gap between them. But the gap or time interval should be sufficiently long for the practice or fatigue effect from the first condition to completely die out. If the practice, or a fatigue effect produced in the performance of the first task of the experimental condition persists to influence the performance in the control condition, then your independent variable influences this condition also. It will then fail to be a control condition.

You can overcome the above difficulty if you choose to introduce the control condition first, to be followed by the experimental condition. You first introduce the test task for one or two trials, then let your subject perform the other task for practice or fatigue effect to build up. After this, you again let the subject perform the test task. It will be possible for you to complete the experiment in one session only. You will also notice that you are using here a modified design of experiment. Your independent variable is sandwiched between two tests of the dependent variable. The design is accordingly called pretest-post-test or before-and-after design. It can be expressed in the following manner :

Test Task 1—Performance Task 2—Test Task 1. This design

has also been used for judging the effect of training on performance of a task, for comparing different methods of training, for examining the effect of propaganda on the formation of attitudes, and so on. For such uses, this design has one important limitation. This limitation is overcome by using a control condition also, in the following manner :

Exp.Cond. Test Task 1—Performance Task 2—Test Task 1
Cont.Cond. Test Task 1— —Test Task 2

It is, however, not necessary for you to know more details about this design at this stage.

You must have appreciated from the above discussion the importance of deciding about the order of placing the control and experimental conditions. For some experiments your design should be to introduce the control condition first ; in others you should place the experimental condition first and the control condition next. Suppose you have to perform an experiment to examine the statement that perception is influenced by previous suggestion or habit. You select an ambiguous figure for your experiment. An ambiguous figure is one that can be perceived as having different forms or as representing different objects at different moments. One such figure appears as black cross at one moment and as white cross at another moment. Looking at the figure, one is as likely to perceive first the white cross as the black cross. In the experiment, you prepare your subject to be attentive to one form only, say the black cross ; your independent variable is the previous suggestion or preparation to perceive this form. Your dependent variable will be the measure of the time for which this figure is perceived. The condition in which you prepare your subject to perceive the black cross will be the experimental condition. In the control condition, there will be no such preparation. Suppose you decide to use the control condition first. You place the figure before your subject's view and tell him to report what he sees. You use a device for measuring the time for which your subject perceives each form. After you have taken say 10 to 20 trials in this condition, you introduce the experimental condition. But your subject is aware now that he sees two forms of the figure. If you try to suggest or prepare him to perceive the black figure, your instruction will have no effect. But if you use the experimental condition first and tell your subject that you would place the figure of a black cross before him which will appear at one moment and disappear at the other and that he should always indicate when that figure appears and disappears, your instruction will have its weight. You will be able to arrive at a conclusive result.

You will note that in designing an experiment you have to decide three issues: (1) How to manipulate the experimental variable? (2) In what order to place the two or more conditions of the experiment? (3) How to control the extraneous variables? We came across two special designs of experiment, namely the counterbalancing design and the before-and-after design. There are several other designs of experiment also. Many of them are specially applicable to group experiments. In a group experiment you use more than one subject. In the class room you perform individual experiments. You become partners and each one takes alternately the role of the experimenter as well as that of the subject. When a group experiment is performed, the same subjects, or different groups of subjects, may be used for the two or more conditions of the experiment. Some special designs are used when the same groups of subjects are engaged in all conditions. Other designs serve to control the extraneous variables when different subjects are used in different conditions. Our purpose is just to understand the essential principles of experiments and the method of performing individual experiments. We will not be concerned with the designs used in the group experiments. You will, however, find in Appendix I a general discussion on the designs and methods of group experiments.

Recommended Reading

McGuigan, F. J., *Experimental Psychology*, Chaps. 1, 3, 6, New York, Prentice-Hall, 1969.

Postman, E. and Egan, J. P., *Experimental Psychology*, Chap. 1, New York, Harper, 1949.

Townsend, J. C., *Introduction to Experimental Method*, Chaps. 4-7, New York, McGraw-Hill, 1953.

CHAPTER II

Conducting Experiments

Formulation of the Problem

IN THE previous chapter we have explained the general purpose for which an experiment is done. We have also seen that an experiment may be the answer to a question : 'What will happen to B, if I do something to A ?' Such experiment we have called exploratory experiment. An experiment may also answer the question : 'How certain or how probable it is that A and B are related ?' The confirmatory experiment provides the answer to such questions. In the exploratory experiment we have no definite hypothesis to start with, we have not even a provisional answer to our question. For example, you may just explore how a person will behave in social situations if kept on starvation diet, i.e., half-fed, for some time. In a confirmatory experiment we have a provisional answer to the question ; we start with a hypothesis. For example, 'under starvation diet a person is likely to become very much self-centered'. Here we already expect what would happen to B, if something is done to A. Only we want to make it sure.

There is a third kind of experiments also that you may be called upon to perform. We have not mentioned them earlier. In such experiments you put a very simple question : 'What my subject's response would be in a given situation ?' For example, you want to determine how quickly or slowly he reacts to a colour or to a sound, how many letters he can observe in one glance, how quickly or slowly his attention shifts, how correctly he can estimate the length of a line, at what intensity he can perceive a light or a sound stimulus, how soon he gets fatigued, and so on. Such experiments enable us to ascertain some facts about individual subjects. They are said to be experiments in the very limited sense of providing for observation in controlled conditions Such experiments, however, have been very useful in the early stages of the development of psychology as a science. They enabled us to know some general facts about the ways the organism functions.

We find from the above that whatever the kind of the experiment, each one is an attempt to provide an answer to a question. Each one centres round a problem. The first thing that is to be done is therefore to make your mind very clear about your problem. You have to decide very precisely what your problem is going to be and to state it in unambiguous terms, to formulate it. The formulation of the problem defines the main purpose of experiment. All that you do in the experiment, and the way you do it, has a purpose only in so far as it helps in answering the problem. Whatever steps you take will be relevant or meaningful only in relation to the problem. Your focus has always to be on the problem. From the beginning to the end, the problem should occupy a position of vantage in your attention.

If your problem is just to ascertain some fact about your subject you formulate it like, for example, 'to determine the errors in the subject's perception of time', 'to measure the subject's reaction time to a visual stimulus', and so on. If your problem is to explore an independent variable, you will formulate it in some such way, e.g., 'to find out the effect of rest pause on the efficiency of motor performance', 'to determine the changes in respiration produced by a strong smell'. Since you have to answer this type of problems also by conducting an individual, and not a group, experiment, in effect your answer to these problems will not be much different from that to the first type of problems. If your problem is to confirm a hypothesis, it has then to be formulated as a hypothesis. For example, 'Rest pauses reduce fatigue in work', 'Complex reaction time is longer than simple reaction time'. The experiment is then conducted to provide the evidence that will support or reject the hypothesis. You will note that in the first two types of experiments there is no question about formulating a hypothesis, because you have no definite hypothesis.

The Choice of Design

We have seen that design of an experiment raises three

main issues : (1) How to manipulate the independent variable ?—whether to use or not to use separate control condition. (2) In what order to place the different conditions ?—whether the control condition should come before or after the experimental condition. (3) How to control the extraneous variables ?—what to do to keep them constant over all conditions of the experiment ? If the extraneous variables are stimulus variables, their control demands no special design. Similarly, in an individual experiment, the control of the organismic variables needs no special concern. Special design may have to be selected for controlling the transient organism variables, the changing temporary states of the organism that influence the dependent variable. When this is the case, the experimenter has to make the correct choice of design.

Some experiments need no design for any one of the above three purposes. The experiment is completed by a set of trials in one condition only. For example, you want to measure your subject's simple reaction time to a stimulus, say light or sound. In a simple reaction time experiment, the subject always receives the same stimulus to which he always responds in the same manner. Here all that you have to do is to take whatever number of trials you choose in the same condition and find the average of the trials. In some other experiments you have only to decide about using or not using a separate control condition and about its placement before or after the experimental condition ; you have not to take any decision about a special design for controlling the extraneous variables. Below you find an example of such an experiment.

You want to find the effect of rest pause on the decline in the efficiency of work. You use a special apparatus, called Ergograph, for the experiment. In a hand ergograph, the subject's forearm is fixed to a board. His first finger is inserted in a loop which is attached to a string ; the other end of the string holds a suspended weight which remains constant. The subject is to pull the weight at fixed intervals, say two seconds, by moving the finger forward and backward. The rate of the movement is controlled by another apparatus called Metronome which produces a ticking sound at fixed intervals. The subject bends his finger, and thus pulls the loop, on the first tick, and straightens his finger at the next tick. The strength with which the subject pulls the weight every time is automatically recorded in the shape of vertical lines successively formed on a smoked paper attached to a rotating drum, which is concealed from the subject's view. The subject's task is extremely simple, bending and straightening the first joint of the first finger alternately at fixed intervals. It is purely repetitive also, as he has to do identically the same thing again and again. There is no practice effect as there is no question of any improvement in the performance. Fatigue effect or decline in efficiency will occur gradually, but it is itself the dependent variable and not an extraneous independent variable. There is no problem, therefore, of keeping practice or fatigue effect constant. The extraneous stimulus variables are controlled by the procedures adopted in obtaining data for the experiment.

Your independent variable in the experiment is the rest pause. Suppose you have decided it to be of the duration of 20 seconds administered after every 5 pulls in the experimental condition. The control condition for the experiment will be continuous pulls, i.e., without rest pauses. You will require one control and one experimental condition. Your next question will be about their order; which one should occur first? This matter will be related to the decision about the total number of pulls in the two conditions. The total number of pulls in each condition is an important stimulus variable. It has to remain constant, otherwise you cannot compare the two conditions for the average strength with which the weight was pulled; this is your dependent variable as the decline in efficiency will be measured in terms of the difference in the average size of the vertical lines formed on the smoked paper. You postpone the decision about the number of pulls in each condition and leave it to be determined with the progress of the experiment in the control condition. You decide, therefore, to take the control condition first. You start the experiment. You observe the vertical lines formed on the smoked paper. You will know how the lines are formed when we will describe the Ergograph in more details at a later stage. When you note that the lines are gradually becoming smaller and smaller in length, i.e., a progressive decline is taking place in the strength of the pulls, you stop the control condition and count the number of lines. You decide to allot the same number to the experimental condition also. You will notice that in the control condition you did not let the subject's finger completely freeze so that he could not pull any more. You would have done this, had your problem been a simple one, namely, to find how readily your subject gets completely fatigued. Had you done this in the experiment we are describing, you would have required a fairly long time, more than thirty minutes, for the subject's finger to have completely recovered from fatigue. The experimental condition could then be introduced only after that. If you had not waited that long, the fatigue set in one condition would have effected the performance in the next condition. The discontinuous performance, i.e., with rest pauses, would then have been no better than the continuous performance, i.e., without rest pauses.

You will have seen that in the experiment described above there was no need for a special design to control the extraneous variables. Such variables, as the rate of movement, the part of the finger involved in the movement, the weight pulled, the amount of work, i.e., number of pulls, done in each condition, were all successfully controlled by the procedure you adopted. Your procedure has also prevented a transient organismic variable to come into play. You have concealed from the subject the record of his performance. Knowledge of one's performance has come out to be an important organismic variable that influences the dependent variable. It motivates the subject for better performance by applying stronger effort when he notices his performance deteriorating.

You will complain that our discussion about the design of the experiment has been unduly dilated. In fact this was done with a purpose. You should have noticed that design is not always necessary for an experiment. You have to decide, every time you plan an experiment, whether the experiment calls for a design. You will also notice that special designs satisfy special requirements. All experiments do not need a special design. You will appreciate that decision about the order in which two or more conditions of the experiments should be placed is not an arbitrary act ; it requires the exercise of a keen practical judgment. You would note that procedure has a wider meaning than design. It relates to all matters about obtaining and recording facts to answer your problem, as you will see in the following section. It enables you also to control the extraneous variables. It can prevent the operation of some extraneous organismic variable too. Above all, you find that no step one takes in an experiment is arbitrary or mechanical. Each one calls for a practical judgment keeping in view the entire situation ; every time you have to take a special decision. There is no fool-proof method for conducting an experiment ; an experiment always requires intelligent handling. Further, the clear awareness of the problem, a definite idea of the independent and dependent variables with which you are primarily concerned, serves you as the guide-light throughout the conduct of the experiment.

By keeping the above facts in view alone you will learn how to use the experimental method for solving a problem in psychology, within or outside your courses. Conducting an experiment successfully requires not only the knowledge of the related literature ; it is also a matter of acquiring skill which is the result of intelligent practice. You learn here by doing and not only by reading. But the doing has to be no less intelligent than the reading. It can be anything, but mechanical.

Procedure

In an experiment we seek to discover or confirm a relationship between variables. To be able to do so we have to observe facts. Unlike naturalistic observation, in an experiment the facts are to be observed under conditions controlled by the experimenter. The observed facts lead us to a result or a conclusion which becomes the answer to the question raised in the experiment. They constitute the data for the experiment. They enable us to arrive at the result of the experiment. The procedure of an experiment deals with the several things done for obtaining and recording facts or data. These are described below.

1. Administration of the Independent Variable

The first thing you have to do in the experiment in order to obtain data is to give a concrete shape to the independent variable. In formulating your problem you state the independent variable in very general or abstract terms. Let us go back to the example of finding the relationship between rest pause and efficiency of performance. In actual practice, the rest pause may be long or short, of this or that duration. It may be one or several rest pauses. The rest pauses may be introduced at regular or at irregular intervals. They may be applied only in the beginning, the middle, or near the end of performance, or they may be applied at all stages of the progress of the work. One cannot explore all of the above possiblities in one experiment. He has to choose one among them and thus give a definite, concrete and specific shape to the independent variable. For example, in the above experiment your independent variable was a rest pause of twenty seconds duration, administered several times, and after every five pulls. You had thus specified or defined the particular way in which the independent variable was administered or applied in the experiment. In other words, you had stated it in operational terms, as it is technically called, that is, you had defined the specific manner in which the independent variable was made to operate in the experiment.

2. Selection of the Task

To decide about the specific mode of applying the independent variable, sometimes you have to select a task through which you can bring about the independent variable. Suppose your independent variable is knowledge of result. This is an organismic variable. It is also a temporary or a transient variable ; it is the subject's awareness of how he is performing the task in hand. To make this variable operate in an experiment, you have to make the choice of a definite task. The task may be one out of several possible tasks. It may be repeatedly drawing lines of a definite length, without using a foot scale, at the end of which the experimenter every time reports the amount of error made by the subject. It may be cancelling one or two specified letters wherever they occur on a printed page. It may be picking up small metal balls with a tweezer, one after the other, to fill up a glass tube standing on a board. There may be thousand and one other tasks in which knowledge of result may be an independent variable. You have to select one task and apply or administer knowledge of result through the medium of that task in the experiment.

Selection of a specific task may be important sometimes also for obtaining observation of the dependent variable. For example, in reaction time experiments, the standard task is to press a telegraphic key. Or, in the experiment on the effect of distraction on the efficiency of work, the dependent variable would involve some definite task. The task, for example, may be solving arithmetical problems, assembling the parts of a cycle bell, reciting a poem from memory, and so on.

You should not think that every experiment requires the selection of a task. In some experiments you do not engage your subject in any task. He may be sitting quite idle. Suppose you want to determine the effect of a strong smell on your subject's respiration. Here the subject has no task to perform. You will thus notice that it is not necessary to utilize a special task for every experiment. You have to judge whether your problem requires the employment of a task or not. If it does, you have to think and decide what should be the appropriate task for the experiment.

3. Measures of Dependent Variables

In selecting a task for your experiment you have to consider whether the subject's performance in the task is measurable. We should understand the different ways of measuring the dependent variable : (*i*) One way is to measure the speed of performance, i.e., how quickly or slowly the subject completes a performance. For example, in learning a maze, you note the time the subject takes in moving his pencil from the entrance to the centre of the maze, or in a test of skill in manual work you measure the speed at which the subject fills up the glass tube with the metal balls picked up by a tweezer. (*ii*) Another measure may be the frequency of the response. How often does the subject breathe in and breathe out within a specified time when, say, in a state of fear ? How many times does he see the black cross in the ambiguous figure ? (*iii*) Still other measure of the dependent variable is the amount of output, or number of things done, within a fixed time You find out how many problems in addition, for example, the subject completed within a specified time. It may also be a mere count of correct responses, for example, how many words the subject could correctly recall from a list learned, say, thirty minutes ago. (*iv*) A fourth measure is the delay in making a response. Technically this has been called a measure of latency. Here you measure the time it takes for a stimulus to evoke a response. Reaction time is a measure of latency. Latency of the response is measured in verbal learning also. The subject is shown a list of, say, paired words and after that he is required to reproduce the second item of the pair when the first item is shown. The delay, or the time taken, in recalling the second item is a measure of latency. (*v*) Still another kind of measure is to determine the magnitude of response. To find out the amount of energy the subject applied to a manual task, you measure the magnitude of pressure exerted by him in, for example, a hand dynamometer. You will find a description of this apparatus in a later chapter. (*vi*) The dependent variable is also measured by counting the errors in a performance, or finding the discrepancy or difference between, say, the length of the line drawn by the subject and the length required to be drawn in the experiment.

You will have noticed from the above that there are several ways of measuring the dependent variable. The data of your experiment are derived from the measures of the dependent variable. It is very important, therefore, that you select a measure that is most convenient as well as most suitable for the purpose of obtaining data. Here too your choice should not be arbitrary. You have to keep your problem and the other aspects of your procedure in view in order to make an appropriate choice.

4. Introspective Data

The kinds of data we mentioned above are behavioural. They form part of the responses made by the subject that can be observed by the experimenter. They constitute the subject's overt behaviour. Some of these the experimenter can observe without any special aid, e.g., the number of words the subject correctly recalls from memory. For others, he may use a special recording device or apparatus, for example, reaction time, or change in the subject's breathing. There are still other facts that the experimenter cannot directly know. These may constitute important data for the experiment. Suppose you want to test the hypothesis that unpleasant stimuli produce change in respiration. You select a set of pictures of some dreadful scenes, say, a severely wounded person lying in a pool of blood, a human corpse (dead body) being eaten by vultures, a cremation or burial scene, etc. You believe that each one would produce an unpleasant feeling in your subject. But you may notice that the sight of the pictures causes no change in the subject's respiration. Your results do not seem to support your hypothesis. The reason is that you have missed some important data ; you do not know whether the pictures did actually produce unpleasant feelings in your subject. The subject alone can tell you if they did so. You ask your subject to report his feelings when he was looking at the pictures. You find him telling that he had no special feeling to report. Every time, he was trying to find out how successfully the artist depicted the scene shown in a picture. How did the pictures compare with each other in this respect ? You now discover that you had not succeeded in applying your independent variable, namely, **unpleasant stimuli** to the subject ; the stimuli were neutral for the subject.

The data that you missed in the above experiment are not behavioural data. They are introspective data. You obtain them when the subject reports about them from his introspection or self-observation. Nonetheless, they are very important data for your experiment. Take another example. You seek to test the hypothesis that unfavourable criticism and discouraging remarks on the subject's performance, in the presence of another person, make the subject's performance deteriorate or become poor. You use two conditions for the experiment. In the control condition you watch the subject's performance quietly with the other person sitting by your side. In the experimental condition you criticise the subject's performance, tell that it is poor, much below what is excepted of an adult student, and so on. When you compare the subject's performance in the two conditions, you may find no difference, or find the performance in the experimental condition better. You then obtain the subject's introspection about his feelings and attitudes at the time of the performance. You discover that your criticism, instead of discouraging the subject, presented a challenge to him. He was motivated to apply all his energy to the task and consequently his performance improved.

In one sense, for the experimenter, the introspective data are also behavioural data. They constitute the subject's introspection, they are an account of his mental state made on the basis of self-observation. But they are reported to the experimenter in words, written or spoken. When the experimenter looks at the verbal report or listens to it, it is nothing different for him from any other record of the subject's behaviour. We have seen how the forward and backward movements of the subject's finger in an ergograph are recorded by the vertical lines on a smoked paper. This is a record of the subject motor behaviour. The introspective report is a similar record of the subject's verbal behaviour which the experimenter objectively observes. The experimenter makes use of both in his experiment in order to arrive at an answer to his problem. The difference is only in the source of the data. The source of the data is not a recording apparatus. It is, on the other hand, the subject himself ; the source of the data is the subject's introspection.

The introspective data are valuable data. But they are not essential data. You do not require them in all experiments, in order to arrive at the result of the experiment. In some experiments they have no place. Suppose you are performing an experiment just to measure your subject's complex reaction time. In a complex reaction time the subject has to react in different ways to different stimuli. There may be lights of, say, four different colours, one light shown at one time. The subject has a set of four different keys or buttons numbered 1 to 4. He has to react by pressing key No. 1, say, to the red light, key No. 2 to the green light, and so on. The lights are presented in chance order ; the subject does not know which light would appear at the moment. Several trials are taken and the reaction time is measured ; finally the average complex reaction time of the subject is found out. For the purpose of your result the data on the subject's complex reaction time are all that you need. Subject's introspection may be out of place here. However, suppose you put a question in the experiment, namely, why complex reaction time is longer than simple reaction time ? Introspective data will then have a use. The subject might tell you how he expected a particular stimulus at a moment and was prepared for that, but actually he got another stimulus. The preparation for the first stimulus created a difficulty in the choice of the correct key to be pressed This did not happen in the other condition where the same stimulus was repeated.

You will notice from the above that you have to decide in every case whether the subject's introspection will supply you any valuable data in answering your problem. You should not make it a routine affair to obtain the subject's introspection. In most experiments reported in standard journals you do not come across the subject's introspective report. They are not found useful for the purpose of the problem that is investigated in the experiment. When you take your subject's introspection, you have to use it, otherwise do not take it.

5. Recording Data

As noted above, the procedure of the experiment also involves a consideration of the appropriate device for recording data. The result of an experiment is drawn from the data obtained in the experiment. An accurate and systematic recording of the data and their neat and clear presentation are therefore the essential requirements of an experiment. The data should be recorded simultaneously with their observation by the experimenter. The experimenter should leave nothing to his memory. To ensure accurate recording of data, some mechanical devices have also been used. You will find them mentioned under our account of apparatus. In most experiments, however, the experimenter has to record the data himself. We will illustrate the method of recording data in the chapter on reporting an experiment.

6. Apparatus

As we noted earlier, the procedure of an experiment involves such matters as using a specific method of applying or administering the independent variable ; sometimes a special task is also employed for this purpose. Procedure also involves the method of observing the dependent variable ; for this too a special task may sometimes be employed. Lastly, procedure involves the method of recording the data obtained in the experiment. An apparatus is a standard mechanical device that performs one or all of these three functions. A complete multiple choice apparatus used in experiments on reaction time provides for the presentation of alternative stimuli ; it contains also a device for making alternative responses ; in addition, it employs a mechanism for accurate measurement and recording of the subject's reaction time. In other cases a separate apparatus is used for a separate function. For example, a tachistoscope provides a very brief exposure of a visual material—what you can see in one glance; a memory drum provides the presentation of a list of verbal items—words, digits, nonsense syllables—in such a manner that each item stays before the subject's view for a definite time, say, two to four seconds, and is then replaced by another item, and so on. Another kind of apparatus provides a task in which the subject engages and his responses are observed. The ergograph is such an apparatus. The mirror drawing apparatus also belongs to this category. It provides a standard situation for copying a figure by looking at its reflection in a mirror. Still other kinds of apparatus serve to produce an automatic record of the subject s responses. The Kymograph or rotating drum is one such apparatus. The drum has a smoked paper pasted around it and moves at a fixed rate. A marker is touching the smoked surface. The subject's responses are automatically recorded by the movement of the marker across the smoked surface of the moving drum. The smoked paper with the marks on it is dipped, afterwards, in a chemical solution and the record is thus made permanent. We will describe some common apparatus used in experiments in more details at a later stage.

The use of an apparatus in an experiment has one very great advantage. Many controls of an experiment are automatically secured when using an apparatus. For example, when using an apparatus it is possible to present identically the same stimulus, say, light of the same colour, of the same intensity, for the same length of time, throughout the experiment. Similarly you can engage the subject in identically the same task, performed in exactly the same manner, in the same situation, for example, in the ergograph, which could not otherwise be possible. The apparatus also provides automatically an absolutely perfect and reliable record of the subject's responses, which would otherwise require a good deal of attention and care on the part of the experimenter. However, though an apparatus is very valuable, it is not always indispensable. Many good experiments have been done without using any special kind of brass or metal apparatus. In fact, as a student of laboratory methods in Psychology, it is more useful for you to devise your own substitutes for an apparatus. This will lend you an insight into the fundamental requirements of the experimental method. The invention of a new apparatus in psychology has always followed the preparation of an improvised device employed by an intelligent experimenter. He thought out a new problem; he also thought out a new device for obtaining data for his problem in order to arrive at a conclusive result. He secured some card board pieces and other sundry articles and assembled them to give a concrete shape to his idea. He noticed that it worked. He then consulted an artisan and the device was converted into a solid brass apparatus. This writer himself invented quite a few apparatus in exactly the same manner described here.

7. Instruction

In most experiments you have to give some instruction to your subject; you tell him what he is required to do. If he has to perform a task, you describe in detail the method of performing the task. For example, in measuring complex reaction time you explain to your subject what stimuli will be presented to him, what responses he can possibly make, and which response he has to make to a particular stimulus. Or, in an experiment in verbal learning you have to tell your subject about the nature of the list that is to be shown to him, that he has to observe each item very attentively as he will have to report from memory what he observed, and so on. The purpose of the instruction is to prepare the subject for what you expect him to do in the experiment.

The instruction serves another purpose also. You use it for administering the independent variable. This is done when the independent variable that is to be manipulated in the experiment is an organismic variable. Suppose you are trying to find out the difference between sensory and muscular reaction times. You use the same apparatus for measuring both. Everything else is also the same. The only difference will be in the instruction given to the subject. For sensory reaction time, you tell your subject to keep his attention focussed on the stimulus, say a red light, and press the key immediately as he sees the light. In the muscular reaction time you tell him to focus his attention on the response, i.e., pressing of the key, and press it as soon as the light appears. The difference is in the emphasis created within the subject on the stimulus, in one case, and on the response in the other. Your purpose in the experiment is to find out whether this difference in emphasis effects the dependent variable, i.e., the length of the reaction time. You have noticed a similar function of the instruction in the experiment on the effect of previous preparation on the perception of an ambiguous figure (p. 12). The introduction of the figure as the black cross sets up the readiness to perceive the black cross, rather than the white cross. Let us take a still other example You want to determine the difference between intentional learning and incidental learning. In the intentional learning condition you tell your subject that he has to learn and remember a list of, say, three-lettered words that will be presented to him trial after trial. At the end of the trials he has to reproduce as many items from the list as he remembers. For incidental learning you present to the subject a similar list for the same number of times, but this time you give him a different instruction. You tell him that you are required to prepare several copies of a list of words for which you would take help from the subject. The items on the list would appear one after the other on memory drum. The subject has to copy each item on a blank paper supplied to him. In the intentional learning trials the instruction serves to arouse in the subject the conscious intention to learn and remember the list. In the incidental learning trials, the instruction prepares the subject just to copy the list without a conscious intention to learn the list. In the first case he knows because of your instruction that you will test his memory for the list. In the second he does not know this. After the subject has prepared the desired number of copies, you remove him and ask him to recollect the words from the list. In this case his learning of the list was incidental, as his intention was to copy and not to learn the list. The independent variable, namely, conscious intention to learn was manipulated in the experiment through the instruction you gave to the subject.

The instruction also serves to keep some extraneous organismic variable constant throughout the experiment. For example, you may be using a cancellation task for an experiment on the level of aspiration. In a level of aspiration experiment the subject is required to set a goal which he aspires to attain. Suppose you instruct your subject to cancel the letters, say, E and G from a sheet having the letters of the English alphabets printed in capitals several times in a haphazard manner.

Such a cancellation sheet is specially prepared for use in experiments. You use several such sheets in the experiment, trial after trial. Each time as you introduce a sheet, you ask your subject to tell how much time he aspired to take in cancelling all of the said letters E and G. The subject thus sets a goal for which he works in a given trial. The experimenter measures and reports to the subject the time actually taken by him in completing the sheet. The same thing is done in a number of trials ; each time the subject sets a goal and the experimenter reports his attainment. The experimenter observes the changes that take place in the subject's goal setting behaviour from trial to trial. The experimenter, however, does not instruct the subject merely what the subject is required to do, namely, cancel the said letters and every time set a goal before starting. He also tells the subject that many people lack the ability to notice minute details quickly and correctly which is very important for everyone to possess, and that he was going to test how quickly and correctly the subject could perceive some specified letters from among a complex of other letters. The experimenter tells all this to keep the subject working throughout the experiment at a high level of motivation, to keep him trying to show the best of himself all the time. Had the experimenter not included this in the instruction and just introduced the task of cancelling letters, the subject's interest would have soon declined. This would have affected the subject's goal setting behaviour. In other situations too the experimenter so frames his instruction as to keep the subject maintaining the same rate or speed of performance, working with the same care, paying the same amount of attention to the task in hand, and so on throughout the two or more conditions of the experiment.

You will appreciate, from what has been said above, the very important functions served by the instruction given in an experiment. Above all, it is the most effective tool in the hand of the experimenter to control the transient organismic variables, the temporary conditions arising within the subject that might affect the dependent variable. It has, therefore, to be very carefully planned. It should tell only what is necessary for the purpose of the experiment. It should state nothing less and nothing more than what is actually needed. The language of the instruction should be simple, non-technical, straightforward and clear. Suppose the following instruction is given in an experiment on complex reaction time :

"I am going to measure your complex reaction time. You will receive different kinds of stimulus from the Multiple Choice Box—red, green, blue and white. The box contains a set of buttons to be pressed. You have to make different responses to the different stimuli. I will give you the ready signal and will then present the stimulus. Respond immediately. After I have measured your complex reaction time, I will measure your simple reaction time. Then I will present to you the same stimulus and you have to make the same response. This will be easier for you and your reaction time will be less here."

The above instruction may not appear to you as inadequate and as confusing as it is because you are familiar with the technical terms like 'Complex reaction time', 'Multiple Choice Box', 'Stimulus and response', 'Ready signal', and so on. You may not feel uneasy when you are told that after your complex reaction time has been measured, your simple reaction time will also be measured ; you know that a complex reaction time experiment uses the simple reaction time measure as a control. The information that simple reaction time is shorter than complex reaction time does not affect you because you already possess this knowledge. All that is said may be all right for the purpose of your practical course since you have to act both as a subject and an experimenter in the same experiment. But this will never happen when you conduct an experiment for answering a research problem. Perhaps, you will never act as a subject, and perhaps your subjects will not of necessity be students of Psychology having also to do practicals in a psychology laboratory. Your subjects may not be knowing anything about Psychology. They may not be able even to understand the language a psychologist uses. The subject may be what is called unsophisticated, one who is completely unaware of what is being done in fact and for what purpose. He may be just co-operating with you by doing all that you want him to do. It is very necessary then for you to learn how to frame your instruction that suits a lay person of average education, and, especially, having no education in Psychology.

Now look at the following instruction and compare it with that we have examined above.

"We are going to do some interesting things. You see here", pointing to the Multiple choice apparatus, "light bulbs of four different colours—red, green, blue and white. You also see four buttons with a letter inscribed on each, R, G, B or W, standing for red, green, blue or white. Each button is electrically connected with a particular bulb. In the experiment, you will find each bulb lighted one after the other in a chance or irregular order. When you see the red light, press the button with the letter R on it and the light will be off. Similarly when you see the green light press the button for green, and so on. Every time, I will tell you 'Ready' before a light is shown. Be attentive. Immediately as you see a light press the button for that light. If you press the correct button the light will be off. Try to be as quick as possible. I am going to measure how quickly you press the button after you see a light. Do you understand everything ? All right."

The instruction for the sample reaction time in the control condition, is given as follows :

"You have to do what you did before. But now you will see only the red light appearing every time. Whenever you see the red light, press the button for that light so that the light is off. Be attentive to the red bulb and press its button immediately as you see the red light."

You note that the instructions for the two conditions of the experiment are not mixed up. It was no use telling the subject about the second condition of the experiment at the time the first condition was introduced In fact telling that would have confused him. Also, telling everything at one time would have led the subject to think that the experimenter was going to engage him much too long. Further, having started anticipating the second condition before the first was over, his interest in the first condition would have declined. But if you give him the instruction for the second condition, after having completed the trials in the first condition, he is likely to welcome the change.

In some experiments, the instructions for the two or more conditions may have much in common. In such a case the general facts may be told as a part of the first instruction.

The other instructions then include the special things that the subject has to do in the conditions that follow. The above instruction illustrates this point.

You will note that framing an instruction, deciding about its content and language, calls for an act of judgment. The correct judgment will require a clear understanding of the problem and of the important controls to be used in the experiment. You cannot decide about the instruction in isolation from the rest of what other things you have to do in the experiment.

Utilization of Data

You adopt a procedure for obtaining data and use some device for recording and presenting data. Our next problem is the utilization of data for arriving at a result In an experiment we manipulate the independent variable and observe what happens to the dependent variable. We cannot, however, come to any result from a single observation ; the observed change in the dependent variable may be due to chance and not to the manipulation of the independent variable. But if we repeat each condition of the experiment several times, that is, take several trials in each condition, and observe that the same kind of change takes place in the dependent variable, we feel confident that the observed change is not due to chance. Chance events are not consistent. When you toss a coin in the air, its turning head or tail is a chance event. If you repeat the tossing several times, you will never find head showing up every time or tail showing up every time. In fact you will observe head turning up fifty per cent of the times and tail turning up the other fifty per cent of the times. It so happens because both events are equally possible and it is just a matter of chance that the one or the other occurs. Suppose you toss a coin ten times and notice that head shows up all the times or fails only once or twice, you will become suspicious about the genuineness of the coin ; you think that the coin is loaded on one side. You do this because you feel sure that a chance event cannot be consistent over a number of observations.

It is clear from the above that in order to arrive at a conclusive result of an experiment, you have to repeat the observations. Repeating observations is the same as taking several trials. No single trial, in other words, can lead you to any conclusion. What you observe and record in the several trials of the experiment, constitutes your raw data. When you look at the raw data you may get some idea about their general trend, but you cannot have a clear idea : you cannot come to a definite result. The raw data have to be summarised. In order to summarise them you have to subject them to a process of transformation, you treat the raw data quantitatively ; you apply some arithmetical operations to them. As a result of this the details of the data get condensed and take on a quantitative expression.

Number of Observations

Before we describe the ways of quantitatively treating the data, let us answer one question. We have said that we repeat our observations—take several trials in the experiment. One may ask how many trials one should take in order to arrive at a conclusive result. For some experiments that you have to conduct, the question does not arise. As we noticed earlier (p. 21) the dependent variable may itself be measured in terms of the number of trials. For example, the experiment on the relationship between meaningfulness and speed of learning (p. 4). You measure the dependent variable, namely, speed of learning by counting the number of trials taken by your subject for learning each of the meaningful and non-meaningful lists. Similarly in trying to find the effect of learning one task on the learning of another task, you count the number of trials required by the subject to learn each task and then mark the difference. If the second task is learnt in fewer trials, you conclude that the first task learning has facilitated the second task learning.

In other experiments the number of trials itself may be the independent variable that you manipulate in the experiment. Suppose you want to find out the effect of the level or strength of learning on the subject's memory for what he learned. You take in the experiment, say, three conditions, using three different lists of equal difficulty, one for each condition, each list consisting, say, of 12 nonsense syllables. In one condition you let your subject repeat the list till he is able to correctly reproduce 5 or 6 items from the list. In the second condition, he repeats the list till he can correctly reproduce all items of the list. In the third condition, you make him overlearn the list, i.e., let him repeat it in as many more trials as he takes for its errorless reproduction. In each condition you ask your subject to recall what he remembered from the list after an interval of, say, thirty minutes. You notice that your subject's recall was best when he overlearned the list. You come to the conclusion that there is a relationship between the number of learning trials or level of learning and the retention of what has been learned. Number of trials is, thus, an independent variable here.

In other experiments too where number of trials may be an extraneous independent variable, and not the experimental variable, the problem about the number of trails is sometimes automatically settled. Such was the case in the experiment on the effect of rest pause on the efficiency of work (p. 16). Nevertheless, in some experiments you have to decide at the outset about the number of trials to be taken. For such experiments our general answer will be : the larger the number of observations, the more reliable will be the result. But you may ask : how large ? The answer depends upon the time at your disposal. In class-room experiments, you have hardly a couple of hours to complete an experiment. You have known from this chapter all that you have to do in conducting an experiment. The next chapter will tell you about reporting an experiment. In the class-room experiment, generally, you conduct an experiment within a couple of hours and write out the report at home. In conducting the experiment also you devote your time mainly to collecting and recording data ; the treatment of data you do at home while preparing the report. When you sit for a practical examination you may be given two to three hours for both conducting and reporting an experiment. The time at your disposal is less in this case. You have to exercise your practical judgment regarding the distribution of the time to the different parts of the job. The time needed for the different parts of the work also differs from experiment to experiment. The time that you devote for obtaining data will, therefore, depend upon the nature of the experiment. Again, even in collecting data, which is one part of the job, you can take more trials within the same time in one experiment, than in another. For example, in an experiment on simple reaction time you can have more observations than in an experiment on complex reaction time, within the same length of time. You have to consider the nature of your problem, weigh every part of the total work to be done, and then fix the time for obtaining data. Having done this, estimate the number of observations possible within this time and then fix the number. You have never to forget that of all other things you do in an experiment, the reliability of your result depends upon the number of observations or trials; they supply the evidence on which you base your result. Take, therefore, as many trials as you possibly can without neglecting the other things you have to do in the experiment. Do not have a predetermined answer to the question about the number of trials.

I may remind you that all the time in this book we are trying to understand the method of conducting individual experiments. The purpose is just to give you the preparatory training. When you take up special problems to investigate, at a later stage of advanced studies and research in psychology, you will then perform group experiments (p. 15). In group experiments one multiplies his observations not only by taking several trials with one subject, but one or more trials with several subjects. In group experiments even when the number of trials is a dependent variable or it is the experimental variable itself, as noted above, the question about the number of observations remains to be answered. In group experiments you add to your observations by multiplying the number of subjects. The question changes into: how many subjects to be included in the experiment in order to arrive at a conclusive result? Our general answer will be the same, namely, the larger the number of observations, the higher the probability of the correctness of the result, the greater the likelihood for the same result to be obtained in future. We will not go into further details regarding this matter, because our purpose here is not to learn the method of group experiments.

Treatment of Result

Let us go back to the problem of treatment of raw data. Whatever is done in an experiment has a value if it yields a result that is likely to hold of other similar cases in future. For example, when you come to a result about your subject's simple reaction time, you expect him generally to react as fastly or as slowly in a similar situation in future also. As we saw above, you cannot come to any conclusion from a single observation. You have to take several observations. Each one will differ somewhat from most other observations. You will notice, however, that most of them are quite close and only a few differ very widely from these. Suppose you have taken 100 trials or observations in the experiment. You find that most reaction times of your subject, say as many as 80 to 85, lie between 140 to 160 milliseconds—a millisecond is one thousandth of a second. Only the remaining 15 to 20 reaction times are outside this range, i.e., below 140 ms. or above 160 ms. You come to the conclusion that if you accept 150 ms., which is midway between 140 ms. and 160 ms. as the usual length of your subject's reaction time, you will not be more than 10 ms. in error in estimating his future reaction time in 80 cases out of 100. The same result is achieved when you calculate the Mean value for the 100 reaction times of your subject. The Mean is a value of observations to which most observations will approximate or fall near. It is the value which is most likely to be repeated in future. You can verify this by performing a simple experiment on yourself. Draw a 5 centimetre or 50 millimetre line at the top of a blank sheet of paper using a scale. Abandon the scale and take a ruler which has no scale points on it. Draw 100 lines below the standard line of 5 cm. so that each line you draw looks equal to it. Now measure and record the length of each line. Add all lengths and divide the sum by 100. This gives you the Mean. Suppose it comes to be 4.8 cm. or 48 mm. Compare this length with the lengths of the individual lines drawn. You will observe that most lines will be quite close to the Mean value and only a few will considerably deviate or depart from this value. This will happen, however, if you have seriously tried to draw lines that appear to be equal to the standard line. Now compare the Mean with the standard ; this gives you the Mean error. You can now safely conclude about yourself that if you attempt to draw a 5 cm. line in future by looking at a line of this length, you are most likely to make an error which will be near to 2 mm.

We notice from the above that the Mean gives us the best

estimate of the future occurrence of an event. Hence, after having made several observations of the dependent variable, we find out the Mean of the observations. The result based on the Mean of the observations will give us a measure of the observations which is most likely to be repeated in future. Accordingly, the results of many of the experiments that you will conduct will be stated in terms of the Mean of the values observed in the several trials. To summarise your raw data, the simplest statistical treatment to which you subject your data is the calculation of the Mean value. As we saw, the Mean also gives you the best estimate of the future occurrence of an event ; it is the value which is most likely to be repeated in future observations.

Besides calculating the Mean of the raw data, you also calculate the standard deviation. We have seen that the raw data will not be altogether identical with the Mean Most of them will no doubt be quite close to the Mean, but quite a few will fall very much apart from the Mean. The standard deviation will give you the average estimate of how much the observations deviate from the Mean. With some subjects the deviation may be quite large ; with others it may be small. Supposing, the Mean reaction time of two subjects is about the same, say, 165 ms., but the standard deviations differ widely. The SD of one subject is, say, 20 ms. ; that of another is 5 ms. You can say that the first subject is much less steady in his reactions than the second subject; the RT of the first subject fluctuates very widely, his responses are very much variable.

We have taken an example from the simplest type of experiments (p. 36), while trying to understand the purpose of converting our raw data into the Mean value and finding its SD. Let us now consider the value of finding the Mean and the SD in experiments where we are interested in discovering or confirming a relationship between two variables. Suppose we are conducting an experiment on the effect of knowledge of result on simple reaction time. Having obtained the raw data for the control and experimental conditions of the experiment, you calculate their Means and SDs. You find the Mean RT with knowledge of result to be smaller than that without knowledge of result, as expected ; you may also find that the SD of the first condition is smaller than that for the second condition.

You will come to the conclusion that knowledge of result produces an improvement in one's performance, the response gets faster. You will also conclude that with knowledge of result the performance gets more steady; it shows less fluctuation or variability; knowing his RT in one trial, the subject strives for reducing its magnitude in the next trial. This does not happen without knowledge of result; the subject's RT becomes sometimes much too long. You notice that comparison between the SDs throws further light on the difference in the raw data, which, perhaps, would have remained undetected.

Limits of Chance Difference

You might put a question. Will any amount of difference between the Means in the two conditions of the experiment suffice to lead one to the conclusion that knowledge of result produces improvement in performance? Shall we not get any difference between the Means of the observations obtained from the same subject on different days working under the same condition of the experiment? The answer is that you might get different Means on the different days; they may not be altogether the same. But if this is so, why then should you think that the difference between the Means of the control and the experimental conditions is due to the influence of the independent variable, e.g., knowledge of result, which is provided only in the experimental condition? Our answer will be that the difference between Means obtained at different times under the same condition will be small, while the difference between the Means of the control and the experimental conditions will be large. We always expect a small difference as a result of chance, and only when a difference is large enough we conclude that the difference is not due to chance; it is due to the presence of the independent variable in one condition and its absence from the other condition. But the answer will not satisfy you. You will put another question: How large? Luckily we possess an answer to your question. It is possible to find the extent of the difference that may be due to chance only. Having known this, we can compare this chance difference with the extent of the difference we obtain between the Means of the two conditions. If the extent of the obtained difference is the same as the extent of the difference that may be due to chance, we conclude that the difference between the two conditions is due to chance and not due to the independent variable manipulated in the experiment. Let us understand how we can find out the extent or limit of the difference that may be due to chance.

Suppose we get a subject who is always willing to cooperate with us. We call him for 50 days and on each day we take 100 trials of his RT, providing him each day the knowledge of result. We calculate the 50 Means for the 50 days. The Means will not be the same. But most Means will be quite close and only a few will fall far from others. We have a statistical method which can tell how many Means will be close to each other and how close they will be. For this purpose we have to calculate the SE for any one Mean and find out what is called the Standard Error of that Mean by using the following formula :—

$$SE_{Mean} = \frac{\sigma}{\sqrt{N-1}}$$

N is the number of observations on which the Mean is based and σ is the notation for SD. The Standard Error of the single Mean tells us how far two-thirds of the 50 Means we may have calculated for the 50 different days will lie from the Mean for which the SE_M has been calculated. Suppose the Mean found on a particular day is 156 ms and the SD is 14 ms. The SE Mean calculated by the above formula will be 2 ms. We can conclude that about 33 Means, that is, 68% or two-thirds of the 50 Means of my subject will fall within the range of 156 ms.−2ms. and 156 ms.+2 ms., or 154 ms. and 158 ms. Any Mean value outside this range, i.e., larger than 158 ms. or smaller than 154 ms. will belong to the remaining 17, that is, 32%, or one-third of the Means. This may also be stated as : the probability of any Mean falling outside this range is 1 in 3. By multiplying the SE_M by 2, we can establish a range within which 95 per cent of the 50 Means are likely to fall. This range will be 156 ms.−2×2 ms. and 156 ms. +2×2 ms. or 152 ms. to 160 ms ; 95 p. c. of all Means will fall within this range. Any Mean falling outside this range is likely to be one of the remaining five in 100, or two or three in 50 Means ; its probability will be 1 in 20 or 5 in 100. Similarly by multiplying the SE_M by 2.58, you can fix the limits for 99 means out of 100. The range will then be 156 ms. -2.58×2 ms. and 156 ms. $+ 2.58 \times 2$ ms. or roughly 151 to 161 ms. In this case you expect hardly one Mean out of the fifty to be outside this range. Now if you had measured the RTs of your subject also in the control condition, that is without letting him know the result, and calculated the Mean, you could decide with a certain degree of confidence whether it differs from the Mean of the Experimental condition just by chance. You know the limits for chance and you also know the likelihood or probability of the Means following within the limits. Thus, if the control condition Mean falls outside the range of 154 to 158, the probability of its not differing from the experimental condition Mean is 1 in 3. If it falls outside the range of 152 to 160, the probability is further reduced; it will now differ from the Experimental Mean only in 5 cases out of 100; its probability will be 1 in 20. Arguing the other way round, the probability of the control Mean being really different from the Experimental Mean will be 19 in 20. We can, therefore, conclude more confidently that the control Mean differs, rather than does not differ, from the Experimental Mean. Further, if the Control Mean falls outside the range of 151 to 161 ms., the probability of its not differing from the Experimental Mean is reduced to 1 in 100; that of its differing from the Experimental Mean is raised to 99 in 100. We can conclude with very high level of confidence that the Control Mean differs from the Experimental Mean not just by chance; the two Means do really differ and are, therefore, expected to differ in future also.

Standard Error of Difference

You have noticed that it is possible to determine the extent of the difference that may occur as due to just chance. You find this by calculating the Standard Error of the Mean. You can use an alternative method where you can find out the Standard Error of the difference between the Means of the Control and the Experimental conditions. This gives you more directly a measure of the extent of the difference that may exist between any two Means on account of mere chance. You can compare the difference that you actually get with the difference that you expect as due to cahnce. You can also determine how much larger the obtained difference should be in order that you may arrive at a result with full confidence. For this purpose, you will find the ratio that the obtained difference is of the SE difference. If the obtained difference is twice as large as the SE difference, then the difference falls outside the range within which 95% of the chance difference are likely to fall. One can conclude that the probability of that large difference to be due to chance is only 5 in 100 or 1 in 20, and that of its not being due to chance is 95 in 100 or 19 in 20. You have seen earlier that we achieved the same result by taking 2 times the SE of the Mean. If the ratio of the obtained difference to the Standard Error of difference is near about 3, i.e., the obtained difference is three times as large as the SE difference, we will argue that the probability of that large difference being due to chance is only 1 in 100, and therefore it is very highly probable that the difference is not due to chance. Here too we could have achieved the same result by multiplying the Standard Error of one Mean by 3 and then judging whether the obtained difference exceeds the limit.

Critical Ratio

We saw above that in order to compare the obtained difference and the SE difference we find the ratio between the two. A ratio is found by dividing one number by another number. If the obtained difference is twice as large as the SE difference, the ratio is 2 ; if it is 3 times as large, the ratio is 3. The ratio thus tells us how large an obtained difference is. As we saw above, our conclusion about the difference being due to or not being due to chance depends upon the largeness of the obtained difference or the size of the ratio. Hence the ratio has been called Critical Ratio. It decides whether the Mean in the experimental condition is really different from the Mean in the control condition. In other words, it tells us whether the independent variable actually influences the dependent variable. It becomes a test of the hypothesis we formulate in the experiment. The small letter t has been used as the notation for the critical ratio. Thus

$$t \text{ or } CR = \frac{Obt_{diff.}}{SE_{diff.}}$$

A difference that is due to chance is said to be insignificant. The one that is not due to chance is said to be significant. The difference between the Mean RTs in the two conditions of the experiment on knowledge of result, would be significant if t is 2 or more. It would be insignificant if t is less than 2. The result that we arrive at in an experiment is, thus, tested by using the critical ratio. The test is accordingly called t test. We have seen that the probability of our result being true increases with the size of t ; when t is 2, the probability of the result as not being due to chance is 19 in 20 ; when t is roughly 3, the probability of our result being not due to chance is much higher, i.e., 99 in 100. When the probability is high we are more sure or confident about our conclusion. If it is low, we are less sure or confident. The value of t, therefore, also determines the level of confidence with which we accept our result. When it is roughly 3 or more, the level of confidence is higher than when t is more than 2 but less than 3. A t of 2 guarantees the truth of our result in 95 out of 100 cases ; the result might fail in 5 out of 100. It is, therefore, said that with a t value of 2, or more, we establish our result at 5 per cent confidence level. Mind here that the per cent is defined in terms of failure of the result. We are confident about the result because the chance of its failure, the odd against it, is low, i.e., 1 in 20. Similarly with a t is about 3 or more, we establish the result at 1 per cent confidence level ; here again our confidence still rises because the chance of the failure of our result is only 1 in 100. Confidence rises as the chance of failure is reduced.

The method for calculating the SE difference is given in the appendix. Any standard book on statistics will tell you why 2 times SE_M or about 3 times SE_M gives you the limits of 95% or 99% for chance occurrence.

You have noticed from the above account that the treatment of the result of an experiment is generally statistical. You summarise your raw data by using a measure of central tendency and in most cases also of variability. You come to a conclusion by subjecting the summarised results to a further treatment. This treatment gives you the basis for the final conclusion. It tells whether you have really been able to discover a new relationship, or to confirm a relationship stated in the form of a hypothesis. You have, thus, been able to utilize your data for the purpose of your experiment—for answering the question raised in the experiment.

When we will describe different kinds of experiments, you will notice that we do not always use the t test to arrive at a conclusion. In some cases our purpose is served by using a simpler method. Suppose you conduct an experiment to examine the hypothesis that for learning a list of, say, nonsense syllables distributed practice, i.e., with a small interval between trials, is a better method of learning than massed or continuous practice. Suppose, further, that your subject required 6 trials to learn a list of nonsense syllables by distributing the trials and 9 trials to learn a comparable list by practising without a break between trials. There is an absolute saving of three trials by the distributed practice method. This saving of 3 trials is in comparison to the 9 trials of massed practice. In other words there is a relative saving of one-third or thirty-three per cent. Your treatment of the result has been very simple : $\frac{9-6}{9} \times 100$. Your conclusion will be that distributed practice provided a saving of thirty-three per cent. You will note that the relative gain or saving gives a more definite picture of your result than does the absolute gain. Suppose massed practice had taken 12 instead of 9 trials and distributed practice 9 instead of 6 trials. In this case too the absolute saving is of three trials. But the relative saving is less, namely, twenty-five per cent :

$$\frac{12-9}{12} \times 100 \text{ or } 25$$

You will come across still other methods of treating the result. You have, therefore, not to apply any method of treatment arbitrarily. Like all other matters in conducting an experiment, you have to exercise your practical judgment about the appropriate method of treating the result.

Chapter III

Reporting an Experiment

The Importance of Reporting

After you have performed an experiment and arrived at a result you report the experiment. When an experiment is an attempt to discover new facts or to verify a hypothesis, the result of the experiment is reported in a standard journal so that other experimenters may also come to know about your findings and accept or reject them. For this purpose it is necessary that they should also know about the procedure you adopted in conducting the experiment. Then alone they can judge whether you used a suitable design, followed the proper method of collecting data, summarised and treated the data adequately and arrived at a conclusion that logically followed from the results. If they are satisfied with all this they will accept your conclusion and use it as a basis for formulating a new hypothesis or studying some new facts. Otherwise, they will reject your result, pointing out the defects in your investigation. This enables you, or some one else interested in the problem, to conduct another experiment after correcting the errors. The obtained findings will, perhaps, then be free from the defects that affected its predecessor. This is the way science progresses. Every scientist benefits both from the truths arrived at and the mistakes committed by other scientists.

You will appreciate now that it is no less important to report an experiment clearly and comprehensively. Every student of experimental psychology has, therefore, to learn not only the correct method of conducting an experiment. He has to learn also the correct method of reporting an experiment. Below you find the report of an experiment which may serve as a guide while reporting an experiment that you conduct. You will note that the report is divided into several sections that are adhered to more or less closely in reports of most experiments.

A Model Report : Complex Reaction Time

Reaction time is the time that lapses between the presence of a stimulus and the occurrence of the response made to it. When the same stimulus is repeated and everytime the S (subject) has to make the same response, the reaction time is called simple reaction time. On the other hand, when several stimuli are presented one after the other in chance order and S is required to make one kind of response to one stimulus and another kind of response to another stimulus, or, when S is required to respond to one stimulus, and not to respond to another stimulus, the RT (Reaction Time) is called complex RT.

In the simple RT S is specifically prepared to receive the stimulus which he expects to be repeated every time during the course of the experiment. He is, thus, set to act in the same manner—to take the same position, assume the same posture, use the same muscle systems while responding. The persistence of the same perceptual and muscular set, having to use the same receptor and motor mechanisms, facilitates the perceptual as well as the response processes. This is reflected in the quickness of the response—the RT is small. On the other hand, in complex RT there is an abrupt change from stimulus to stimulus, and from response to response. There can be no special preparedness, no set either to perceive or to act in a specific way. The situation becomes complex and difficult for S. S's RT lengthens on this account. For the same reason, the variability of the RT is also likely to be larger in complex RT. When S happens to get the stimulus that he expects, the RT will be smaller in the trial ; when he happens to get one that is different from what he expects, the RT will be larger. In this experiment an attempt is made to measure S's complex RT in a situation containing more than one stimulus, each one presented in a random order and each one demanding a different response, and to compare it with his simple RT in order to find out the difference between the two.

Hypothesis : (1) S's complex RT will be longer than his simple RT

(2) The variability of the complex RT will be relatively larger than that of the simple RT.

Method

Apparatus : Multiple Choice Reaction Time apparatus provided with (1) four sets of light points : red, green, yellow and white ; (2) four sets of response buttons and (3) a chronoscope.

Subject : Final Degree class male student of average health, aged 19 years.

Design of the Experiment : The experiment was designed in the ABBA order ; A stands for simple RT, B for complex RT. This design was used to counterbalance practice and fatigue effects. Twenty trials were taken under each of the A—simple RT, and B—complex RT, conditions, as shown below :

Table 1

ORDER OF CONDITIONS

	Simple	Complex	Complex	Simple
No. of Trials	10	10	10	10

Procedure : S was seated comfortably at a table facing the side of the apparatus that contained the light points and the response buttons. His first finger rested on the metal disc fixed at the middle of the board that contained the buttons set equidistantly from the metal disc. He was given the following instruction for condition A—simple RT.

"Here you are going to do something quite interesting. You see four light bulbs—Red, Green, Yellow and White. You also see four buttons each bearing a letter symbol : R, G, Y and W. A particular button is connected with a particular bulb. It is possible to light a particular bulb at a time. When you press the button connected with the bulb the light will be off. However, you will now find only one bulb—the red one, lighted every time. You have to press its button immediately as you see the light. Do you generally work with your right hand or left hand ? Please keep the first finger of that hand resting on this disc. Every time, before the red light is on, I will ask you to get ready. After a short while, the red light will be on. You have to press immediately the button for red. I am trying to find out how quickly you can act. The moment I say 'Ready', become attentive to the red bulb, and the moment you see the red light, press its button. Do you understand ? That's right."

Following was the instruction for condition B—complex RT. "Now all the four bulbs will be lighted, one at a time. The moment you see a light press the button for that light and the light will be off. If you press the button for another light that is not on, the light will not be off. It will be off only when the correct button is pressed. Always press, therefore, the correct button—the button connected with the light that is on. Here I am going to find out how quickly you can act in a complex situation. Let your first finger be resting on the disc. When I say 'Ready', be attentive to the bulbs, and immediately as you see a particular light, press its button. Do you understand ?"

For the second part of condition A, S was instructed that he was to do what he did in the beginning of the experiment; only the Red light would appear every time and he would immediately press its button.

For the complex RT condition, E (Experimenter) took 5 trials for each of the four lights, administered in chance order.

The length of the foreperiod was kept constant by mental counting, namely, two seconds, in both conditions. To make sure whether S responded after he had perceived the stimulus, catch tests were also introduced in simple RT condition, i.e., some time the Ready signal was given without being followed by the stimulus. If S reacted without receiving the stimulus, he was instructed not to do so, which prevented him from doing this in future.

After the trials in both conditions were concluded, S's introspection was also taken. He was asked to describe his experiences while responding to the two conditions of the experiments—how he felt and whether he experienced any special difficulty.

Introspective Report : "The work was very interesting. I always tried to press as quickly as I could. But some time I feel I did not press very quickly. It was easy to press the single button when only red light was appearing. But when the different lights came at different times, I felt perplexed. I took longer time to press. At first I tried to guess which light would come. But the guess did not work. So I gave up guessing. I waited for the light to be on and then pressed its button. In the beginning I had some difficulty in selecting the correct button. But afterwards I had no difficulty. I wonder how I performed in the experiment !"

Result

Raw data are reproduced in the Appendix.

Table 2

MEAN, SD AND SE_M FOR THE SIMPLE AND COMPLEX RT'S AS WELL AS THE SE DIFF. BETWEEN MEANS, t, p AND C.V.

Reaction Time in Milliseconds

	Simple	Complex
Mean	190.35	430.80
SD	11.65	27.84
SE_M	2.67	6.39
CV	6.12	6.44

$SE_{diff.}$ 6.29

t 35

p $\angle$ .01

Table 2 shows that the Mean for the complex RT is significantly much larger than that for the simple RT. The relative variability of the RT's in the two conditions is not very different ; the coefficients of variability are quite close.

Table 3

MEAN AND SD TO RED LIGHT IN THE TWO CONDITIONS

	Simple	Complex
N	20	5
Mean	190.35	433.40
SD	11.65	43.55

Table 3 gives the Means and SD's for the RT to red light in the two conditions. As compared to the Mean of the simple RT, the Mean of the complex RT is about as large as that for the complex RT to all the four light stimuli treated together (Table 2). The variability, however, for the complex RT to red light is more than one and a half time that for the complex RT to all the four stimuli ; the two SD's are 43.55 and 27.84, respectively (Table 2).

Table 4

MEAN RT'S FOR THE FIRST 10 AND THE NEXT 10 TRIALS UNDER EACH CONDITION

Condition	RT First Half	Second Half
Simple	194.70	186.00
Complex	453.20	408.40

Table 4 shows that the Mean RT for the second half of the trials in each condition is smaller than that for the first half.

Discussion

Our first hypothesis, namely, that complex RT is longer than simple RT has been strongly supported by the results obtained. The value of t is 35 which is significant at much above the 1 per cent level of confidence (Table 2). Same is evidently the case with the complex RT to the red light (Table 3).

Our second hypothesis seems to lack support when we consider the variability of the complex RT's to all the four kinds of stimuli treated together (Table 3). It seems that in the complex situation S did not expect any special stimulus to appear and was, therefore, equally unprepared for each one. S's introspection also corroborates this point. Hence, though there was considerable increase in the length of the RT's, their relative variability remained unaffected, when compared to the simple RT's. But when we consider the variability of the 5 complex RT's to the red light, our hypothesis seems to be substantiated (Table 3). It appears that the set formed during the first 10 trials of the uniform presentation of the red light, at times, facilitated S's reaction to this light also in the complex situation ; this resulted in reduction in the length of the RT. At other times the long interrupted and infrequent appearance of the red light in the series, produced a resistance to the set to respond to this stimulus which further delayed the response to the red light. The RT's became, as a result, most erratic and variable.

We further note that practice influenced the RT's in both conditions (Table 4). This is clear also from the inspection of the raw data; RT's in both conditions gradually decrease. Our results support the general finding about the effect of practice on RT.

Our raw data also bring another point to light. Set has a facilitating influence in a uniform situation. It has an interfering effect when there is a change in the situation. The first RT in the complex situation is considerably large; it is 489 ms. With the gradual dissolution of the set, there is a gradual reduction in the length of the complex RT's ; the RT to red, when this stimulus occurred second time in the series, is an exception. This we have explained earlier as due to the resistance to set.

The facilitative effect of set is also marked in the steep rise in simple RT in the trial immediately following the complex RT series. The RT of 213 ms. was higher than the RT in the very first trial of the simple RT series and much higher than that for the tenth trial of that series which was 188 ms. only. This happened because of the dissolution of set during the course of the complex RT trials.

Conclusion

We can draw the following conclusions :

1. Complex RT is longer than simple RT.
2. Complex RT may also be relatively more variable than simple RT.
3. Practice influences the Reaction Time.
4. Preparatory set is a factor in RT.

Reference

Woodworth, R. S. and Schlosberg, H., *Experimental Psychology*, (1954), Chap. 2, pp. 8-38.

Appendix

Raw Data

A. Simple		B. Complex		B. Complex		A. Simple	
SN	Light RT	SN	Light RT	SN	Light RT	SN	Light RT
1	R 210	1	G 489	11	G 418	11	R 213
2	R 198	2	Y 468	12	Y 425	12	R 199
3	R 203	3	R 438	13	R 412	13	R 194
4	R 189	4	W 456	14	Y 408	14	R 189
5	R 193	5	Y 462	15	W 415	15	R 184
6	R 202	6	W 426	16	R 405	16	R 186
7	R 183	7	R 489	17	G 416	17	R 174
8	R 191	8	G 448	18	W 388	18	R 178
9	R 190	9	R 423	19	W 400	19	R 168
10	R 188	10	Y 433	20	G 397	20	R 175

Review of the above Report

You read above a complete report of an experiment. You noticed that the report is headed by the title of the experiment. The title defines the broad area in which the experiment falls. It does not state the problem. In order to formulate the problem one has to prepare the ground, to clarify the concepts used and describe other relevant facts and findings. In some cases, however, the problem itself is used as the title unless its statement is very long. The part of the report that is meant to prepare the ground for formulating the problem forms the introduction to the experiment. The report of an experiment, thus, begins with a concise introduction. This is followed by the statement of the specific problem that is investigated in the experiment and formulation of the hypothesis or hypotheses that are to be examined.

Under Method you have important details about the apparatus. No mention need be made of such accessories as a battery, connecting wires, etc., for example, when, say, an electrically operated apparatus is used. Besides the apparatus, there may be other important materials used in some experiments, like lists of words or syllables, a cancellation sheet, a pack of playing cards, and so on. These should also be mentioned. The sub-heading then should be Apparatus and Materials. In some experiments there may be no special apparatus. The sub-heading would then consist of only Materials. Materials like paper and pencil used for recording data should not be mentioned.

Design of the experiment also comes under Method. So do the details of the procedure which also include 'Instruction to S'.

Introspection, when taken, is placed at the end of the procedure. As noted earlier (p. 25), introspection is not necessary for all experiments. In fact in most reported experiments, introspection does not occur. When introspection is taken, it must be used while discussing the results, as you notice in the above report. Merely taking introspection without using it, makes it altogether superfluous.

In the above report, you must have noticed a clear difference between the language of the instruction and that of the rest of the report. The language of instruction is not only simple and straightforward; it is also non-technical. The instruction is meant to be understood by a person who may happen to know not even the A B C of psychology. The language of the rest of the report is somewhat terse and technical. In fact you will find it also difficult as compared to the language used in the earlier chapters of this book. The reason is that the report of an experiment is meant for a psychologist who is fully familiar with the vocabulary of psychology. The report is not intended for a lay reader—one who is not aware of psychological terms and techniques. The report is, therefore, written in a technical and scientific style. You have to learn to express yourself in the technical language of psychology. The writing of the report gives you a training for this. Maybe, when you read the above report, at places you find its language difficult for you to understand. But as the report is meant to be a model for you, it would not have been proper to use a different style of writing. You have to learn the standard mode of expression used in the science of psychology.

You must have noticed that the report of an experiment is written in the past tense. The report is the account of an experiment that has already been conducted. At the time of writing the report, the experiment has become a thing of the past. It would be highly improper, therefore, to use the present or the future tense in the report. When you plan an experiment, you use the future tense ; you propose to conduct an experiment whose details you work out before conducting it. At the time of planning, the experiment is still to be conducted. But at the time of reporting, the experiment has already been conducted. Hence the use of the past tense in the report.

In the above report the broad heading, namely, Method, is followed by the broad heading, namely, Result. Under this you summarise your data and present the summary in the form of tables. For each table you also use a title. The title tells you what the table represents. The statement made in the table is also clarified ; the clarification is placed after the table. You find that you have a table of Raw Data also. But this table finds its place at the end of the report, as an appendix to the report.

In many reports you will come across a graph, or graphs. The graph presents the results for visual inspection. Graphs are very useful in making comparisons of the data obtained in the two or more conditions of an experiment. They give you a picture of the raw data, and also, sometimes, of the summarised results. We could have prepared a graph for the raw data of the experiment reported here. By looking at the graph you could have known the increase or decrease in the reaction times from trial to trial. It was, however, not convenient to prepare a graph. The Mean Complex RT is more than twice as large as the Mean Simple RT (Table 2). For preparing a graph of moderate size, within an area, say, 3" wide and 4" long, we would have been required to use very large units of steps against which the RT's for the forty trials of the experiment would have been plotted. But the range within which the RT's vary in each condition is so small that the difference in RT's of the different trials within each condition could not have been shown clearly. The graph would, then, have served no purpose. That is why the above report does not include a graph. You will find in experiments, particularly, on learning and remembering and forgetting, that graphs are very helpful in presenting a detailed picture of your data. You can discover some special features of your results by just looking at the graph.

The description of the results in the form of tables, and graphs also where possible, is followed by discussion of the results. In the discussion you examine your problem and the hypothesis, where formulated, in the light of your results. The results form the evidence for or against your hypothesis. You weigh each part of the result in order to come to a conclusion. You try to explain on the basis of your data why your result failed to support your hypothesis, if this happens. You may also refer to other reported results and see how your result compares with them. You make use of your data to explain the discrepancy wherever found.

Writing the discussion of one's result requires the application of his thinking and reasoning capacities to the full. Whatever conclusion one draws for or against his hypothesis, or about certain findings not anticipated in the statement of the problem, must directly follow from the results. The data must convincingly lead to it.

You should have noted in the above discussion that first an overall comparison has been made between the two conditions of the experiment. This is followed by detailed analysis of the data. For this purpose one refers to the raw data and to the graph prepared on the basis of the raw data, where convenient. The data express certain facts that are lost in their treatment. You have to develop the art of comprehending what the data manifest ; you have to learn the language of the data. When you look at the data carefully and examine their inter-relationships, you will discover certain facts that are missed in the summarised data.

You will appreciate that writing a good report is a matter of skill one acquires by practice. The skill is born of intelligent performance of the experiment and judicious utilization of the data. A mechanical approach will never make you learn how to conduct an experiment and how to report it. Intelligent practice will alone enable you to acquire the desired skill. Reading the reports of experiments published in standard journals will lend you the necessary insight for developing skill.

Recommended Readings

CHAPTERS II AND III

McGuigan, F. J., *Experimental Psychology*, Chapters 1-4, Prentice-Hall of India Private Ltd., 1969.

Townsend, John C., *Introduction to Experimental Method*, Chapters 8 to 11 and Chapter 17, McGraw-Hill, 1953.

CHAPTER IV

Psychophysical Experiments

Psychophysics

A GROUP of scientists who later called themselves psychophysicists became interested in the scientific study of the psychological processes of which one becomes aware in self-observation or introspection. These scientists were trained in the methods of the physical sciences and they sought to develop similar methods for the study of the psychological processes. They were impressed by the close relationship between the properties of the physical stimulus and the characteristics of mental events. The sensation of colour, for example, is related to the length of the light wave, that of brightness to the strength of the light stimulus. Similarly, the sensation of loudness is related to the intensity of the sound stimulus, that of tone to the frequency of the sound wave. Such relationships between the physical properties of the stimulus and the attributes of sensations are noticeable in respect of all kinds of sensations ; the physical and the psychological dimensions are closely related. The psychophysicists thought that a systematic study of the relationship could enable them to discover some laws governing the relationship. They called themselves psychophysicists because of their interest in the study of the relationship between the physical and the psychological. The study of the relationship—its description and interpretation—they called the science of psychophysics.

The close relationship between the physical and the psychological led the psychophysicists to think that it may be possible to measure the characteristics of the psychological events just as it is possible to measure the properties of physical objects. To measure the characteristics of objects, we use a scale of measurement ; we have a scale for measuring length, weight, density, etc., of physical objects. The scale uses a unit of measurement which is the same for all ranges of the measured characteristic. For example, we measure length in units of inch or meter, weight in units of ounce or gram, which remain constant for all lengths or all weights. The scale, further, begins with a zero value, which implies absence of the measured characteristic. The psychophysicists thought that for measuring the characteristics of the psychological events too one should develop a similar scale. The zero value of such a scale, its origin, would be at the point where the mental process first occurs. The psychophysicists noted that in spite of the close relationship between the two dimensions—the physical and the psychological, the zero value of the psychological scale is not the same as the origin of the physical scale. There is no mental response to the very low values of the physical stimulus. In other words, the physical value of the stimulus should reach a particular level beyond zero before it can elicit a mental response. In the area of visual sensation, for example, the intensity of the light stimulus should be a little above zero for the sensation of light to occur. Similarly, the intensity of the stimulus should further increase before one can experience the sensation of colour. The same principle holds for the other kinds of sensations.

Stimulus Threshold—RL

The psychophysicists called that value of the stimulus above zero at which a sensation takes place and below which one experiences no sensation, the least noticeable value of the stimulus. They gave a technical name to this minimal value. They called it '*limen*' in German, which is translated as *threshold* in English. The least noticeable value of a stimulus was thus called the Stimulus Threshold. The German word for stimulus is *Reis*. The stimulus threshold was termed in German as *Reis Limen*. RL is the abbreviation for *Reis Limen*, and stands, thus, for the least noticeable value of a stimulus. It was found that the least noticeable value of a stimulus is not identical in all observations ; it undergoes some change from trial to trial. The RL was, therefore, defined to be that value of a stimulus which was noticeable in 50 per cent of observations and not noticeable in the remaining 50 per cent. We will see that the psychophysicists developed systematic mehtods for finding the RL or the stimulus threshold for all kinds of sensations.

It has been found that individuals differ in respect of the value of RL ; the least noticeable value of a stimulus is not the same for all. Some persons can notice a stimulus at a much lower value when compared to some other persons. The RL, thus, also becomes a measure of sensitivity to a stimulus or of sensory acuteness. Persons differ in visual acuity, auditory acuity, and so on ; some are less and some are more sensitive to a particular class of stimuli.

Difference Threshold—DL

The RL provided the zero for the psychological scale. The psychophysicists further noticed that like its zero value, the unit of measurement in the psychological scale is not identical with that of the physical scale. For every unit of increase or decrease in the value of a stimulus, there is not the same unit of increase or decrease in the intensity of the sensation. Further, while the unit remains the same throughout the physical scale, the unit increases with the progress of the psychological scale. The physical difference between 4 grams and 5 grams is the same as that between 60 grams and 61 grams. But the psychological difference, the difference which one can notice by lifting the weights, is not the same. While 4 grams and 5 grams may be noticeably different, 60 grams and 61 grams will be noticeably the same—one is not expected to differentiate between them. The unit of noticeable difference, therefore, increases with increase in the value of the stimulus ; the unit of the psychological scale is not constant for all ranges of the scale.

The psychophysicists determined the noticeable difference between the values of a stimulus in respect of each one of the kinds of sensations, visual, auditory, tactual, thermal, and so on. In every case they found that the unit of the noticeable difference, the extent of the difference between any two values of a stimulus at which one can be aware of the difference, changed with change in the value of the stimulus. They called the just noticeable difference to any value of a stimulus the differential threshold or *Differential limen* ; it is abbreviated to DL. The DL was also called the JND or just noticeable difference. Here again, like RL, the DL was not identically the same for all trials taken by the same subject for the same value of a stimulus. It slightly varied from trial to trial. The DL was, accordingly, defined as the minimum difference between any two values of a stimulus that was noticed 50 per cent of the times and unnoticed the remaining 50 per cent of the times. The DL also came to be used as a measure of one's discriminative power; individuals differ in the size of the DL obtained for the same value of a stimulus. Some persons can discriminate between any two values that fall at a much smaller distance, as compared to others.

Weber's Law

The finding that the unit of the psychological dimension is not constant for the different ranges of the corresponding physical scale, at first created an obstacle in the attempt to develop measures of the psychological processes. Weber solved the difficulty by discovering that though the unit of the psychological scale is not absolutely constant, it is relatively constant. The DL for a stimulus bears a constant ratio to the stimulus irrespective of the value of the stimulus. In other words, though the DL increases with increase in the size of the stimulus, the increase is always proportional to the size of the stimulus. Thus, if an addition of 1 gram makes an appreciable difference to a weight of 20 grams, an addition of 5 grams will make an appreciable difference to a weight of 100 grams. The DL increases in the same proportion as the stimulus. For this example, it is 1/20 or .05 grams, which will be a constant ratio, according to Weber, for all values of weight. The ratio came to be called Weber's ratio or Weber Fraction. Weber claimed that each kind of sensation has a fixed ratio that is constant. Weber's law, namely, that the just noticeable difference to a stimulus bears a constant ratio to the stimulus, was stated in the form of the following equation:

$$K=\frac{\Delta R}{R},\ K=\text{constant},\ \Delta R=DL,\ R=\text{Stimulus value.}$$

Weber's ratios were found for all kinds of sensations. For light intensity it was around 1/100; for weight the fraction was about 1/30; for sound intensity the ratio was between 1/4 and 1/5, and so on. Other investigators, however, found Weber's fraction to be fairly constant only for the middle ranges of stimulus values; it increased rapidly for the extreme values of a stimulus.

Fechner's Law

Fechner modified Weber's Law and used it for a direct measurement of the intensity of sensations. Weber found that in order that a particular stimulus value be just noticeably different from another value, the other value should be increased by a constant fraction of the first value. Thus if Weber's ratio for a particular kind of sensation is 1/5, a stimulus of the value of 10 should be increased by 1/5 of its magnitude, i. e., by 2 to be just noticeably different from 10; it should be 12. Again the other value that would be just noticeably different from 12 would be 1/5 of 12 added to 12, or 14. 4. Still other magnitude of the stimulus that would be sensed as different should be 1/5 of 14,4 added to 14.4 or 17.28, and so on. We notice in this case that the just noticeably different values can also be determined by using a constant multiple of 6/5; $10\times\frac{6}{5}=12$; $12\times\frac{6}{5}=14.4$ and $14.4\times\frac{6}{5}=17.28$, and so on. Fechner, thus, pointed out that by multiplying the stimulus magnitude each time by constant value, we would produce one unit change in the resulting sensation. Starting with 10 as the initial magnitude, the first change will occur at 12, the second at 14.4, and the third at 17.28 and so on. We notice, therefore, that while the stimulus value progresses by the process of multiplication, the sensation increases by the process of addition. Increase by the process of multiplication is called geometrical progression; that by the process of addition is called arithmetical progression. If two variables so correspond with each other that when one increases geometrically, the other increases arithmetically, the relation between them is termed logarithmic. Hence the sensation values may be thought as the logarithms of the corresponding stimulus values. Those who are familiar with the use of Log Tables know that: Log 1=0, Log 10=1, Log 100=2, Log 1000=3, Log 10000=4, and so on. Fechner's discovery of the logarithmic relationship between values of the stimulus and units of sensation led him to restate Weber's Law as: "sensations are proportional to the logarithm of the exciting stimuli." Fechner expressed the law in the form of the following equation :

$$S = C \text{Log } R; \; S = \text{sensation}, \; C = \text{Weber's constant}, \; R = \text{stimulus magnitude}$$

Fechner, thus, provided an equation for the direct measurement of sensation.

Psychophysical Methods

For a study of the relationship between the physical and the psychological dimensions, the psychophysicists developed three different methods of collection and treatment of data. A brief description of each one is given below :

1. **The Method of Mean or Average Error, also Called the Method of Adjustment or the Method of Reproduction** : As the name suggests, the method is used to determine the average magnitude of error in one's perception of the value of a stimulus. In using this method, the experimenter repeatedly presents to the subject a stimulus of a fixed or constant value, called the standard stimulus, together with a variable stimulus, that is, a stimulus whose value can be changed, also called the comparison stimulus. The subject can increase or decrease the magnitude of the variable stimulus until it appears to him to be equal to the standard stimulus ; the subject is required to adjust the variable stimulus to equality to the standard stimulus. The difference between the value of the standard stimulus and the value of the variable stimulus which S makes equal to the standard stimulus gives an estimate of the magnitude of the error S makes in perceiving the standard stimulus. The Mean of the differences obtained from several observations provides the Average Error or Mean Error in perception. Since S adjusts the variable stimulus to equality to the standard stimulus, the method is also called the Method of Adjustment. Sometimes, the constant stimulus is alone presented to S and he is asked to reproduce the stimulus. For example, he may be shown a line of a fixed length and he may be required to draw other lines of the same length. A comparison of the length of the line presented with the average length of the lines drawn by S gives an estimate of S's error of perception of the constant

line. Hence the other name of the method, namely, the Method of Reproduction.

2. **The Method of Limits, also Called the Method of Just Noticeable Stimulus Difference, or the Method of Minimal Change, or the Method of Successive or Serial Exploration** : This method has been principally used for the determination of the RL or the DL. RL is the lower or upper limit of a stimulus value that can be barely noticed, the just noticeable value of the stimulus, or that value of the stimulus which produces a change in the S's response (p. 56). Similarly DL is the limit of the difference between two values of a stimulus that can be noticed—the just noticeable difference, or the minimal difference that can produce a change in the perception of the stimulus (p. 57). The procedure for determining the RL or the DL by this method involves the presentation of the variable stimulus in a successive or serial order, that is, by gradually increasing or decreasing its amount. Hence the other name, i. e., the method of successive or serial exploration.

3. **The Method of Constant Stimuli or the Method of Frequency** : The chief purpose of this method too is to determine the RL or DL. This method is very similar to the method of limits. Here also different values of a stimulus are presented to S. Each time, for determining RL, S has to report whether he notices the stimulus or fails to notice it, To determine DL, S has to report whether a particular value of the stimulus is the same or different from a standard stimulus which is kept constant. The two methods differ only in the mode of presentation of the variable stimulus. In the method of limits E presents the variable stimulus in a regular increasing or decreasing order ; in the constant stimuli method, E changes the value of the variable stimulus in an irregular or chance order ; a large value of the stimulus may be abruptly followed by a very small value, a still larger value, or by one of medium size. It is just a matter of chance which value of the variable stimulus follows or precedes which other value. The S cannot anticipate whether he would get a larger or a smaller value at the next instant. However, though different values of the variable stimulus are presented in chance order, the same values are presented throughout the entire sets of observations E decides to take in the experiment. That is why it is called

the Method of Constant Stimuli. The name Frequency Method relates to the manner in which the data are treated by this method. The frequency of each kind of responses E makes in respect of each value of the variable stimulus is counted and the RL or DL, as the case may be, is calculated on this basis.

The Method of Constant Stimuli is similar to the Method of Limits also in another respect, as compared to the Method of Average Error. In the method of average error, S manipulates the variable stimulus—he increases or decreases it himself, or he reproduces the standard stimulus. In the other two methods, E manipulates the variable stimulus; S only judges and makes a verbal response to express his judgment.

The application of each one of the psychophysical methods is being illustrated in the remaining part of this chapter.

The Method of Average Error

Determination of the Extent of the Muller-Lyer Illusion by the Method of Average Error : Illusion is a form of perception that takes place in unusual surroundings. There are two kinds of illusion : temporary illusions and permanent illusions. The Muller-Lyer illusion is a permanent illusion, i. e., it always occurs with every person. In this illusion two straight lines of equal length are perceived as unequal. Each of the two straight lines ends with a pair of oblique lines on each side, but the directions of the oblique lines differ in the two straight lines. In one straight line, the oblique lines are turned inward to form arrowheads, in the other they are directed outward to form feather-heads. The feather-headed line is perceived longer than the arrow-headed line. Physically they are equal, but subjectively or psychologically they are unequal. This illusion is called an optical illusion, since it involves an error in the visual perception of length.

In spite of the Muller-Lyer illusion being a permanent one, individuals differ in the extent of the error. An attempt is made to verify the occurrence of the illusion and to determine the extent to which S is liable to this illusion.

Method

Subject : A male undergraduate student.

Apparatus : The Muller-Lyer illusion board with the arrow-headed line of a fixed length of 50 mm.

Procedure : E gave the following instruction to S :

"You notice a line here that is divided into two lines: one having feather-heads and the other having arrow-heads. It is possible for you to shift the part that has feather-heads, back and forth, and thus increase or decrease its length. You have to increase the length of the feather-headed line when you find it smaller than the arrow-headed line, so that you make the two lines equal. You have to decrease its length when you find it longer than the arrow-headed line and thereby make the two lines equal. While shifting back and forth, please stop at the point when you are sure that the two lines look equal to you. Do you understand ?"

In 50 per cent of observations E set the variable line at much greater length so that in order to make the two lines equal, S had to move inward, i. e., toward himself, that portion of the apparatus that was bearing the feather-headed line. In the remaining 50 per cent of trials, the variable was set at a much smaller length, so that, to make the two lines equal, S had to move the feather-headed portion outward, i. e. away from himself. This was done to neutralise the Movement Error[1]. Similarly, in 50 per cent of the trials E handed over the apparatus to S so that the feather-headed line was to the right of the arrow-headed line. In the other 50 per cent of the trials, E turned the apparatus round to 180°, before handing it over to S, so that the feather-headed line appeared on the left of the arrow-headed line. This was done to counter-balance the Space Error[2].

In order to counter-balance practice and fatigue effects, the experiment was planned in the following manner :

R	L	L	R
OIIOOIIO	OIIOOIIO	OIIOOIIO	OIIOOIIO
R=Right	L=Left	O=Outward	I=Inward

As would appear from the above design, in all 32 trials were taken, 16 standard to the right, 16 standard to the left; 16 involving outer movement and 16 inward movement.

Every time after S adjusted the variable length to equality to the standard length, E took the apparatus from him and looking at its back recorded the actual length of the variable line at which S adjusted it to equality to the standard line.

Result

Table 1

RAW DATA SHOWING THE ACTUAL LENGTH OF THE VARIABLE LINE IN MILLIMETERS

	R		L		L		R	
	I	O	I	O	I	O	I	O
	48	49	47	46	47	46	47	48
	49	49	47	47	48	45	48	48
	47	47	46	47	46	47	48	48
	49	46	45	46	46	47	49	47
Sum	193	191	185	186	187	185	192	191

Table 2

MEAN AND SD FOR RIGHT AND LEFT, INWARD AND OUTWARD, FIRST HALF AND SECOND HALF, AND TOTAL, TOGETHER WITH THE SE DIFF, t AND p

	Right	Left	Inw.	Out.	1st Half	Second Half	Total
Sum	767	743	757	753	755	755	1510
Mean	47.94	46.44	47.31	47.06	47.19	47.19	47.19
SD	0.75	0.62	1.25	1.19	1.14	0.89	1.02
Diff.	1.50		0.25		0.00		
SE diff.	0.59		0.37				
t	2.54						
p	$< .02 > .01$						

PSE[3]=47.19, CE[4]=2.81, S_e=0.75, M_e=0.125

Discussion

Looking at Table 1, we notice that S has consistently set the feather-headed line at a smaller length; in each case he has perceived a smaller length of this line to be equal to the physically larger length of the standard line, i.e., 50 mm. The Mean value of his settings is 47.19 mm which is subjectively equal for him to an arrow-headed line of 50 mm. The constant Error is 2.81 mm. which means that S has over-estimated the length of the feather-headed line by 2.81 mm. or about 3 mm.

The difference between the Right and the Left Means is 1.50 mm. and the *t* value is more than 2, which is significant at 2 per cent confidence level. The magnitude of the error exceeds by 0.75 mm. when the standard is to the left of the variable and it is reduced by that value when the standard is to the right of the variable. The net amount of the error due to the illusion, after making adjustment for the space error, is 2.06 mm. or about 2 mm.

S makes no significant movement error ; the difference in this respect (Table 2) is only .25, which being less than the SE diff., is evidently within the limit of chance.

Practice or fatigue has no effect on S's behaviour. The Mean values for the two halves of the performance are identical.

Conclusion

The Muller-Lyer illusion has occurred in case of the subject. The extent of the illusion is about 3 mm. which is reduced to about 2 mm. after adjustment for space error. Though practice has generally been found to reduce the extent of the illusion, our results do not support this finding.

Explanation of Terms

In the experiment reported above we have used several terms which are explained below :

I. **Movement Error[1] and Space Error[2] :** We tried to find out the difference in the subject's visual perception of two straight lines resulting from the difference in the endings of the two lines. The independent variable that we have manipulated in the experiment is the endings of the two lines and the dependent variable that we are observing is the subject's perception of the length of the two lines. There are two other independent variables also that may influence the perception. These are (1) the inward and outward movements made by the S in adjusting the length of the variable line which produce difference in the sensation of movement, or the kinaesthetic sensation produced by the movement of a bodily organ.

This difference too, besides the difference in the visual sensations produced by the different endings of the two lines, may influence the difference in S's perception of the length of the two lines. In order to estimate the length of an object with your eyes closed, you move your hand across its entire length from one end to the other; the kinaesthetic sensation provides the sensory cue for your perception of length. (2) The difference in the relative position of the two lines may as well influence the perception of the lines. The images produced by the two lines in the left and right retinae of the subject are not identical. This fact has been called retinal disparity. The relative position of the lines may, therefore, be another independent variable. To determine the influence of these extraneous independent variables (p. 6), 50 per cent of the times E required S to move inward and 50 per cent of the times outward. Similarly, 50 per cent of the times the standard line was to the right and 50 per cent of the times it was to the left. In psycho-physical experiments these extraneous variables have been called errors and named as **movement error and space error**. Movement error is intelligible to you as it is the result of movement. But why call the error resulting from the relative position of the two lines as space error ? You might be knowing that when two or more objects exist together in space, they acquire some spatial quality; one will be to the right or left of the other, or, above or below the other, as the case may be. Hence, when the relative position of two sets of stimuli, or of two objects that are presented together, influences the result of an experiment, the factor of space comes in. This factor will have to be dealt with in all experiments where two or more sets of stimuli have to be presented together. You will find later, when we describe the use of the other psycho-physical methods, that some time the standard and variable stimuli are not presented together; they come one after the other. You will also see that in such cases we come across what is called **time** error. This is so, because the question of time arises when one object or event precedes or follows another object or event, when one comes **before** or **after** the other, when one event is described as **now** and the other as **then.** Co-existence or simultaneous occurrence is the category of space; succession, or occurring one after the other, is the category of time.

It should be clear from the above that space and time errors are related to the mode of presentation of the standard and variable stimuli. If your procedure requires them to be presented together, you must do something to determine the space error. If they have to follow or succeed each other, you have to do something to bring out the time error.

II. **Point of Subjective Equality** (**PSE**)[3] : We have noticed that on the average, the feather-headed line of the length of 47.19 mm. is perceived by the subject as equal to the arrow-headed line of the length of 50 mm. ; the 47.19 mm. line is subjectively or psychologically equal to the 50 mm. line. Thus 47.19 mm. is the point which defines the limit of the variable line perceived equal to the standard line. Hence the term point of Subjective Equality.

III. **Constant Error**[4] : You have noticed that the error in the perception of the feather-headed line has only one direction ; in spite of being equal, this line is always perceived longer than the arrow-headed line. Its length is always over-estimated. You have noticed earlier that an error may also occur in both directions (p.39). In drawing several lines equal to a given standard line, sometimes you under-draw and sometimes you over-draw ; these are errors of both over-estimation and under-estimation. If you sum up the two kinds of errors the result will be zero — the pluses will cancel the minuses. When the errors are in both directions so that together they cancel each other, we call them variable or unsystematic errors. They are also called chance errors. The measures of variability—average deviation or standard deviation—give us the average amount of the variable errors. In finding the average deviation you ignore the sign of the deviations. In finding the standard deviations, you square the deviations and then add them—by squaring, the minus deviations also become plus. If you do not ignore the sign of the deviations, or do not square them, their sum would be zero. When the errors generally tend to be in one direction, so that their sum is significantly more than zero, they are called constant errors or systematic errors. We come across these two kinds of errors also in other than the psychophysical experiments, but we do not call them errors. When we measure the dependent variable in an experiment on the basis of several observations taken under each condition of the experiment, we find the difference between the results of different conditions and then apply a test of significance (p. 42). The test makes us more or less sure whether the difference between the two or more sets of observations taken under different conditions is due to chance or variable error, or it is due to a real difference between the sets of conditions.

Movement Error, Space Error and Time Error are also constant errors. They influence the perception of the subject beyond the limits of chance; they too determine the difference in the subject's perception. In the general language of experiments, they too are significant independent variables extraneous to the experiment in hand; the experiment in hand is concerned with the difference in the context of the visual stimuli provided by the two lines, i.e., one ending with arrow heads, the other with feather heads. In the above experiment we are interested in the constant error produced by this difference. The constant error is obtained by subtracting PSE from the standard length. The space error and the movement error are obtained in the following manner:

$$S_e = \frac{M_R - M_L}{2} \qquad M_e = \frac{M_o - M_I}{2}$$

S_e = Space error; M_e = Movement error;
M_R = Mean right; M_L = Mean left;
M_o = Mean outward; M_I = Mean inward

Having determined the two kinds of error and having known whether they are significant or not, we deduct them from the CE obtained in the experiment. In the above experiment M_e was not significant; S_e alone was found to be significant (Table 2). S_e was equal to 0.75 mm. By subtracting this amount from CE we obtain the net amount of error due to the optical illusion. This amount was found to be 2.06 mm.

Problems Related to the Experiment

1. **Determination of the Error in Perception of Visual Length or Visual Area**: For visual length, S may be asked to reproduce a standard length several times. The mean of the reproduced lines will be the PSE. The CE will be the difference between the standard length and the PSE. CE may be plus or minus. A plus CE will mean S's tendency to underestimate the standard length; minus CE will reflect his tendency to overestimate the standard length.

For determination of the error of visual area, a card board device can be prepared having two rectangles. The area of one rectangle will be constant; that of the other should be adjustable, i.e., could be increased or decreased by shifting back and forth one part of the apparatus. The experiment will then be done in a manner very similar to the experiment on Muller-Lyer illusion.

2. **Determination of the Extent of the Horizontal-Vertical Illusion** : This illusion is produced by the simultaneous perception of two straight lines, one horizontal and the other vertical, illustrated by the following diagram :

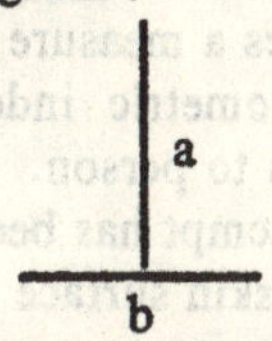

Lines *a* and *b* are physically equal, but psychologically or subjectively line *a* is longer than line *b*. In this problem, error in perception depends upon the relative direction of the two lines. The constant error to be determined will be the space error of direction.

3. **The Effect of the Knowledge of the Result on the Extent of the Muller-Lyer or the Horizontal-Vertical Illusion** : Here S will be informed about the error made in each trial in one set of trials. In another set of trials the knowledge will be withheld.

4. **Effect of Bisection of the Horizontal Line on the Magnitude of the Horizontal-Vertical Illusion** : It has been found that the extent of the illusion is greater in the inverted ⊤ shaped arrangement (⊥) of the two lines than in the ⊤ shaped or └ shaped arrangement, or when the two lines are separated by a gap (|_). This result can be verified by designing and conducting an experiment using the method of average error.

5 **Error of Estimation of the Size of a Coin** : In this experiment the standard will be a round coin. S will be required to increase or decrease the size of a lighted disc by manipulating a knob, so that the size of the disc appears to S to be equal to the size of the coin.

You can think of several other problems to which the method of average error can be applied.

The Method of Limits I

Determination of the Two-Point Threshold by the Method of Limits : When two points on the skin surface are touched simultaneously, one gets the perception of two points only when the two points are separated by a minimal distance. When the separation is smaller than this distance, S gets the perception of one point only, though physically two points are being stimulated at the same time. This minimal distance at which S gets sensation of two points in 50 per cent of the trials and of one point in the other 50 per cent of trials, has been called the 2-point threshold or spatial threshold. It is also called the aesthesiometric index since it provides a measure of the sensitivity of the skin surface. The aesthesiometric index varies from region to region and also from person to person.

In this experiment an attempt has been made to determine the two-point threshold for the skin surface of the S's right palm.

Method

Subject : A female undergraduate student.

Apparatus : Aesthesiometer.

Procedure : A 2-cm. line was drawn on the surface of the S's right palm. The S's forearm extended under a screen so that her palm was invisible to S.

E gave the following instruction to S :

"I will touch your palm sometimes with one pencil point and sometimes with two pencil points. You have to report every time whether one or two points are touching your palm. Try to be very attentive. Every time before your palm is touched you will be given ready signal. Do you understand ?"

E took a few preliminary trials to find out the range within which S's judgment varied between almost all judgments of one point and all judgments of two points. The range was found to be from 8 mm. to 15 mm. After this E started the actual experiment. He took 20 trials in alternate ascending and descending series[1], the separation between the two points of the aesthesiometer being gradually increased or decreased in steps of 1 mm. The trial series were of unequal length[2].

At times E applied only one point of the aesthesiometer as a check stimulus[3].

Result

Table 1

RAW DATA

Distance in mm.	d	a	d	a	d	a	d	a	d	a	d	a	d	a	d	a	d	a	d	a
15	2						2				2				2					
14	2		2				2		2		2				2		2			
13	2		2		2		2		2		2		2		2		2		2	
12	2	2	2	2	2		1		2	2	2	2	2	2	1		1		1	2
11	1	1	2	1	1	2		2	1	1	1	1	1	1		2		2		1
10		1	1	1		1		1		1		1		1		1		1		1
9		1		1		1		1		1		1				1		1		1
8				1				1				1						1		
T	11.5	11.5	10.5	11.5	11.5	10.5	12.5	10.5	11.5	11.5	11.5	11.5	11.5	11.5	12.5	10.5	12.5	10.5	12.5	11.5

a=ascending d=descending $\Sigma T = 221$, Mean=11.45

Table 2

MEAN, STANDARD DEVIATION AND STANDARD ERROR

	Ascending Series	Desending Series	First Half	Second Half	All Series
Mean	11.00	11.90	11.30	11.60	11.45
SD	0.671	0.735	0.60	0.943	0.837
SE_M	0.335	0.267	0.30	0.314	
Diff.	0.90		0.30		
$SE_{diff.}$	0.428		0.434		
t	2.10*		0.69		
p.	$<.10>.05$				

*t=2.09. p=<.05

Discussion

The two-point limen for the S's right palm has been found to be 11.45 mm. The Mean for the descending series is larger than that for the ascending series; the difference between the two Means is 0.90 mm.; the *t* value of 2.10 is near to the 5 per cent significance value of 2.09. The difference may thus be treated to be barely significant. This shows that S's judgments are influenced by the expectation error; S has a tendency to anticipate a change before the occasion for a change in his judgment arises.

There is no evidence of practice or fatigue effect; the Means for the two halves of the series are almost equal; the *t* of 0.69 is insignificant.

Explanation of the Terms Used and the Procedure Adopted in the above Report

1. **Ascending and Descending Series**[1]: E presented the stimulus in ascending and descending series; one series started with so large a value of the stimulus distance between the two points that it always produced the response 'Two'; the distance gradually decreased by small steps until S reported 'One'. The next series started with such a small distance that always produced the response 'One', the distance was gradually increased until S's response was 'Two'. Each series was stopped with the first change in the judgment. The alternate descending and ascending series were

used to find out the constant error of habituation or that of expectation if either one influenced S's judgment. Some S's are likely to repeat the same response even when there is an occasion to change the response—they are resistent to change; others are likely to change a response before the situation actually demanded the change—they are eager to change. The first ones are liable to habituation error; they will persist to respond by 'two' in the descending series and 'one' in the ascending series even on getting the impression of one point or of two points touched, respectively. In the descending series their threshold will be lower—the change of response from 'two' to 'one' would generally occur a little later than it should. In the ascending series their threshold will be higher—the change of response from 'one' to 'two' would generally occur a little later than actually demanded by the impression they get. The ascending and the descendings series taken together would then cancel the habituation error. The second type of S's are liable to expectation error. Experiencing a change in their impression from 'one' to 'two' or from 'two' to 'one', they expect the change to occur and report it earlier than the real occasion for a change of response arises. In the descending series they will respond by 'one' a little earlier than getting a clear impression of being touched by one point, and in the ascending series they will respond by 'two' a little earlier than getting a clear sensation of two points. The threshold for the descending series will be larger than that for the ascending series. The Mean of all series taken together will here again cancel the expectation error.

By separately calculating the Means for the ascending and the descending series and by comparing them, it would be possible to know whether S was influenced by either tendency and became, thus, liable to either the habituation error or the expectation error. If the Mean for the descending series is smaller than the Mean for the ascending series, we get evidence of the constant error of habituation; if the case is just the reverse, there is evidence of the constant error of expectation. In the above experiment we noted evidence of the expectation error, the Mean for the descending series was larger than that for the ascending series.

Since the two kinds of errors tend in different directions you cannot expect the occurrence of both in the same S. In fact the two kinds of errors may throw a light on an inherent tendency in S—on a trait of his personality. The more conservative type of person tends to persist in the same behaviour and shows a resistence to change unless compelled by circumstances. On the other hand, the more radical type is impatient to change even when the situation does not demand change. Experiments can be planned to ascertain the relationship between liability to the constant error of habituation or expectation and the trait of perseveration or of radicalism. A paper-and-pencil test of conservatism and radicalism, or a performance test of the tendency to persevere or to change, may be used for this purpose, besides an experiment using the method of limits.

2. **Series of Unequal Lengths** : If all series were of the same length, i.e., they all started at the same value, S might have formed a set to change his response after a fixed number of steps in each series in a routine manner, without giving full attention to the impression that he actually got. Starting the series not always from the same step avoided the formation of the set and made S more careful in making the response.

3. **Check Stimulus :** This stimulus is used to ascertain whether S is reporting mechanically, i.e., without relating his response to the impression that he actually gets. If his response is mechanical, he would some time give a response of 'two' when only one point actually touched his skin.

4. **T or Transition Point** : Table one shows the transition point or T for each series. The transition point is the midpoint of the step below which the change in response occurs in the descending series and above which a change of response occurs in the ascending series. Each transition point becomes, thus, the threshold value for the series. A Mean of the threshold values of all series gives us the best estimate of the S's two-point threshold. You should bear in mind that the two-point threshold is a RL value. The stimulus is the distance between two points which is increased or decreased. The two-point threshold is the distance between two points that is barely noticeable to the subject. When the two points are perceived as **one** the distance is not noticed. When they are perceived as **two** the distance becomes noticeable. It should not be confused with DL which requires a comparison between a standard stimulus and a variable stimulus. Here we have only a variable stimulus, namely the distance between the two points which is changed in regular order.

Other Problems

1. **Comparison between the Aesthesiometric Indices for any Two or more Selected Parts of the Body, e.g., Finger Tip, Forehand, Forearm, etc.**

2. **Determination of the Effect of Muscular Fatigue on the Two-Point Threshold :** The experiment will be done according to the fore-test—after-test design (p. 11). The aesthesiometric index for the same region of the upper surface of the S's forearm, or of his palm, will be determined twice with a gap in between during which S will work on an ergograph or a hand dynamometer until he shows clear signs of muscular fatigue (Appendix III).

3. **Determination of the RL for Hue, Using the Method of Limits :** This experiment can be done by using a photometer. This is an apparatus for increasing and decreasing the intensity of a light shown to the subject. Using a coloured light, you determine the intensity of the light at which S can perceive the hue or colour of the light in 50 per cent of observations. Since photometers are not generally available in a psychological laboratory, a colour rotator can be used for the purpose. One coloured disc, say red, and one white disc are so fixed on the wheel of the colour rotator that only a certain portion of each disc is visible at a time. In the ascending series, the visible portion of the red disc should be so small, to begin with, that when the wheel is rotated S perceives no colour. The visible portion of the red disc will be then increased by small degrees in the series and S will report his perception at each step. The descending series will start with a portion of the red disc large enough to produce a clear perception of colour. The visible part of the red disc will then be gradually decreased in regular steps and S will every time report his perception, until S fails to see the rotating wheel as red.

The method of limits can also be used for determining the proportion of complementary colours, e.g., red and bluish green, or yellow and blue, whose mixture produces a colourless sensation. Similarly, the proportion of the non-complementary colours whose mixture produces a difference in hue can also be determined, e.g., the proportions of red and yellow that produce orange. There are three laws of colour mixture. You can know about them from any text book of general psychology. The method of limits can be used to demonstrate these laws.

RL values can be determined by the method of limits for all sense modalities, using in each case a suitable apparatus. You can determine, e.g., the RL for auditory acuity or the minimum distance at which S can hear the ticking of a time piece, or a click produced by an acoumeter (Appendix III).

4. **Demonstration of the Gestalt Law of Closure in the Perception of Geometrical Figure :** The circumfrance of say a circle may be broken into several arcs as shown in the following figures :

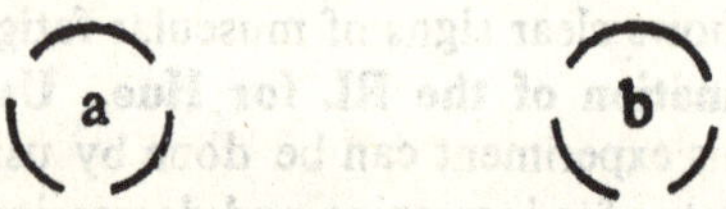

If figure *a* is exposed to you for a simple moment by a tachistoscope (Appendix III) and you are asked to report what you see, most likely you will say 'a circle'. This happens because the figure is perceived as a unified whole ; the gaps in the figure are closed. But if the gaps are wide enough as in figure *b*, you are most likely not to report the perception of a circle. By the method of limits you can determine the minimum gap between the arcs of a circle for your perception to be governed by the law of closure.

5. All the problems that were earlier suggested for experiments by the method of average error, can be dealt with by the method of limits.

The Method of Limits II

Determination of the DL for Visual Length, Using the Method of Limits : DL is the difference threshold or the least noitceable difference between any two values of a stimulus. It has been found that there is no point-to-point correspondence between the change in the physical values of a stimulus and the change in the resulting responses ; change in the response occurs only when the change in the physical value of a stimulus reaches a certain limit. This limit varies with the size of the physical stimulus. The larger the value of a stimulus, the larger the required amount of increment or decrement in the value for the change to be noticeable. Weber noticed a relationship between the size of the physical stimulus and the size of the corresponding DL. Weber's law stated that the increase or decrease in the size of the DL is proportional to the increase or decrease in the size of the stimulus. However, we are not concerned with this matter in the present experiment. Our object is to determine the minimum change in the given length of a straight line that can be perceived as such by the subject. Since individuals differ in this respect, my S's DL for visual length may be large or small and, thus, throw a light on his power of discrimination between visible lengths or distances.

Method

Subject : A male undergraduate student.

Material : A set of 13 white cards, 4"×2", each having a straight line in the middle drawn in black ink, the length of the lines ranging from 14 mm. to 26 mm. One additional card having a 20 mm. line used as standard.

Procedure : S was seated at a table facing E. E gave the following instruction :

"I will place before you two white cards each having a black line. You have to compare the length of the lines and decide whether the line on the right is longer than, equal to, or shorter than the line on the left. Please look at the two lines and give your judgment carefully. When you cannot make up your mind, tell that you are doubtful. Do you understand".

The variable lines were presented in alternate ascending and descending series. The series were of unequal lengths. In all 10 series were taken. In 5 series, the standard line was on the right and in the other 5 series the standard line was on the left. This was done to neutralise the space error. The series with the altered positions of the standard and variable cards were introduced in random order. Since S was every time required to judge the line on the right in comparison to the line on the left, when the standard occurred to the right, his judgment was reversed at the time of recording. The 'doubtful' responses were recorded as equal.

Result

Table 1

RAW DATA AND TREATMENT OF DATA

Length in mm.	R a	L d	L a	R d	L a	R d	L a	L d	R a	R d	
26		L						L			
25		L		L				L		L	
24		L		L		L		L		L	
23		L		L		L	L	L	L	=	
22	L	=	L	L	L	=	=	=	=	L	
21	=	=	=	L	=	=	=	=	=	=	
S 20	=	=	=	=	L	=	=	=	S	=	
19	S	=	S	S	S	S	S	S	S	S	
18	S	S	S		S		S		S		
17	S		S		S		S		S		
16	S		S				S		S		
15	S		S						S		
14	S										
Tu[1]	21.5	22.5	21.5	20.5	21.5	22.5	22.5	22.5	22.5	23.5	Σ Tu=221, MTu=22.10
Tl[1]	19.5	18.5	19.5	19.5	19.5	19.5	19.5	19.5	20.5	19.5	Σ Tl=195, MTl=19.50
PSE[2]	20.5	20.5	20.5	20.0	20.5	21.0	21.0	21.0	21.5	21.5	Σ PSE=208, MPSE=20.80

IU[3]$=22.10-19.50=2.60$ mm. $DL=\frac{IU}{2}=\frac{2.60}{2}=1.30$ mm.

$PSE=\frac{22.10+19.50}{2}=\frac{41.60}{2}=20.80$ mm., $CE=PSE-St=0{\cdot}80$ mm.

$PSE_a=20.80$ mm , $PSE_d=20\ 80$ mm., $PSE_R=20.90$ mm.,

$PSE_L=20.70$ mm., $Se=\frac{0.20\text{ mm.}}{2}=0.10$ mm.

Discussion

S's DL for the standard length of 20 mm. is 1.30 mm. which is 6·5% of the standard length. S can thus correctly perceive the difference in the length of a 20 mm. line only when it is increased by 1.30 mm. Between 19.50 mm. and 22.10 mm. his judgment about any difference in length is uncertain ; the variable length of 20.80. mm. is most likely to appear to S as equal to 20 mm. The constant error being 0.80 mm., S over-estimates the standard length to this extent. The error is uninfluenced by the factors of habituation or expectation ; the PSE values for the ascending and descending series are identical. The space error (Se) is much too small to call for any special consideration.

The DL being only 6.5% of the standard, S is fairly sensitive to difference in length

Explanation of the Terms Used and the Procedure Adopted in the Experiment

1. **Transition :** T or transition marks the point of change in S's response. Tl (lower transition) marks for the ascending series, the first change from a 'S' (shorter) to a 'non-S' response ; Tu (upper transition) marks the first change from a 'non-S' response to a 'L' (longer) response. In the first series (Table 1) these occur between 19 and 20, whose midpoint is 19.5, and between 21 and 22, whose midpoint is 21.5, respectively. For the descending series, Tu marks the first change from L to non-L response and Tl marks the first change after that from non-S to S response. In the fifth series which is an ascending one, subject makes an L response after S response and then makes an = response which is followed by an L response. Similarly in the last series which is a descending one, the = response is followed by a L response after which the subject again makes the = response. Tu and Tl for these series have been determined according to the rules just mentioned. In the fifth series Tl is the midpoint of the steps 19 and 20, the first change from S to non-S, and Tu is the midpoint of the steps 21 and 22, the first change from non-S to L. Similarly the rule for the descending series has been applied to the last series, and so the Tu and Tl for this series are 23.5 and 19.5 respectively. However, while collecting data, such irregular series may be discarded and additional series may be taken in order to complete the desired number of series.

2. **PSE[2] :** Point of subjective Equality is the theoretical value of the variable stimulus which is most likely to appear equal to the standard stimulus or where plus and minus judgments balance. We have already explained PSE earlier (p. 67). We can determine the PSE for each series; it is the step or midpoint of the steps eliciting 'equal' response. The best estimate of the PSE for the entire set of observations is the Mean of the PSE values of the individual series. The PSE can be determined by an alternative method also :

$$PSE = \frac{Tu + Tl}{2}$$

PSE found by the two methods should be identical. CE or constant error is found by subtracting the standard stimulus value from PSE (PSE − St)

3. IU[3] : The Interval of Uncertainty marks the range within which neither 'short' nor 'long' responses predominate. It is the difference between Tu and Tl. DL or difference limen is half interval of uncertainty or $\frac{Tu - Tl}{2}$

Other terms used have already been explained in the preceding experiments.

Other Problems

1. **Determination of DL for Grey, Using the Method of Limits :** Here too the colour rotator will be used (p. 75). Two interlocking white and black discs of smaller size will be superimposed upon two interlocking larger white and black discs, so that only the outer portions of the larger discs will be visible. The larger discs will be set at 180° each, so that half of the black disc and half of the white disc will be visible. The proportion will remain constant throughout the experiment. The smaller discs will be set at different angles in different trials. S will be required to report in each trial whether the grey produced by the smaller discs, when the wheel is rotated, was darker, lighter or of the same shade as the grey produced by the large discs. In the ascending series the proportion of the black disc will be gradually increased, to produce darker and darker grey ; in the descending series the proportion of the black discs will be gradually decreased to produce lighter and lighter grey.

2. **Determination of the DL for a Given Distance between Two Points Touched on the Skin Surface :** A constant distance between two points of an aesthesiometer clearly perceived as two when touching the skin surface will be used as the standard. A set of variable distances between two points, starting with a value smaller than the standard distance, but clearly perceived when applied to the skin surface, and increasing in regular steps, will be used for comparison with the standard distance in alternate increasing and decreasing series. To neutralise the time error, in 50 per cent of the series the standard distance will precede the variable distances; in the other 50 per cent, the standard distance will follow the variable distances. The change in the order of the standard and variable distances will however be made in a random unsystematic manner.

The method of limits can be used for determination of the DL within any sense modality, e.g., DL for pitch and loudness in the area of audition, for taste and smell in the gustatory and olfactory areas, respectively, and so on. Appropriate apparatus has been prepared for the purpose of exploring a particular sense modality.

Method of Constant Stimuli I

Determination of the Subject's Span of Apprehension, Using the Method of Constant Stimuli : In a single glance, an individual will be clearly aware of only a small portion of the present mass of stimuli so that he is able to give correctly the details of what he observed. If the same kind of stimuli are very briefly exposed to S several times so that each time he can give a single glance to them, the average amount of correct details that he reports constitutes his span of apprehension. Individuals differ in their span of apprehension; some can catch more distinct and clear details in one glance than others. The difference in span of apprehension also depends upon the nature of the stimulus, e.g., the span of apprehension is larger for words than for unrelated letters. The object of the experiment is to determine S's span of apprehension for letters.

Method

Subject : A 13-year old school boy.

Apparatus : Disc Tachistoscope.

Materials : A set of 8 cards of the same size, each one

containing different numbers of alphabets in random order ranging from 3 to 10. In no case the alphabets constituted a word.

Procedure : E exposed the cards to S, one after the other, in a random order. A card was fixed on the card-holder, S was then given 'Ready' signal after which the latch that held the disc in the starting position was released. The rotation of the disc provided an exposure of 60 ms. or about 1/15 of a second. S was then to report the letters that he could observe. Each card was exposed 10 times.

E gave the following instruction :

"You will see a card having some letters written on it. The card will appear before your view for a single moment only. You have to be very careful, as you have to report the letters that you see. When I give you the 'ready' signal, look at the white dot on the black board. The card bearing the letters will appear for a single moment at this place. Be careful and attentive. Do you understand ?"

E prepared a plan for the exposure of the cards so that each card could be exposed ten times, though the order of exposure was random. E recorded S's report of what he saw after each exposure.

Results

Table 1

RAW DATA SHOWING RIGHT (+) AND WRONG (−) APPREHENSION OF EACH CARD FROM TRIAL TO TRIAL

No. Letter Stimulus	Trials									
	1	2	3	4	5	6	7	8	9	10
10	−	−	−	−	−	−	−	−	−	−
9	−	+	−	−	−	−	+	−	−	−
8	−	−	−	+	−	+	−	−	+	+
7	−	+	+	−	−	+	−	+	−	−
6	+	−	+	+	+	−	+	−	+	−
5	+	−	+	+	−	+	+	−	+	+
4	+	+	+	+	+	−	+	+	+	+
3	+	+	+	+	+	+	+	+	+	+

Table 2

FREQUENCY AND PROPORTION OF RIGHT AND WRONG APPREHENSION OF EACH CARD

No. Letter Stimuli	Frequency R	Frequency W	Proportion p	Proportion q
10	0	10	0.00	1.00
9	2	8	0.20	0.80
8	4	6	0.40	0.60
7	4	6	0.40	0.60
6	6	4	0.60	0.40
5	7	3	0.70	0.30
4	9	1	0.90	0.10
3	10	0	1.00	0.00
			Sum p=3.20	Sum q=2.80

Treatment of Result

$$RL = A - i/2 - i \text{ sum } p = 10 - .50 - 3.20 = 6.30$$

$$RL = B + i/2 + i \text{ sum } q = 3 + .50 + 2.80 = 6.30$$

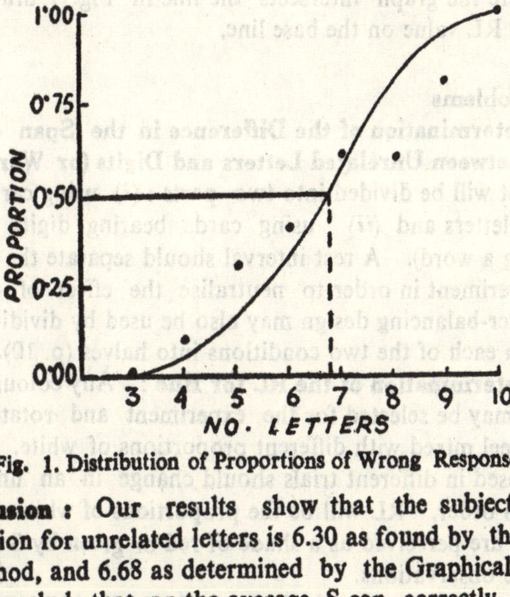

Fig. 1. Distribution of Proportions of Wrong Responses.

Conclusion : Our results show that the subject's span of apprehension for unrelated letters is 6.30 as found by the Summation[1] Method, and 6.68 as determined by the Graphical[2] Method. We may conclude that, on the average, S can correctly apprehend letters when their number is below seven.

Explanation of Terms Used and the Procedure Adopted

The RL has been computed by the summation[1] as well as the graphical[2] method. The formula for the summation method is RL=A−i/2−sum p=B+i/2+sum q.

Sum p and sum q are found by adding up the proportions in the p and q columns, respectively. The proportion for the value of the stimulus for which all responses are either right or wrong has been left out in adding the columns (Table 2). A is the Apical value, i.e., the value of the stimulus for which all responses are wrong and just below which the responses are divided between right and wrong. B is the Basal value, i e., the value for which all responses are right and just above which the responses are divided between right and wrong. i/2 is half step interval. The alternative formula for RL is used as a check on the calculation. The RL should be the same according to either formula.

For calculating RL by the graphical method, the proportions of wrong responses have been plotted on graph paper (Fig. 1) and a smooth ogive passing close to the points has been drawn by free hand. A perpendicular dropped on the base line from the point where the graph intersects the line in Fig. 1 drawn at .50, marks the RL value on the base line.

Other Problems

1. **Determination of the Difference in the Span of Apprehension between Unrelated Letters and Digits (or Words) :** The experiment will be divided into two parts : (*i*) using cards bearing unrelated letters and (*ii*) using cards bearing digits or (letters composing a word). A rest interval should separate the two parts of the experiment in order to neutralise the effect of eye strain. The counter-balancing design may also be used by dividing the sets of trials in each of the two conditions into halves (p. 10).

2. **Determination of the RL for Hue :** Any colour, say, red or green, may be selected for the experiment and rotated on the colour wheel mixed with different proportions of white. The proportions used in different trials should change in an unsystematic or random order. RL will be the proportions of white and red or green that are perceived as a shade of red or green by S in 50 per cent of the observations.

All other problems to which the method of limits applies can be dealt with by the method of constant stimuli also.

Method of Constant Stimuli II

Verification of Weber's Law in Respect of DL for Lifted Weight : We fail to notice every increment or decrement to the value of a stimulus ; a stimulus may increase in size or intensity without one's being able to appreciate the change. Only when the amount of the increment or decrement reaches a certain limit, one can notice the difference. The limit of noticeable difference has been called the difference threshold or DL. The DL, however, does not remain the same for all values of a stimulus ; it increases or decreases with the size or intensity of the stimulus. Weber discovered that the DL remains relatively the same for different values of a stimulus. He stated his finding in the form of a law. Weber's law says that the noticeable difference to the value of a stimulus bears a constant ratio to the stimulus ; DL for any stimulus increases or decreases in the same proportion as the value of the stimulus. If the value of a stimulus increases, say, by $\frac{1}{4}$, the DL also increases by the same ratio. For example, if the DL for 20-candle power light is 1-candle power, the DL for 100-candle power light will be 5-candle power. This constant ratio has also been called Weber's fraction. Weber claims this law to be applicable to all sense modalities, and for all values of the stimulus for a particular class of sensations. It states, according to him, a lawful relationship between the physical and the psychological dimensions. The law has been found to be true for all kinds of sensations, but not for all values of a kind of stimulus. It holds only for the intermediate and not for the extreme values of a stimulus.

In this experiment an attempt was made to examine the correctness of Weber's law for the sensation produced by lifting a weight.

Hypothesis : The DL found for each one of two or more different weights will be the same fraction of the respective weights.

Method

Subject : An adult postgraduate student.

Apparatus and Materials : (1) Two sets of seven wooden, plastic or tin containers of the same size and colour but differing in weight by a constant unit ; the cases in one set weighing from 45 to 75 grams, and those in the other weighing from 70 to 130 grams.

Two additional containers, one weighing 60 grams and the other 100 grams. (2) A metronome.

Procedure : The experiment was divided into two parts. Part I used the first set of 7 comparison weights, differing by units of 5 grams, with the weight of 60 grams as the standard. Part II used the other set of comparison weights differing by units of 10 grams, with 100 grams as the standard.

For each part of the experiment, E prepared a plan for the presentation of the comparison weights and the standard weight so that though the comparison weights were presented in a random order, as required by the method of constant stimuli ; each comparison weight was presented the same number of times together with the standard weight. Also, in order to neutralise time error (p. 66), 50 per cent of the times the standard was presented first and the remaining 50 per cent of times it was presented next to the comparison weight.

E gave the following instruction to S : "Here I am going to judge your capacity for the discrimination of weights. I will place one weight between your thumb and first finger. The moment you hear the first tick, lift the weight by moving only your wrist. When you hear the next tick place the weight back on the table. I will then let you hold another weight to be lifted in the same manner as the first one. You have to judge and report whether the second weight is heavier or lighter than the first one, or both are equal. If you cannot decide or you are in doubt tell this. Try your best to make a judgment and only when you fail to do so, tell that you are uncertain. In this manner, every time you have to decide between two weights whether the second one is heavier or lighter than the first one, or they are equal. Every time your judgment will be about the second weight in relation to the first weight. Be very careful and attentive. Do you understand ?"

S extended his forearm that rested on the table in the same position below the base of a screen ; the screen separated him from E and kept the weights out of his view.

E recorded S's responses on a record sheet previously prepared. E reversed S's judgment in those cases where the standard was presented next to the comparsion weight.

Results

Table 1*A*

RAW DATA

Trials	1	2	3	4	5	6	7	8	9	10
Weights										
75	+	+	+	+	+	+	+	+	+	+
70	+	+	+	=	+	+	+	+	+	+
65	=	+	+	−	=	=	+	+	=	+
S 60	=	+	+	=	=	−	+	=	=	=
55	−	=	=	−	=	−	=	=	−	+
50	−	−	−	−	−	−	−	−	=	−
45	−	−	−	−	−	−	−	−	−	−

Table 1*B*

RAW DATA

Trials	1	2	3	4	5	6	7	8	9	10
Weights										
130	+	+	+	+	=	+	+	+	+	+
120	+	+	+	+	+	=	=	+	+	+
110	+	=	+	=	=	+	+	+	+	+
S 100	+	+	−	−	=	+	=	+	=	=
90	−	−	+	=	−	=	+	=	−	−
80	−	−	−	+	−	−	−	−	=	−
70	−	−	=	+	−	−	−	−	−	−

Table 2*A*

FREQUENCIES AND PROPORTIONS OF THE THREE-CATEGORY JUDGMENTS WITH STANDARD AS 60 GR.

Weight		Frequency			Proportions		
		+	=	−	p	m	q
A	75	10.	0.	0.	1.0	0.0	0.0
	70	9.	1.	0.	0.9	0.1	0.0
	65	5.	4.	1.	0.5	0.4	0.1
	60	3.	6.	1.	0.3	0.6	0.1
	55	1.	5.	4.	0.1	0.5	0.4
	50	0.	1.	9.	0.0	0.1	0.9
B	45	0.	0.	10.	0.0	0.0	1.0
	Sum				1.8	1.7	1.5

Treatment of Result

$$Lu = A - i/2 - i \text{ sum } p = 75 - 5/2 - 5\times 1.8 = 75 - 2.5 - 9.0 = 63.50$$

$$Ll = B + i/2 + i \text{ sum } q = 45 + 5/2 + 5\times 1.5 = 45 + 2.5 + 7.5 = 55.00$$

$$IU = 63.50 - 55.00 = 8.50 \qquad PSE = \frac{63.50 + 55.00}{2} = 59.25 \qquad CE = 59.25 - 60.00 = -0.75$$

$$DL = \frac{8.50}{2} = 4.25 \qquad DL = \frac{5\times 1.7}{2} = 4.25 \qquad K_1 = \frac{4.25}{60} = 0.071$$

Table 2*B*

FREQUENCY AND PROPORTIONS OF THE THREE-CATEGORY JUDGMENTS WITH STANDARD AS 100 GR.

Weights		Frequency			Proportions		
		+	=	−	p	m	q
A	140	10	0	0	1.0	0.0	0.0
	130	9	1	0	0.9	0.1	0.0
	120	8	2	0	0.8	0.2	0.0
	110	7	3	0	0.7	0.3	0.0
	100	4	4	2	0.4	0.4	0.2
	90	2	3	5	0.2	0.3	0.5
	80	1	1	8	0.1	0.1	0.8
	70	1	1	8	0.1	0.1	0.8
B	60	0	0	10	0.0	0.0	1.0
Sum					3.2	1.5	2.3

$$Lu = A - i/2 - i \text{ sum } p = 140 - 10/2 - 10\times 3.2 = 140 - 5 - 32 = 103$$

$$L_l = B + i/2 + i \text{ sum } q = 60 + 10/2 + 10\times 2.3 = 60 + 5 + 23 = 88$$

$$IU = 103 - 88 = 15 \qquad PSE = \frac{103 + 88}{2} = 95.5 \qquad CE = 95.5 - 100 = -4.5$$

$$DL = \frac{15}{2} = 7.5 \qquad DL = \frac{10\times 1.5}{2} = 7.5 \qquad K = \frac{7.5}{100} = 0.075$$

Table 3

DL AND K FOR THE TWO STANDARD VALUES OF THE STIMULUS

Standard Stimulus	Summation Method		Graphic Method	
	DL	K	DL	K
60	4.25	0.071	4.45	0.074
100	7.50	0.075	5.50	0·055
Diff.		0.004		.019

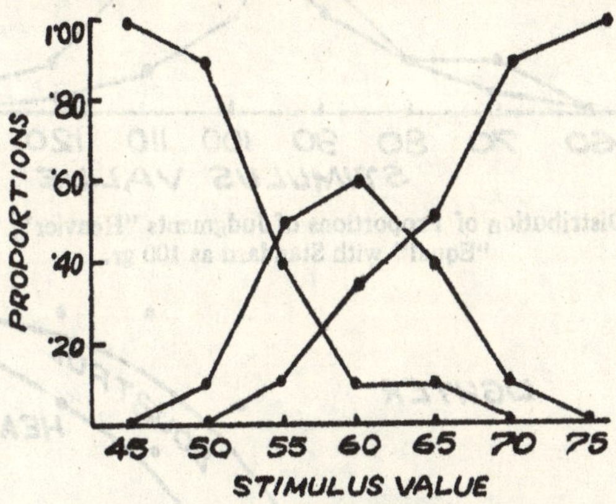

Fig. 1. Distribution of Proportions of Judgments, "Heavier", "Lighter", "Equal" with Standard as 60 gr.

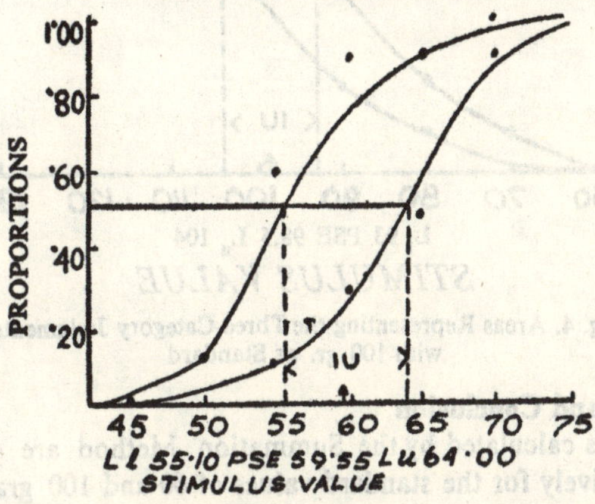

Fig. 2. Areas Representing the Three-Category Judgments with Standard as 60 gr.

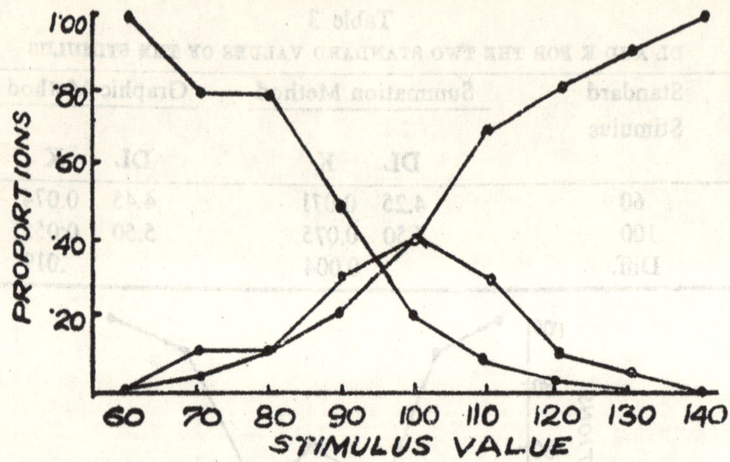

Fig 3. Distribution of Proportions of Judgments "Heavier", "Lighter", "Equal" with Standard as 100 gr.

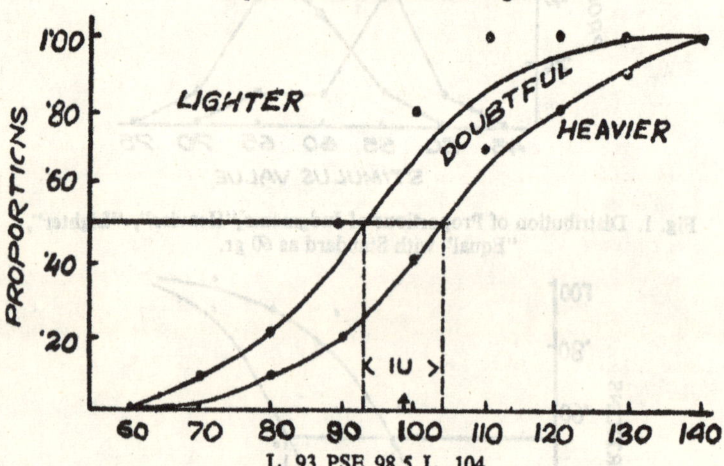

L_l 93 PSE 98.5 L_u 104

STIMULUS VALUE

Fig. 4. Areas Representing the Three-Category Judgments with 100 gr. as Standard

Discussion and Conclusion

The DL's calculated by the Summation Method are 4.25 and 7.50 respectively for the standard values of 60 and 100 grams. The K values are 0·071 and 0.075, the difference being 0.004, which is too small to be considered significant. The DL's for the standard values of 60 and 100 grams found by the graphical method are 4.45 and 5.50 respectively; the respective K values are 0.074 and 0.055. The difference between the K values in this case is somewhat larger. The graphic DL's have, however, been determined by drawing freehand smooth curves in Fig. 2 and Fig. 4. The larger difference found between the two Weber's ratio's may be due to this. We can, therefore, better trust the result obtained by Summation Method which yielded almost equal ratios for the two different standard weights. Our results thus support Weber's law.

Though Weber's law has been confirmed by our results, we cannot arrive at a definite conclusion for two reasons. First, a proper verification of Weber's law requires one to take at least 100 judgments for each variable stimulus. Second, as we have already noted earlier, it has been consistently found that Weber's law does not hold for all values of a stimulus. It fails when the Weber's ratios are found for the extreme values of the stimulus. For these two reasons we cannot treat our results conclusive.

Explanation of Terms and Procedure Adopted

The DL has been computed by two methods. The first method is the summation Method we illustrated in the calculation of RL (p. 84). Here we have three categories of responses and hence the frequencies of the judgments for each variable stimulus have been counted and classified under three categories. The frequencies have been converted into proportions and placed under three columns in Tables 2*A* and 2*B*, since $p+m+q=1$, (m stands for = or ?). The sum of the frequencies for each variable stimulus is equal to 10, and the sum of the corresponding proportions is equal to 1. This is a check on the correctness of the frequencies and the proportions. The proportions within each column have been separately summed up (sum p, sum m, sum q). The Apical (A) and Basal (B) values have been determined as for computing RL (p. 84); they are the values of the variable stimulus at which all responses are of one category and immediately below or above which the responses are distributed in more than one categories. The proportions for A or B have been left out while finding out sum p and sum q (Tables 2*A* and 2*B*).

You will note one difference between Table 2*A* and 2*B*. In Table 2*A*, the apical and basal values are the highest and the lowest-stimulus values, respectively, used in the experiment. In Table 2*B*, on the other hand, the apical value is one step higher and the basal value one step lower than those used in the actual experiment. The reason is that neither 130 gr., the highest value, nor 70 gr., the lowest value used in the experiment obtained cent per cent responses of the same category. These cannot, therefore, be treated as apical and basal values for the purpose of the calculation of the Upper Limen and the Lower Limen, respectively. We have assumed that the next higher and the next lower values, namely, 140 gr., and 60 gr. will obtain cent per cent responses of the same category, and have, accordingly, used them for the calculation.

Like the method of limits (p. 78) where we find out the Mean Tu and Mean T_l in order to calculate the DL, in the method of constant stimuli we find the Upper Limen (Lu) and the Lower Limen (L_l) for the same purpose. These are found by using the same formula as used for finding RL and the terms used in the formula have already been explained (p. 84).

Other calculations and other terms are the same as already used and explained in connection with the determination of the DL by the method of limits.

You will note that DL has been calculated also by the formula : $DL = \frac{\text{i sum m}}{2}$ (p. 88). This is used as a check. Both formulas should give identical results.

We noticed that in taking the data, time error was controlled ; S was asked to judge the second weight in relation to the first weight but the order in which the two weights were presented was reversed in 50 per cent of trials ; S's judgment was also reversed when the standard weight was presented after the comparison weight. This was done because S's judgment in every trial was based on the comparison between the sense impression from the second weight with the sense image left by the first weight. This difference could affect the judgment of S if the standard weight was always presented in the same order in relation to the comparison weight.

Two other controls of the extraneous variables were also made in the experiment : (1) the weights were to be lifted from the same position, to the same height, held by the same fingers of the same hand, by the movement of the same set of muscles (wrist muscles), and of the same intensity. If these variables were not kept constant, the kinaesthetic cues that formed the basis for the sensation of weight would have altered from trial to trial, not only on account of the difference in the weights, but because of the changing conditions of lifting the weight. (2) The time for which each weight was lifted was kept constant by using a metronome. The metronome was set at 60 per min. S lifted a weight at the first tick and held it back on the table at the next tick. This was done to prevent sensory adaptation, a very common phenomenon applying to all sense modalities, namely, the prolongation of a sensation reduces its intensity.

The second method used for finding the DL was the Graphical Method (p. 89). Three distribution curves have been plotted from the proportions of judgments in each category (Tables 2*A* and 2*B*, Figs. 1 and 3). Further, the proportions of 'heavier' and 'equal to' judgments have been combined and the combined proportions have been plotted in Figs. 2 and 4, besides the points for the proportions of heavier judgments. Free-hand smooth S-shaped curves have then been drawn passing close to the respective points. The two S-shaped curves divide the entire area into three parts as shown in Figs. 2 and 4. Vertical lines have been dropped on the base line from the points at which the two S-shaped curves intersect the horizontal line drawn at .50. The vertical lines determine the points on the base line that give 50 per cent of the lighter judgments and 50 per cent of the heavier judgments, respectively. These points define the upper and the lower DL values. The DL can be calculated from these values as in the Summation Method, $DL = \frac{L_l - L_u}{2} = \frac{1U}{2}$

Other Problems

1. Determination of the DL by Using Two-Category Judgments : In the above experiment S was permitted to express his judgments in three categories, namely, 'Heavier', 'Lighter', and 'Equal'; where he was uncertain or doubtful, his response was recorded as 'Equal'. It is possible to calculate DL also when S expresses his judgments in terms of two categories only. For example, he may be instructed to report whether the weight lifted next is heavier or lighter than the weight lifted first. When he finds it difficult to decide, he is persuaded to make a decision. If even then a certain S persists that he cannot decide, E passes on to another comparison and after that again introduces the weight for which S was not able to decide. In this manner, E obtains the desired number of definite judgments, say 10, as in the above experiment, for each variable weight. E then counts from his record the frequencies of 'heavier' and 'lighter' judgments and converts the frequencies into percentages. The DL is then calculated using either the graphic method or the linear interpolation method.

The calculation of DL using only two categories of judgments is illustrated below :

Weight	Frequency Heavier	Frequency Lighter	Percent H	Percent L
75	10	0	100	0
70	9	1	90	10
65	7	3	70	30
60	6	4	60	40
55	2	8	20	80
50	1	9	10	90
45	0	10	0	100

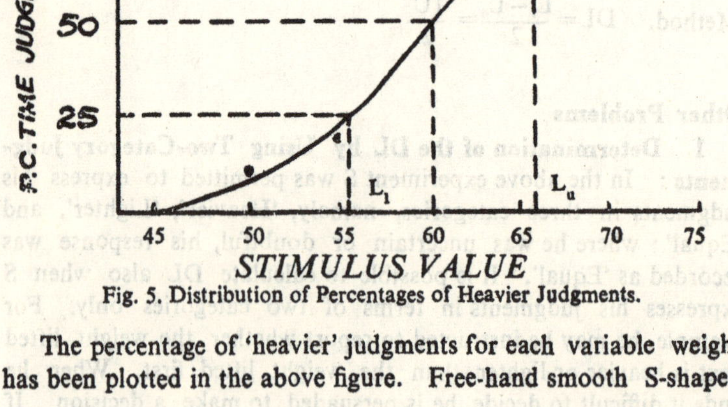

Fig. 5. Distribution of Percentages of Heavier Judgments.

The percentage of 'heavier' judgments for each variable weight has been plotted in the above figure. Free-hand smooth S-shaped graph has then been drawn passing close to the respective points. Horizontal lines have then been drawn starting at 25 per cent and 75 per cent points and a perpendicular has been dropped at each point where each line intersects the graph. The points on the base line represent the lower threshold (L_1), and the Upper Threshold (L_u), respectively. Having thus determined the L_1 and the L_u, the DL can be determined as when using three-category judgments (p. 93).

The linear interpolation method is the same as used for calculating the Median (Q2), the 25th percentile (Q1) and the 75th percentile (Q3). Q1 will be found in the following manner :

$$55+5[(25-20)/(60-20)]=55.625$$

55 is the value of the step above which Q1 will be located ; 5 is the step interval ; 25 is the required percentage for the first quarter ; 20 is the per cent for 55; 60 is the per cent for the step at which Q1 will be located. The difference between 60 and 20 gives us the frequency of this step, as here we are dealing with cumulative frequencies and not the obtained frequencies as found in a frequency distribution table. Q3 will be obtained in the following manner :

$$Q3=65+5[(75-70)/(90-70)]=66.25$$

Q1 and Q3 are the Lower and the Upper thresholds, respectively. DL will then be calculated by the usual method.

2. **Determination of the DL for Visual Area, Using the Constant Stimuli Method** : A standard size, say 40 mm. × 60 mm. rectangle will be compared in random order with a set of other rectangles of variable sizes ; three or four of the rectangles will have smaller and three or four larger areas in comparison to the standard rectangle.

The Method of Constant Stimuli can be used for all kinds of problems where the method of limits can apply.

Recommended Readings

Postman, L., and Egan, J. P., *Experimental Psychology*, Chapter 4, Harper, New York, 1649.

Underwood, B. J., *Experimental Psychology*, Chapters 3 and 5, Appleton, New York, 1966.

Woodworth, R. S. and Schlosberg, H., *Experimental Psychology*, Chapter 8, Holt, New York, 1954.

Chapter V

Attention

Attention is not a name for any specific mental function, as is perception, learning, remembering, or thinking. It may characterise all mental activities. We have, thus, attentive or inattentive perception, learning, remembering, thinking, and so on. Attention has, accordingly, been described in various ways, for example, as a state of preparedness for the exercise of a mental activity, as the quality of clearness or vagueness accompanying any mental function, as a process of setting the stimulus mass into figure-ground relationship, etc. Attention is, thus, a general name for a multitude of facts and processes each one of which sheds a light on what we ordinarily understand by the term, such as span of attention, distraction of attention, fluctuation of attention, shift of attention, and division of attention. We will describe the experiments related to these facts.

Span of Attention or Apprehension

An experiment on the determination of the subjects' span of attention has already been reported earlier (p. 81). We have also described a problem on the difference in the span of attention between different kinds of unrelated visual materials like digits, letters, geometrical figures, dots (p. 84). For determining S's span of attention for letters, digits or figures, we require S to describe what he observes. For dots, however that are identical in nature, S has only to state the number of dots he observes. It thus becomes the span for number of seen objects; S may be asked to state the number even when the stimulus consists of letters or figures. But when we ask S to describe what he observes we may call the span of attention, thus determined, as the span of apprehension. Apprehension in this context is taken to mean not only 'to catch' the stimulus but also to **know** what one catches. For most experiments, therefore, span of attention really becomes span of apprehension.

We may have several problems concerning the effect of some independent variable on the span of attention like organisation or grouping of stimulus materials, heterogeneity of stimulus materials, distracting stimuli, or knowledge of result, and so on. We take up in this chapter some of these problems.

Effect of Organisation of the Stimulus Materials on the Span of Attention : The span of attention when actually measured becomes the span of apprehension. S has not only to report **that** he is aware of the stimulus. He has also to report **what** he is aware of. Then alone we can be sure about the correctness or incorrectness of what S reports. It may as well be said, therefore, what we measure is S's span of observation or preception. The Gestalt psychologists have shown that what we perceive at a moment is an organised whole. The span of attention depends, therefore, not only on the number of the stimulus materials of which one becomes aware in a single act of attention. It also depends upon the degree to which the stimuli can be organised or grouped as a unified whole. Grouping, organisation, relatedness, or membership-character also, therefore, becomes an important determiner of the span of attention or apprehension. The span for related stimulus materials, i.e., those that are grouped or constitute unified wholes, will be larger than the span for unrelated or ungrouped stimulus materials.

You can plan an experiment to examine the above hypothesis by manipulating organisation, i.e., using different levels of organisation of the stimulus materials. At the lowest level you may have unrelated letters, at the next higher level related letters, i.e., words, and going still higher you can have related words, i.e., sentences. For this purpose, three sets of cards have to be prepared, one set of, say, ten cards for each level. For example :

Set 1 E W R O R H K B K O H
Set 2 A T P E N P A T R E D
Set 3 H E S A W T H E C A T

To keep all cards comparable, the second and third sets should have two- or three-lettered simple words only, as in the above example. You will mark that each card contains seven different letters of which four letters have been repeated. The spacing of the letters should be the same on all cards.

To counter-balance the sequence effect (p.10), the A B C C B A design has to be used in exposing the cards to S. The exposure time shouid be very brief, about 60 ms., so that only a single glance of the stimulus material is possible. S is to be provided with a small sheet of paper after each exposure to write down what he observes. S's introspection is taken after all cards have been exposed. The response sheets are to be arranged in order from trials 1 to 10, separately for the three sets. E has to count the number of correct letters on each sheet and prepare a table of results using a separate column for each set, besides the first column for the serial number of trials. Three separate graphs are also to be plotted on the same graph paper for each set of cards, using number of trials from 1 to 10 as the X axis and number of letters correctly apprehended as the Y axis. Separate means and standard deviations are to be computed for each set and, if possible, t test of significance of difference (p. 41) is also applied. The results are to be discussed as to whether they support the hypotheses. Use is made also of the detailed data in the discussion, as well as of S's introspection.

You may note one interesting fact in the data. S may not perceive the words on the cards as isolated units, since all letters are equally spaced. The Gestalt factor of proximity or nearness has been prevented from operating here. On this account S's span may not differ for the different sets of stimulus materials. It may also happen that S discovers the word cards or sentence cards as such after he has already taken a few trials with them. His span for these cards will then show a sudden change, producing an abrupt rise in the curve. The detailed data will indicate if this happens. S's introspection may also throw a light on this matter.

Effect of Heterogeneity of the Stimulus Materials on the Span of Apprehension : In this experiment, besides the homogeneous materials, namely, only letters or only digits, E has to use also heterogeneous materials, i.e., a set of letters and digits randomly distributed on the card. In apprehending the heterogeneous card, the factor of similarity will operate in the separate groupings of the two kinds of materials, but the factor of proximity will favour the grouping of the materials that are close to each other in spite of their dissimilarity. The two factors will thus operate in opposite directions. On the other hand, when digits or letters are exposed alone, they are likely to be more easily grouped because of similarity ; it would be possible for S to catch more materials in a single act of attention. It is expected, therefore, that the span of attention for heterogeneous materials will be less than that for homogeneous materials. However, in the heterogeneous card, the dissimilarity of the two kinds of materials may make their discrimination easier and they may be set into two small units ; this may facilitate their apprehension. This point has to be kept in view while discussing the result of the experiment.

The experiment can be planned in the same manner as that for determining the effect of organisation on the span of apprehension. Here too E has to prepare three sets of cards—one set of digits, another of letters, and a third of letters and digits randomly mixed, as shown below :

Set 1	Set 2	Set 3
2 9 3	B R W	4 P L
6 4 5 1	L O K N	7 3 B 8
3 6 8	C T F	K T 6

Effect of Knowledge of Result on the Span of Apprehension : The experiment can be performed in much the same way as dealing with the problems described above. E may decide to take 10 trials with knowledge of result (KR) and 10 trials without knowledge of results (WKR). The counterbalancing design will be used also in this experiment. For measuring the span, homogeneous or heterogeneous materials may be used. The size of the materials, i.e., their number, should exceed the limit within which one is likely to observe and correctly report the materials ; it should be, say, 10 to 12 on a card. E can manage with 10 such cards and use the same cards in the two conditions. The cards may be numbered serially and the order of their presentation in each condition may be randomly decided (Appendix I).

The hypotheses will be that in KR condition the span will be larger than that in the WKR condition. This will be due to the reinforcing effect of knowledge of result. S may every time set a goal for his correct apprehension and may be rewarded by reaching or exceeding the goal, or punished by not being able to do so. Or he may compare his result in one trial with that in the previous trial and may be motivated to achieve better.

The presentation of the data, tabular and graphic, and the

treatment of the data will be done in much the same manner as for the effect of grouping, or of heterogeneity, on the span of apprehension. Besides noting whether the hypothesis was supported by the result, the discussion will also bear upon any progressive change noted in the KR condition. This might further support the reinforcement theory. S's introspection too may provide supportive evidence. The observed effect of any change from WKR to KR and back to WKR will also be noted. Close inspection of the detailed results may bring to light still other facts.

Distraction and Span of Apprehension

For an experiment on the effect of distraction on the span of apprehension too you have to do very much the same as in the case of the effect on the span of apprehension of the other indepeddent variables mentioned above. For your guidance the complete report of an experiment on the effect of distraction is given below.

The Effect of an Auditory Distractor on the Span of Apprehension : The span of apprehension is the amount of the given stimulus materials one can catch and correctly report in a single act of attention. The span of apprehension may vary from person to person. It may also vary with the kind of the stimulus material, e.g., letters, figures, digits, or with the change in a transient organismic variable, e.g., eye strain, S's motivation, etc. There may be factors in the environment like irrelevant auditory, visual or any other kind of stimuli, that may influence S's span of apprehension. Several experiments have been reported on the effect of noise on performance. The results have been conflicting. Sometimes noise has been found to go with improvement rather than deterioration in S's performance. It has been argued that under ordinary circumstances one holds in reserve a certain amount of his energy, while applying himself to a task. This excess energy is used during extraordinary circumstances. That is why in difficult and stressful situations sometimes one shows marked improvement in his performance. Special devices have been used to measure the muscular effort exerted by S while performing a task. It has been found that there is increase in muscle tension when one is working under distraction. Thus, more energy is applied to the task performed in distracting surroundings. However, it has been noted that the cumulative effect of noise is generally harmful. Difference has also been found between the effect of continuous and that of discontinuous or intermittant noise. One gets negatively adapted to continuous noise which then ceases to influence the performance.

In the experiment reported here an attempt was made to determine the effects of continuous and intermittant irrelevant auditory stimuli on the span of apprehension. The following hypotheses were examined : (1) The span of apprehension will be larger under quiet than in noisy surroundings. (2) Intermittant noise will affect the span more than continuous noise.

Method

Subject : A female undergraduate student.

Apparatus and Materials : Disc tachistoscope adjusted to provide an exposure of 60 ms.

A set of 10 2″×3″ cards ; each having 5 letters and 5 digits randomly distributed on it.

A wooden stick for producing noise by striking against a table.

Procedure : The experiment was done under three conditions : (1) Quiet (Q), (2) continuous Noise (CN), and (3) Intermittant Noise (IN). Data were taken under the three conditions according to the following design :

	Condition					
	Q	CN	IN	IN	CN	Q
Trials	5	5	5	5	5	5

Same set of cards were used under all conditions, but the order of the cards changed from condition to condition in a random manner.

Instruction to S : "When I say ready, please look at the white mark on this black board" pointing to the fixation board. "At this very place a white card will appear for a single moment. It will have some letters and numbers on it. You have to write down what you observe in the card on a sheet of paper that I will give you. Be very careful and attentive. I am going to see how many letters and numbers you are able to observe correctly in a single glance. Do you understand? After we have finished the experiment, I would ask you to write down how you felt during the course of the experiment; whether you experienced any difficulty or had any special facility in observing and reporting."

S's Introspection: "I wonder why that much noise was produced. It somehow very much irritated me. I think I could observe better when there was no noise. With the noise on I had to make special effort to observe the card. I had difficulty in concentration. By the way, I wonder how did I fare".

Result

Table 1

NO. CORRECT APPREHENSION PER TRIAL IN EACH CONDITION

Trials	Condition					
	Q	CN	IN	IN	CN	Q
1	6	3	4	5	4	4
2	7	4	3	5	7	5
3	5	5	5	4	6	7
4	7	5	4	5	6	6
5	6	6	4	5	5	7
Total	31	23	20	24	28	29

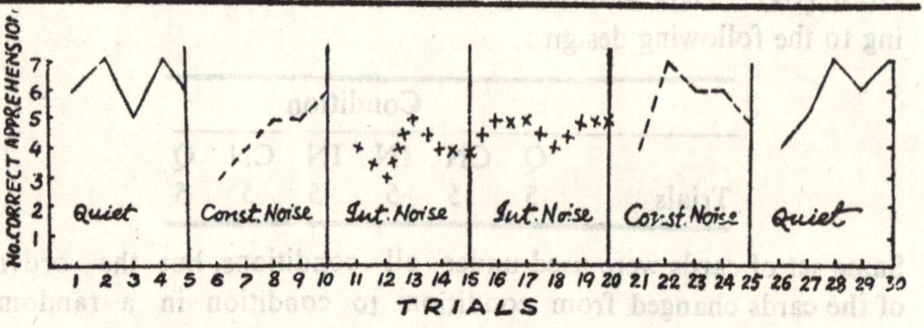

Fig. 1. No Correct Apprehension in Q, CN and IN Conditions

Table 2

TOTAL, MEAN AND SD OF CORRECT APPREHENSION IN EACH CONDITION

	Condition		
	Q	CN	IN
Total	60	51	44
Mean	6.0	5.1	4.4
SD	1.0	1.14	0.66

The largest Mean Span was found in the quiet condition, next to that in the continuous noise condition and the smallest in the intermittant noise condition (Table 2). The lowest absolute variability is noticeable in the intermittant noise condition and the highest in the continuous noise condition.

Discussion

The results support our hypotheses. S's span was adversely affected by noise. Further, S got adapted to continuous noise; the difference in the Mean span is larger between quiet and intermittant noise, namely 1.6, than between quiet and continuous noise which is 0·9. S's introspection also supports our findings; S got 'irritated' by noise, and experienced difficulty in 'concentrating' to the stimulus materials.

Detailed examination of the data shows that the distraction produced by continuous noise is maximum immediately after the introduction of the continuous noise in the quiet condition. The shift from the quiet to the noise situation reduced the number of correct apprehension from 6 to 3, to the extent of exactly 50 per cent (Table 1 and Fig. 1). The span gradually increases from trial to trial which shows S's negative adaptation to the continuous noise. We find similar evidence of negative adaptation to the continuous noise in the next series of 5 trials in this condition. Except for the span in the first trial of this series, the span for the other trials in the series is about the same as for the trials in the quiet condition. The detailed data, therefore, indicate not much difference between the quiet and continuous noise conditions. The difference between the Means for the two conditions is mainly due to the effect of change from one condition to the other which dies out when S becomes adapted to the change. The fact that change itself becomes a distractor is apparent from the span in the first trial of the second series under the quiet condition; the span is only 4 which is the lowest value in this condition. Adaptation to the noise makes it's absence catch S's attention which affects his concentration to the stimulus materials. One may be unaware of the ticking of the time-piece lying on one's table. But the moment the ticking is stopped, the change distracts one's attention from the task in hand.

The span in intermittant noise condition is generally smaller for almost all trials than the span in the two other conditions

(Table 1 and Fig.1). There is some evidence of negative adaptation, however, in this condition too. The modal span for this condition is 4 in the first five series, while it is 5 in the next five series. The adaptation to the noise, however, is not as perfect when the noise is intermittant as in the case of continuous noise. The fact that the variability of the span is lowest in this condition indicates that S makes special effort to concentrate which keeps his span at almost constant level throughout the series.

We may conclude that it is possible to apprehend more facts when one is working in a quiet situation than working in the midst of noise. However, it is possible to become adapted to the noise and then experience no impairment in the efficiency of work. Such negative adaptation is difficult to achieve when one is exposed to discontinuous noise, one that comes and goes in an unsystematic manner.

The above experiment may suggest other problems. One such problem will be : the distracting effect of noise on the span of apprehension as a function of the complexity of the materials or task to which attention is given. A simple task does not require much concentrated attention and can therefore be performed even if some attention is taken up by other stimuli. But when the task is complex, this is not possible as the complexity of the task demands more concentrated attention for its successful performance. The experiment on this problem may be divided into two parts. In the first part use only homogeneous materials, say only a set of letters, digits or geometrical figures, and measure S's span under quiet and noise conditions. In the second part use heterogeneous materials, say, letters, digits and figures, all randomly distributed on the same card. Here too measure S's span in both noise and quiet conditions. Since more discriminative attention is to be given to the complex card, attention is likely to be more strongly distracted by the noise. Some loss in the span of attention may occur on account of the complexity of the task even in quiet condition. But if your hypothesis is correct, the loss will be greater on account of complexity in the noise condition. The difference between the span in quiet and noise conditions for homogeneous materials when compared to the same difference for heterogeneous materials will, thus, provide an answer to the problem.

We have seen that an individual may apply more energy to the task in hand and thus counteract the distraction from irrelevant stimuli. Measures of the muscular effort exerted when a task is done in noisy surroundings have shown an increase in the effort. But the result has not been consistent. S's attitude toward the task and his habit of concentration are also significant independent variables to influence his performance. Hence, the distractibility of a person by irrelevant stimuli may provide a measure of his attitude to the task as well as of his habit of concentration. The more concentrated attention one can give to a task the less the chance of his being distracted by irrelevant external or internal stimuli. Individuals differ in the ability to give concentrated attention to the task in hand. This point must be kept in mind while discussing the result of an experiment on the problem of distraction.

In the above discussion we have dealt with the effect of distraction on the span of attention. As we have said at the outset, attention characterises all mental functions ; it is a necessary condition for the performance of all voluntary activities. The greater the attention one gives to a task, the better, within the limits of his abilities, his performance is likely to be. Experiments on the effect of irrelevant noise or other distracting stimuli can, therefore, be performed by using any kind of sensory-motor or mental task. In fact, scores of experiments have been performed and reported on the effect of noise on industrial efficiency. You can also perform an experiment on the effect of noise—continuous and discontinuous, on, say letter cancellation, a substitution task, arithmetical work, and so on. The reported experiment on the effect of noise on the S's span of apprehension will guide you in planning and performing an experiment on any one of these problems.

There are some other facts related to attention like fluctuation of attention, shift of attention and division of attention.

Fluctuation of Attention

It involves what may be called the waxing and waning of attention. When attention is given to a very mild stimulus like a distant sound or a faint figure, the stimulus appears to come and go. At one moment, the stimulus comes within one's attention and at another moment it passes out. Fluctuation of attention is different from shift of attention where attention passes from one stimulus to another stimulus or from one part of a complex stimulus to another part. In fluctuation of attention, attention is all the time given to the same stimulus which appears and then disappears.

Experiments on fluctuation of attention can be done by using an auditory or a visual stimulus. For an auditory stimulus one may use a time-piece placed at a distance from the S so that he does not hear its ticking ceaselessly but with breaks or gaps. To provide a faint visual stimulus, use a Masson's Disc. It is a circular card board having a broken line connecting its centre with the circumference. The disc is shown below :

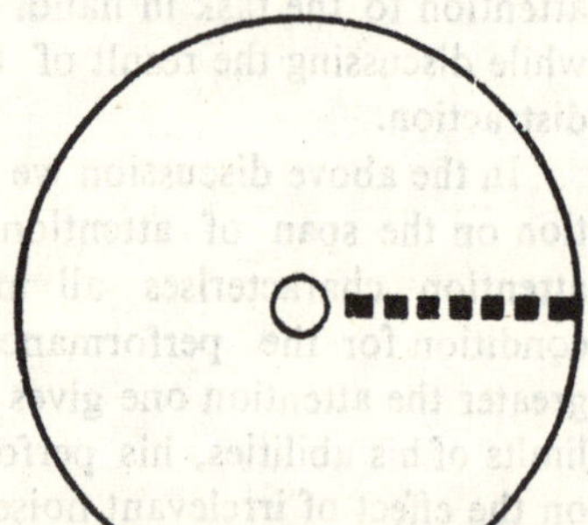

Fix the disc on a rotator (Appendix III). When rotated, the disc looks like having as many faint circles as the broken parts of the line. S is asked to fixate one circle all the time. The circle will appear to come and go. Its appearance is called the positive phase of the fluctuation and its disappearance the negative phase. The two phases together form a cycle.

An experiment may be done to determine the rate of fluctuation. For this purpose, you have to use a telegraphic key, a time-marker, a chronometer—all connected by electric wires with the positive and negative poles of a battery, the stylus of the time-marker and the pointer of the chronometer touching the smoked surface of a rotating drum (Appendix III). S has to press the telegraphic key when the circle he is fixating disappears and release it when it re-appears. When the key is pressed, an electric circuit is made and the marker becomes magnetised ; the stylus is pulled down. When the key is released the circuit is broken and the marker is demagnetised ; the stylus goes up. The alternate up and down movements of the stylus at the two intervals trace a curve on the rotating smoked paper that the stylus is touching; the curve is like : 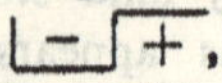, which represents the positive and negative phases in the cycle. A succession of such cycles over a period of time is shown below :

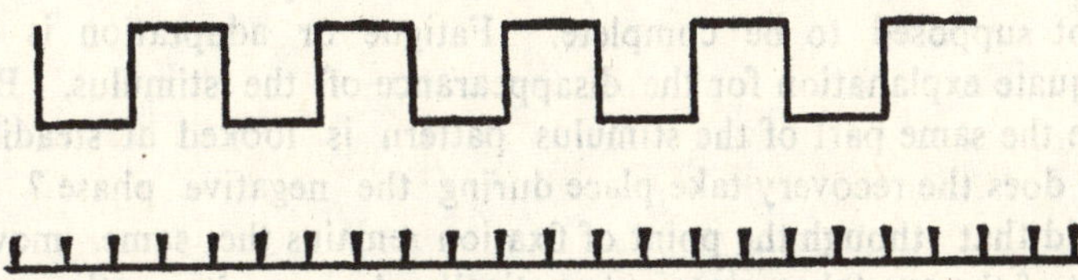

The pointer of the chronometer moves up and down at regular intervals of .25 sec., .50 sec or 1 sec., as desired. Since it is touching the rotating drum, it traces a time line on the smoked paper. The time line is also shown in the above Figure. The rate of fluctuation can be easily determined from the graph. Select, say, 10 cycles of fluctuation and using a divider set its two points at a distance which is the same as the total length of the 10 cycles. Bring the divider to the time line and count the units of time covered by the distance. You will thus get the time for the 10 cycles. You can then calculate the time per cycle which will be the rate of fluctuation. If you are interested in the time taken by the positive and negative phases separately, measure the time for each phase, of each cycle by the same method and record your data in a table using separate columns for the positive phase, the negative phase and the total cycle. For example, you may want to determine the change in the rate of fluctuation and in the relative duration of the positive and negative phases with the progress of time. You can find out the ratio of the positive phase to the negative phase per cycle, or calculate separate Means for the positive and negative phases, as well as for the cycles. To determine the effect of fatigue or practice you can compare the first 10 with the last 10 cycles, or the first half of the total cycles with the second half.

Fluctuation of attention has been explained in different ways. A plausible explanation is that constant stimulation of a part of the retina produces fatigue in that part. The efficiency of the receptors in that part is lowered and the weak stimulus therefore fails to evoke a response in the receptors. The stimulus object disappears. The receptors recover during the negative phase and are ready to respond to the weak stimulus ; the object re-appears. The occurrence of fatigue in the retina has also been called retinal adaptation. The explanation however is not supposed to be complete. Fatigue or adaptation is an adequate explanation for the disappearance of the stimulus. But since the same part of the stimulus pattern is looked at steadily, how does the recovery take place during the negative phase ? It is said that though the point of fixation remains the same, movement of the eye takes place automatically. As a result, another part of the retina is brought into play. The part of the retina that was stimulated at the previous moment, thus, gets time to recover. Experiments devised to examine the part played by eye movement however do not yield a conclusive result. An alternative hypothesis to explain fluctuation is the occurrence of cortical rather than sensory adaptation. It appears that both sensory as well as cortical adaptation play their parts in fluctuation of attention.

A relationship has been noticed also between fluctuation in blood supply, or oxygen supply, and fluctuation of attention. Interruption in supply of blood or oxygen lowers the efficiency of the receptors and so a weak or faint stimulus fails to evoke a response. Restoration of the supply increases their efficiency. The hypothetical relationship between fluctuation of attention and the cycle of breathing, i. e., inspiration, or breathing in, and expiration, or breathing out, can be experimentally examined. We will describe in a later chapter an experiment on the effect on respiration of the change in feeling. You can obtain simultaneous records of fluctuation of attention and of the cycles of breathing and examine if there is any observed relationship between them.

We will deal with an experiment under perception of form which will also illustrate the phenomenon of shift of attention.

Doing Two Things at a Time or Division of Attention

It is possible to do two things at a time. One can copy from a page and also listen to a story. Whether this involves a division of attention is still an open question. If one of the two tasks is automatic, one can perform it without giving attention to it, i.e., it may pass into marginal attention, e. g., writing the letter X one after the other, or even writing the alphabets over and again. The other task may then alone be in the focus of attention, e. g., listening to a prose passage to enable oneself to answer questions on its content. The simultaneous performance of the two tasks will not involve a division of attention since only one task is engaging attention. In another case there may be a rapid back and forth shift of attention from one task to the other ; one task engages attention at one moment and the other task at the next moment. The process is very similar to what happens when one looks at an ambiguous figure. In such a figure at one moment one sees one form and at the next moment another form (p. 12). Similarly, when a student listens to the lecture in the class room and also takes notes from the lecture, his attention shifts, back and forth, from the lecture-listening to the notes-taking. At first the student experiences difficulty in the simultaneous performance of the two tasks. With practice he is able to do this. Experiments done on the simultaneous performance of two novel tasks provide an answer to the question, namely, whether it is possible to divide attention. *If attention could be divided the two tasks should be performed as efficiently together as separately.* But this has not been the case ; the output is considerably decreased in both tasks when they are performed simultaneously.

An experiment can be easily planned on the problem, namely, whether simultaneous performance of two tasks involves a division of attention. The following hypothesis will be verified :

There will be a decrement in the output of either tasks when they are performed simultaneously as compared to their separate performance.

Materials : (1) Twenty lists of unrelated 3 to 4 lettered words, each list containing, say, 10 words. (2) Cancellation sheets. (3) Stop watch.

Procedure : Read out audibly and slowly, at the rate of about 1 sec. a word, the first five lists to S, one after the other. Ask S to reproduce the words he remembers from each list immediately after each one has been read out, and record his responses ; the lists should be read at 30 sec. intervals. Measure the total time taken in this part of the experiment. After this is over, present to S a cancellation sheet and instruct him to cancel each one of two letters wherever they occur ; you decide which two letters are to be cancelled, say, C and R. The cancellation task is to be performed by S for the same time as taken by the five word-lists. Provide as many cancellation sheets one after the other as required. Give a rest of 5 mins. and then introduce both tasks together. Read out another 10 lists one after the other at the same pace as the first 5 lists, while S both listens to and reproduces the words he remembers from each list, after it has been read out, and also cancels the letters from cancellation sheets. Record S's responses in each list. Also record the total time in each half of this part of the experiment. Allow another 5 mins. rest and then introduce the cancellation task alone for the same time as in the first part of the experiment, followed by listening to and reproducing the remaining five words lists.

The design of the experiment will be as follows :

TASK					
Single		Double		Single	
5 word-lists	Cancellation	5 word-lists & cancellation	5 word-lists & cancellation	Cancellation	5 word-lists

Instruction to S : Word lists "I will read out a list of 10 words to you slowly. Listen to it attentively and after I have read out, tell me the words you remember. In this way, I will read out a few similar lists and in each case after I have read out a list you have to tell what you remember."

Cancellation : "Here is a printed sheet. You have to cancel C and R wherever they occur on the sheet. I will give you a start signal. Work quickly and accurately. Stop when I ask you to stop. After you have finished one sheet, I will give you another if required."

Word Lists and Cancellation : "This time you have to listen to the list of words and immediately tell me the words you remember. But at the same time you have also to cancel the letters from the sheet. You have to perform both tasks together. Thus, when I read out the list and while you reproduce the words you remember, do not stop to cancel the letters. It is possible to do this and you can perform the two tasks at the same time. Always go on also cancelling while listening and reproducing the words."

Take S's introspection about how he felt during the course of the experiment and in performing the single and the double tasks. Whether he experienced any special difficulty ; how he felt his performance was, good or poor, and in which task.

The results will consist of (1) the number of words correctly reproduced from each list which E had recorded after reading out each list and (2) total numbers of the two letters cancelled and of those missed during the first, each of the two halves of the second, and the third parts of the experiment. The results will be presented in the following tabular and graphic forms :

Table 1

NO. CORRECT REPRODUCTION

Word Lists	Single Task	Double Task	Double Task	Single Task
1				
2				
3				
4				
5				
Time				

Table 2

NO. CANCELLED AND NO. MISSED

	Single Task	Double Task	Double Task	Single Task
Cancelled				
Missed				
Time				

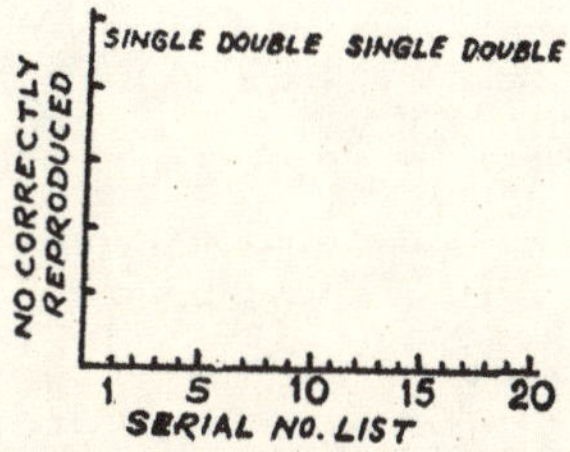

Fig. 1. No. Correctly Reproduced in Each List

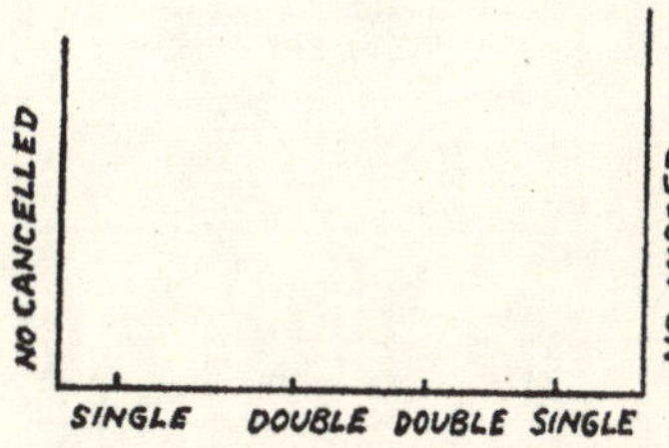

Fig. 2. Nature of Task Engagement

The treatment of result will involve calculation of Means and SD's of correct reproductions in the 10 trials of single and the 10 trials of double tasks, and calculation of the obtained differences between the four sessions, namely, single, double, double, single, in respects of no. correctly reproduced, no. cancelled and no. missed. If desired, the difference between the Means of correct reproduction may also be tested for significance, particularly when the difference is not large enough to be evidently significant. The discussion will, centre round the following points :

(1) Verification of the hypothesis concerning superior performance of the single task on considering the overall results and the detailed data.

(2) Relevance of the automaiization hypotheses if the difference between single- and double-task situations is small, for the cancellation task, and difference between the two havles of the double-task situations, as well as the single task situation, is considerably larger for cancellation.

(3) Relevance of shift hypothesis if the difference between single- and double-task situations is about equally large for both tasks, and the difference between the two halves of the single- as well as the double-task situation is about the same for cancellation and word reproduction.

(4) Any other point made out from the results.

Recommended Reading

Woodworth, R. S. and Schlosberg, H., *Experimental Psychology*, Chapter 4, Holt, New York, 1954.

CHAPTER VI

Perception

PERCEPTION is the knowledge of an object that is 'here' and 'now'. One does not, however, perceive all that is 'here' and 'now'. At any moment, one is influenced by a mass of stimuli that impinge upon his external and internal sense organs. All this is 'here' and 'now' to him. But he perceives only a small part of the total stimulus field. This part is segregated from the rest. It stands out against the rest and constitutes the object that is perceived. The mere segregation of a part of the stimulus field is the simplest act of perception. The part that is segregated appears to have a form or shape ; it is a figure. The rest of the stimulus field has no form ; it gets at the moment into the background. The simplest act of perception, thus, involves the setting of the stimulus field into figure-ground relationship. The figure stands out against the ground. It is a unified whole. It has some characteristics that make it different from the ground. The figure has form or shape which the ground does not have. The figure tends to appear as extending nearer to the perceiver ; the ground seems to recede back from the perceiver. The figure has clear outlines, which the ground does not have, and so on.

The Gestalt psychologists have pointed out a set of factors outside and inside the organism that favour the grouping or organisation of the stimulus field in one way rather than another. The external factors are those of similarity, proximity or nearness, common fate, good continuation, and closure. Past experience, a momentary set, needs, values and attitudes constitute the organismic factors. Experiments have been conducted to demonstrate how these factors operate in perception. Suggestions regarding an experiment on the Gestalt law of closure have been made in Chapter IV (p. 76).

It is easy to plan an experiment to demonstrate the organisation of the stimulus field into figure-ground relationship. The material to be used for this purpose is the so-called ambiguous figure—a figure that has no constant form. Some such figures have a reversible perspective; different parts of the stimulus form into figure and ground at different moments; what constitutes the ground at one moment is perceived as figure at another moment. The change from figure to ground occurs without a change in the stimulus pattern. The diagrams given below can serve as suitable materials for the experiment.

Any one of these drawings may be selected for the experiment. The drawing should be pasted on 4″×3″ stiff card board. It should be placed on the table, resting on a back stand, at a distance of about 12″ from S. S has to look steadily at the centre of the drawing and report the change in what he perceives. Suppose you select the Rubin's Cross for your experiment. S has to report when he sees the black cross and when he sees the white cross. To obtain an objective record of S's report, the same set of apparatus is to be used as described earlier (p. 106) for measuring fluctuation of attention S has to press the telegraphic key when he sees one figure, say, the black cross, and release the key when he sees the other figure, namely, the white cross. You may have a very simple problem, namely, determination

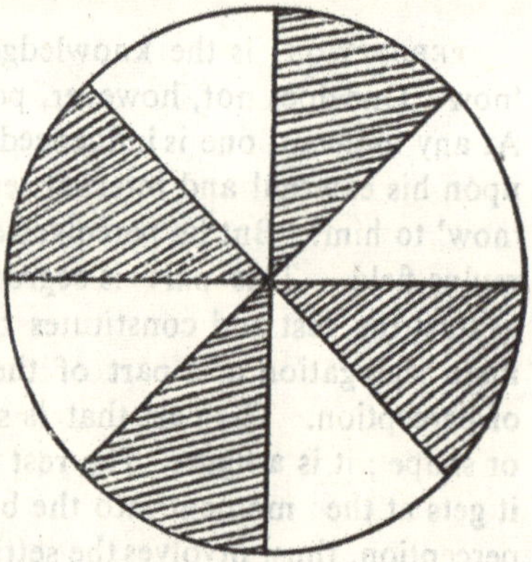

Fig. 1. Rubins Cross

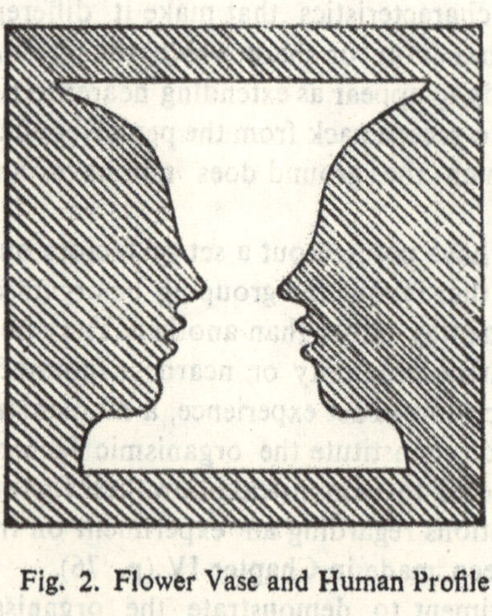

Fig. 2. Flower Vase and Human Profile

of the rate of shift from the black to the white figure. From the tracings on the smoked paper and the time line, you can find out the average number of alternations or shifts within a given time, say 5 minutes. You can also examine the progressive changes in the rate of alternation to answer such problem as the effect of continued observation, or of retinal fatigue, on the rate of alternation in a reversible figure. For this purpose, you may compare the rate of shift, say, in the first 5 minutes and the last 5 minutes of continued observation, or for the first 10 cycles and the last 10 cycles. The recording of data and treatment of result will be done in very much the same manner as for fluctuation of attention (p. 107).

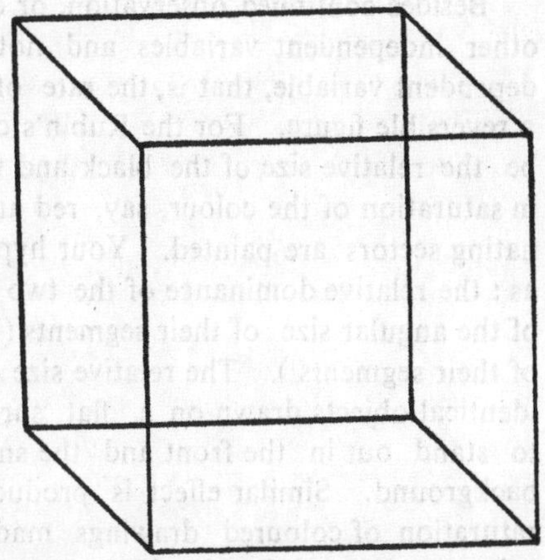

Fig. 3

The rate of alternation in a reversible figure has been noted to be slow at first and becomes more and more rapid with continued observation. The shift from one figure to another can be explained, as in the case of fluctuation of attention (p. 108), in terms of retinal fatigue or adaptation. The cumulative affect of fatigue that results from continuous observation lowers the efficiency of the retinal receptors. The receptors in the eyes that are involved when one figure is seen do not completely recover during the time the receptors involved in the other figure come into play. Both sets of receptors, therefore, develop adaptation more readily than in the initial stage of the perception. This makes the change more rapid. Hull explains the change in the rate of alternation by using the concept of reactive inhibition (IR); the repeated occurrence of a response produces a condition that interferes with the recurrence of that response. Continued observation results in the development of IR which cuts short the course of either perceptual respone. This makes the change more rapid.

Besides continued observation, or eye strain, you can introduce other independent variables and note their influence on the dependent variable, that is, the rate of shift in the perception of a reversible figure. For the Rubin's cross, one such variable may be the relative size of the black and white sectors, or difference in saturation of the colour, say, red and pink, in which the alternating sectors are painted. Your hypothesis then may be stated as : the relative dominance of the two sets of figures is the function of the angular size of their segments (of the colour or saturation of their segments). The relative size of the figures of otherwise identical objects drawn on a flat surface makes the bigger one to stand out in the front and the smaller one to recede in the background. Similar effect is produced by the difference in the saturation of coloured drawings made on the same surface ; the brighter coloured drawing looks nearer to the perceiver than the lighter coloured one. The rate of shift in a reversible perspective is, therefore, likely to be influenced by the difference in the size or colour saturation of the parts of the drawing.

In the problems stated above, you manipulate the stimulus variable, namely, size or colour of the parts of the diagram. You may also manipulate an organismic variable and measure the difference in the rate of the alternation. One such variable is set. Set may be defined as the state of preparedness for a particular kind of response. Our every day perception is influenced by set. We are predisposed to perceive some objects as edible and others as inedible ; we have developed a habit to perceive them as such. A good example of the predisposition to perceive some objects in the same manner in spite of the difference in stimulation from the objects is what has been described as the phenomenon of perceptual constancy. The retinal image of a person looked at from a distance is smaller than the retinal image when he is quite close. Still the perceived size of the person remains the same. Similarly the retinal image of the plate lying on the dining table is not circular when looked at by a person sitting at the table. Still the plate is perceived as circular. We get an instance of colour constancy when we find that a heap of coal looks equally black, or the white exterior of a building equally white, under the strong light of the midday sun and the twilight of a cloudy evening. The change in the intensity of light reflected by the perceived object does not affect the perception of its colour.

Besides the more or less permanent set to perceive, there may be a temporary set also. Your perception may be determined by the need of the organism at the moment. In an experiment, a group of hungry and a group of satiated S's were exposed, for a single moment, a set of figures that had no definite form to represent an object. The hungry S's perceived more food or food related objects than did the satiated S's.

A set can be directly manipulated by the instruction to S (p. 27). For example, you may use Fig. 2 (p. 114). Suppose the middle portion that is perceived as flower vase is painted red and the sides seen as human faces are painted green. The drawing is placed behind a screen. S is told "Behind the screen there is a drawing of **red flower vase**. I will remove the screen and then looking at the centre of the drawing you will note that the **flower vase** appears for one moment and then disappears at the next moment. It will thus appear and disappear from your view though you are all the time looking at it." The screen is then removed. Your S is most likely to perceive the flower vase and may not be able to discover the green profiles for some time. You have specially prepared him to perceive one particular form rather than the other.

Following is the report of an experiment in which a temporary set has been manipulated through instruction to S :

Effect of Instructionally Induced Mental Set on the Preception of a Reversible Perspective

A diagram or drawing is said to have a perspective when its parts are perceived as having a figure-ground relationship ; one part stands out as a perceived object against the remaining part that serves as the ground. A reversible perspective implies the appearance of the same part as figure at one moment and as ground at the next moment ; what was seen as figure becomes the ground and what formed the ground is seen as figure. There is, thus, an alternate shift in the figure-ground relationship. Gestalt psychologists have viewed the organisation of the stimulus situation into figure and ground as the simplest form of perception and have described it as primitive organisation. They have also indicated a group of external and internal factors that account for this organisation. A mental set is an internal factor. Set is a predisposition or a state of preparedness for a particular kind of response. It accounts for the greater likelihood for the present stimuli to be perceived as having one rather than another form or characteristic. Set has been manipulated in experiments in diverse ways. One device is to so frame the instruction to S that he becomes specially prepared to make the desired response. The set that is made to operate in this manner has been described, accordingly, as instructionally induced set.

In this experiment an attempt was made to examine the influence of an instructional set on the rate of shift in a reversible perspective.

Hypothesis : The set induced in the subject to prevent the occurrence of shift would reduce the rate of alternation in a reversible figure.

Method

Subject : A male postgraduate student.

Apparatus and Material : (1) Morse Telegraphic key. Time-Marker. Accumulator. Kymograph. (2) A card board disc divided into eight alternately white and black sectors of equal size.

Procedure : The disc rested on the table supported by a back stand at a distance of 12″ from S and facing S.

Data were obtained under two conditions : Control and Experimental, according to the following design :

	Condition			
	Cont.	Exp.	Exp.	Cont.
No. of cycles	10	10	10	10

Instruction to S

Control Condition : "Please look at the centre of this drawing. You will see here a black figure at one moment and a white figure at the next moment. Press this key and keep pressing as long as you see the black figure. Release the key immediately as you see the white figure. In this manner you have to press and release the key as long as the experiment continues."

Experimental Condition : "You have been pressing and releasing the key on perceiving the black and the white figures, respectively. Now try to hold the figure as it appears. Do not let it slip out of your view. Try to prevent its disappearance. When you see the black figure hold it before your view, and when you see the white figure hold it too. But do not forget to release when the black figure disappears or to press when the white figure disappears. You just make up your mind to hold the figure, to keep it before you, to prevent the change. But never fail to release or press when the change does actually take place."

Result

Table 1

TIME IN SECONDS PER CYCLE IN THE CONTROL AND EXPERIMENTAL CONDITIONS

Control		Experimental		Experimental		Control	
Serial No.	Time	Serial No.	Time	Serial No.	Time	Serial No.	Time
1	4	11	8	21	7	31	3
2	5	12	9	22	6	32	4
3	4	13	9	23	8	33	3
4	5	14	10	24	7	34	3
5	4	15	8	25	7	35	4
6	4	16	11	26	6	36	4
7	5	17	8	27	7	37	3
8	4	18	7	28	6	38	4
9	4	19	8	29	8	39	5
10	5	20	9	30	7	40	3

Introspection : "I tried to prevent the change but I could not succeed. The change did take place. Perhaps I could not do what you wanted me to do. I do not know."

Table 2

MEAN, SD AND OBT. DIFF. BETWEEN MEANS OF CONTROL AND EXPERIMENTAL CONDITIONS

	Control			Experimental		
	1st half	2nd half	Total	1st half	2nd half	Total
Mean	4.4	3.6	4.0	8.7	6.9	7.8
SD			0.71			1.47
Diff. Between Exp. and Control					3.8	

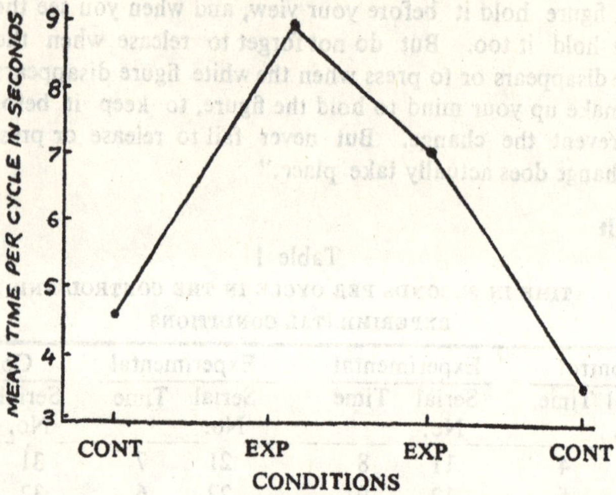

Fig. 1

Our results (Table 2) show that the mean time per cycle is 4.0 secs. in the Control Condition, but it is twice as much, namely, 7.8 secs. in the Experimental condition; the difference between the two means is 3.8. The difference is relatively quite large and can safely be treated as a real difference without applying a test of significance. The mean for the first half of the data is larger than the mean for the second half in both conditions.

Discussion

The results support our hypothesis. The instructional set to prevent the shift has affected S's perception ; the shift from one figure to the other is much slower in the experimental condition. Set as an organismic factor does influence form perception. S's introspection reveals that he adhered to the instruction given by E ; he tried to prevent the occurrence of the change.

The results support the general finding that the rate of shift becomes faster under prolonged observation. The change in the second half of both control and Experimental conditions is quicker; the differences between the means of the first half and those of the second half are 0.8 secs. and 1.8 secs. respectively (Table 2, Fig. 1). This is due to retinal adaptation. Persistent stimulation of the retinal receptors involved, lowers their efficiency, thus, making the appearance of a particular figure less durable.

References

Woodworth, R. S. and Schlosberg, H., *Experimental Psychology*, Methueng & Co. Ltd., Rev. Ed., 1954, Chapter 4, pp. 76-78.

You can manipulate a set also in another way. Instead of asking the subject to retain a figure or prevent its disappearance, which may be called perseveration set, you may direct S to look for the other figure when he sees one figure, to bring about the shift more quickly ; this may be called an expectancy set. In this case, if set influences the perception, the mean for the experimental condition will be smaller than that for the control condition.

Space Perception

In the experiments on perception described above we have dealt with perception of form. There are other kinds of perception also on which experiments have been done, namely, perception of space, perception of time and perception of movement. We will take up space perception and time perception.

Our common sense view of space is that it holds or contains objects. We believe that objects exist in space. But in fact, we can have no direct knowledge of space apart from the objects. We observe spatial characteristics of objects which are described as length, breadth, width or depth, size or area, distance or direction. Objects are perceived to possess these spatial characteristics. Experiments on space perception also, therefore, involve perception of length, area, depth or distance. In Chapter IV we have described some experiments on perception of seen or visual length (p. 68) and perception of visual area or size (p. 68). The experiment we described on the determination of the aestheriometric index (p. 69) will also come under space perception ; the index is called spatial threshold as it defines the perceived limit of two-point distance on the skin surface.

Length—horizontal or vertical, size and area are characteristics of a flat surface. They comprise our knowledge of what are called the two dimensions of space. Our knowledge of the third dimension of space involves perception of depth or distance. When you perceive a cube you are aware of its height, its length and also of its depth or relative distance, from the observer, of its sides other than the front one.

The perception of the first two dimensions of space can be explained in terms of the images cast by objects on the retina. The retinal image is flat ; it has a size or area. Looked at from the same distance, a small size object projects a smaller image on the retina than does a large size object. But how do we come to perceive the third dimension of space, depth or distance, when the retinal image is flat or only bidimensional ? A set of visual cues has been noted to constitute the basis for the perception of depth or distance. They have been classified as monocular or binocular. The monocular cues, as the name suggests, operate even when an object is seen with a single eye. The binocular cues come into play when both eyes are functioning together. Any text-book on psychology gives an account of the visual cues in perception of depth and distance.

The cues for perception of depth or distance are provided not only by the visual receptors. The auditory receptors also play an important part in perception of the relative distance between the perceiver and the objects around him. The kinaesthetic sense provides still another source of perception of spatial characteristics of objects. The blind man's perception of size, area, depth or distance is derived from the qualitative difference in the sensations produced by his bodily movements. Ingenious experiments have been devised on the kinaesthetic perception of space. We will not describe them in this book, and will confine ourselves only to the description of an experiment on the visual perception of depth or distance.

For an experiment on the accuracy of perception of visual depth you can use the psychophysical method of average error or that of limits (p. 61). The apparatus to be used is the so-called visual depth perception apparatus, described in the Appendix III. It consists of a box whose front side has a window through which S can perceive the interior of the box. Inside there are two vertical sticks, mounted side by side on parallel rods. One of them is fixed and its position cannot be changed ; it lies midway between the front and back sides of the box ; the other can be moved back and forth by rotating a knob fixed on the long side of the box. S has to adjust the variable rod so that it is in line with the stationary rod, that is, gets in the same frontal parallel plane as the stationary one. Another stick enables the E to determine the distance in millimeters between the two planes in which the rods are localised by S ; this distance defines the magnitude of error. The experiment will be done under two conditions : (1) Monocular and (2) Binocular. The hypothesis will be that accuracy of depth perception increases under binocular vision. The counterbalancing design may be used to neutralise the effect of sequence. The treatment of data has to be done as described in Chapter IV.

Perception of Time

We perceive time as we perceive space ; we become directly aware of time in which events take place and objects exist. We know whether an event lasted long or short, whether it happened before or after another event, just as we know whether an object is large or small, whether it is to the right or left of another object. We use some device for measuring time, as we do for measuring space. But measured time provides us an indirect knowledge of time ; we actually infer time from the perception of relative positions of the hands of a clock or watch ; we perceive space and estimate time on this basis. We perceive time when we discriminate long or short time, or note the difference between any two intervals of time, without consulting a time measuring device.

In the previous section we have referred to experiments dealing with error in perception of space. We will consider here the experiments on the accuracy of perception of time and the factors that influence it. As in the case of perception of space, we will be concerned not only with the magnitude of the error but also with its direction—time too, like space, may be over-estimated or underestimated. Further, like experiments on perception of space, a set of standard methods have been used for collection and treatment of data on perception of time. An account of the same is given below.

1. **Method of Reproduction** : S is required to reproduce a constant time interval produced by E, called the stimulus interval. The mean difference over a number of trials between the magnitude of the stimulus interval and those of the reproduced intervals gives an estimate of S's error of time perception. If the mean reproduced interval is longer than the stimulus interval, the error is one of over-estimation, and if shorter, the error is of under-estimation. You will identify in this method the psychophysical method of Mean or Average Error (p. 60).

2. **Method of Comparison** : Here E presents a constant

standard interval and one of a set of variable comparison intervals, one after the other, in a random sequence. S has to judge about the second interval whether it is longer or shorter than the first, or they are equal. E may present the variable intervals in a regular increasing or decreasing order for comparison with the standard interval (Method of Limits), or the variable intervals may bc presented in a random order (Method of Constant stimuli).

3. **Method of Estimation :** This is the easiest method for collecting data on time perception. S is asked to indicate the passage of a given time interval, say 10 secs., by pressing and releasing a telegraphic key alternately, each for 10 secs. He goes on pressing for 10 secs. and then releasing for the next 10 secs. and so on, without making use of any time measuring device. E acquaints S, in the beginning, with the time interval by tapping twice, say on the table, at a measured interval ; E uses a stop watch for the purpose of measuring the time interval. He then asks S to press and release the key for the same interval. In order to record S's responses and to obtain an accurate measurement of the time for which S actually pressed or released the key, E uses the same set-up as proposed for experiment on perception of a reversible figure (p. 114). The experiment can, however, also be done by handing over a stop watch to S, with its dial facing E and made, thus, invisible to S. E sets the stop watch at the starting position every time and passes it on to S asking him to press the button of the stop watch twice at the given time interval, holding it in a manner that the dial is invisible to him. E records from the stop watch the time for each trial.

When using the method of reproduction E produces the stimulus interval by tapping on the telegraphic key twice, the two taps spaced at a measured time interval, and S too taps twice to produce the same time interval. Two separate telegraphic keys may be used, one for E and one for S ; each having its own separate connection with a separate time marker, and thereby producing separate graphs on the smoked drum. Or, for producing the stimulus interval E may use a stop watch and press it and then stop it after the desired time interval, with the back of the watch facing S, and the clicks produced being within his hearing. E then sets the stop watch at the starting position and passes it on to S who starts the stop watch and then stops it, in order to produce the same interval, without looking at its dial.

For the method of comparison, E produces two intervals, one after the other—he makes two taps spaced at one interval, and then again another two taps spaced at the other interval. S is to judge the second interval in relation to the first. When using a stop watch, E may start and stop the watch, and thus produce two clicks for one interval, and then again press and stop it for the other interval. S is to judge the differences between the two intervals.

Besides using a gap between two momentary events, i.e., two taps or two clicks, E may use a single event lasting for a given period of time, like a continuous sound stimulus spreading over, or a flash of light enduring for, a fixed time. S may then be required to produce a sound or light having the same duration. Similarly, E produces two sounds or two lights of different durations and requires S to judge the difference. We shall describe below some experiments on the perception of time.

Determination of the Extent and Direction of Error in the Subject's Perception of Time

The experiment may be conducted by using any one of the three methods described above. Suppose, we use the method of reproduction. The apparatus to be used for recording the data will be the same as for the experiment on the perception of a reversible figure (p. 114). Only, here we use two telegraphic keys, one for S and one for E, each having its own separate circuit of connection with time marker. E and S will be sitting on the same side of the table, and a screen will hide the kymograph from S. S will be instructed as "I will press and immediately release my key and after a time interval I will again press and release it. You have to press and release your key also at the same time interval twice. Please be very attentive and let not your mind wander. I am going to see how correctly you can repeat a time interval. When I first press and release my key, you have to carefully observe after what time I again press and release it. When I have pressed and released next, you press and release your key and after the same time as I did press and release it again. I will give you a ready signal each time, before I first press my key. Do you understand ?" E selects a definite time interval as the stimulus interval, say 5 secs.

For the simple problem of determining S's error in perception of time, twenty trials would serve the purpose. The pressing and releasing of the key at intervals will make vertical hatchings producing a graph on the smoked paper like the following:

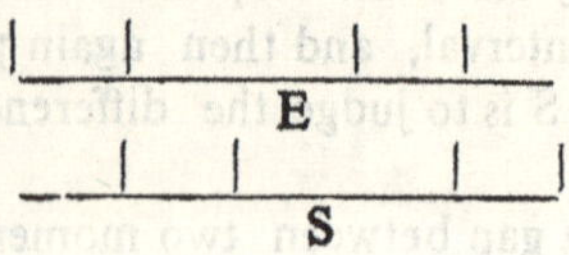

Using the time-line traced on the smoked paper, E measures the duration of the reproduced intervals (p. 107) and records the data in the form of a table. Mean and SD are calculated for the 20 observations. The difference between the constant stimulus interval produced by E and the Mean time found from the data would give S's constant error (p. 67) in perception of time. The SD would show fluctuations in S's perception of time which may be wide or narrow according to the value of the SD. A wide fluctuation may be explained as due to S's varying capacity to concentrate and to keep off distracting thoughts during the course of the experiment. S's introspection, which has also to be taken, may throw further light on the matter.

S's error in perception of time may tend more strongly in the positive or the negative direction. If his Mean is larger than the stimulus interval produced by E, S overestimated the time; if it is shorter, S underestimated the time.

It is not very necessary for E to use a key for producing the stimulus interval and thus obtain a record of his own performance also. E may tap on the table twice, spacing his tapping at a fixed time interval measured by a stop watch—he taps with one hand and simultaneously starts the stop watch which he holds in the other hand, and then stops the watch and at the same time taps again. Nevertheless, the record of E's performance too will show how best he was successful in producing the same stimulus interval. The record of E's performance may be used also in another way. E may not produce a constant stimulus interval, for which he has also to use a stop watch. In utilizing the data, then, a detailed record will be prepared not only of S's reproduced time, but also of the stimulus intervals produced by E, from trial to trial. Means will be calculated for both sets of data, and the difference in the Means will be interpreted in the manner described above. SD will be calculated only for S's Mean.

In experiments on time perception, E has to take an important precaution. S may mentally count when E is producing the stimulus interval and repeat the same counting process while reproducing the interval. Counting at the same pace, he may succeed in reproducing the interval accurately. S may use the same device also when the method of estimation is used. While taking S's introspection, E may find out from him whether he used this device. It may not be wise to suggest him, before taking the data, to avoid this. He may not co-operate and use the device despite E's instruction to the contrary ; had he not been forewarned, perhaps this would not have occurred to him.

The experiment can be done by using the estimation method also. There may be a confusion in the interpretation of the result obtained by this method. The Mean that is found for S's estimations of the constant time interval that E instructs him to estimate, is the actual or measured time ; S's error of estimation has to be found with reference to this Mean value. Supposing the time to be estimated is 10 secs. and S's Mean comes to 8 secs. In this case S has judged, on the average, 8 secs., the actual time, to be equal to 10 secs. He has overestimated the time. Supposing, his Mean comes to 12 secs., S has then perceived 12 secs. as 10 secs. He has underestimated.

Perception of Long and Short Time

There are a set of variables that have been found to influence the accuracy of time perception. One such variable is the short or long duration of the perceived time interval. Experiments have been done on perception of varying lengths of time. It has been found that the extent of the error decreases as one proceeds from a very short time ; it becomes minimum when one reaches about 1 sec. interval (0.8 secs.), and then goes on increasing with increase in the time interval. The point of time at which there is minimum error has been described as **indifference interval**. It is also found that very short time is generally overestimated, while a long interval of time is generally underestimated. You can verify this finding by using two time intervals, say, 0.5 secs. and 15 secs. The data can be collected by using either the reproduction or the estimation method. The counterbalancing design (p. 9) may be used. For this experiment, the rate of movement of the kymograph should be very slow so that the divisions of the line traced on the drum have an easily measurable length.

Perception of Filled and Unfilled Time

Another variable influencing the perception of time is the vacant or filled character of the perceived time. In order to find the difference in the accuracy of perception of filled and unfilled time, data are to be taken under two conditions. In one condition S remains otherwise idle all through the experiment. In the other condition he is engaged in a task, like copying from a printed page, solving arithmetical problems, taking dictation from a passage, etc. The data may be obtained either by the method of estimation or that of reproduction. The hypothesis will be (1) perception of empty time is more accurate than that of filled time, since in perceiving filled time S's attention is divided between perception of the time and performance of the task, which is likely to lower the efficiency of the perception ; (2) filled time will be underestimated while empty time will be overestimated.

The obtained result may not, however, support the hypothesis. Though S may be apparently idle during the empty time interval, his mind may wander and the time may, therefore, really be filled with implicit thought processes. There will be no difference, then, between the two conditions of the experiment—both involve filled time. To make them different, instruction to S should emphasise that he should keep his mind vacant—should not allow any idea to occupy his mind. S's introspection will also throw light on this point. The hypothesis may not be substantiated also for another reason. The task filling the time may be dull or uninteresting to S ; it may produce monotony. The time, though filled, may on this account be overestimated. This fact would be revealed in S's introspection. The following report of an experiment illustrates the influence of monotony on time perception.

Perception of Time as a Measure of Task Monotony

Time like space can be directly perceived ; we can discriminate long or short time without consulting a time-measuring instrument.

Psychologists have not been able, however, to identify the sensory processes that mediate time perception. It has been suggested that the introceptive receptors provide the sensory cues for time perception, but the evidence so far has not been conclusive. Like space, perception of time may be more or less accurate, and the error, also in this case, may be positive or negative—time too may be overestimated or underestimated. Several factors have been identified as influencing the accuracy of time perception and the direction that the error may take. There may be more or less permanent organismic factors—individuals may differ in the accuracy of time perception. The accuracy may depend also on the condition of freshness or fatigue in the perceiver, the length of the interval perceived, the empty or filled character of the interval, the nature of the task engaging the time. In this experiment an attempt was made to determine the effect of engagement in a repetitive, dull, monotony producing task on S's perception of time. It has been found that a monotonous task is more likely to be overestimated than underestimated. Time seems to move at snail's pace in watching a dull picture in the cinema house ; it flees while reading a breath-taking detective story. Industrial psychologists have, accordingly, used perception of time as a measure of monotony, or psychological fatigue, as distinguished from physical or industrial fatigue.

Hypothesis : Time engaged in a monotonous task will be overestimated.

Method

Subject : A graduate right-handed male student.

Apparatus and Material : (1) Morse Telegraphic key ; (2) Kymograph ; (3) Time-Marker ; (4) Chronometer ; (5) Two wooden trays, one of them containing 20 wooden cubes.

Procedure : Data were collected by the method of estimation. S was first given by E an idea of the passage of 60 secs. E tapped the key twice, spaced at an interval of 60 secs., looking at a stop watch. The experiment was divided into two conditions : (1) Experimental and (2) Control. In the experimental condition S had to pick up and transfer the cubes one by one to the empty tray and then transfer them back to the first tray and to go on repeating this performance. In the control condition he took from E a dictation of a printed passage. In both conditions S kept the first finger of his left hand near the key in order to press and release it as required. The Control condition was introduced before the Experimental. A rest pause of 15 minutes separated the two conditions.

Instruction to S

Control Condition : "I will press this key and wait for just 60 seconds and will then press it again. I am doing this to give you an idea of 60 seconds duration. Be very attentive. Ready. You now know how long it takes for 60 seconds to pass. You have to press this key continuously for 60 seconds and then release it for another 60 seconds. You have to keep the first finger of your left hand near the key. Press the key for 60 secs. and release it for another 60 seconds. In this way you have to go on pressing for 60 seconds and releasing for 60 secs. unless I ask you to stop. Here are a few sheets of blank paper. You have to use them for writing a passage that I will dictate. You have to take dictation from me and also go on pressing and releasing the key alternately for 60 secs. Do you understand ?"

Experimental Condition : Here are two trays. There are 20 cubes in one tray. You have to remove each one of them to the other tray, one by one. After this is done, you have to again take them back to the first tray. In this way you have to fill one tray, then empty it, then fill the empty one and so on. You have also to press the key for 60 secs. and then release it for another 60 secs. as you did while I was giving you dictation. Do you understand ?"

Result

Table 1

TIME IN SECONDS

Condition			
Trial	Control	Trial	Experimental
1	64	1	47
2	62	2	51
3	63	3	45
4	65	4	40
5	59	5	42
6	60	6	32
7	58	7	35
8	57	8	34
9	54	9	35
10	56	10	32

Table 2

MEAN TIME IN SECOND, SD, AND t IN THE CONTROL AND EXPERIMENTAL CONDITIONS

	Control		Experimental
Mean	59.8		39.3
SD	2.44		5.25
SE_{diff}		4.50	
Obt_{diff}		20.50	
t		4.55	

Table 3

CONSTANT ERROR AND DIRECTION OF ERROR

	Control	Experiment
CE	0.2	20.7
Direc.	Plus	Plus

In Control condition S perceives 59.8 secs., on the average, as aqual to 60 secs.; his constant error is only 0.2 secs. In the Experiment condition S perceives 39.3 secs. as equal to 60 secs.; his constant error is 20.7. The difference is very highly significant. S has very much overestimated the time in the experimental condition. His estimation of time in the control condition is almost correct.

Discussion

S has overestimated the time while he was performing the cube-transfer task. The actual time is about two-thirds of the perceived time. His perception of time while taking dictation is almost accurate. The repetitive character of the task produced in the S the feeling of boredom which further increased with the repetition of the task ; the error increased after the 5th trial. Our results support our hypothesis, namely, a montonous task performance leads to overestimation of time.

The accuracy in the perception of time engaged in dictation takes us to the conclusion that S reacted to this task neither as dull nor as interesting. His overall attitude to the task was neutral. We notice rather a slight decline in S's interest after the fourth trial. In fact, there was a slight tendency to underestimate the time in the first four trials ; in each case the actual time was more than 60 secs. But thereafter, a tendency to overestimate the time appears, though it is not very marked ; the actual time in five out of six trials was less than 60 secs. After all taking dictation is a mechanical activity and one might gradually get bored if the task is continued for some time.

Our final conclusion will be that one can identify a task to be monotonous to a person on measuring his perception of the time given to the task.

Recommended Reading

Fraisse, P., *The Psychology of Time*, Harper & Row, New York, 1963.

Geldard, F. A., *Fundamentals of Psychology*, Chapters 14, 15, Wiley, New York, 1962.

Osgood, C. E., *Method and Theory in Experimentat Psychology*, Chapters 5, 6, 7, Oxford University Press, New York, 1953.

Postman, E. and Egan, J. P., *Experimental Psychology*, Chapters 4, 6, Harper, New York, 1949.

Underwood, B. J., *Experimental Psychology*, Chapter 2, Appleton, New York, 1966.

Woodworth, R. S. and Schlosberg, H., *Experimental Psychology*, Chapter 14, Holt, New York, 1954.

Chapter VII

Sensory-Motor Learning

Learning is more or less a permanent modification of behaviour resulting from experience. If the modification of behaviour is not the result of experience, it is called maturation ; the modification in behaviour takes place automatically with the growth of the body. It is, however, difficult to separate learning from maturation. They are very much interdependent. We cannot expect a child to learn how to walk before he is able to stand up, and to learn to stand up before he is able to sit up. At the same time, the child is not able to sit up, stand up or walk all at once. He is able to perform this only gradually being trained to perfection by practice or experience.

The modification of behaviour in learning is to be distinguished from another modification of behaviour which may be the result of fatigue. The latter is temporary and disappears after rest. Further, the change in behaviour produced by learning is marked by improvement in the behaviour ; the change due to fatigue results in impairment of behaviour. The improvement in behaviour can be measured in terms of increment in number of responses within a fixed time, decrement in time in performing the activity, increase in speed of performance, or decrease in the errors made in performance. The same measures are used to determine the change produced by fatigue. In this case, however, the change is in the other direction, i.e., decrease in number of responses, or increase in time or errors.

We can distinguish between performance and learning. Performance is the observed behaviour. Learning is more or less permanent change within the organism which cannot be directly observed ; it can only be inferred ; the term retention is also used for the change within the organism. Thus, what is learned is retained; the learned activity can be repeated afterwards in more or less the same manner because of its retention. What is retained has also been called the after-effect of the performance. Thus, the change within the organism called learning, the after-effect of an experience or performance, and retention of what one experiences or learns are more or less interchangeable expressions; they convey about the same meaning.

Learning Curves

It follows from what has been said above that learning cannot be directly measured. We can only measure the performance which manifests learning. We can represent learning graphically; we can plot learning curves. They are shown below. The measure of learning used in plotting the given curves is the number of responses.

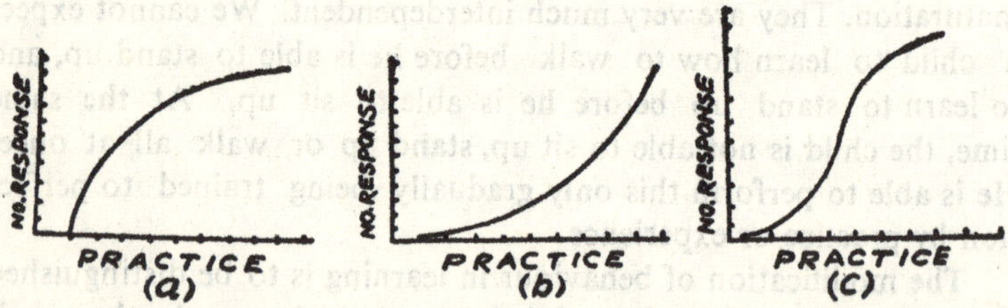

The first curve shows a rapid and steep rise in the beginning; the rise becomes slow or gradual afterwards. It means that the change in performance—increase in response—is greater at first and becomes less and less afterwards; the improvement is more rapid at first and gets slow afterwards. Such curve is called a negatively accelerated curve; the rate of gain or progress, acceleration, becomes less and less with increase in practice. The second curve is called positively accelerated curve. The rate of gain here increases with practice; it is slow at first and becomes more and more rapid afterwards. The third curve possesses both features. It starts as a positively accelerated curve and then changes into a negatively accelerated curve. Such a curve has been called a sigmoid or S-shaped curve.

The learning carve you have seen above shows a regular rise; every trial or unit of practice shows some gain; the amount of the gain, however, may be large or small as compared to the gains in the preceding trials. You can seldom get such regular curves, if you plot them on the basis of the data obtained from a single subject. You can get such curves only when you pool the data obtained from a large number of subjects engaged in learning the same task. For individual data you will get a curve which would be something like this:

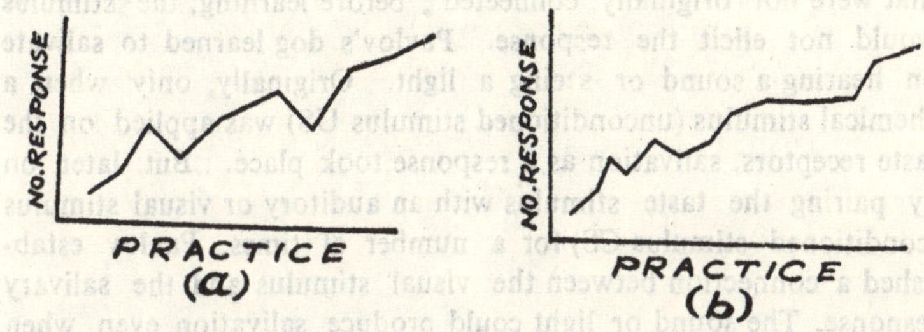

The curves do not show only rise throughout. A rise is followed by a fall in some parts of the curve. You will note in curve (*b*) a period of neither rise nor fall, a stage in learning when there is no observed gain or loss from practice. Such period of no gain is called a plateau.

The completion of the learning, that is, the stage beyond which there is no further gain from practice, can also be noted in a learning curve. The curve levels off ; it shows no further rise. This stage indicates what has been called the physiological limit—the maximum an individual can achieve from practice within the limits of his inherent capacities. The physiological limit is to be distinguished from the plateau ; in the latter case there is further rise in the curve ; when the physiological limit is reached, the curve shows no further improvement.

Before we consider the experiments on learning, we will make a broad distinction between kinds of learning. The simplest kind of learning consists of establishing an association between a single stimulus and a single response. The typical example of such simple kind of learning is the conditioned reflex. The more complex forms of learning also involve association but neither the stimulus nor the response is as simple. The entire performance consists of a series of associations between sensory and motor elements. There is a third kind of learning called verbal learning. This kind of learning involves symbols or signs for stimulus and responses ; the association established by learning is between symbols.

The Conditioned Reflex

Experiments on conditioned reflex were first suggested by Pavlov, a Russian physiologist. In simple language, it consists of establishing a connection between a stimulus and a response that were not originally connected ; before learning, the stimulus would not elicit the response. Pavlov's dog learned to salivate on hearing a sound or seeing a light. Originally, only when a chemical stimulus (unconditioned stimulus US) was applied on the taste receptors, salivation as a response took place. But later on by pairing the taste stimulus with an auditory or visual stimulus (conditioned stimulus CS) for a number of times, Pavlov established a connection between the visual stimulus and the salivary response. The sound or light could produce salivation even when presented without a food object. The experiment was done on children, and even on adults, and conditioned response was established.

The conditioned reflex experiments led to the discovery of a set of facts. If a conditioned reflex has been established, the CS could be used for establishing a connection between the response and some other stimulus. Thus a CS, say, sound is made to elicit the response of salivation after its repeated pairing with the US, namely, food object. Afterwards the sound stimulus is paired, say, with a visual stimulus several times until the visual stimulus by itself elicits the salivary response. The first conditioning, namely, between sound and salivation, is called first order conditioning ; the second conditioning between the light and salivation is called second order conditioning.

Another fact has been called stimulus generalisation. The conditioned response (CR) is evoked not only by the conditioned stimulus (CS) but also by other stimuli similar to it. If the response has been experimentally conditioned to a light stimulus of a given intensity or colour, it will be elicited also by lights of other intensities or colours. This has been called stimulus generalisation.

Still another fact is called experimental extinction. After the CR has been established by pairing a US and a CS, the CS will evoke the response. But if every time the CS alone is presented in future, the strength of the response will gradually decrease till it will cease to be elicited ; if the food stimulus is never used and only the bell is rung, the amount of saliva will gradually become less and less, and the time interval between the ringing of the bell and the process of salivation will gradually increase. This time interval has been called latency and the latency of the response has also been used as a measure of response strength (p. 22). The repeated presentation of CS alone will ultimately reach a stage when it would cease to produce salivation The association between the CS and CR has been extinguished ; this is called extinction. The pairing of the US and the CS is called reinforcement ; the presentation of the CS without the US is called non-reinforcement. Experimental extinction is thus the result of a succession of non-reinforced trials, i.e., those in which CS is not paired with US. In this connection, another interesting fact was also discovered. Continuous presentation of CS without US produces extinction. However, if no further trials are taken for some time and thereafter CS is again presented alone, i.e , without US, it may elicit the response (CR). This has been called spontaneous recovery ; the association is recovered without reinforcement. However, if no reinforcement is further made, there will be a permanent extinction and the CS will not be able to evoke CR even after a time gap. Resistance to extinction has also been used as a measure of response strength. If the association between CS and CR is strong, it would need much larger number of non-reinforced trials in order to produce extinction.

Conditioning experiments have also been used to produce discrimination between stimuli. A conditioned reflex is first established, say, between a visual stimulus and the salivary response. At first the response will take place even if the intensity or colour of the light is changed (stimulus generalisation). But if the US is paired only with one intensity or one colour of the light stimulus and it is not paired with any other intensity or colour, the response will become linked with only that intensity or colour. In future, only the reinforced intensity or colour of the light stimulus will produce the response. The organism has learned to discriminate between the intensities or colours of the light stimulus. Discrimination, thus, operates in a direction opposite to stimulus generalisation.

Two experiments on conditioning are described below :

Hand-withdrawal Reflex : Any shock stimulus elicits the automatic withdrawal of the hand. A mild electric shock is used in this experiment as the US and the hand-withdrawal as the UR. The hand-withdrawal conditioning apparatus is described in Appendix. S's hand is placed on the metal plates. E presses the switch which delivers electric shock and S's hand automatically withdraws. S is instructed not to resist the withdrawal of his hand. A buzzer is used to present the CS. E first uses the electric shock alone a number of times to see whether the hand-withdrawal does take place. He then uses the buzzer alone to ascertain that the buzzer does not produce the response. Then he pairs the two ; he starts first the buzzer, then after 0.5 seconds releases the switch to apply the shock stimulus. The stimulus pairs are repeated at intervals of 15 secs. Thereafter, in between the paired stimuli, E introduces in chance order only the buzzer to test whether the CR is elicited. When E notes that CR is elicted by the test trials, i. e., the buzzer given without the shock, invariably, he then takes 5 test trials consecutively. The CR is then extinguished by successive presentations of the buzzer alone.

E records the number of paired trials after which the irregularly interspersed test trials produced the CR, the number of test trials in which CR was not evoked, and the number of paired trials after which the successive test trials showed regular occurrence of the CR. Similarly, he records in the extinction series the trials on which the CR did not occur, and the number of extinction trials needed to prevent the occurrence of CR in 5 successive trials.

The Eye-lid Closure Reflex : The sudden entry of a puff of air automatically produces the closure of the eyelid. The puff of air, thus, is the US for the eyelid closure which is the UR. It is possible to condition the response to another stimulus, e. g., a sound, light or touch stimulus. The apparatus to be used is described in Appendix III. The puff of air is administered by E and the dripping of S's eye-lid is automatically recorded on a rotating drum. Similar procedure as that for the hand-withdrawal reflex is to be adopted for experiment on the eyelid-closure reflex.

Learning of Psychomotor Skills or Sensory-Motor Learning

We have noted above (p. 135) that a more complex type of learning involves a series of stimulus-response connections. The learning, however, does not consist merely of acquiring these bits of connections but also integrating or organizing them into a complex pattern. An example of such learning we find in copying alphabets, typewriting, etc., that involve a pattern of complex behaviour that can be analyzed into bits of stimulus-response connections. Some experiments illustrating the processes involved in the acquisition of psycho-motor skills are described below.

Mirror Tracing : Learning is a modification of behaviour resulting from experience. When the child learns to copy the alphabets from a printed page, he encounters lot of difficulties. He looks at the drawing of the alphabet and makes a series of movements with his hand. While looking at the alphabet, he moves his eyes up and down, and sideways. As long as the movements of his hand do not correspond with the movements of the eyes, his drawing is not successful ; there is no coordination between the eye and hand movements. By practice he learns to make only those movements of the hand that correspond with the movements of the eyes. The eye-hand coordination is established ; both move in corresponding directions. As adults, we have acquired perfect coordination between eye and hand movements in copying a printed page ; we encounter no difficulty ; in fact copying becomes the easiest task for us to perform. But when we are asked to copy the same alphabets by looking at their reflection in a mirror, we encounter perhaps as much difficulty as we faced when learning to write the alphabets as a child. The reason is that in this case the eye-hand coordination established by practice does not work. The up and down directions of the alphabets are reversed when seen in a mirror. To copy the alphabets, therefore, the hand should move in a direction opposite to the eyes' movement. A new eye-hand coordination is required in order to accomplish the task. This is interfered with by the previously established coordination. Hence the enormous difficulty experienced in drawing a visual pattern seen in a mirror. Mirror tracing has, accordingly, been used as an excellent device to demonstrate the process of sensory-motor learning. A star pattern, shown below, which requires several up and down, and sideways movements, in order to be copied, has been generally used for the mirror-tracing experiment.

The apparatus to be used in the experiment is the so-called mirror-tracing apparatus (Appendix III). It consists of a mirror vertically fixed on the far side of an wooden board. Direct observation of the board is prevented by a screen fixed at a height from the board so that it does not obstruct the movement of S's hand along the board. The star pattern is placed on the board, fixed on it by drawing pins. S is instructed to trace the star, while looking at the mirror, by keeping his pencil between the inner and outer boundaries of the star. Crossing the boundary is treated as error. The direction of the movement is indicated in the star pattern (Fig. 1). In tracing, S makes anti-clockwise movement, i.e., moves from right to left which reverses the usual movement from left to right. E takes several trials, say 20, each time using a separate sheet bearing the star pattern. The sheets are numbered to indicate the order of the trials from the beginning to the end. Every time S has to start at the same point. E gives S the start signal and also starts the stop watch to measure S's time in completing the pattern. Besides time score, E also finds out error score for each trial.

Fig. 1

E prepares two graphs of S's learning, a time graph showing the change in time and an error graph showing the number of errors from trial to trial. E also records from his objective observation of S's behaviour how S attacks the problem, and notes the marks of S's feelings from his facial expressions, his features, remarks made, and other responses. S also gives an introspection about the nature of the difficulty encountered by him, any rule or principle that helped him in overcoming the difficulty, whether he used only the hit-and-miss method, and so on. The discussion will centre round the nature of the learning process, utilizing both the objective and the subjective data, the curve of learning, occurrence of a plateau, etc.

Maze Learning : A maze consists of several paths and turnings ; some of the paths are blind—they have no opening. In order to get out of the maze one has to choose the correct turning or choice point. The blind paths are also called blind alleys ; wrong choice of a turning leads one into a blind alley. The maze has been extensively used for experiments on animal learning. However, different types of human mazes have also been devised. Some of these have been so planned as to prevent S from getting a view of the maze in order that S can learn the correct path only by a trial-and-error (Appendix III). The sensory cues involved in such maze learning experiments are the kinaesthetic ones—the sensations of movement provided by the stimulation of the proprioceptres. Below is a description of an experiment on maze learning.

Problem : To demonstrate and examine the process of human learning in the acquisition of a pattern of sensory-motor connections.

Apparatus and Materials : The maze learning box. A brass plate with the slotted maze pattern. A stop watch. The box is placed on the table in front of S, the open side of the box facing S. E inserts a sheet of blank paper under the slotted brass plate and helps S to place his pencil point at the centre of the maze ; E's hand should not touch the brass plate. E then gives the start signal and instructs S to move his pencil through the grooves in order to be able to get out of the maze. E times S's performance. He replaces the used sheet by another. The sheets are numbered so as to indicate the order of trials. The trials are stopped when S's learning reaches the stage of two errorless trials. Both time and error scores are found. The number of choice points wrongly selected constitutes the error score. S gives his introspection about the method by which he learned the maze ; whether it was just trial-and-error, or he worked out a plan ; how he was able to discriminate between the correct and incorrect moves at each choice point ; whether he used kinaesthetic cues, or verbal aids like 'first turn left, then right, ignore the first turn, choose the second turn,' etc. Did he construct a visual picture of the total maze which helped him to get through the right path, or did he learn a series of separate movements ? E also makes use of objective observation. He plots both time and error curves. In discussion, he concentrates upon S's mode of attack, the nature of the learning curve, plateaus in learning curve, and also answers the points about the nature of S's learning process.

Another kind of Maze, called 'the punch-board maze (Appendix III) can also be used in an experiment on learning. It consists of two pieces of punched wooden boards, upper and lower, of identical size. The upper piece has drilled into it ten to twelve rows of holes, each row consisting of four or five holes ; in addition, there is a single hole at the top and another at the bottom. For one hole of each row in the upper piece there is a hole in the corresponding position in the lower piece randomly distributed over its surface. Each one of the top and bottom holes too has a hole in the corresponding position in the lower piece. For each trial, a soft paper is placed under the upper piece and S is required to insert his pencil, starting with the top hole, in that hole of each row that has a corresponding hole in the lower piece. Each trial is finished after S reaches the bottom hole, and inserts his pencil therein. S is never given a chance of looking at the lower piece. If he hits the correct hole, his pencil will pierce through the paper and pass into the lower piece; otherwise, the pencil would only make a mark on the paper. For each trial, E gives the start signal and, using a stop watch, measures the time taken. S gives his introspection and E also observes S's behaviour. E counts from the sheet the number of correct hits from trial to trial. With 10 rows in the upper piece, the maximum number of correct responses will be 12. Both time and error responses are recorded. Separate curves are plotted for each kind of score. The discussion centres round the same points as in the experiment on the slotted maze, described above.

Another device that has been very widely used in experiments on complex sensory motor behaviour is the so-called pursuit rotor (Appendix III). The pursuit rotor measures S's tracking behaviour. It consists of a rotating table (turn-table) ordinarily used for playing gramaphone records. The turn-table has a small metal disc on it—4 inches in diameter. S is given a stylus electrically connected with the turn-table. S is required to keep the stylus on the disc, while the turn table is rotating. When the stylus gets into contact with the disc, an electric circuit is made. A record of the time for which the stylus is on the disc is obtained. A time marker and the Kymograph are used for recording (p. 106). The entire experimental session may be divided into units of 1-min. S's score will be the percent of the time in secs. the stylus was on the disc.

Recommended Reading

Geldard, F. A., *Fundamentals of Psychology*, Chapters 4 and 11, Wiley, New York, 1972.

Munn, N. L., *Introduction to Psychology*, Chapter 10, Oxford and I.B.H., New Delhi, 1967.

Osgood, C. E., *Method and Theory in Experimental Psychology*, Chapter 8, Oxford University Press, New York, 1953.

Postman, L. and Egan, J. P., Chapters, 13, 14, Harper, New York, 1949.

Underwood, B. J., *Experimental Psychology*, Chapter 10, Appleton, New York, 1966.

Woodworth, R. S. and Schlosberg, H., *Experimental Psychology*, Chapters 18, 19 and 21, Holt, New York, 1954.

CHAPTER VIII

Verbal Learning

Learning Materials

In experiments on verbal learning we use such materials as words, numbers, figures and nonsense combination of letters. Experiments on verbal learning became very popular with psychologists after Ebbinghaus introduced the nonsense syllables. Before that the verbal materials used in learning experiments consisted of prose passages, poems, or words. There was one great limitation in using these materials; their difficulty level could not be objectively determined. Two passages of the same length may not be equally difficult for the same or for different persons. Even while using words having the same number of letters, one cannot be sure that they are equally difficult to learn. Compare the words 'drub' and 'drum'. The first word may be unknown to many, while the second one is familiar even to the beginning students of English. The requirements of experimental control could not be satisfied, therefore, when one used such kinds of verbal materials in learning experiments. Nonsense syllables were invented by Ebbinghaus to remove this defect. It consists of two consonants with a vowel in between; the syllable is not a word to be found in a dictionary. But this is not enough for the syllable to be nonsense or meaningless. In the psychological sense meaning is nothing but association. A word has meaning because it is associated with some object, action, event, or situation in the experience of the person who understands its meaning. The German word Frau is nonsense for you since you cannot associate it with any other word, object, event, or behaviour with which you are familiar. All that you understand from the word is that it contains the four English letters F R A U; it is otherwise meaningless to you.

It is easy to make any number of nonsense syllables using the 21 consonants and the five vowels. But it is not easy to make sure that the syllable thus formed is nonsense. It may have no association for you ; but it may have some association for your subject. Different systematic investigations have been made to determine what is called the association value of nonsense syllables. Different methods have been used in such investigations. In one such method a sample of, say, 100 S's is used. Each S is given a particular syllable and asked to tell whatever comes to his mind while giving his attention to that syllable. Each S is given, say, one minute for the purpose. Adding the number of associations given to each syllable by each one of the 100 S's and finding the mean number gives the association value of each syllable in terms of percentage. In this way, different lists of nonsense syllables have been prepared, each one having an association value ranging say from 5% to 80%. The association value of the syllable is then treated as its difficulty value. A syllable having high, say 60 per cent, association value is likely, on the average, to be learned more quickly than one having 20 per cent association value.

With the difficulty value of the nonsense syllable known, one can use a list containing nonsense syllables of the same difficulty value ; two lists, e.g., may be of the same difficulty value, though containing different sets of nonsense syllables, since both lists contain nonsense syllables of the same association value.

In recent times nonsense syllables are being substituted by a combination of consonants, e.g., HXP. We use the more comprehensive term 'trigram' now which may be a combination of two consonants and a vowel (CVC) or of three consonants (C C C). The CCC trigram is to be preferred to the CVC. The latter can be pronounced like a word and may thus suggest a word similarly pronounced which may make its learning less difficult. Consonant trigrams (CCC) cannot be pronounced while learning the trigram ; for learning them all that is needed is to associate the three letters as a single unit. Nevertheless, the CCC trigrams too may have a high association value, e.g., RMS which is an abbreviation of Railway Mail Service, or even XPL which may easily suggest the word **expel**. Some trigrams may have advantage over others in this respect. Further, some consonants occur more frequently together than do others, e.g., K and N quite often go together in the English language ; on the other hand, C and F and G and K are seldom found to occur in juxtaposition, i.e., immediately one after the other. List of trigrams have been prepared keeping these facts in view.

As we noted above, lists of nonsense syllables, or of consonant trigrams, have been prepared in the English language and they are used in verbal learning experiments. Their use as such is, however, limited to those whose mother tongue is English. The same syllables or trigrams may have different difficulty values for those whose mother tongue is other than English. A nonsense syllable in one language may be a meaningful word in another, e.g., WUH is meaningless in English, but it is a very familiar word in an Indian language meaning **he, she or that** or, the CCC trigram KSM may be a nonsense trigram of very low association value but it sounds very similar to the Hindi word 'KASAM' which means oath or swearing. The standard English lists of nonsense syllables or CCC trigrams, therefore, may not work with other than those whose mother tongue is English. For experiments on such persons whose mother tongue is not English, one has to construct his own nonsense syllables or CCC trigrams, until standard lists for the language concerned have been prepared on the basis of research The hints given below may be used for preparing your own list of nonsense syllables.

(1) Write down the consonants at the top of a sheet of paper.

(2) Starting with the first consonant B, pick up another remote consonant, say, G, and insert between them each one of the five vowels, one after the other. Judge the resulting combination for its association value ; in this particular case each combination will be a word. Select the next consonant H. Again examine the five combinations. Perhaps, none is an English word. But some may be words, or may have an association value, in your own language. BAH, for instance, is a word meaning sexual potency; it has also an association with **wah** which is an exclamation conveying praise or appreciation. Apply your imagination and similarly examine the other combinations. Select the one or more that has no association value in your judgment. Then select some other consonant, combine it with another remote consonant and examine the alternative combinations. In this manner, form as many combinations as required for the length of

the list you desire to prepare ; keep a few extra ones in reserve. As shown earlier, the component letters that are in close proximity in the alphabetical series should not occur in the same nonsense syllable. Each syllable should contain the consonants that fall apart in the alphabetical series.

(3) Selecting from those that you have finally made, prepare the list or lists of the desired number of nonsense syllables. In listing the nonsense items, you have to take some precaution: (*i*) Adjacent items should have no common components. (*ii*) The components of adjacent items should not be such as are in close proximity in the alphabetical series, e.g., CAG and DOH should not succeed each other in the list. (*iii*) The vowels should not occur one after the other in the same order as in the alphabetical series. For example, while listing 10 items, the order of the vowels should not be AEIOU followed by AEIOU. The vowels should appear on the list in a chance or random order.

Some of the hints and precautions suggested above will be applicable also while preparing the CCC trigrams. In addition you have to see that the sequence of the letters does not repeat the sequence of those letters frequently found in words (p. 146).

Trigrams are to be preferred for Indian subjects. In most of the Indian languages the vowel sound is not represented by a letter in the alphabetical series ; there are only minute notations for the vowel sounds. A nonsense syllable in such a language may contain only two letters with the vowel sign. A CCC trigram can, in this case, be easily prepared by using any three letters.

We have noticed that a nonsense syllable (CVC), as well as a consonants trigram (CCC), is a very appropriate material for experiments on verbal learning. This does not mean that meaningful material like words, or a connected passage, is a taboo for such experiments. In fact, words have been used quite often because they can be listed like the nonsense items, and the same learning procedure is appropriate to words also. Further, the familiarity value of words in the English language has been found by empirical research on the frequency of the use of the words in the English speaking population. The difficulty value of the words is in this sense determined. Use is made of list of words of high familiarity value, so that the learning does not involve the acquisition of the words but of the association of the words as elements of the particular list. But unless the familiarity value of words of a language other than English has been similarly determined, they cannot be considered a proper material for experiments on verbal learning. Connected passages, prose or poetry, are used for special types of experiments, i.e., those where the dependant variable is the learning of ideas, of the central theme, etc.

Methods of Verbal Learning

Serial Learning : A list of items, CVC or CCC, is exposed on a memory drum (Appendix III). If no memory drum is available, the items may be written in bold letters, each item on a separate, say, 1″×2″ card. The cards are piled face up behind a screen in the order which is to be maintained throughout the experiment. E practices to count mentally, say from 1 to 5, at a pace that covers 2 sec. S is instructed to read out the word or spell the letters composing the item, when a card is presented to him. E presents the top card to S for 2 sec., then removes it and keeps it face down on his side of the screen. He then presents the second card for 2 sec. and places it face down on the first card, and so on, until all cards are exposed to S. S is then given 20 sec. to reproduce the items he remembers, every time trying to reproduce them in the same order as presented by E. E then turns the piled cards upside down so that the first card is face up, and starts the next trial. The procedure is repeated till S is able to reproduce each item correctly and in the order the cards were presented. Every time E records S's responses on a separate sheet. The sheet contains the list of items in the first column, besides several blank columns. Each column is used for recording S's reproductions from trial to trial. The learning is called serial learning because S not only learns the items but also the order in which they are listed. If the instruction given to S merely says that he has to reproduce all items correctly, without also requiring S to reproduce them in their order of presentation, the method will be called free recall or simple reproduction method. Whether E uses the method of serial learning or that of free recall, in either case he stops the trials after two correct or faultless reproductions. This is done to make sure that S would not make any error if further trials were taken. Two faultless reproductions are, thus, used as what is called the criterion of learning.

Level of Learning : Criterion of learning defines the level or strength of learning. When the learning has reached the stage of faultless reproduction, the criterion used is that of simple, cent-per-cent, complete, or perfect learning. Before this stage is reached, the learning is said to be incomplete, imperfect or partial. For example, the learning trials may be stopped when S correctly reproduces one-fourth, one-third, half or two-thirds, and so on, of the total number of items on the list. The learning level or strength will then be 25 p.c., 33 p.c., 50 p.c., 66 p.c., etc. Each one will be called partial learning, and the learning in these different cases will be of unequal strength. Strength or level of learning is, thus, determined by finding the percentage of the ratio between the number of items correctly reproduced at the end of the trials and the number of items in the list. Thus, we can think of all possible levels between 0 learning, i.e., before practice, and cent-per-cent or perfect learning.

Beyond perfect learning too there may be other levels of learning. The measure of these levels will be in terms of what is called over-learning. Having learned a list to the criterion of faultless reproduction, any further trial will produce over-learning. The ratio between the number of additional trials and that required to reach the stage of perfect learning gives a measure of over-learning. Suppose simple or perfect learning has been achieved in 8 trials, and four additional trials are further taken ; over-learning will be $\frac{4}{8} \times 100$ or 50 per cent. In this manner we can have all measures of over-learning. To conclude, the criterion used gives us the measure of level or strength of learning which may vary on both sides of simple or perfect learning ; those falling below simple learning will be called partial learning, and those falling above it will be called over-learning.

Method of Anticipation and Prompting or Method of Serial Anticipation : This method is similar in result to that of serial learning. But the procedure is different. In this method the items are at first exposed one after the other, each one for 2 sec. as for serial learning, without requiring S to reproduce those he remembers. E then presents the first item for 2 secs. and requires S to anticipate the next item, which is then presented for 2 sec. and S again has to anticipate the next one and so on. S thus has to anticipate an item before it is exposed and checks his anticipation when that item appears. Trial after trial is taken till S is able to correctly anticipate all successive items. Each item in the list functions both as stimulus and response, except the first one which serves only as a stimulus. Seeing one item, S anticipates the next item ; his anticipation is thus his response to the exposed stimulus item. The first item in the list serves as the cue item and it is an extra item as it does not come into reckoning while one determines S's score in a trial ; the score is the total number of correct anticipations. For this reason, the cue item may be just a set of 3 zeros : 000

This method is called anticipation method because every time an item appears, S has to anticipate the item immediately following it before it is shown. Since the next item is also shown after an interval, generally, of 2 sec., it serves as a prompting to S for checking his anticipation. S knows whether his anticipation is correct or incorrect and this knowledge helps in the fixation of the correct response ; the correct response is reinforced and the incorrect response is non-reinforced.

You will note that learning by the method of anticipation and prompting involves stimulus response connections. The process may be compared to the connection between a sensory stimulus and a motor response that we came across in conditioning experiments (p. 137). The process of conditioning may be used to explain the stimulus response connection also in the case of serial learning. Each item is a stimulus which evokes in S its verbal response, that is, when the item is presented S pronounces or spells it. The next item that follows is another stimulus which elicits its own verbal response. The entire process may be represented as:

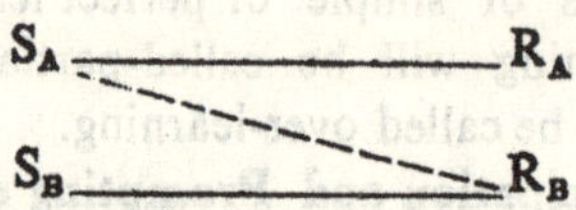

The learning consists of conditioning R_B to S_A, so that S_A in future evokes R_B. The learning of the total list involves a chaining of conditioned responses. Except the cue item and the end item, all items function both as stimulus and response. The response to one item becomes the stimulus for the next following item. You can compare this to the process that takes place when one learns a series of movements comprising a single act, one movement evoking another movement. The simple act of walking can be used as an illustration. As you step forward, one leg moves ahead of the other. When the first leg moves your body swings forward, and when the second leg moves, your body swings backward. The forward stepping motor response causes stimulation of the kinaesthetic receptors : the kinaesthetic stimuli evoke the forward-body-swing response. The body swing in its turn stimulates the forward movement of the other leg which stimulates the backward swing of the body, which again stimulates the forward movement of the first leg and so on. The child has had to learn this series of to-and-fro movements—one movement evoking another movement—of only those members of the body that are essential for walking, inhibiting all other irrelevant movements.

The learning produced by anticipation and prompting method is similar in its result to that produced by the serial learning method. There is one difference. In the first case both stimulus and response events are explicit. One item is shown to S to which he makes an explicit response by anticipating the next item. In serial learning also stimulus response connections are formed ; one item on the list evokes the next item which evokes that following it, and so on. But in this case, when S correctly reproduces one item in the given order, part of the stimulus-response event is explicit and part of it is implicit. You do not, therefore, observe the stimulus response chaining in this case as you do in the learning achieved by anticipation and prompting method. The outcome of serial learning is in fact similar to the observed series of responses involved in a chain of movements. The kinaesthetic stimuli are implicit ; you observe only the responses.

There is, however, one marked difference in the learning process between the two methods. In anticipation and prompting there is positiver einforcement of the correct responses and negative reinforcement of the incorrect ones ; S knows whether he is anticipating correctly by checking his anticipation when the next item appears. There is no such reinforcement in serial learning ; S does not know whether the items reproduced by him, or the sequence in which they are reproduced, is correct. If reinforcement plays a part in learning, as claimed by some learning theorists, prompting and anticipation should have an advantage over serial learning as a method of learning. You can perform an experiment to examine this hypothesis. Let your S learn a CVC or CCC list by the method of serial learning to the criterion of two errorless reproductions, allowing an interval of 20 sec. between trials. Let him then learn, after an interval of, say, 10 ms., another comparable list, i.e., containing items of the same difficulty value, by the method of anticipation and prompting. Stop after S reaches the criterion of two errorless anticipations. Then test S for serial learning of this list, i.e., repuire him to reproduce the items in the correct order. If he makes an error, present the entire list as in the serial learning method and test for serial learning. Score S's rate of learning of the two lists in terms of (*i*) the number of trials required to reproduce the two lists in the correct order ; (*ii*) the number of correct responses from trial to trial. The latter is, generally, to be converted into percentage. Plot learning curves for the two lists on the same base, using per cent of correct responses as the ordinate or X axis and trials as the abscissa or Y axis. If reinforcement plays a part in learning, S should take less trials to reproduce the items serially in the second list, and his correct responses from trial to trial will also be larger for this list.

Serial Position Effect

While using the method of serial learning or serial anticipation, one notices a peculiar phenomenon which has been termed the **serial position effect.** This is to be noted when one counts the number of times each item of a list is correctly reproduced or anticipated while S is learning the list from trial to trial. A graph is plotted using the frequency of occurrence of correct reproduction, or anticipation, converted into percentage as the X axis and the serial order of the items as the base or Y axis. Such a graph is shown in Figs. *a* and *b*. The graph is bow shaped and has,

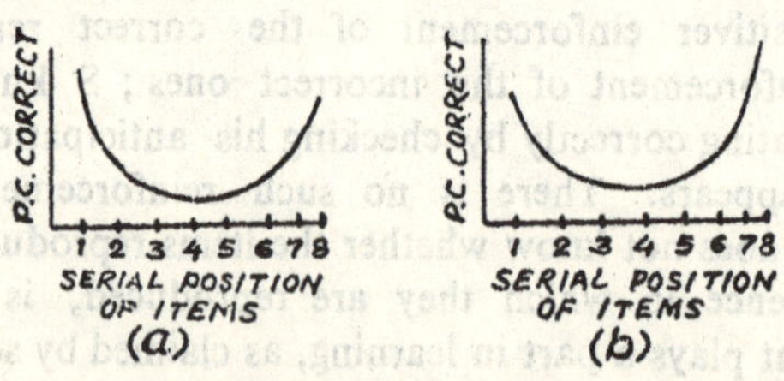

accordingly, been called the **bow shaped serial position curve.** This happens because the beginning items are the easiest to learn, next are items at the end of this list ; the middle items are the hardest to learn, though all items have the same difficulty value. The serial position curve for free recall has the same general bow shape, but in this case the items at the end of the list are most frequently recalled [Fig. (*b*)], the beginning items come next; the middle items, here too, are least frequently recalled.

The serial position effect has been described as the outcome of primacy and finality effects. S's interest in the beginning items is more wholesome and gradually declines with the presentation of similar items on the list. The items at the end of the list provide a break from the monotony which has a satisfying effect. As a result, the beginning and end items are more likely to be recalled than the middle ones. Being once recalled, the probability of their recall in subsequent trials further increases. Hence they come out to be most frequently reproduced items.

The serial position effect is also explained as due to inhibitory tendencies in learning. When a list is presented for free or serial recall, or for serial anticipation, each item becomes associated not only with the item immediately preceding or following it, but with all other items. We encounter, in other words, both immediate and remote associations. The associations of the beginning and end items have only one direction—forward or backward ; other items have bidirectional associations ; they are associated with those preceding as well as those following them. As a result, the item that immediately follows the item which is exposed has to compete, in order to be anticipated or recalled, with several other items with which the exposed item is associated, and the number of such remote associations is larger for the middle than the beginning or end items. The greater competition exerts greater interference on the correct recall or anticipation of the immediately following item. Successful recall or anticipation, accordingly, becomes more difficult for the middle items than for the beginning or end ones. It seems, however, that both factors, namely, the greater inhibitory influence of remote associations as well as primacy and finality account for the serial position effect.

You can conduct an experiment to find out the difference in the serial position effect between free-recall and serial recall or serial anticipation. You have to note the frequency of correct reproduction of each item of a list. The absolute frequency is then to be converted into percent frequency for which you have to divide the absolute frequency by the number of trials taken to reach the criterion of two errorless reproduction or anticipation

(p. 148). The resulting quotient is then to be multiplied by 100. Two serial position curves are plotted for the two lists, on the same base.

Clustering of Items

The serial position effect, however, is noticeable in free recall only when the items of a list are unrelated, i.e., the different items do not have any **special** kind of association with other items. A list, e.g., may contain items so that one item may be such as can be paired with another item in the list, such as black and white, large and small, father and son, etc., though the related items may not occupy adjacent positions in the list. In another list the items may be such that they can be organised into separate units, each containing two or more items of the same class. For example in a 12-item list five items are names of animals, four items are names of flowers, and three items are names of articles of furniture, though the items are randomly distributed on the list. For both types of lists the serial position effect is likely to be replaced by the clustering effect ; items closely associated are likely to be recalled in pairs ; similarly, items that fall in the same class may have the same frequency of occurrence in recall. The hypotheses may be verified in an experiment using two comparable word lists, i.e., both containing very familiar words having about the same number of letters ; in one list all items are unrelated, in the other, two or more items fall within the same class. You may have another problem where a comparison is made between free recall and serial learning or serial anticipation, using in both cases comparable lists containing related items. Free recall of such a list is likely to be easier than its serial learning or serial anticipation ; the tendency for the clustering of the related items will interfere with the requirement of learning them in the original order.

The clustering of items in recall gives an advantage, in learning, to a related-items list. Hence, when using the free recall method, a list of related items is easier to learn than that of unrelated items. The items may be such that they can be classified within a **single** category, e.g., all items may be names of pieces of furniture, of flowers, or fall in a still broader category like animate, etc. Or, the items may fall in **more than one** class or category, such as animals, vegetables, fruits. They may also be such as can be grammatically classified into verbs, nouns, adjectives, etc. A list containing all items of the same class and a list containing items that can be classified under more than one category, differ in their levels of organisation. You may then have a problem on the relationship between the level of organisation of items in a list and rate of learning.

The Method of Paired Associates—PA

In this method you have to use a list of paired items. Each item in the list has two components and S has to learn to associate the two components so that when the first one is given he can reproduce the second one. This type of learning occurs when you learn to remember the names of persons, meanings of words, colours or other signs or symbols for objects, telephone and car numbers, etc. Given a word you can recall its equivalent in your own language ; seeing the face of a man you are reminded of his name ; seeing one animal you call it a dog, another a cat, and so on. In all these cases, there is a pairing, and the learning involves association between the members of the pair.

Anticipation Method of PA Learning : Of the two members or terms constituting a paired-item, the first one functions as a stimulus and, hence, it is called the stimulus term ; the second one functions as a response and is accordingly called a response term. The procedure is to expose the pairs one after the other in a preliminary trial ; exposing each pair for 4 sec. Thereafter, the stimulus term is alone exposed for 2 sec. and S is required to anticipate the response term. After 2 sec. the response term is also exposed for 2 sec. All pairs in a list are exposed in this manner, one after the other ; every time S is to anticipate the response term on the presentation of the stimulus term. In this way, trial after trial is taken till S is able to anticipate all response terms correctly. The criterion of learning is two errorless anticipations. An interval of 20 sec. is introduced between trials ; it is, accordingly, called inter-trial interval. In the absence of a Memory Drum (Appendix III), one may prepare two cards for each pair and at first present both together, thereafter one card is presented for 2 sec. followed by the other one.

We may note the main difference between PA (Paired-associates) learning and serial anticipation. In the latter, the association between the items is vertical, you move down the list from item to item ; each item has a double stimulus response functions. In PA learning the association is lateral or side-ways ; the left term is associated with the right term, and each term serves a single function ; the left term is the stimulus and the right term the response.

In order to make sure in PA learning that your S does not learn the response term serially, i.e., without learning to associate it with its stimulus term, you have to make use of a very important control. While using a memory drum, you prepare three or four alternative lists, all having the same paired items but arranged in different orders. The alternative lists are used in different trials in a random sequence. With this control, S cannot serially learn the response terms. His learning will depend upon associating the side terms only. When using paired cards, as suggested above, it is easier for you to change the order of the presentation of the pairs from trial to trial. Keep the different pairs of cards in a line on your side of the screen. Pick up any pair arbitrarily and present the stimulus and response terms one after the other, each for 2 sec. determined by mental counting (p. 148). Restore the cards to their places on the table and then pick up any other pair, and so on.

Recall Method of PA Learning : You may also adopt a modified procedure for PA learning. The procedure that we explained is called the Anticipation Method ; the modified one is the Recall Method In the recall method, you expose the pairs—both terms, exposed at one time, for 2 sec., one after the other, till the list of items is completed. You then expose the stimulus terms only for 2 sec. each during which S has to anticipate the response term ; you do not expose the response term. Every trial thus involves two steps : (1) Acquisition of the association by presenting both terms ; (2) Test of the association by presenting only the stimulus term. You will mark one important difference between the two types of procedures, from the point of view of theory of learning. The anticipation method provides S the opportunity to check his response for correction ; the recall method withholds this opportunity. The reinforcement principle is made to operate in the first case ; it plays no obvious part in the second case. Here again test the reinforcement principle by comparing PA learning by the anticipation method with that by the recall method (p 151). While using the recall method, present each paired item for 2 sec.

only in the acquisition part as well as in the test part of a trial, so that the total time per item in each trial is comparable with the total time of 4 sec. per item when using the anticipation method. This control is important because a relationship has been noted, in experiments, between probability of recall and presentation time ; probability of correct recall increases with the increase in presentation time upto certain limit. You can conduct an experiment, using either the free recall, serial learning, serial anticipation, or PA learning method, to verify this finding. Expose the items of one list for, say, 2 sec. each, and those of the other list for, say, 6 sec. each.

PA Learning and Conditioning : Paired-associates learning can also be explained according to the principle of conditioning. The association between the stimulus and response terms of the paired items can be represented as in learning by serial anticipation. When A and B are presented as stimuli, each evokes its own

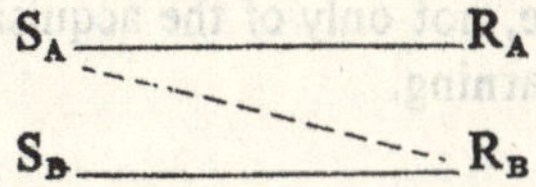

verbal response (p. 150). Pairing of A and B, enable S_A to evoke R_B in the absence of S_B. This interpretation of A-B associations fits very closely when the recall method of PA learning is used (p. 156). The anticipation method (p. 155) can also be interpreted by the conditioning principle, but not the so-called classical conditioning whose model we find in the work of Pavlov (p. 136). In this case the principle of operant conditioning applies. In operant or instrumental conditioning, S is free to make any response in the stimulus situation. One of the responses that he makes is followed by another stimulus that functions as a reward. This response is thus said to be reinforced ; other responses that S may make do not produce the reward stimulus ; they are not reinforced. An association is formed between the stimulus and the rewarded response. In PA learning situation, after the preliminary trial is over, S may respond to the stimulus term exposed by anticipating any one of the response terms he came across in the preliminary trial, besides other similar responses not included in the list, which have therefore been described as extra-experimental associations. The exposure of the correct response term after the expiry of 2 sec.

reinforces his anticipation if it is correct, and non-reinforces it if it is incorrect. We may be reminded here of Skinner's Box where only pushing of the lever produces the reward stimulus, namely, the pellet of food, but making other responses does not present the pellet of food. Gradually the animal learns to press the lever and obtain the food pellet. In this case the food pellet functions as a physical reinforcer or reward. In PA learning the presentation of the correct response-term functions as a psychological reward or reinforcer. We find the principle of operant or instrumental conditioning applying also to complex sensory-motor learning (p. 138) e.g., maze learning, where stimulus-response associations that lead to exit from the maze are learned by practice. The exit which marks at the human level the completion of the task functions as a psychological reward.

The discussion about the application of the conditioning theory to learning will prepare you to follow the experiments reported in standard journals. The various facts about conditioning have been found to be true, not only of the acquisition of motor skills, but also of verbal learning.

Experiments on Verbal Learning

We have already incidentally suggested several experiments on verbal learning. We will now deal with them more directly. The simplest experiments are those that are intended to determine S's rate of learning for different kinds of verbal materials.

Different measures of the dependent variable have been used in verbal learning experiments. The more frequently used ones are the number of trials required to reach the criterion, the per-cent of correct responses from trial to trial, the per-cent of errors from trial to trial, the latency of the response. The latency of response, however, is a difficult measure without some special measuring device.

Other kinds of problems in verbal learning using singly presented items like three-lettered words, nonsense syllable, consonant trigrams, may be concerned with independent variables that may be classified under two large heads : (A) Type of Learning material. (B) Method of Learning. Under Type of Learning Material, we have (1) meaningfulness of the learning material, (2) amount of material or length of list, (3) Interrelatedness of items within the list, (4) similarity between items, also called intra-list similarity. Under (B) Method of Learning we have (1) distribution or spacing of practice, (2) part *versus* whole learning, (3) intentional *versus* incidental learning. I may remind the reader that here we are using **method** in a different sense. We have earlier described the **methods** of free-recall, serial learning, serial anticipation and paired-associates learning. In these cases we are referring to the outcome of the learning process namely, acquisition of the power to recall items from the list freely or in the original order, stimulus-response chaining of items, or learning to associate the members of a pair. In the latter case we refer to the procedure conducive to learning or, more simply stated, method of presentation of material. You will understand this difference when we have dealt with the methods of learning in the latter sense at the end of the chapter.

Type of Learning Material

1. Meaningfulness : Meaning in psychology implies the associations that a stimulus may have, and difference in meaning, therefore, depends upon the difference in the association value of the learning material (p. 144). Familiar words have very high association value while nonsense syllables or nonsense consonants may be so prepared as to have very low association value. To examine the effect of meaning on the rate of learning, one may use a list of very familiar three-lettered words and another list of CVC or CCC trigrams. Besides the number of item-components, the number of items in the lists, i.e., the length of the lists or amount of learning material, should also be the same. In addition, such other factors should be kept constant as the exposure time per item, the mode of presentation of items—visual or auditory, the learning method—free-recall, serial learning, serial anticipation, or paired-associates learning, the criterion of learning, and the apparatus or device used for presentation of the learning material. These are the extraneous independent variables which have to be controlled in order that the result is conclusive (p. 6).

Everything else being equal, meaningful materials are easier to learn than nonsense materials. This happens because when we learn a list of items, the learning involves acquisition of the items and also the learning of the association between items. Meaningful items are familiar to S ; they are already known to him. He has not got to learn them in the sense that he has to learn a CVC or CCC trigram that has been previously unknown to him. In other words, the integration of the elements of the item, i.e., the letters composing the item, is not new to him when an item is a familiar word ; each item forms an integral whole, a single unit. All that he has to learn is the association of these word units in the list, so that the extra-experimental associations of these words are not revived when he tries, trial after trial, to reproduce the items of the list. In the case of a CVC or CCC trigram, the elements of the item, i.e., the letters composing the trigram, have to be integrated as a unit. Only after the response integration, as the process is called, has been achieved, the learning of the association of items in the list would be possible.

While preparing a list of words, one has to bear in mind that the immediate memory span for unrelated words is 7 to 8 items ; if a list contains seven or eight words, S may correctly reproduce all in a single trial. The word lists, therefore, should be long enough to exceed this limit. It should contain at least 10 and preferably more than 10 items.

As you will note from the above account, the experiment will have to be divided into the parts, each one using one list. Since the experimental variable is meaningfulness, you may call the part of the experiment using the word list as the experimental condition and the other as the control condition. The question might arise as to which one should be used first. The answer will be to use the control condition first and then the experimental. If the meaningful list is first learned, the change to the nonsense list may create an undesirable feeling in S ; the unfamiliarity of the items may be more striking because of their difference from the items of the word list and S may anticipate greater difficulty in learning this list. His interest might, therefore, be affceted ; he may work with a lower motivation. In order to minimise the effect of this organismic independent variable (p. 4), it would be safer to use the control list first to be followed by the experimental list. Of course, E should provide for sufficient interval between the two conditions, say, 20 mins.

The result will be based upon the comparison between the number of trials taken and the percentage of correct responses from trial to trial.

2. **Interrelatedness** : We have already referred earlier (p. 145) to the problem about the relatedness of the learning material and the rate of learning. Here we have to use two lists of words, one

falling in the same class, or having two or more items of the same class, and the other having no apparent relationship between them. The related items list will be easier to learn by the free recall method, though it may be difficult to learn by the serial learning or serial anticipation method. In learning the related items list by the free recall method (p. 148), two or more items hang together and are also likely to occur together in recall. This may be verified by identifying the items recalled from trial to trial. While in learning an unrelated items list one has to acquire fresh association between single items. This accounts for the ease in the acquisition or learning of the related items lists. S's introspection would throw further light on the matter. The introspection might show that S clearly identifies the class to which a set of items belong, or the type of association that they may have. We have already suggested several problems under the Clustering of Items (p. 145) which we need not repeat here.

3. **Amount of Learning Material :** A longer list obviously requires more effort to learn than a shorter one. But the question here arises whether the increase in effort and time is proportional to the increase in the number of items ; will a 20-item list require twice as many trials as a 10-item list. It has been found that the increase in effort and item becomes disproportionately greater with the increase in the amount of the learning material. An experiment may be conducted to verify this finding. Three lists of words or nonsense trigrams may be used, the number of items in the lists differing in a given proportion, e. g., the number of items in one list is two-thirds of that in a second list and half of that in a third list. If a CCC trigram list is prepared, a list of six trigrams as the shortest one will serve the purpose ; the other two lists may be of 9 and 12 tiems respectively. In a word-list, the shortest one has to be of at least 10 items (p. 160). The number of trials required for each list to reach the same learning criterion may then provide the required data. The proportional difference between the lengths of the lists and that between trials taken to learn each list will serve as the answer to the problem. A graphic presentation of the results is also possible by converting the proportions into percentage. The x axis will represent the three lists and the y axis the percentage ; one graph will show the percentage of items in the

respective lists and the other the percentage of trials required to learn them. The graph for example will be as follows :

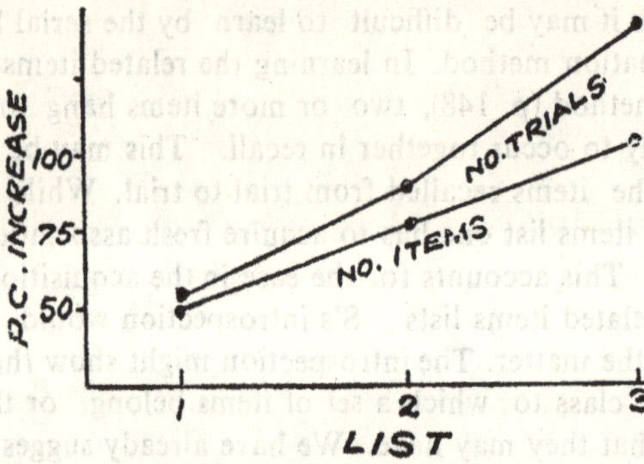

As we have noted earlier (p. 152), we use not only the number of trials as the measure of learning. We also measure learning in terms of the number of correct responses from trial to trial. If the lists are of different lengths, we will note that the number of correct responses per trial increases with the length of the lists, though the increase will not be in the same proportion as the difference between the length of the lists. This happens because of the relationship between presentation time and probability of recall. A longer list requires longer time to be presented than does a shorter list. We may equate the presentation time by making the exposure time per item longer for the shorter list. Thus, having a 10-item and a 20-item lists, we may expose the first list at the rate of 4 sec. per item and the second list at the rate of 2 sec. per item. The total presentation time will then be the same, i. e., 40 sec. for the two lists. In this case the recall in a given trial may be equal for the two lists. We may verify this hypothesis by conducting an experiment.

What is important for learning is the total time in learning ; the manner in which the time is distributed between the exposure of the items and the number of trials does not affect the learning. In other words, a shorter exposure of items would require larger number of trials to learn the list than will a longer exposure of items. If a list having, say, 10 items exposed at the rate of 2 sec. per item takes, on the average, say 8.8 trials or a total time in learning of 176 sec., the same list exposed at the rate of 6 sec. per item is likely to take about 3 trials or a total time of 180 sec. This result has, however, been found for group experiments. You can use this as a problem for individual experiment also. You have to prepare two comparable CVC or CCC lists, say, of 8 items each. Provide 2 sec. exposure time for learning the first list and, say, 3 or 4 sec. for learning the second list. You have to see that your S gives full attention to the items even when the exposure time is long. Compare the results with respect to both the number of trials and the number of correct recall from trial to trial. You will expect fewer trials and more correct response from trial to trial when the exposure time is 3 sec. If you, further, find that the total time in learning, which would be the product of the exposure time multiplied by the number of items and the number of trials taken to reach the criterion, is roughly the same for the two lists, your hypothesis stands supported by your result.

4. **Intra-list Similarity** : Rate of learning is affected also by similarity between the items of a list. If the list is meaningful, similarity of items m ght result in higher order organisation of the items and thus make the list easier to learn (p. 154). But with nonsense materials, similarity may have an adverse effect on learning by creating confusion between the items. We have noted that the learning of a list of nonsense trigrams is more difficult than that of words, because S has to learn to integrate the components of an item before he can learn to associate the items within the list (p. 160). If the elements composing each item altogether differ from item to item, the integration becomes easier. But if two or more items have common elements, each element, thus, having a diverse association with other elements, response integration becomes more difficult. This will affect the rate of learning. It will influence the rate of learning still greatly when the serial recall, serial anticipation, or paired associates learning method is used. The similarity between the items will create confusion which would affect the correct ordering of the items. More trials will be needed to discriminate the items from each other so that each one is given its correct position in recall or anticipation. In PA learning the confusion will result in a displacement of the response term because of the confusion between similar items. In any case, the rate of learning will be affected.

To perform an experiment on the effect of intra-list similarity, you can prepare either a CVC or CCC list. Suppose, you prefer

CVC list of 10 items. You will need twenty consonants for the list. You can then prepare one list using different consonants in each item. The vowels however will have to be repeated since they are only five. The other list may use, say, only 10 consonants, each consonant repeated twice. It may be more convenient to prepare a CCC list containing, say, only seven items. The first list will then use 21 consonants and the items will all be dissimilar. The second list may use 7 consonants each repeated three times or 14 consonants, only seven repeated twice. Following lists may serve as an example :

List I	*List II*
BZL	BKW
FJY	PZM
CQS	KQV
GMW	MZG
HDT	DRJ
PXN	QWN
KVR	RJC

In the above lists you will note that items of List I have no common element while those of List II have seven letters occurring twice. Let your S learn the two lists either by the serial recall or the serial anticipation method. Allow 30 ms. interval between the learning of the two lists. Compare the learning of the two lists both in respect of number of trials needed to reach the criterion as well as the percentage of correct responses from trial to trial. If you find a difference in the learning of the two lists in favour of the dissimilar item lists, you come to the conclusion that similarity of the items in the second list is responsible for this difference ; similarity between the items has caused what is called intra-serial inhibition or inhibition within the series. You will come across another term, namely inter-serial inhibition, or inhibition between two series, at a later stage. You will find there that the learning of a second list may be affected by the factor of inter-serial inhibition ; the learning of List I may inhibit the learning of List II. This will also happen bacause of similarity of some elements between the two lists. When you conduct an experiment on intra-serial inhibition, the factor of inter-serial inhibition may also come into play. Thus, if you let your S learn the dissimilar items list first and then the similar items lists, the difficulty in the learning of the second list will be caused both by intra-list similarity and inter-list similarity. After all both lists have been prepared by combining the same elements ; 14 consonants appear in both lists. You may suppose that if you reverse the sequence, i. e., introduce the similar-item list first, the learning of this list will be affected only by intra-list inhibition. But then the learning of the dissimilar-items list may be affected by inter-serial inhibition. In this case if the learning of the first list is made difficult by intra-list similarity, that of the second list is made difficult by inter-list similarity. In an individual experiment it is difficult for you to overcome this limitation, specially when you have to complete the experiment in the same session. You may, however, use this point in discussing your result.

There is one evidence of inter-serial inhibition which, if it occurs, gives you a strong basis to argue that inter-serial inhibition has taken place. It is called intrusion ; while learning the second list, your S may recall or anticipate an item he has already learned in the first list. The response integration (p. 160) your S requires to learn is interfered with by the response integration he has already acquired in the first list; the previous learning has produced a tendency in him to repeat the same response. This response being incorrect only gradually drops out with the progress of second-list learning. Hence the difficulty in the learning of the second list.

You will note that you can make the problem on the effect of intra-list similarity more difficult by using the degree of inter-list similarity as your independent variable and prepare for the purpose two experimental lists, one using only seven consonants, each repeated thrice, and the other using 14 consonants, only seven repeated twice, in addition you have the control list repeating no consonant. The three lists may then be learned either by the serial recall or the serial anticipation method. You may dispense with the control list for want of time. In this case, each experimental list will function as a control for the other (p. 6). You can also use the PA learning method. You may use a CCC trigram as the response term and a three-letter familiar word as the stimulus term in each item. The two lists will have different words as stimulus terms in each ; one list will have altogether dissimilar trigrams, and the other more or less similar trigrams, as response terms. The matter may be made still more complicated. Both stimulus and response terms may consist of CCC trigrams and the common elements may be distributed between stimulus and response items ; the stimulus term of one item may share a component with the response term of another item. You may think of other ways also of introducing intra-list similarity.

Methods of Learning

Distribution of Practice : S may learn a maze or memorise a list of trigrams or words by continuous practice, or he may take some rest after one or more trials. In the first case he is learning by the method of massed or uninterrupted practice, in the second, by the method of distributed or spaced practice. It has been usually found that spacing of practice in psychomotor learning makes the learning easier than massing of practice. Experiments have been done on different types of psychomotor tasks that we described in Chapter VII. It has also been found that all durations or lengths of rest interval between trials do not produce the same result. There is, what is called, an optimum duration of rest interval for a particular kind of task and maximum benefit is achieved from distribution of practice when this optimum duration is used. There is also another significant finding. The rest interval may be introduced at different stages of the learning ; it may be provided after every trial, after every two trials, and so on. The gain in learning will not be the same. Thus, we can conceive of an optimum location of rest interval which too may not be the same for all kinds of tasks. Besides location, one may find a difference in effect of distribution of practice with a difference in the spacing of the rest interval ; the rest interval may be introduced at the beginning, middle, or near the end of the practice period.

Individual experiments on the effect of distribution of practice on learning a psychomotor task cannot, however, be successfully conducted. E has to obtain data for both massing and spacing of practice. The task in both conditions must be identical or at least comparable, i. e., should involve the same kind and level of skill for learning. With an identical task, practice in one condition will have a positive transfer effect on practice in the other condition. If distributed practice follows massed practice much of the obtained gain in distributed practice may be due to mere practice effect. If the order is reversed, mass practice may come out to be equally easy or difficult ; the disadvantage from massing may be offset by the gain from practice. The result in either case will be inconclusive. It is difficult to devise different psychomotor tasks of comparable difficulty, i. e., involving the same kind of skill and being equal in difficulty. Even if such comparable learning tasks could be devised, the transfer effect will be very considerable, since the two tasks will call for the same kind of skills or patterns of responses. At the human level, more particularly, it is impossible to eliminate transfer effect when learning, for example, two mazes, having the same number of choice points—involving the same number of correct or incorrect moves, allowing for the same direction of movement, requiring the same minimum time, etc., under two conditions of learning. Only group experiments can provide a satisfactory answer to the problem of distribution of practice in psychomotor learning. In such experiments, identical task is used in both conditions, but the S's engaged in the two conditions are not be the same (Appendix I). We will not go into further details of the matter since we have decided to confine ourselves only to individual experiments.

Individual experiments on the effect of distribution of practice on verbal learning can be easily performed ; we can easily prepare two different, but comparable, lists of verbal items. The transfer effect in this case will be negligible because the learning of lists of verbal items does not require any special skill ; whatever the content of the list, the learning may be accomplished in a more or less routine and mechanical manner. A preliminary practice with the kind of verbal items, using identical procedure, would minimise whatever transfer effect may be produced in the learning. Complete report of an experiment on the problem of massing and spacing of practice will make us understand the procedure to be adopted in such experiments.

Differential Effect of Massed *versus* Spaced Practice on the Rate of Verbal Learning : While learning a task, one may perform the task, trial after trial, without any rest between trials, until he gets mastery over the task. On the other hand, one may take a short rest after every trial, or after two or more trials. In the first case, we have massed practice, in the second spaced practice. It has been found in several experiments that spaced practice has an advantage over massed practice—less practice is needed to achieve the same level of proficiency in performing the task when the performance is interspersed with small rest intervals. The gain from spacing of practice has been explained in various ways. The repeated performance of any task produces boredom which results in impairement of performance. This may be due to a decline in S's motivation ; he does not apply as much effort in performing the task and this in the long run affects the learning. If the work period is interspersed with rest intervals then S's motivation remains at the optimal level for a longer time.

There is another factor also that influences S's performance. It has been noted that every response an organism makes in performing a task creates a condition within the organism that interferes with the future occurrence of the response. A noted learning psychologist, C. M. Hull, has called this Reactive Inhibition (IR)—the inhibition produced by reaction or response. Continuous performance results in the gradual accumulation of IR which after some time becomes strong enough to interfere with the tendency to perform the task and shows itself in the deterioration in performance, what we generally call, fatigue effect. But before it becomes that strong, it affects the rate of improvement from practice and prolongs the effect on the learning of the task. If rest is provided from time to time, IR is prevented from accumulating ; it is dissipated or wears out ; the organism recovers from its effect. As a result, there is no set-back in improvement from practice.

There is still another effect produced by rest that results in gain in learning for spaced practice. The neural changes produced in the organism by practice are prevented from consolidating, or becoming stable when there is no rest interval. With rest interval, these neural changes persist in the absence of external stimulation and get, therefore, more easily fixed or stabilised. The cumulative effect of practice, from trial to trial, consequently, becomes greater, and thereby, makes the rate of learning faster.

We may mention even another factor, particularly influencing the learning of a verbal task. When one learns a list of verbal items, each item gets associated with other items. It is directly associated with the items that immediately follow or precede it, and remotely associated with each of the other items (p.153). These remote associations produce a hindrance in learning since they compete with the direct associations. The remote associations are weakened during the period of rest or no-practice. Spacing of practice, thereby makes the learning easier because of less interference from the remote associations.

In this experiment an attempt is made to verify the following hypothesis :

Spacing of practice makes the learning of verbal materials easier.

Method

Subject : An undergraduate male student.

Materials : Two comparable lists of 4-letter high frequency words, each containing twelve items as shown below :

List 1	*List 2*
OOO	XXX
HALL	SNOW
NOSE	CORN
SALT	FAIR
ROAD	TANK
FAME	WOOD
BOAT	FROG
HAIR	SHOE
DUST	GOAT
BIRD	FISH
RICE	DOLL
LOCK	ROOM
TREE	GIRL

Procedure : The serial anticipation method was used for learning. List 1 was used for the control condition, namely, massing of practice, while List 2 functioned for the experimental condition, namely, spacing of practice. The control condition was introduced first. Since no memory drum was available, E printed each item in capital letters on a separate 2″×1″ card. The cards were piled face up on E's side of a screen in the listed order. E picked up the top card and placed it on the table, in front of S, for 2 sec. after which it was placed face down on E's side of the screen. E timed the exposure by mental counting. E exposed the next card as he did the first one for another 2 sec. and so on All cards were piled face down one above the other after each one was exposed. E turned the pile upside down so that now the first card was on the top face up. E then started the test trials. He exposed a card and S was required to anticipate the word on the next card. The next card was then exposed after 2 sec.

and so on. E recorded S's anticipations on a sheet lying on his side of the screen. The same procedure was repeated from trial to trial till S was able to anticipate all items correctly in two successive trials.

The same general procedure was adopted for both conditions. Only, in the experimental condition E introduced a rest of 20 sec. after every trial. A 10 min. interval separated the learning of the two lists.

Instruction to S : "I will place before you several cards one after the other. Each card has printed on it a 4-lettered word. You have to read out each word as it is placed before you. After I have shown you all cards, I will test your memory for the words. For this purpose, when I place a card before you, you have to reproduce the word on the card that I showed you next to this card. I will give you 2 sec. for this after which I will show you the next card. You have then to anticipate the word that follows the word on this card, and so on. In this manner, I will take several trials and stop when you are able to correctly anticipate the word that immediately follows, after seeing the word that is shown to you. You have to be very attentive. Do you understand ?"

Results

Introspection : "In the beginning I found that the word I reproduced was different from the word that was shown. I felt very much discouraged and thought that the task was difficult for me. But gradually I noted that I was becoming more and more successful. Perhaps the second list of words that I learned was easier. I was soon able to reproduce correctly the next word".

Table 1
NUMBER CORRECTLY ANTICIPATED FROM TRIAL TO TRIAL

Trial	Massed	Spaced
1	6	5
2	7	7
3	7	8
4	8	10
5	9	10

Table 2
FREQUENCY OF CORRECT ANTICIPATIONS

Item	Massed	Spaced
1	9	7
2	8	6
3	9	5
4	7	5
5	5	5

Table 1 (*Cond.*)

Trial	Massed	Spaced
6	10	11
7	10	12
8	11	12
9	12	
10	12	

Table 2 (*Cond.*)

Item	Massed	Spaced
6	4	4
7	3	3
8	5	5
9	5	6
10	7	6
11	9	5
12	9	6

Table 3

NUMBER OF TRIALS TO CRITERION AND GAIN FROM SPACING OF TRIALS

	No. Trials	Time
Massed	9	240
Spaced	7	312
Diff.	2	72
% Gain	22	
% Loss		30

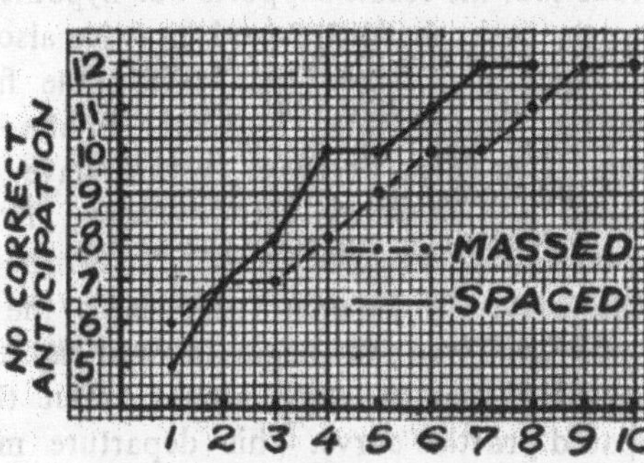

Fig. 1. No. Correctly Anticipated from Trial to Trial.

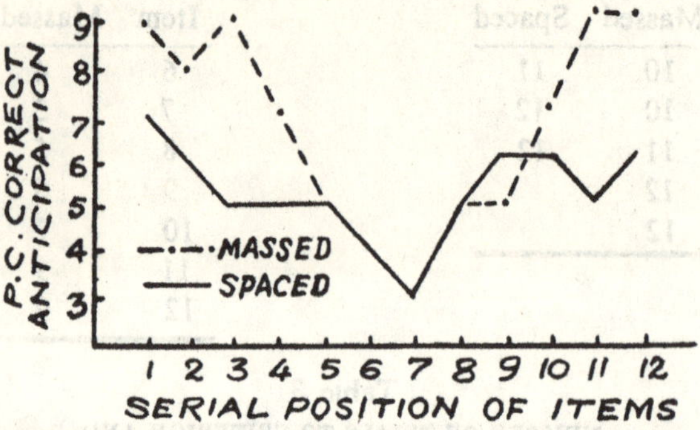

Fig. 2. Serial Position and Frequency of Anticipation.

Discussion

Spaced or distributed practice showed 22 per cent gain in effort as compared to massed practice though there was 30 per cent loss in time taken (Table 3). Massing of practice thus came out to be an easier method of learning the list of words. Since the total time included that spent on rest between trials, the time devoted to practice was also much less in spaced practice—192 sec. Hence we may conclude that the result supports our hypothesis.

We notice the gain in distributed practice also from trial to trial. Table 1 and Fig. 1 show that except the first trial, the number of correct anticipations is greater in almost all trials of spaced practice. The gain, perhaps, would have been larger if List 1 learning had not influenced List 2 learning. This is shown in Fig. 2 which presents the serial position curve for the two types of learning. The curve for massed practice is the typical bow-shaped serial position curve; the beginning and end items are more frequently anticipated than the middle items. But this is not as true for the spaced practice curve. This departure may be due to the interference in the learning of the second list after the first list learning. Inspection of the raw data (Appendix) shows several intrusions from the first list; Doll, Coat, Fair and Frog were substituted by Hall, Boat, Race and Tree from the first list. As a result S correctly anticipated only 5 items in the first trial of List 2 while he had anticipated 6 in the first trial of List 1.

We also note in the result one interesting phenomenon, namely, similarity as a potent factor in interference. The similarity of rhyme—Hall and Doll, Boat and Goat—led to the substitution of the one for the other. Besides intrusion from the first list, we notice the substitution of extra-list items, namely, Bank for Tank, Feet for Goat. Bank or Feet does not occur in any list. The clang association between the two words Bank and Tank accounts for the substitution. The association of shoe with feet makes feet come after shoe. The occurrence of an altogether new item in recall or anticipation has been called importation.

Our results present an instance also of the clustering effect—related items tend to be linked up and recalled in pairs. In the first three trials of List 1 we notice repeated displacement of Fame by Dust after Road. Perhaps the relatedness between Dust and Road prevented the correct anticipation of Fame after Road. The clustering of Dust and Road may also be explained as due to a strong extra-experimental association between these two words that prevailed upon the association to be acquired between Road and Fame in the experimental list. We get several other instances of clustering also, e. g., Fish and Tank, Tank and Frog, Wood and Tree, and so on in the second list.

We may conclude from the above discussion that distributed practice has an advantage over massed practice ; it calls for less effort in learning. The advantage, however, is offset by the loss in total time. If restriction is put on time, distributed practice may lose its advantage over massed practice.

The advantage from spacing can be explained in terms of what we said in the introduction. One fact seems, however, to be supported by our result. We notice greater confusion between immediate associations and remote association in the learning of the first list as the cause of the errors of anticipation—Lock replaced Boat after Fame, in second trial for example, or Rice replaced Road, after Salt. Further, there are more frequent cases of failure of anticipation. In the second list, we get more cases of clustering effect to account for the errors, rather than of interference due to confusion between remote and immediate associations, or of failure of anticipation.

We may have several other related problems. We may compare the effect of spacing of trials as a function of the difference between the methods used for learning—free recall *versus* serial recall or serial anticipation ; free or serial recall and paired-associates learning. It has been found that PA learning does not

Appendix

RAW DATA

Serial No. of Trials

List 1

Serial No. of Items	1	2	3	4	5	6	7	8	9	10
1	Hall	Hall	Hall	Hall	Hall	Hall	Hall	Hall	Hall	Hall
2	Hair	Nose	Nose	Nose	Nose	Nose	Nose	Nose	Nose	Nose
3	Salt	Salt	Salt	Salt	Salt	Salt	Salt	Salt	Salt	Salt
4	Rice	Road	Rica	Road	Road	Road	Road	Road	Road	Road
5	Dust	Dust	Dust	Fame	X	Fame	Fame	Fame	Fame	Fame
6	X	Lock	X	X	X	Boat	Boat	Boat	Boat	Boat
7	Bird	X	X	X	Dust	X	Hair	Hair	Hair	Hair
8	X	X	Bird	Boad	Dust	Dust	Dust	Dust	Dust	Dust
9	X	X	Rice	Bird	Rice	Bird	Bird	Bird	Bird	Bird
10	X	Rice	X	Rice	Rice	Rice	Rice	Rice	Rice	Rice
11	Lock	Lock	Lock	Lock	Lock	Lock	Lock	Lock	Lock	Lock
12	Tree	Tree	Tree	Tree	Tree	Tree	Tree	Tree	Tree	Tree

List 2

Serial No. of Items	1	2	3	4	5	6	7	8
1	Snow	Snow	Snow	Snow	Snow	Snow	Snow	Snow
2	Tank	Corn	Corn	Corn	Corn	Corn	Corn	Corn
3	Rice	Fair	Wood	Fair	Fair	Fair	Fair	Fair
4	Fish	Tank	Bank	Tank	Tank	Tank	Tank	Tank
5	Fish	Fish	Wood	Wood	Wood	Wood	Wood	Wood
6	Tree	Tree	Frog	Tree	Frog	Frog	Frog	Frog
7	Tank	Fish	Tank	Fish	Shoe	Shoe	Shoe	Shoe
8	Boat	Feet	Goat	Goat	Goat	Goat	Goat	Goat
9	X	Fish	Fish	Fish	Fish	Fish	Fish	Fish
10	Hall	Doll	Doll	Doll	Doll	Doll	Doll	Doll
11	Girl	X	Room	Room	Room	Room	Room	Room
12	X	Girl	Girl	Girl	Girl	Girl	Girl	Girl

produce any advantage to spacing of practice. You may also plan and conduct an experiment to ascertain the differential gain from spacing between meaningful and nonsense materials.

Several experiments have been reported on the effect of differential spacing of trials or location of the rest interval, and on the duration of rest interval. There is an optimum duration and an optimum location of rest interval which might vary from task to task. Experiments can be conducted to verify these findings.

Part Learning and Whole Learning

One can learn a verbal material, e. g., a prose passage, or a poem, by dividing the entire material into parts and then learning it by separately memorising each part. For example, one may memorise the first stanza of a poem repeatedly reading it, and then pass on to the next stanza and also learn it by heart before passing on to the next stanza, and so on, till he has learned by heart each stanza of the poem. He may then try to recite the entire poem from his memory. On the other hand, he may repeatedly read the entire poem, stanza by stanza, until he can recite the whole poem correctly. The question arises as to which method of memorising the poem is easier. The answer has not been conclusive. Part learning method has one advantage—one has not to wait long to be rewarded for his effort. He repeats the part several times and obtains the reward of having been able to repeat it from memory. On the other hand, in learning by whole method, he has to repeat the entire material several times till he is able to reproduce it correctly—the reward is very much delayed. Prompt reinforcement, or quick reward, rather than delayed reinforcement or belated reward, keeps S's motivation at the optimal level throughout the learning. Whole learning method has its own advantage—the entire material is learned as an integrated whole, while part learning requires additional effort to integrate the parts—each part stands as an isolated unit. The result of an experiment on part *versus* whole method depends, however, on a number of variables, viz. nature of the learning material—whether easy or difficult, having closely related, partially related, or unrelated contents, the personality of the learner—whether young or old, intelligent or dull, his previous learning habit, etc., and so on.

For an experiment on part *versus* whole learning, you may

take 20 sentences for part method and 20 sentences for whole method from the same prose passage. Divide each set of 20 sentences into 4 sections, so that each section contains 5 sentences. Paste the sentences within each section on a separate sheet. For the part method, present the first sheet to S for 30 seconds and test his reproduction. Repeat the same till S reaches the criterion of two faultless reproductions. Record the number of repetitions needed. Do the same with the second sheet, and so on. After S has been able to learn the sentences on each sheet, ask him to reproduce all the 20 sentences in the order in which they were presented on the separate sheets. Record the errors of reproduction. In case there are errors or failure to reproduce all sentences, present all sheets one after the other, each for 30 sec., and test S's reproduction for the entire set of sentences. Repeat this till S is able to reproduce all sentences correctly. Record the number of trials needed for the purpose. Allow a rest of 20 ms. Then take up the learning by the whole method for which the second set of sentences is to be used. In this case present the four sheets one after the other, each for 30 sec., and test S's reproduction for the entire set. Repeat the procedure till S reaches the stage of two faultless reproductions. Take S's introspection for the ease or difficulty in learning the two sets of sentences, and how he felt in the two parts of the experiment. Calculate the total time taken by S for each set in reaching the criterion of 2 faultless reproductions of the entire set. Add, further, the numbers of trials taken by S to learn the sentences within each section by the part method and divide the total by 4, the number of sections, to determine the number of trials taken to learn the entire set. Add the value thus found to the total number of additional trials taken to reproduce the entire set in the original order. This will give the total number of trials required by S to reach the criterion for learning the entire set of twenty sentences. Find the difference between this value and the total number of trials taken to reach the learning criterion by the whole method. Prepare two graphs also on the same base. In discussing your results, use the points mentioned in the above paragraph.

Intentional Learning and Incidential Learning

We learn many things without having a conscious intention to learn. Such learning is called incidental learning. If, on the other hand, S makes a conscious effort to learn, the learning is called intentional learning. For example, a student may learn the names of his class mates on repeatedly hearing the teachers call these names in the class room. He makes no effort to learn the names. On the other hand, a student may be required, as a part of his history lesson, to learn not only the historical events but also the names of persons associated with those events.

Experiment on incidental *versus* intentional learning can be done in one of two ways : (1) E uses comparable sets of materials, e. g , two lists of CCC trigrams of equal difficulty. One list is exposed to S with the instruction to learn the trigrams so that he is able to reproduce them correctly. The other list is exposed to him, say, for preparing several copies of the same. In the first case E gives the instruction : "You will be shown a list of 3-lettered nonsense words which you have to learn so that you can correctly reproduce them from memory. Spell each word as it is shown and then write on a sheet of paper as many as you remember. The list will be shown to you several times." E makes the needed modification in the instruction when a memory drum is not used. The instruction for incidental learning will be : "I have to take your help in preparing several copies of a list of 3-lettered nonsense words. You will see each word one after the other and you have to copy on a sheet of paper each one as you see it. After you have thus prepared one copy, the list of words will be shown to you again in the same manner and you have to prepare the copy. I require six copies of the list". E removes each copy after a trial is over and keeps it on his side of the screen. After the six trials are over, E tells S : "You have prepared six copies. I would like now to know if you can recall from memory the words you have copied. This is just to find out if you are able to remember things you are not specially asked to remember".

The incidental learning trials are taken first and after 20 ms. E introduces the list for intentional learning. E takes 6 trials on this list also. The items of both lists are exposed for 3 sec. each, long enough for S to copy the item. E compares the number of items S is able to reproduce correctly after six exposures under each instruction. Since the number of items in the two lists are the same, E may not convert the raw data into percentage values by dividing the number correctly reproduced by the total number of items and multiplying by 100.

(2) E prepares a kind of material which also contains some thing other than what S is instructed to learn. For example E prepares a list of 7 CCC trigrams, each one written in one of seven different but familiar colours at the centre of a 2″×2″ card. The cards are exposed to S one after the other under the instruction for intentional learning, namely, that he has to reproduce after each complete exposure the trigrams that he remembers. E takes, say, six trials and records S's correct reproductions from trial to trial. After the trials are over, E presents to S a list of the seven items written in black letters and asks him to name from his memory the colour of each item. E tells S: "You should have noticed that each nonsense word I showed you was written in a different colour. I would like to know whether you remember the colour of each word. Write against the word the colour in which it was written". To make sure whether S can correctly name the seven colours, E may show him seven patches of colours giving the name of each one.

E may use another kind of material that can be more easily prepared. He may use 3 or 4-lettered familiar words, say, 10 in number, each one written in the centre of a card and each card having a different drawing of figures on its top and bottom borders. The following may serve as an example :

MAN	×××
PIG	UUU
ICE	▲▲▲
GUN	OOO
FIT	△△△
BAG	▰▰▰
NET	●●●
FAR	⦣⦣⦣
ROD	⊥⊥⊥
CAT	▱▱▱

E shows the cards to S with the instruction to learn the words, by the usual, say, free-recall method, and records the number of trials taken to reach the criterion of cent per cent learning. He then presents to S a sheet containing on the left column the list of words in a changed order, each word forming a row with all the 10 sets of drawings. S is asked to match each word with the drawing that accompanied it on the card. The correct matchings will give the incidental learning score.

Your results will show better learning when explicit instruction to learn is given. The reason may be that instruction has a motivating effect on S. Motivation being an important factor in learning, absence of conscious motivation to learn may lead to poor performance in incidental learning. Higher motivation is also ensured in intentional learning, the experimental situation, because S's ego is involved in the learning task—he takes it as a challenge to his learning ability. In incidental learning the task in respect of which S's ability is tested remains disguised from him, e. g., he does not even anticipate that his ability for memorising the verbal material, recalling colours, or matching designs, is being tested. Further, the intentional learning trials may enable S to check his reproductions in one trial for their success or failure when the items are exposed to him in the following trial. The correct responses, being thus rewarded, are reinforced while the incorrect ones are non-reinforced and drop out. Incidental learning provides no occasion for this.

The difference between intentional and incidental learning is paralleled by a difference between the so-called recitation or active method and mere reading or passive method. Experiments have been reported that prove the superiority of the recitation method. The procedure has been a simple one. In the passive method, S is presented a verbal material which he reads a number of times till he is able to reproduce it. In the active or recitation method, S has to recapitulate or recite from his memory whatever he remembers after each reading. The total time taken to memorise the materials becomes the base for comparison between the two methods. It has been found, invariably, that less time is required to learn by the recitation method. You can perform an experiment to verify this finding. The same factors can account for better performance by the recitation method that explain the advantage in intentional learning over incidental learning.

Verbal Conditioning

We have noted how the principle of conditioning applies to sensory-motor learning (p. 136). We have also noted the principle of conditioning involved in serial anticipation (p. 150) and paired-associates learning (p. 157) methods used in experiments on verbal learning. We will describe an experiment illustrating a more direct and clear application of conditioning in verbal learning.

For an experiment on verbal conditioning, prepare a list of 100 very familiar verbs in the past tense, for example, ran, gave, pulled, etc. Write each word on a separate 3″ × 5″ card. On the same card also write the six pronouns—I, We, He, She, You and They. Divide the cards randomly into two piles, each containing 50 cards. Instruct S to construct sentences using the verb and one of the pronouns. Present each card with a blank sheet of paper for S to write the sentence. The blank sheets should be numbered serially. Say 'good' in a 'flat unemotional tone' each time S constructs a sentence using the first person pronouns, i. e., I and We. Say nothing when S uses another pronoun. After the first pile of cards has been done with, start with the second pile. This time say 'good' when S uses You, and say, nothing when S uses I, We, or any other pronoun. Count the frequency of the choice of each pronoun in respect of each pile. Plot a separate curve on the same base for the two piles ; use the six pronouns as the x axis and the frequencies, converted into percentage, as the y axis. In discussing your results, take note of the progressive changes in the frequencies, supporting the effect of differential reinforcement on the change in the relative strength of the tendency to choose the reinforced responses. After the introduction of the second pile, mark the gradual weakening of this tendency for want of the reinforcement appropriate to the first pile, and the gradual shift in the tendency to choose the pronoun reinforced in the second pile. Comment on any other data pertinent to the other facts about conditioning (p. 136).

Recommended Readings

Geldard, F. A., *Fundamentals of Psychology*, Chapter 11, Wiley, New York, 1962.

Munn, N. L., *Introduction to Psychology*, Chapter 10, Oxford and IBH, New Delhi, 1967.

Osgood, C. E., *Method and Theory in Psychology*, Chapter 12, Oxford University Press, New York, 1953.

Postman, L. and Egan, J. P., *Experimental Psychology*, Chapter 14, Harper, New York, 1949.

Underwood, B. J., *Experimental Psychology*, Chapters 10, 11, Appleton, New York, 1966.

Woodworth, R. S. and Schlosberg, H., *Experimental Psychology*, Chapters 23, 25, Holt, New York, 1954.

CHAPTER IX

Transfer of Training

THE ACQUISITION of one skill, sensory-motor or verbal, helps or hinders the acquisition of another skill. This phenomenon has been called transfer. Learning the process of addition facilitates the learning of multiplication. The latter, together with the acquisition of the process of subtraction, paves the way for the learning of division. Learning type-writing by the hunt-and-peck method hinders the subsequent learning of the same skill by the so-called touch-system. Different theories has been advanced to explain the transfer phenomenon. The oldest one is the so-called doctrine of cross-education or formal discipline. This theory influenced the old practice of making children learn the classical subjects, like Latin, Sanskrit, or Arabic, and mathematical tables before they were made to study the school subjects. It was believed that learning these tough subjects provided exercise of the higher mental faculties like memory, attention, reasoning, etc. The development of the basic mental faculties made the learning of the other subjects easier ; there was a positive transfer effect. The theory, however, has become outdated ; a person may be good at reasoning, or have a good memory, so far as one kind of material is concerned, but not for others. It has been replaced by two other theories : (1) Theory of identical elements and (2) Theory of common method or common principle. According to the identical elements theory, the basis of transfer from one task to another, or from one learning material to another, is the presence of common elements between them, e. g., learning to assemble the parts of a time-piece facilitates learning to mend a wrist watch because the two have several common parts. The theory of common method or principle says that acquiring the method, rule or principle applied in performing one task helps the performance of another task if the same method, rule or principle applies there too. Having learned to solve one puzzle by discovering the rule applied therein, facilitates the solution of similar other puzzles. It is difficult to say which theory is more acceptable; one theory applies to one and another theory to another kind of task or learning situation.

The following is the description of a simple experiment on transfer in sensory-motor learning.

Transfer in Sensory-Motor Learning

Bilateral Transfer : Transfer in learning may be positive or negative. When the previous learning of a task in one situation makes its subsequent performance or learning in another situation easier, or when the learning of one task facilitates the performance or learning of another task, we get an instance of positive transfer. On the other hand, when the previous learning makes the subsequent learning more difficult, we get negative transfer. When one learning does not influence another learning, we get zero transfer. Transfer effects may be noticed both in sensory-motor learning as well as verbal learning or learning of concepts or ideas. Transfer in sensory-motor learning has been further classified as motor transfer or pattern transfer. In motor transfer, the acquisition of a skill by one member of the body helps the performance of the skill by another member of the body. If the two parts or members of the body are symmetrical, i. e., are corresponding members of the right and left sides, like right hand and left hand, right foot and left foot, right eye and left eye, and so on, the transfer is called bilateral transfer, i. e., transfer from one side to another. Pattern transfer involves transfer from learning one pattern of sensory-motor task to another similar pattern.

For an cxperiment on bilateral transfer, the mirror tracing task (p. 139) provides a good material. The problem is to determine the effect of practice by the preferred hand on performance of the same task by the non-preferred hand. E has to find out at the outset whether S is right-handed or left-handed.

The fore- and after-test design (p. 11) is to be used. We have described the procedure for the mirror tracing experiment (p. 140). Using the same procedure, E takes two trials from S's non-preferred hand. He then takes several trials by the S's preferred hand, say 10 to 12 or more. He again takes two test trials by the non-preferred hand. Both time and error curves are plotted for the total number of trials, using number of trials as the harizontal axis (abscissa) and time or error as the vertical axis (ordinate). Introspection of the subject is also taken. S is required to throw light on the difficulty encountered and how he overcame the difficulty. You may discover from S's introspection, e. g., that he tried to resist the spontaneous movement of his hand and to force himself to move in a direction opposite to that in which the hand tended to move and that he did the same in the test trials. If this fact comes out in the introspection you get an evidence of the common principle theory of transfer. The treatment of result will involve a comparison between the score of the second fore-test trial and the average of the scores in the two after-test trials. The obtained difference between the scores is to be converted into percentage difference using the formula

$$\frac{\text{Second} - \text{Average Last Two}}{\text{Second}} \times 100$$

The value thus found gives the transfer score, which in this case will be positive.

The discussion will centre round the learning curve—the nature of the curve, plateau, if any, abrupt change in the curve, the points from S's introspection, evidence for or against the rival theories, etc.

There can be several other problems on transfer effect in mirror tracing. One such problem will be transfer from one eye to the other. The two preliminary trials will be taken with one eye. This will be followed by practice with the other eye. The test trials will then be taken with the first eye. To use only one eye, you may prepare a card-board cover with strings attached to its ends. The strings are tied to the head so that one eye is covered.

Another problem may be the effect of change of orientation of movement on transfer in mirror tracing. The preliminary test trials may involve anti-clockwise movement while the practice trials clockwise movement. In this case, obviously, the same hand is to be used for both orientations of movement. In another problem, one may manipulate not only the orientation of movement but also the hand ; practice is done in one orientation, from left to right, using preferred hand, while the test involves another orientation, from right to left, and the non-preferred hand. In still another problem, one may try to explore transfer effect by changing the location of the mirror, from the front to the right or left side.

Pattern Transfer : In an experiment on pattern transfer, one uses different patterns of drawing for the practice and the test series. One may have a preliminary trial on a maze pattern followed by practice on the star pattern and then take final test on the maze pattern. Both patterns, however, are to be traced from their mirror images.

Transfer can be studied also in maze learning. S may learn one maze and is then instructed to learn another equally difficult maze pattern. The problem will be whether learning one maze facilitates learning another maze. In this case, the design may be a simple one. The first maze learning is followed by the second maze learning with sufficient rest in between ; S learns A, learns B. E will plot two curves for each type of scores, viz., error and time. Each curve will be plotted on the same base for both A and B. He will compare the mean number of trials and the mean amount of errors for reaching the criterion of two errorless performance. He will comment in the discussion on the difference between the two kinds of scores and will try to interpret the difference, if any. In addition, he will find out from S's introspection, and also from his own objective observation of S's performance, what method of learning S had adopted, whether it was the hit-and-miss method —random movement,or a planned attack on the problem, and what kinds of cues, kinaesthetic, visual or verbal, S availed of (p. 140).

Still another problem on transfer in maze learning will be the effect of practice in one orientation of the pattern on the learning of the same pattern in a different orientation, say fixing the slotted pattern on the board by rotating it 90° or 180°. Still another problem may be reversing S's movement in the second set of trials—instead of starting from the point of entry, S starts from the centre of the maze and exits from the point of entry.

We have described the experiments on positive transfer and habit facilitation in the acquisition of sensory-motor skills. As we noted earlier, a previous learning may also create difficulty, may hinder the process of a subsequent learning. The second learning in this case would have been less difficult if it were not preceded by the first learning. Following is the report of an experiment on negative transfer or habit interference :

Habit Interference : It was commonly believed that training in one skill facilitates the training in another similar skill. Earlier method of education was influenced by the so-called doctrine of formal discipline or cross-education. Much emphasis was laid on rote memory because it was presumed that memory practice would help the learning of all subjects in future. Later investigations, however, have contradicted this notion. The acquisition of one skill does not always help the acquisition of other similar skills ; it sometimes also hinders ; at other times, one learning has no effect on another learning. We have thus three kinds of transfer situations : (1) positive transfer or habit facilitation when the acquisition of one habit helps the formation of another ; (2) negative transfer or habit interference when an earlier habit creates additional difficulty in the formation of another habit, and (3) zero transfer when the first habit has no effect on the second habit formation. In this experiment attempt was made to verify the occurrence of habit interference in the acquisition of a sensory-motor task. Both positive and negative transfer occur when there is some element of similarity between the two learning tasks ; in the absence of any similarity, zero transfer takes place. Because of the similarity between the two situations, the responses acquired in performing the first task tend to be elicited when the second task is performed, the conditioning principle of stimulus generalisation (p. 137) comes into play. But despite their similarity, the responses learnt in the first task may not only be inappropriate but also incompatible with the responses required for the second task. It is, therefore, necessary that the first task response should be unlearned before the responses appropriate to the second task uninterruptedly occur. This fact increases the difficulty in the acquisition of the second task response. The learning of the second task responses would, accordingly, be less difficult if there were no such interference from the acquisition of the first task responses.

Hypothesis : Two similar tasks requiring incompatible responses for their successful performance would interfer with each other's learning.

Method

Subject : A male undergraduate student aged 19 years.

Material : (1) Card sorting tray having 24 compartments, each compartment having pasted on its side wall one of six playing cards in a suit. (2) A pack of cards with six cards in each of the four suits. (3) Stop watch.

Procedure : The tray was placed on the table so that its near side was even with the edge of the table. S stood on that side and the pack of cards, thoroughly shuffled by E, was placed on the table, face down. S used his non-preferred hand, which was discovered by E on enquiry from S, and picked up the top card from the pack and placed it in the appropriate compartment.

Instruction : "This tray has 24 compartments, as you see; each compartment has a particular card pasted on its side. Here is a pack of twenty-four cards. Your task is to pick up each card, using your left hand" (to a right-handed subject) "and place it in the same compartment as the suit and number of the card you have picked up." I am going to see how fast you can learn to sort out the cards correctly in their respective compartments in the shortest possible time. Every time I will give you a 'start' signal because I will measure the time you take in completing the task. Do you understand ?"

E took 20 trials, giving 30 sec. interval between trials during which he noted the time and error, collected the cards and shuffled them. He then turned the tray so that the far side of the tray was now even with the edge of the table. E then took another 5 trials in this altered orientation of the tray.

Objective Observation : S started with enthusiasm, though he looked tense at first. Gradually, with the progress of the trials he appeared to take it easy and often smiled on reaching the end of a trial. With the change in the orientation, he started in the same spirit, but soon became very tense. He pressed his lips and often also bit his lower lip, clenched the fist of the free hand, seemed to be restive. He exclaimed "what is happening now ?"

Introspection : "The task was difficult in the beginning but later on it became easier for me. When the box was placed in the changed position, I had much difficulty in performing the task. My hand was moving in the other direction and every time I had to correct myself. I had to give much greater attention to the task in order to avoid errors."

Results

Table 1

RAW DATA SHOWING TIME IN SECONDS AND ERROR IN THE FIRST AND SECOND ORIENTATIONS

	First			First			Second	
Trials	Time	Error	Trials	Time	Error	Trials	Time	Error
1	150	6	11	74	0	1	168	6
2	152	5	12	75	0	2	158	4
3	148	4	13	75	0	3	150	3
4	140	4	14	62	0	4	148	1
5	147	3	15	65	0	5	140	1
6	135	1	16	55	0			
7	104	2	17	52	0			
8	105	1	18	54	0			
9	98	0	19	47	0			
10	96	1	20	42	0			

Table 2

MEAN, SD, SE DIFF. BETWEEN MEANS FOR TIME SCORE AND THE CRITICAL RATIO ; MEAN ERROR

	Orientation	First		Second
Time	Mean	93.50		152.80
	SD	37.72		9.52
	$SE_{diff.}$		6.68	
	t		8.90	
Error	Mean	1.35		3.00

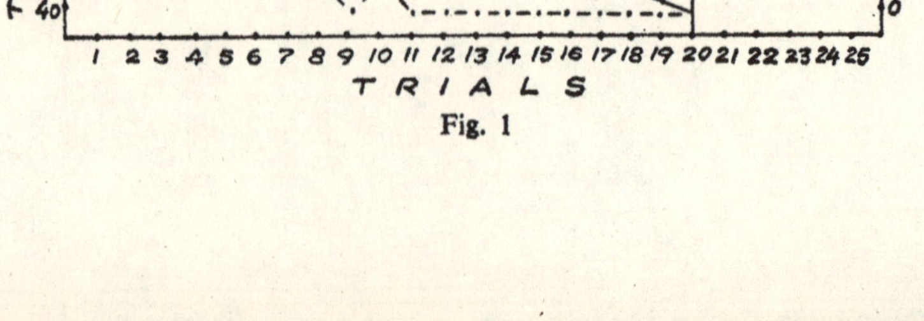

Fig. 1

The mean difference in time between S's performance in the two orientations is highly significant, t being equal to 8.90. The difference in the error is equally great ; S made, on an average, more than twice as many errors in the second orientation as in the first.

Discussion

We find that S has taken significantly much more time, on an average, in performing the card sorting task when the orientation of the tray was reversed (Table 2). Same is the case with the errors. The learning of the task in the first orientation, thus, interfered with its performance and learning in the reversed orientation. Had S learnt the task in the second orientation, before he learned it in the first orientation, he would have taken as much time and committed as many errors as he did in the first orientation, since the task in the two situations was identical, the difference was only in the orientation of the tray. The difference in time and error between the two orientations can, thus, be interpreted as due to the interference exerted by the first learning.

Apart from the overall difference between the two means, we notice considerable difference in the initial trials between the two orientations (Table 1). The curve (Fig. 1) which shows a gradual fall from trial to trial in the first orientation, abruptly rises with the change in the orientation and reaches a height above that in the first orientation so far as time score is concerned.

E's objective observation of S's behaviour also indicated experience of greater difficulty on his part in performing the task in the reversed orientation. He became more 'tense', 'pressed his lips', 'bit the lower lip' and 'clenched his fist'. He also exclaimed in disgust : "What is happening now ?"

S's introspection supports the objective findings. S found the performance of the task in the changed orientation 'much difficult'. The association he had formed between the visual impression of a card and the movement of his hand interfered with the acquisition of the new association required when the movement took place in the reversed orientation.

The results are consistent with our hypothesis, namely, that if two similar tasks requiring incompatible responses for their successful performance are learnt one after the other, the first task causes a hindrance in the acquisition of the second task. In other words, our results provide clear evidence of habit interference.

Transfer in Verbal Learning

We have dealt with transfer in sensory-motor learning and have also seen that transfer may be positive, negative, or zero. We come across transfer in verbal learning also. In verbal learning transfer can be best illustrated when using the method of paired-associates learning. But before we take up transfer in PA learning, we will deal with some facts that would help us in understanding transfer in PA learning.

Backward Association in PA Learning

We have noted that PA learning involves the learning of an association between the stimulus and the response terms. You test the learning by exposing the stimulus term alone and require your S to anticipate the response term. The association is called forward association as S learns to associate the response term with the stimulus term. A question arises as to whether the learning of the forward association results also in the acquisition of the backward association. In other words, given the stimulus term, S can anticipate the response term. But can S also reproduce the stimulus term if you give him the response term ? Having learned to move forward from stimulus to response, can S also move backward from response to stimulus ? It has been found that in PA learning S does not acquire only forward association. He also acquires, as a result, backward association. You can verify the finding by conducting an experiment. Let your S learn a PA list by the usual procedure. You then test him by exposing the response term alone and asking him to reproduce the stimulus term. You may find that he is able to do so in respect of some items, if not all. You come to the conclusion that PA learning involves also the acquisition of backward association. You may take up another problem : does the learning of forward association facilitate the acquisition of backward association ? Here again let S learn a PA list by the usual method. Then test for backward association. If S fails either partly or wholly in the test, you take further trials in which you expose the response term first, let S reproduce the stimulus term, and then expose the stimulus term. If you find that S takes fewer trials in acquiring the backward association as compared to his learning of the forward association, you conclude that the learning of forward association facilitates the acquisition of backward association.

Two Steps in P.A. Learning : We have earlier noted (p. 159) that learning a list of nonsense items requires both the integration of the individual items as well as their association in the list (p.160). This applies to PA learning also. S acquires response integration, that is integration of the elements composing the response term, as well as its association with the stimulus term. You may verify this conclusion by conducting an experiment on PA learning where you use two comparable lists of paired items. You may have 3-lettered familiar words as stimulus items in the two lists, each one paired with a CCC trigram as response term. Let S first learn only the CCC trigrams of the first list by the free recall method, presenting them in different orders from trial to trial. Then start the PA learning trials for the second list. Allow a rest of, say, 10 minutes after which start PA learning trials for the first list. Compare your S's rate of PA learning for the two lists. You will find that the first list is easier to learn than the second list. The reason is that since S has to acquire response integration as well as learn the association between the stimulus and response terms, the learning of the second list becomes more difficult. The problem may also be stated as the effect of response familiarity on PA learning. The result will support the view that PA learning involves two steps, namely, response integration and association learning ; the latter comprises both forward and backward associations.

Transfer in PA Learning : We have noticed that transfer, whether positive or negative, cannot be possible without similarity (p. 186). If two tasks are altogether different, transfer from the one to the other will be zero. It is easy to manipulate similarity in PA learning even at a very simple level by making the stimulus or response terms identical in the two lists learned one after the other. We may then visualise three situations of transfer in PA learning : (1) having the same stimulus terms in both lists, (2) having the same response terms in both lists, and (3) having different stimulus as well as response term in the two lists. Such learning situations can be symbolically represented and each representation may be called a transfer paradigm. We have thus :

(1) A–B, A–C ; (2) A–B, C–B ; and (3) A–B, C–D.

In the above paradigms (1) and (2), you will note that the common term has the same function, it is either stimulus or response in both lists. We will, therefore, describe them as Single-Function (SF) paradigms. We may have Double-Function (DF) paradigms also, such as:

(1) A−B, C−A ; and (2) A−B, B−C

We can, thus, visualise four transfer paradigms in PA learning, besides the zero transfer paradigm, viz, (1) A−B, A−C ; (2) A−B, C−B ; (3) A−B, C−A ; (4) A−B, B−C.

In all PA learning transfer paradigms, the first list is called **acquisition** list and the second list is called **test** list. In learning the first list, S newly acquires the association between the two terms of the paired item ; the second list is used to test the effect of the first list learning on the second list learning—what is called transfer effect. Hence the second is named as the **test** list. The trials on the first list are called **acquisition trials** ; those on the second list are called **test trials.**

We have some important findings on transfer in PA learning : (1) The identical response paradigm generally yields positive transfer. The response being the same in both lists, the learning of the **test** list becomes easier since one step, namely, response integration (p. 191), is already covered. All that S has to do is to associate the response term with a new stimulus term in the **test** list. (2) The identical stimulus paradigm quite often produces negative transfer. Since the response changes in the **test** list, the advantage from response learning is not there—the fact that accounts for positive transfer in the identical response paradigm. Further, the same stimulus term occurs also in the **test** list. The association of the stimulus term established with a different response term in the **acquisition** list, tends to evoke the occurrence of the same response when the stimulus term is presented in the **test** list. The test list learning is, therefore, interfered with on this account. S has first to unlearn the association between A and B, and then alone it will be possible for him to learn the new association between A and C. The unlearning of the first association requires additional trials on the **test** list—several non-reinforced trials sufficient to produce extinction (p. 137), besides those needed for building up the new association. Hence the negative transfer, as indicated by the larger number of trials required to learn the test list as compared to the acquisition list. The result, however, is not consistent; one may some time obtain zero or even positive transfer in the identical stimulus paradigm. This may be explained as due to the positive influence of the similarity of the learning tasks as well as the learning procedure ; both lists are learned by the same method. If this influence becomes stronger than the inhibition in the test list learning due to response competition, the transfer effect will be positive ; if both are equal in strength, they will cancel each other and the net result will be zero transfer. Negative transfer will occur if the interference from the acquisition list learning is stronger than the facilitation caused by similarity of task and method.

The double function paradigm has most often produced negative transfer. The reversal of the function of one term from the acquisition to the test list, causes confusion which hampers with the learning of the test list. In the A–B, B–C paradigm, the A–B acquisition involves the learning of B as a response term. Its occurrence as the stimulus term in the test list tends to evoke A because of the backward association formed in A–B learning (p. 190). This inhibits the occurrence of C as the response. Further, C has to be learned as a new term In A–B, C–A paradigm the already established forward association between A–B, evokes B when the response term A is presented after C in the test list. As a result, the presentation of C in the subsequent trials evokes both A and B, only one of which is a correct response. This causes delay—requires more trials—in linking C with A alone. Further, the advantage from response learning is lost since the response term of the acquisition list disappears from the test list.

Following is the report of an experiment on negative transfer or habit interference in verbal learning. Here we are introducing a paradigm which has invariably produced negative transfer and which was not mentioned earlier. In this paradigm we use the same stimulus and response terms in both lists, only the response terms of the first list are rearranged and new pairs of stimulus-response items are thus formed. The paradigm may be symbolically represented as : A–B, A–B′ , you will note the situation to be very similar to what we found in the report of the experiment on habit interference (p. 185). S is required to associate with the stimulus a response that is not only new but also inappropriate to the stimulus in the context of the already learned stimulus-response associations.

Negative Transfer or Habit Interference in Verbal Learning : The effect of one learning on another has been called transfer which may be either positive or negative. In positive transfer the previous learning facilitates the subsequent learning ; in negative transfer what is learned earlier interferes with what is learned later. Transfer, whether positive or negative, depends upon similarity. If two learning tasks are altogether dissimilar there will be no transfer—what is called zero transfer—from one task to the other. Transfer effect may be noted both in sensory-motor and verbal learning. Paired-associates learning has been found to be very appropriate for demonstrating transfer effect.

In this experiment an attempt was made to bring about negative transfer in PA learning by manipulating similarity between the elements of the paired-items in the two learning lists. Negative transfer has also been described as habit interference, specially when the acquisition of one skill adversely affects the acquisition of another skill ; transfer, by the way, may be used in a larger sense, namely, when learning to perform one kind of activity influences the **performance** of another kind of activity. Our problem may, therefore, be also stated as that of habit interference in verbal learning.

A variety of transfer paradigms has been used in experiments on transfer in PA learning. Since our object was to bring about negative transfer, we used the A – B, A – B′ paradigm which has invariably been noticed to produre negative transfer. The following hypothesis was examined :

The acquisition of one habit interferes with the acquisition of another habit, if the two call for incompatible responses to the same stimulus.

Method

Subject : A female undergraduate student of Psychology.

Material : Seven 2″ × 2″ cards each containing 4-lettered words and seven 2″ × 2″ cards each containing consonant trigrams.

Procedure : Using the 14 cards, E prepared two sets of paired items as shown below :

Set 1 (A – B)	*Set 2 (A – B′)*
XTQ – BOOK	XTQ – DUCK
VKP – ROAD	VKP – GOAT
BZM – CART	BZM – HALT
GWN – HALT	GWN – CART
HRF – DUCK	HRF – BOOK
NLC – GOAT	NLC – WORK
JDS – WORK	JDS – ROAD

Set 1 was used as the acquisition set. E at first exposed each pair for 4 sec., timing the exposure by mental counting. He then exposed the stimulus trigram alone for 2 sec. during which S had to anticipate the paired word. The word was then exposed for two seconds together with the trigram. In this manner each paired item was exposed from trial to trial The order of presentation of 'he paired items was altered at random, after the preliminary trial in which both terms of the pair were exposed together for 4 sec. The learning criterion was two errorless anticipations. Using an inter-set interval of 20 ms., E introduced set 2 which became, thus, the test set. The same procedure was followed for the test trials also.

Instruction : "I will show you a combination of 3 consonants paired with a word. There will be seven such pairs. After this I will show you the consonants and you have to reproduce the word paired with it. Then I will show you the word also In this manner I will show you the pairs from trial to trial till you can correctly reproduce each word on seeing the consonants paired with it."

Result

Introspection : "I did not have much difficulty in learning the words because they were all known to me. I had some difficulty in correctly reproducing the word linked with the consonants, since there was nothing to help me in li king them together. However, later on I could succeed in doing all that. But I had a lot of difficulty in reproducing the correct word when the word was paired with a different consonant. When the consonants were shown to me with a different word I got puzzled and felt that there was something wrong. When the co sonants were afterwards shown to me alone I was reminded of the word that was paired with it originally ; the changed word would never come to my mind. I felt altogether lost and sometimes I was not able to reproduce anything".

Table 1

NUMBER CORRECT PER TRIAL, NUMBER OF INTRUSIONS, AND TOTAL NUMBER OF TRIALS TO CRITERION, FOR THE ACQUISITION AND TEST SETS ; DIFFERENCE BETWEEN TOTAL NUMBER OF TRIALS

	Acquisition	Test	
Trials	No. correct	No. correct	No. Intrusions
1	×	×	2
2	1	×	2
3	3	1	2
4	5	3	1
5	5	3	1
6	7	5	1
7		4	1
8		6	1
9		7	×
Total	6	9	
Diff.	3		

S has taken 6 trials for learning set 1 and 9 for learning set 2 ; the difference is of 3 trials ; 50% more trials were needed to learn set 2.

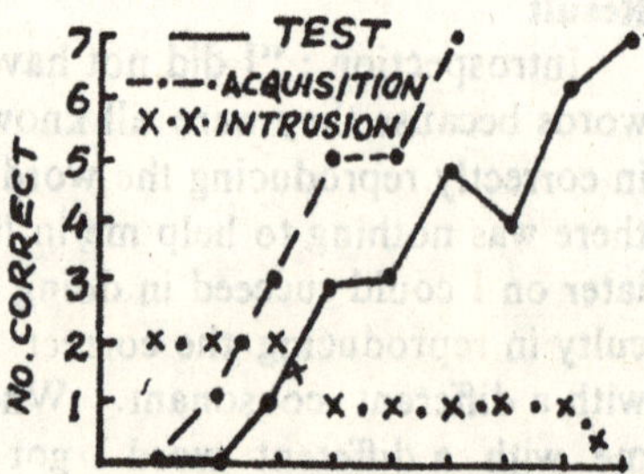

SERIAL NO. OF TRIALS

Fig. 1. No. of Correct Anticipations per Trial for the Acquisition and Test Sets.

Discussion

The results support our hypothesis. The same list of words was used for the two sets of PA items, the difference between the sets being only in respect of the arrangement of the response terms. The acqusition of the second set of paired items called upon S to make a response to a stimulus that was linked up with another stimulus occurring in the list and, thus, incompatible with the one he had already learned to associate with this stimulus. As a result, the learning of the new set of pairs was considerably interfered with by the acquisition of the old set (Table 1, Fig. 1); S needed 50% more trials to learn the test pairs.

The interference in learning is also evidenced by the intrusions from set 1; the already established association between the stimulus and response terms tends to elicit the same response when the stimulus term is presented to S in the second set. The prior learning of the response terms dose not produce any advantage in the learning of the second set of items as the response terms are all familiar words and their number being limited to seven, their acquisition may be presumed to have produced no difficulty. In order to produce the correct response in either set, only the association learning was needed. There was no advantage even from familiarity with the learning method which could have had a positive transfer effect on the second set learning. The two sets are identical in respect of their elements ; only the arrangement of the response terms has been altered in the second set. There is no positive factor, therefore, to offset the negative transfer effect produced by the strong tendency for the stimulus term to elicit the response originally linked with it. Hence the very clear evidence of negative transfer or habit interference. S's introspection also supports our results; he got 'puzzled' at the altered arrangement of the response terms ; he felt much "difficulty" ; the originally paired response disturbed the occurrence of the correct response in the test trials.

We can conclude that our hypothesis regarding the occurrence of negative transfer in the A – B, A – B paradigm is supported by the results.

Appendix

RAW DATA

Acquisition Trials

Trigrams	1	2	3	4	5	6	7
XTQ	Duck	X	Goat	Book	Book	Book	Book
VKP	Last	X	Road	Road	Road	Road	Road
BZM	Book	Cart	Cart	Cart	Cart	Cart	Cart
GWN	X	Work	X	X	Goat	Halt	Halt
HRF	X	Cart	Goat	Work	Goat	Duck	Duck
NLC	Halt	Halt	X	Goat	Goat	Goat	Goat
JDS	Goat	X	Work	Work	Work	Work	Work

TEST TRIALS

Trigrams	1	2	3	4	5	6	7	8	9	10
XTQ	Book	X	Book	Duck	Duck	Duck	Duck	Duck	Duck	Duck
VKP	Cart	Road	X	Work	Road	Goat	Goat	Goat	Goat	Goat
BZM	X	Cart	Halt	Halt	Halt	Halt	Halt	Halt	Halt	Halt
GWN	Halt	X	Duck	X	Book	Cart	X	Cart	Cart	Cart
HRF	X	Work	Duck	Book	Book	Book	Book	Book	Book	Book
NLC	X	X	Road	Goat	Road	Road	Goat	Work	Work	Work
JDS	X	Work	Goat	Book	Goat	Work	Goat	Work	Road	Road

Stimulus Generalisation

We have noted that the A–B, A–C paradigm quite often yields negative transfer (p. 192). We have used the principle of unlearning or experimental extinction (p. 192) as the possible explanation. We can illustrate the conditioning principle of stimulus generalisation (p. 137) also in transfer in PA learning. This will happen when the stimulus terms in the two lists are not identical, but similar. The similarity may vary along a scale from perfect identity as in A–B, A–B, to complete difference as in A–B, C–B. Starting from this end, namely zero similarity, as we increase the similarity between stimulus terms of the two lists we expect greater and greater amount of positive transfer, till we reach the stage of identity of the stimulus term (p. 191). We get here an instance of what has been called the generalisation gradient. It means that when conditioning has been established, a stimulus which is very similar to the conditioned stimulus will evoke the conditioned response more frequently than the less similar conditioned stimulus. In other words, there will be a relationship between the degree of similarity and the frequency of the occurrence of the conditioned response. You can conduct a simple experiment on the effect of similarity between stimulus terms on transfer in P.A. learning. Use in one condition two PA lists, having identical response terms and distinct stimulus terms ; in another condition let the stimulus term of one list have some common elements with that of the other list, e. g., house and mouse, book and cook, so on each one paired with the same response term in the two lists which may be a word or a trigram, as you choose. You will expect stronger positive transfer in the second condition ; the second list learning will be easier in this condition. If possible, use a control also : A–B, C–D ; this is likely to produce zero transfer.

Inter-Serial Inhibition or Facilitation

We have referred to a distinction between intra-serial and inter-serial inhibition (p. 164). We have also illustrated intra-serial inhibition in learning (p. 164). Experiments on transfer in PA learning present an instance of inter-serial inhibition in learning. We have noted in the above report how the learning of the first set of items inhibited the learning of the second set of items. Negative transfer effect in learning may, thus, also be termed as inter-serial inhibition effect Positive transfer will then be the same as inter-serial facilitation. We came across intra-serial facilitation in learning of related items when using the free recall method (p. 161).

Recommended Readings

Geldard, F. A., *Fundamentals of Psychology*, Chapter 5, Wiley, New York, 1962.

Munn, N. L., *Introduction to Psychology*, Chapter 10, Oxford and IBH, New Delhi, 1967.

Osgood, C. E., *Method and Theory in Psychology*, Chapter 12, Oxford University Press, New York, 1953.

Postman, L., and Egan, J. P., *Experimental Psychology*, Chapter 18, Harper, New York, 1949.

Underwood, B. J., *Experimental Psychology*, Chapter 12, Appleton, New York, 1966.

Woodworth, R. S. and Schlosberg H., *Experimental Psychology*, Chapter 24, Holt, New York, 1954.

CHAPTER X

Remembering and Forgetting

WHEN WE are able to remember what we had experienced or learned some time back, we are said to have retained it. When we fail to remember, or we forget what we had experienced or learned we are said not to have retained it. Remembering is, thus, the positive and forgetting the negative aspect of retention. How we retain what we are able to remember, cannot be known directly. It is supposed that every performance, learning, or experience leaves its after-effect or trace. When we recall what we had performed, learned, or experienced, we revive the after-effect or trace, which is, accordingly, called memory trace. The memory trace may be of different degrees of strength. If it is strong enough, we are able to remember, and if it is weak, we forget what it represents. The passage of time has its effect on the memory trace. If it is not used or revived for some time, it gradually fades out.

It will follow from what we said above that experiments on remembering and forgetting involve three different phases. The first phase is that of performance or learning ; unless one has performed or learned something, the question about its remembering and forgetting does not arise. The second phase consists of a time interval. If the performance or learning continues there is no question of its retention ; we retain it during the time we are not performing or learning. The third phase is that of the test of retention. We can determine whether we have retained what we have performed or learned only by trying to remember or recall it. If we can remember it completely, or even partially, we can say that we have been wholly or partly retaining it ; if we cannot do so, we decide that we are no longer retaining it. Following is the paradigm of a general experiment on remembering and forgetting :

Learning—Retention Interval—Test of Retention.

In earlier Chapters, VII and VIII, we have understood the

methods used for experiments on learning—sensory-motor or verbal. In an experiment on remembering and forgetting we introduce a learning task using any one of the methods that is appropriate to our problem. We then let the S have nothing to do with the task. The length of this period will again depend upon the nature of the problem and other factors that will be illustrated when we deal with the experiments on remembering and forgetting. After the expiry of the period, S is given a test of retention which may be one of several types that will be described below.

Let us understand one important difference between learning experiments and experiments on remembering and forgetting. We have seen that in learning experiments too, particularly verbal, we test S's retention of whatever he had observed in a particular learning trial by requiring him to reproduce what he remembers, or to anticipate the next item or the adjacent member of a pair, before it is exposed. In each case, however, we measure **immediate** retention as distinguished from **delayed** retention which is characteristic of experiments on remembering and forgetting. That is why we introduce the test of retention not immediately but only when some time has passed after learning. In learning experiments we have immediate memory test ; in experiments on remembering and forgetting we have delayed memory test.

Methods of Testing Retention

1. **Recall Method** : S is required to reproduce, after a specified period, whatever he had learned. Supposing, S was made to learn a 10-item list of nonsense syllables to the criterion of one faultless reproduction or anticipation. He is then called upon, after, say, 30 ms. to recall the items from the list. The number of items correctly recalled will provide the data on S's retention of what he had learned. To get a precise recall score, we find the ratio between the number of items correctly recalled and the total number of items in the list and multiply the ratio by 100. We may have a range of recall scores from 0 to 100 ; 0 means complete forgetting, and 100 perfect retention ; the different amounts of retention are represented by the percentage values obtained between 0 and 100.

2. **Relearning or Saving Method** : Having learned a list, S's retention is tested after a specified time interval by asking him to recall what he learned. In case there is lack of perfect recall.

or there is no recall, he is again made to learn the list by the same method as on the previous occasion. We, thus, have a set of **relearning** trials and stop when S reaches the criterion of one faultless reproduction. We then compare the number of trials S took to relearn the list with that he took in the first or original learning. If S takes less trials in relearning, we presume that S had not completely forgotten the list, otherwise he should have taken as many trials as in the original learning ; the relearning would have involved no saving. The method has accordingly been described as the saving method. Sometimes S may not be able to recall anything—his recall score may be 0, but the relearning may show some saving which would imply that the recall method was not sensitive enough to indicate retention. In other words, relearning is a more sensitive method of testing retention. To find the saving score, you have to use the following formula :

$$\frac{\text{No. Trials Origin. } \textit{minus} \text{ No. Trials Relearning}}{\text{No. Trials Origin. Learning}} \times 100$$

Here again the score may range between 0 and 100 ; 100 would mean complete recall of the items after the time interval, or perfect retention ; 0 would signify no retention or complete forgetting.

3. **Recognition Method** : This is the most sensitive measure of retention. Here you test retention by presenting to S again the original items mixed up, in a random order, with several new items of the same kind. S is asked to identify those that belonged to the list he had observed or learned. The correct identifications will provide the raw retention score. But the raw score has to be corrected for chance success. May be, among S's correct identifications, one or two have been accidentally corr ct. He really remembers and can correctly recognise, say, 6 out of 10 items, but he has made just a guess about a few more out of which say 2, come out to be a correct hit. You have, therefore, to make a correction for chance by using the following formula :

$$\frac{R-W}{N_1+N_2} \times 100$$

Here R stands for right or correct responses, i. e., those that belonged to the original list and have been correctly identified by S as such **plus** those that did not belong and have been correctly identified as not belonging to the original list. W stands for wrong responses which will consist of those identified as belonging to the list but **not actually** belonging **plus** those identified as **not** belonging but **actually** belonging. In taking the recognition test, you ask S to say 'yes' to those items that he recognizes, and 'No' to those that he does not recognize, as belonging to the original list. N_1 and N_2 stand, respectively, for the number of items in the original list and that of those added at the time of the recognition test. You will always find recognition to be an easier test than recall. This may be verified by an experiment. In this case it would be better to take only a few learning trials, say one or two, unless the retention interval is very long; take the retention test for one list by the recall and for the other by the recognition method. The lists should of equal difficulty.

4. **Reconstruction Method**: Here S is tested for the reproduction of the order or arrangement of stimuli presented to him in a certain order or arranged in a certain manner—temporal or spatial. After the stimuli are presented, their arrangement is disturbed; S has to set them in the presented order. S's score will be the number of presentations needed to reproduce the correct order.

Of the four tests of retention, the most widely used is the recall test. The other tests are applied to suit the special requirements of a problem or of the task used in an experiment.

Experiments on Remembering and Forgetting

There are several independent variables that can be manipulated in experiments on remembering and forgetting. You find below a description of some of these variables.

1. **Meaningfulness**: It has been invariably noted that meaningful materials are better retained than non-meaningful ones. A list of familiar words can be recalled better than a list of nonsense syllables, or of digits, after the same time interval.

2. **Amount of Material**: We have seen earlier that a short list can be learned more easily than a long list (p. 161); the number of trials taken to learn a long list is disproportionately larger than that required to learn a short list. We obtain, however, a reverse finding when we consider the retention of a long list as compared to a short list. The larger the amount of materials learned, the better the retention. This applies equally to meaningful and nonsense materials. The reason is that a larger list is more difficult to learn; it requires more trials than does a shorter list. In other

words, each item of the list is presented more often so that those that have already been learned in the earlier trials get a stronger chance to be overlearned. They will also be better retained. You can verify this finding by using two lists, differing in the number of items. Let your S learn both to the same criterion. Test his retention for the two lists after the same interval, using the recall or the saving method, or both. You may use any learning method you choose.

3. **Level or Strength of Learning** : We have understood how we determine the level or strength of learning (p. 148). A relationship has been noted between retention and level of learning. What is overlearned is better retained than what is simply learned, and what is simply learned is better retained than what is partially learned. Overlearning has, thus, come out to be a very important factor in retention, whether we test retention by the recall or the saving method. The degree of relationship between overlearning and retention, however, is not expected to remain the same through all ranges of level of overlearning. In other words, we should not expect that 100% overlearning would show twice as much gain in retention as 50% overlearning. You can test the finding by examining the statement : 'There is no perfect relationship between overlearning and retention.' You may use, say, three 7-item lists of CCC trigrams. Let S learn one list to the criterion of simple learning, that is, 0 percent overlearning. Let him take 50 percent overlearning trials on the second list and 100 percent overlearning trials on the third list, after reaching the simple learning criterion. Give the recall test in each case, say, after 15 minutes. Draw a curve with the percent of overlearning as the abscissa and the recall score as the ordinate, as given below :

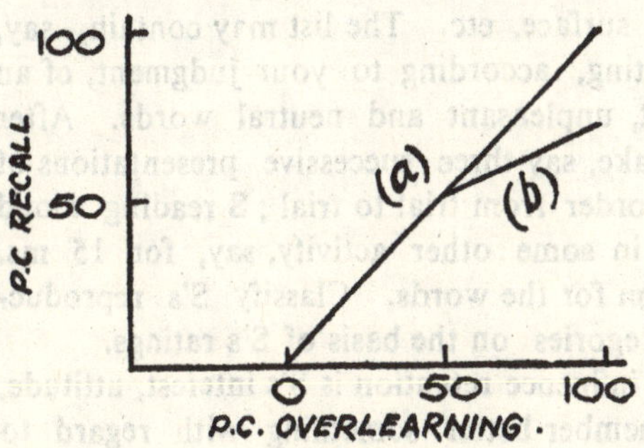

If the relationship is perfect your curve will be a straight line (a), otherwise it will be a curved line which bends as it progresses (b).

4. **Spaced *versus* Massed Practice** : Distribution of prac-

tice has an advantage not only for learning (p. 166) but also for retention. What is learned by the method of spaced practice is also retained better than what is learned by the massed practice method. We have noted (p. 168) that the net-work of associations formed between the parts of a list interfere with association that is relevant to the correct response. The incorrect associations gradually wear out resulting in the gradual increase of the corrcet responses from trial to trial. The rest between trials helps to stabilise the correct associations and to further weaken the incorrect ones. The correct associations, therefore, are stronger and are better retained when the learning is spaced. The recall of the materials learned by the method of spaced practice is likely, therefore, to be better than that of those materials learned by massing practice.

5. **Other Factors** : There are other factors also besides those mentioned above that have been introduced as experimental variables in experiments on remembering and forgetting. One such factor is the affective tone of the learning material. It is suggested that pleasant memories are more lasting than unpleasant memories. A rough and ready method to test this hypothesis will be to ask S to recount some of those experiences from his early life that he remembers vividly. The experiences are then sorted out into two classes according to their pleasant or unpleasant meaning. The result, however, may not be consistent. Sometimes the unpleasant experiences may be better recalled than the pleasant ones. An alternative method may require S to rate words for their feeling tone on a 3-point scale : (1 Having generally pleasant associations, (2) Neutral, i. e., neither pleasant nor unpleasant, and (3) Having generally unpleasant associations. You may have such words as, murder, tree, joy, sweet, hatred, bravery, war. courage, picnic, madness, success, camel, punishment, blood, mango, river, wound, roof, flower, mountain, surface, etc. The list may contain, say, 30 familiar words, consisting, according to your judgment, of an equal number of pleasant, unpleasant and neutral words. After they have been rated, make, say three successive presentations of the words, changing the order from trial to trial ; S reading aloud each word. Engage S in some other activity, say, for 15 ms. and then test his retention for the words. Classify S's reproductions within the three categories on the basis of S's ratings.

Still other variable to influence retention is S's interest, attitude, or values. One may remember better something with regard to which he has a favourable attitude, what one likes, or what one values. Experiments on these factors, however, call for a measure of S's interests, attitudes, or values, for which special measuring devices have to be secured ; we will not be concerned with them in this book.

Curve of Forgetting

As we noted earlier (p. 201), it has been believed that every activity performed by the organism leaves its after-effect, or trace, on the nervous system. The trace is retained after the activity has ceased. It is possible to call back the memory of the activity by reviving the trace. It has accordingly been described as the memory trace. The memory trace, if not revived from time to time, gradually fades out, according to the law of disuse, until it is completely obliterated. The forgetting is due to the fading of the memory trace. This therory has, accordingly, been called the **trace theory** It is also called the **atrophy theory**. Atrophy is the process of gradual wasting away or dying out of a muscle as a result of disuse. If any organ of the body is not used for a considerably long time, the muscles supplied to it cease to function, they die out, and the ability to move the organ is lost. Similarily, if a memory trace is not used in recalling the past experience or activity it represents, it is gradually atrophied ; it fades out.

The trace theory of forgetting presupposes that time is a very important factor in forgetting. Ebbinghaus plotted a curve of forgetting by testing retention of different comparable lists of nonsense syllables after different intervals of time. He found that

TIME INTERVAL IN DAYS

forgetting increases with the increase in the time interval, though the difference in forgetting is greater between intervals of shorter lengths than those of longer duration ; the curve of forgetting shows a steep fall in recall in the beginning, but afterwards it becomes more gradual, as shown above.

It may not be possible for you to plot the curve of forgetting for you will have to measure forgetting also for intervals that may be longer than 24 hours or even a week, as Ebbinghaus did. But you can conduct an experiment to verify the hypothesis, namely, that forgetting is a function of time. You may use three comparable lists of verbal items—words, or trigrams ; let S learn the first list. Engage him, say, for 5 ms in a mild activity, and then test his recall for the list. Let him next learn the second list and again test his recall engaging him in the mild activity, say, for 15 ms. Finally, let him learn the third list and test his recall, say after 30 ms. You will then compare the recall scores for the three different intervals, and also plot a curve using the x-axis as the time line and the ordinate as percent recall.

The curve of forgetting may be alternately explained by another theory of forgetting called the interference theory. We will know more about this theory in the section that follows Briefly, according to this theory, forgetting is due to cross interference between different experiences that we come across in life. Because of this when we attempt to recall one experience, memories of other experiences are also revived and create a confusion. As a result, we fail, either wholly or partly, to recall that experience successfully. If an experience is attempted to be recalled after a longer than a shorter interval then the load of the interfering experiences will be greater to make the attempt less successful. Hence, the loss of memory is not due to the passage of time, but due to the other experiences that fill the time.

Retroactive and Proactive Inhibition

We noted that time is an important element in forgetting. However , one significant finding in the area of remembering and forgetting has reduced the importance of time as such as a cause of forgetting It has been found that when a learning activity is followed by another activity forgetting is greater and it is less when the same activity is followed by rest. This applies to the memory for both activities—the activity which follows and the activity which is followed. Each one, in other words, affects the memory of the other. If the activity that follows influences the memory of the activity that precedes, the process is called retroactive inhibition ; if what precedes affects the memory of what follows, we have an instance of what is called proactive inhibition. The word inhibition means check, and check on memory is the same as forgetting. Retroaction means backward action and proaction means forward action. Thus, retroactive inhibition means forgetting caused by the backward action of one activity on the memory for the activity that precedes Proactive inhibition means forgetting caused by the forward action of an activity on the memory for the activity that follows. You will note that here your dependent variable is **inhibition**, or loss of memory, and the independent variable is retroaction in one case and proaction in the other case.

In an experiment on RI Retroactive Inhibition) or PI (Proactive Inhibition), you measure the dependent variable, namely, forgetting, by using the recall method alone or together with the saving method (p. 202). To administer the independent variable (p. 19), **retroaction**, you introduce in the general design for measuring forgetting another activity in between learning and test of retention. This activity will, therefore, be called interpolated activity ; you, thus, provide for a situation where retroaction—backward action—can be possible. For experiment on PI, you introduce an activity before the activity whose memory is to be tested—this makes the operation of proaction possible. The following is the standard paradigm for experiments on RI :

RETROACTIVE INHIBITION

Condition	Original Learning	Retention Interval	Retention Test Recall	Retention Test Relearning
Experimental	List A	Interpolated Activity	List A	List A
Control	List B	Relaxation	List B	List B

You have to specify the retention interval, say, 10 ms or 20 ms, as the case may be. This interval should be the same for both experimental and control conditions, otherwise difference in the forgetting between the two conditions may be due to the difference in the length of the retention interval—longer time may occasion greater forgetting. The control of this extraneous independent variable (p. 6) namely, time is very important. There is another extraneous variable which also need be controlled, namely, overlearning. The control condition, i.e., one in which retroaction is not allowed to operate, requires S to relax for the time after which retention test is to be taken. You cannot make S completely relax by letting him go to sleep. All that you can do is to prevent him from engaging in any activity. In order to achieve this, you keep him passively engaged, that is, keep him busy in a task that requires no effort on his part, e. g., naming colours shown successively on a rotating drum, looking at photographs, listening to humorous stories, or chatting with E. By this device you control overlearning. For if you, otherwise, leave him to himself during the retention interval, he may rehearse or recapitulate silently the items from the list that you made him learn and whose retention you propose to test. The forgetting then may be less in the control condition because of overlearning and not for want of retroaction. For the interpolated activity you may choose any task—learning, cancellation of letters, coding, working out sums, etc.

Following is the paradigm for an experiment on PI :

PROACTIVE INHIBITION

Condition	Engagement		Retention Interval	Retention Test	
				Recall	Relearning
Control	1. Relaxation	2. Learning List A	15ms.	List A	List A
Experimental	1. Learning List C	2. Learning List B	15ms.	List B	List B

The first engagement in the experimental condition may not necessarily involve learning ; it may be any activity. Relaxation in the case of PI occasions no problem. The retention interval—whatever its length—in the above design it has been shown 15 ms, must be the same in both conditions.

The discovery of RI and PI led to a revision of the theory of remembering and forgetting. The trace theory gave way to what has been named the interference theory. We forget not because the memory traces are lost, but because the responses pertinent to the task that we attempt to recall come into conflict with the responses from other tasks that precede or follow ; this causes failure in recall. The phenomenon is similar to what we come across while discussing the effect of similarity—intra-serial and inter-serial—in learning (p. 165) or transfer (p. 192). The same factor explained the advantage in spacing of practice ; the wrong responses weaken during rest interval and thereby fail to exert much interference with the occurrence of the correct responses (p. 168). The same principle applied also to the interpretation given to the serial position effect (p. 152). Interference, thus, comes out to be a potent factor affecting both immediate and delayed memory (p. 210).

RI is a demonstrable fact ; it has been consistently found that forgetting is greater in the experimental condition (p. 208). You can verify this for yourself. You will get better recall or more saving when the original learning is followed by relaxation. If your retention interval is long enough, the control condition may also show some forgetting. But the time gap being the same in both conditions, the difference in the forgetting will be due to RI. In fact, you report your result by calculating the net RI. The recall scores obtained in the two conditions, give you the percentage forgetting or inhibition, which is the counterpart of the recall score. The difference between the percentages for the two conditions provides you the net amount of RI. You treat your result in the same manner even when you use saving scores as the measure of the dependent variable.

Theory of RI

Two theories have been developed to account for RI : the Perseveration or Anti-consolidation Theory and the Transfer Theory. The first theory has been derived from the trace and the second from the interference theo y of memory (p. 208). Let us first take up the Perseveration Theory There is a fundamental law of mental inertia according to which any nervous activity persists for some time even after the stimulus which arouses the activity has been removed. Technically this has been described as the terminal lag of a neural process. We get an illustration in the occurrence of the so-called after-sensation. If you keep looking at, say, a green patch and then turn your eyes to a white surface, say the wall, you will see dim patch of green or of red on the wall, though there is no such real patch. This happens because of the persistence of the effect of stimulation of the visual receptors even when the stimulation actually ceases. By the way, the **terminal lag** is to be contrasted with what is described as the **initial lag** — a neural process takes some time to build up after the application of the stimulus. The reaction time experiments (p. 45) present an instance of the **initial lag**—the response does not follow immediately on the presentation of the stimulus ; there is a time gap.

The law of mental inertia has also been called the law of perseveration of mental energy. This fundamental principle, coupled with the assumption about memory trace, supplies the basis for the anti-consolidation theory. According to the theory, the after-effects of the activity of learning persist even when the learning trials have stopped. The persistence or perseveration of the after-effects or traces leads to their stabilisation or consolidation—they are fixed. Being stabilised, they are likely to be retained longer and to be remembered better. RI is due to the obstruction in the process of stabilisation or consolidation of the memory traces ; the interpolated activity that occurs after the original learning prevents the persistence of the traces and, thereby, also their consolidation. Hence the traces of the original learning are weak, which results in the poor recall or loss of the memory. This does not happen when the original learning is followed by relaxation which permits the persistence and thereby consolidation of the traces of the original learning.

The Transfer Theory is an extension of the interference theory of memory (p. 208). When S is trying to recall what he learned earlier, his responses are interfered with by the responses that he acquired while engaging in the interpolated task ; a competition of responses takes place that produces the failure in recall. Hence the poorer recall in the experimental condition.

A third theory has appeared on the scene, called the Two-Factor Theory of RI, which is a modification of the transfer theory. This theory does not consider interference to be the only factor in RI ; it is only partly due to the confusion between the responses from the interpolated task and those from the original task whose memory is tested. It is also due to the unlearning of the responses from the original task which is caused by the introduction of the interpolated task. When one is engaged in an interpolated task, there is intrusion (p. 165) of responses from the original task because of habit strength, but being inappropriate to the interpolated task, these responses are rejected or non-reinforced. As a result, these responses gradually become weaker and weaker till they altogether drop out to make room for the correct responses. The principle of extinction (p. 137) that we came across while discussing conditioning comes into play. The originally learned responses are thus unlearned. What happens is very similar to the process of first list unlearning that accounts for negative transfer (p. 192). When one is attempting to recall the original task after the interpolated activity has ceased, the failure in recall is due to unlearning also. RI, according to the Two-Factor Theory, is thus the net result of : (1) interference in recall of the first task responses by the second task responses, and (2) unlearning of the first task responses.

The following report of an experiment on RI will illustrate the points made in the above discussion.

RI as a Function of Similarity : Retroactive Inhibition (RI) means the forgetting of one experience due to the action of another experience that follows. For long, it was believed that time is the main factor to account for forgetting. The lapse of time between the occurrence of an experience and the attempt to remember or recall it causes the atrophy, wasting away, or weakening of its memory traces. Hence the longer the time interval, the greater the forgetting. But it was later discovered that we forget many things not because we have not attempted to revive them, but because of the other activities that take place during the intervening period. In such a case, though the time interval may be the same, the memory of what was learned is poor if the learning is followed by another activity rather than rest or a period of no activity. Experiments on RI demonstrate this fact.

RI has been explained in diverse ways. Perseveration Theory explains RI as due to the lack of stabilisation or anti-consolidation of the memory traces of the task whose memory is tested. This lack of stabilisation is brought about by the intervening task that prevents the persistence of the after-effects of the first task. The Theory of Interference, on the other hand, maintains that RI is due to confusion, response-competition, or interference caused by the intervening task when one is trying to recall the preceding task whose memory is being tested. A third theory, Two-Factor Theory, assumes RI to be due to two causes : (1) unlearning of the responses of the first task during the time one is engaged in the second task, and (2) competition from the second task responses that inhibits the responses of the first task.

The interference theory of forgetting has led to the hypothesis that the greater the similarity between the original and the interpolated task, the greater the forgetting of the original task. Greater similarity would cause greater confusion resulting in greater interference from the second task responses. An attempt was made to examine this crucial hypothesis.

Method

Subject : A male college graduate.

Apparatus and Material : Memory Drum. Four lists, each of 12 familiar four or five lettered words, headed by a three-lettered cue stimulus. One list of 10 nonsense syllables with a set of three circles as the cue stimulus.

Procedure : Data were obtained under three conditions ; control, Experimental I, and Experimental II, using the following design :

Condition	Original Learning	Retention Interval 10 ms.	Retention test	
			Recall	Relearning
Control	List A	Relaxation	List A	List A
Exp. I	List B	Learn List D	List B	List B
Exp. II	List C	Learn List E	List C	List C

In the control condition S relaxed for 10 ms during which E kept on talking to him in a leisurely manner, to prevent S from rehearsing word List A. In Exp. I, learning of list D, which consisted of nonsense syllables, was immediately introduced after the learning of word List B. Word List C in Exp. II was immediately followed by learning of word List E ; each word in the list rhymed with a word in list C; the rhyming words in the two lists differed only in their initial letters ; the remaining three or four letters were identical (Appendix)

All lists were learned by the serial anticipation method ; each item was exposed for 2 sec. in the original lists—lists A, B, & C, and for 4 sec. in the interpolated learning lists, lists D & E. In each case, 8 sec. inter-trial interval was used. A rest of 5 ms was allowed between conditions. The interpolated learning trials were continued for both lists D & E even after the criterion of one anticipation was reached in order to complete the retention interval of 10 ms. Retention was tested both by recall and relearning method.

Instruction:"This is a test of your learning capacity. I will show you a list of words, one after the other; you have to read each word alone. After this I will show you the first word in the list and you have to tell me from your memory the word that occurs next. Then the second word will be shown and you have to supply from your memory the word that comes next, and so on. Do you understand ?" The same instruction was used for learning List D also, only, S was told that the list contained a nonsense combination of three letters which he had to learn as he did the list of words.

Introspection : "The word list was easy to learn at first, but when I had to learn another word list after having learned one word list, I had much difficulty. I do not know why it so happened. Many words were very similar in the two lists and so when I tried to remember a word from this list, I was confused. I had much difficulty in learning the list of words that had no meaning. They were all quite new to me."

Result

Table 1

NO. TRIALS IN ORIGINAL LEARNING AND RELEARNING, ABSOLUTE AND PERCENT RECALL AND SAVING, AND PERCENT FORGETTING, NET RI AND DIFF. IN RI

Condition	No. Trials orig. Learn	Recall Abs.	Recall p.c.	Forgetting p.c.	Net RI	No. Trials Relearning	Saving Abs.	Saving p.c.	Loss p.c.	Net. RI
Control	5	9	75.00	25.00		1	4	80	20	
Exp. I	5	7	58.33	41.67	16.67	3	2	40	60	40.00
Exp. II	6	2	16.67	83.33	58.33	5	1	16.67	83.33	63.33
Diff. bet. Exp. I & Exp. II					41.66					23.33

Table 2

NO. INTRUSIONS IN INTERPOLATED LEARNING, RELEARNING AND RECALL, IN EXP. II

Trial	Intrusions Int. Learn.	Recall	Relearn
1	5	3	6
2	4		3
3	3		1
4	2		

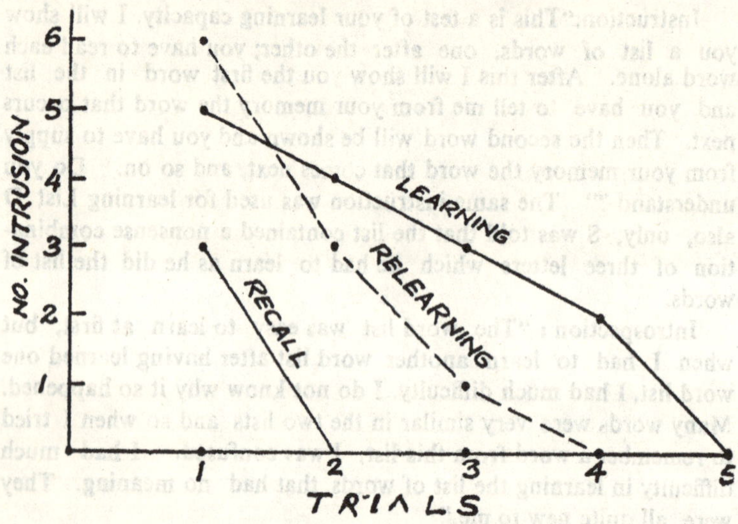

Fig. 1. No. Intrusions, Learning, and Relearning.

Discussion

The results show (Table 1) that forgetting has taken place to the extent of 25 p. c. and 20 p. c. as tested by the recall and saving methods, respectively, in the control condition ; forgetting was 41.67 p c. and 60 p. c. in Exp. I, where the two lists are dissimilar ; it was 83.33 p. c. and 83.33 p. c. in Exp II, when the two lists are very similar. Net RI was 16.67 p. c. and 40 p. c. in Exp. I; it was 58.33 p. c. and 66.33 p. c. in Exp. II. Net RI exceeded in Exp. II, as compared to Exp. I, by 41.66 p. c. and 23.33 p. c. Similarity has, thus, come out to be a factor in RI.

Our results support the Transfer Theory of RI. Greater RI in Exp. II is not due to the anti-consolidation of the memory traces of the original learning, as contended in the Perseveration Theory. The interpolated tasks were introduced immediately after original learning in both experimental conditions ; the effect of anti-consolidation of the memory traces should have been equal in both. But RI is much greater in Exp. II The greater RI is due to the greater confusion created by the interpolated learning at the time of recall or relearning of List C, the original list in this condition. The similarity between Lists C and E caused greater interference at the time of recall or relearning of List C. There are three intrusions from List E in the recall of list C, and 6, 3, and 1 in the first, second and third relearning trials, respectively, of List C (Table 2). The attempt to recall or relearn List C evoked responses not only from List C but also from List E which competed with the former, sometimes gaining the upper hand and sometimes producing the failure of recall.

We further note that the data lend a strong support to the Two-Factor Theory of RI. The loss of memory is due to both unlearning of the original list responses as well as the interference caused by the responses from the interpolated task. While S was learning the interpolated list, responses from the original list were also evoked, but were gradually dropped being incorrect ; the conditioning principle of extinction produced by non-reinforcement seemed to be applicable here. Using Hull's terminology, the strength of the excitatory potential at the back of these responses gradually diminished. As a result, an attempt made to recall these responses after the termination of the interpolated learning trials could not be very successful. This unlearning of the original list responses did not at all occur in the control condition and, presumably, not to a considerable extent also in Exp. I, since nonsense syllables being very different from words could be easily discriminated. Thus, while attempting to learn the interpolated list in Exp. I, the responses from the original list could not be as strongly evoked as to replace an item from the interpolated list. The point is supported by the occurrence of intrusions from the original list during the interpolated learning trials in Exp. II, but not in Exp. I (Appendix: Raw Data). In Exp. II, number of intrusions is 5 in the first, 4 in the second, 3 in the third, and 2 in the fourth trials of the interpolated list (Table 2 and Fig. 1). Had we used a list of dissimilar words, instead of nonsense syllables for interpolated learning in Exp. I, we could expect some evidence of intrusions in this case too, as the discrimination between the responses of the original and interpolated learning lists would not have been as clear cut.

We may conclude that similarity is a factor in RI and that similarity operates both by causing unlearning of what is learned and tested for retention, as well as by creating confusion between the responses appropriate to what is learned and those pertinent to what follows. Our results thus support the Two-Factor Theory of RI.

Appendix

CONTROL CONDITION

List A	Learning Trials					10 ms	Recall	Relearning
XTN	1	2	3	4	5			
Tree	√	√	√	√	√	R	√	√
Cloth	×	√	√	√	√	e	√	√
Dust	√	√	√	√	√	l	√	√
Blue	×	×	√	√	√	a	√	√
Grass	√	√	√	√	√	x	√	√
Cover	×	×	×	×	√	a	×	√
Work	×	×	√	√	√	t	×	√
Rain	×	×	×	×	√	i	×	√
Cake	×	√	√	√	√	o	√	√
Bird	×	×	×	√	√	n	√	√
Back	√	√	√	√	√		√	√
River	√	√	√	√	√		√	√
Total correct	5	7	9	10	12		9	12

Exp. I

List B	Learning Trials					List D	Interpolated Learning Trials								Recall	Relearning Trials		
RVS	1	2	3	4	5	OOO	1	2	3	4	5	6	7	8		1	2	3
Road	√	√	√	√	√	BEH	×	√	√	√	√	√	√	√	√	√	√	√
Mouth	√	√	√	√	√	FUM	√	√	√	√	√	√	√	√	√	√	√	√
Page	×	×	√	√	√	DIR	×	×	√	×	√	√	√	√	×	√	√	√
Soup	×	√	√	√	√	NUJ	×	×	×	×	×	×	√	√	×	×	√	√
Hour	√	√	√	√	√	BOP	×	×	×	×	×	×	×	√	√	√	√	√
Fruit	×	×	×	√	√	QEL	×	×	×	×	×	√	×	√	×	×	×	√
Lamp	×	×	×	×	√	PAB	√	×	√	√	√	√	√	√	√	√	√	√
Goat	×	×	×	√	√	MEK	×	√	√	√	√	√	√	√	√	√	√	√
Fish	×	×	√	√	√	HOF	√	√	√	√	√	√	√	√	√	√	√	√
Kite	√	√	√	√	√	XAJ	√	√	√	√	√	√	√	√	√	√	√	√
Rice	√	√	√	√	√	Total	4	5	7	6	7	8	8	10	7	8	9	10
Coal	×	×	√	√	√	correct												
Total correct	5	6	9	11	12													

Exp.-II

Learning Trials							Interpolated Learning Trials									
List C							List E									Recall
BKL	1	2	3	4	5	6	TOB	1	2	3	4	5	6	7	8	
Ring	×	√	√	√	√	√	Rock	Lock	×	×	×	Rock	Rock	Rock	Rock	King
House	√	√	√	√	√	√	Soon	×	Soon	Soon	Soon	Soon	Soon	Soon	Soon	House
Near	√	√	√	√	√	√	King	×	Ring	Crown	Ring	King	King	King	King	×
Plate	√	×	√	√	√	√	Dear	Near	×	Dear	Dear	Dear	Dear	Dear	Dear	×
Dove	×	×	×	×	√	√	Crown	Brown	Brown	×	×	Crown	Crown	Crown	Crown	Love
Lock	×	×	×	√	√	√	Mouse	House	House	Mouse	Mouse	Mouse	Mouse	Mouse	Mouse	×
Book	×	×	×	×	×	√	Cook	×	Book	Book	×	×	×	Cook	Cook	Book
Nest	×	√	×	×	√	√	Love	Love	Love	Love	Love	Love	Love	Love	Love	×
Seat	×	×	×	×	×	√	Heat	Heat	Heat	Heat	Heat	Heat	Heat	Heat	Heat	Heat
Brown	√	√	√	√	√	√	Luck	×	×	Duck	Duck	×	×	×	Luck	×
Moon	√	√	√	√	√	√	Rest	×	×	Rest	Rest	Rest	Rest	Rest	Rest	×
Duck	√	√	√	√	√	√	Slate	Plate	×	Plate	Slate	×	Slate	Slate	Slate	×
Total Correct	6	7	7	8	10	12	Total correct	2	3	6	7	9	10	11	12	2
							Total Intr.	5	4	3	2					3

Word List C	Relearning Trials				
BKL	1	2	3	4	5
Ring	King	King	Ring	Ring	Ring
House	House	House	House	House	House
Near	Dear	Near	Near	Near	Near
Plate	×	×	×	×	Plate
Dove	Dove	Dove	Dove	Dove	Dove
Lock	×	Rock	Lock	Lock	Lock
Book	Book	Book	Book	Book	Book
Nest	Nest	Nest	Nest	Nest	Nest
Seat	Heat	Seat	Seat	Seat	Seat
Brown	Crown	Crown	×	Brown	Brown
Moon	Soon	×	Moon	×	Moon
Duck	Luck	×	Luck	Duck	Duck
Total Correct	4	6	9	10	12
Total Intr.	6	3	1	0	0

You may complain that within the limited time at your disposal it may not be possible for you to take a control, besides two experimental conditions. You may drop the control condition and even the relearning test. Your purpose is to determine the effect of similarity and to this end the condition using similar tasks would be the experimental and that using dissimilar tasks would be the control condition ; similarity being your experimental variable. Only, you will not be able to ascertain the net amount of RI and thereby determine the difference in RI. But the fact that the occurrence of RI has been consistently supported, and that the retention interval you provided was the same for both conditions, would conclusively lead to the result that the difference in the amount of forgetting between the two conditions is due to the difference in RI. However, when you do not use the relaxation condition, say that you could not do this for want of time.

Other Problem : Temporal Location of the Interpolated Activity

There are several other problems in this area. One such problem was used to test the Perseveration Theory. The following hypothesis was formulated :

RI is a function of the temporal location of the interpolated activity.

We have noted (p. 211) that according to the Perseveration Theory, the introduction of the interpolated activity immediately after the original learning prevents the consolidation of the traces of the latter and hence its memory becomes weak. If this is the case, the provision of a gap between the original learning and the interpolated activity should diminish the amount of RI. To test this hypothesis you may take three conditions. Fix the retention interval, say 15 ms., and divide it into three equal parts. In the first condition introduce the interpolated task for 5 ms. immediately after the original learning and then allow rest for 10 ms. In the second condition introduce 5 ms. rest, then bring in the interpolated task for 5 ms. to be followed by rest for another 5 ms. In the third condition allow 10 ms. rest after the original learning and then introduce the interpolated task for 5 ms. The following design may be adopted :

Condi-tion	Original Learning	Retention Interval 15 Minutes			Retention Test	
		5ms.	5 ms.	5 ms.	Recall	Relearning
I	Task A	Task D	Rest	Rest	Task A	Task A
II	Task B	Rest	Task E	Rest	Task B	Task B
III	Task C	Rest	Rest	Task F	Task C	Task C

According to your hypothesis, you should expect maximum RI in Condition I because of the minimum opportunity for the consolidation of the memory traces, and minimum RI in Condition III, because of the longest duration of disengagement to allow for the perseveration of the traces and their consolidation thereby. To control the independent variable of similarity, you have to use the same kind of task for interpolated learning in all conditions. You have also to allow sufficient rest between conditions, say 10 ms.

Experiments on this problem have not yielded consistent results. Often one finds forgetting to be least in Condition I, which can be explained by the Two-Factor Theory (p. 212). The responses acquired in the first task will be incorrect for the interpolated task. Their non-inforcement during the interpolated task learning will make these responses weak, according to the principle of extinction. The amount of unlearning of the first task responses will, however, be the same in all conditions. Hence the extent of failure to recall the first task after the retention interval will be the same, on this account, for all conditions. But the principle of spontaneous recovery (p. 137) will favour Condition I, where the retention test is not introduced immediately after the interpolated task, as compared to Condition III, where the test is taken immediately after the interpolated task activity. As a result, some of the responses that were weakened during the interpolated task activity would be recovered in Condition I, thereby, reducing the amount of forgetting. Hence the unexpected finding.

Spontaneous Recovery and RI

One may plan an experiment to demonstrate the effect of spontaneous recovery on RI. You may use two conditions. In one condition the interpolated task is prolonged, after the original learning, to cover the entire duration of the retention interval In the other case, the first part of the duration is used for the interpolated task, the rest is given to relaxation. If spontaneous recovery takes place, forgetting will be less in the second condition. However, the result may not be conclusive, since by letting S prolong the interpolated task, you increase the strength or level of its learning ; a relation has been noted between RI and the level of learning. Experiment on RI as a function of learning strength is described below.

RI as a Function of the Level of Original Learning : We have noticed that similarity is the chief factor to account for most of the inhibitions caused both in learning (p. 164) as well as remembering and forgetting (p. 214). Similarity produces confusion so that competition between responses associated with the items of the same series—intra-serial similarity, or with the items belonging to different series—inter-serial similarity, inhibit the correct response ; this accounts for the delay or difficulty in learning as well as remembering. The confusion is due to want of discrimination or differentiation between the items within a single series or those belonging to different series. Practice sharpens the discrimination so that with the progress of the learning the differentiation becomes more and more effective in ruling out the incorrect responses. Hence, the greater the level or strength of the learning the sharper will be the discrimination both within or between the series. In case of RI, one may argue that the stronger the level of the original learning or that of the interpolated, the sharper the discrimination between the elements of the one and those of the other, and, accordingly, the less the confusion between the two ; the less will also be the inhibition in remembering. It is difficult to plan an experiment where one may use the level of the original learning as the independent variable for testing RI, since what is partially learned is more easily forgotten than what is completely learned or overlearned, and what is completely learned is more easily forgotten than what is overlearned (p. 205), irrespective of the learning being followed by rest or by some other activity One may, however, overcome this difficulty by planning two experiments on RI. In one experiment, the original list may be overlearned, to the same level, in both conditions, namely, that of relaxation and that of interpolated learning, and RI be calculated. In the other experiment original learning may be simple in both conditions, and RI also found. According to our hypothesis net RI will be larger in amount in the second experiment where original learning was of a lower level. In both experiments the level of the interpolated learning, the nature of the task, and that of the material, should be kept constant.

RI as a Function of the Level of Interpolated Learning : Manipulation of the level of interpolated learning is easier, since we are not testing the retention of the interpolated task. You may use three conditions in the experiment, differing in the strength of the interpolated learning : (1) partial learning, (2) simple learning and (3) overlearning. If the length of the learning list is kept constant in the three conditions, the condition of overlearning would require the longest time. To keep the retention interval constant, you have to let S relax after the criterion of partial or simple learning has been achieved. The factor of spontaneous recovery (p. 137) may then influence the recall scores in the condition of simple or partial learning. In spite of this, if you find the recall better in the overlearning condition your result will be conclusive. However, you may not be sure of the result since the advantage from spontaneous recovery may exceed the gain from the finer differentiation between the original and the interpolated learning lists. There is one way to overcome this difficulty. Use lists of different lengths in the three conditions, the shortest where overlearning is to be produced and the longest where the interpolated learning is aimed to be partial. Use in Condition 1 a list of, say, 9 nonsense syllables for simple learning. The time taken by S to reach the stage of simple learning may then be used as the length of the retention interval. Use a longer list, say, of 12 syllables in Condition 2, and a shorter list, say, of 7 syllables in Condition 3. The original learning should be of the same level in all three conditions.

Proactive Inhibition

The design of experiment on PI has already been given earlier (p. 210). Now that we have understood how experiments on RI can be planned, performing an experiment on PI should not be difficult ; no special description of an experiment on PI, need, therefore, be made. We may, however, describe an experiment dealing with the differential amount of forgetting in RI and PI.

In an experiment on PI, S relaxes in the control and engages in some activity in the experimental condition for the same time, before another task of equal difficulty is introduced in both conditions as the next step (p. 210). The retention of this task is tested after allowing for a retention interval of the same length in both conditions. We expect the recall to be poorer in the experimental condition. In experiments on RI, the engagement in the interpolated task itself provides the retention interval for the experimental condition, and the control condition makes for a relaxation for the same length of time, before the retention test is given. Following will be the design of the combined experiment on PI and RI:

Exp. I Proactive Inhibition

Condition I. Relaxation. Learn Task A. Rest Int. Test Task A
Condition II. Learn Task C. Learn Task B. Rest. Int. Test Task B

Exp. II. Retroactive Inhibition

Condition I. Learn Task A. Ralax. Test Task A
Condition II. Learn Task B. Learn Task C. Test Task B

Retention is tested after the same time interval in both experiments. In PI, we presume that retention is affected by the preceding, and in RI by the following, task engagement. According to the Two-Factor Theory of RI, we expect the failure in recall to be due to (1) unlearning of Task B responses because of the non-reinforcement of these responses during the engagement with Task C, and (2) interference from Task C at the time of recall of Task B. In case of PI, there is no unlearning of Task B to affect its recall after the retention interval. Whatever failure in recall might occur will be due to the interference from Task C responses. Even this interference will not be as great as in the RI situation. In the PI situation Task C responses will have been affected by unlearning during the period of Task B learning, on account of non-reinforcement. They will be less strong to interfere with the recall of Task B. As a net result, the inhibition or loss of memory is expected to be significantly greater in RI than in PI. In fact, it was the comparison between the results of PI and RI experiments that led to the formulation of the Two-Factor Theory of RI.

Reminiscence

We have seen that spaced practice has an advantage in learning over massed practice (p. 166). The advantage is noticeable not only when learning is measured by the number of trials taken to reach the criterion, but also by the number of correct responses from trial to trial. This latter is gain is described as reminiscence. Reminiscence is better recall a little while after practice than immediately after practice. In more general terms, reminiscence is improvement in performance after a period of no overt practice. As such, reminiscence is opposed to forgetting. For an experiment on reminiscence, let your S learn by the serial anticipation method (p. 149) two lists of, say, CCC trigrams, each having six to seven items. While S is learning the first list, stop after, say, 5 trials, and allow him 40 sec. rest, during which he is engaged in a very mild activity to prevent rehearsal. Then take the next trial. In the second list pass on to the 6th trial, without any break. Keep detailed record of S's responses from trial to trial. The following will be the design of the experiment :

Cond.	Learning Trial						
Exp.	1	2	3	4	5	Rest	6
Cont.	1	2	3	4	5	6	

Consider S's performance in the 6th trial. You will expect more correct responses in this trial in the Experimental condition. You may further notice that the items missed in the control and added to the correct responses in the experimental condition are those falling in the middle of the list.

Experiments on reminiscence have been done by using different lengths of interval for test of reminiscence. The least reminiscence effect has been found for an interval of 20 to 30 sec. There are several other interesting findings that have also been used for explaining the phenomenon of reminiscence. Reminiscence is better when the partial learning, after which reminiscence is tested, has been accomplished by massing rather than by spacing of practice. It is better for items in the middle of the list than those at the ends of the list. It is better when items of a list are exposed for a shorter period, say, 2 sec., than for a longer period, say, 4 sec. each. It increases with increase in intra-list similarity. Reminiscence effect does not occur in PA learning. You can use each one of the above findings as a problem and conduct an experiment to verify the finding.

The general theory of interference as a factor in remembering and forgetting applies also to the reminiscence effect. While attempting to learn a list, a network of associations is formed between a given item and the other items in the list. The number of such associations is larger for the middle items than for the end items. The adjacent associations are stronger than the remote associations. In the beginning stages, the incorrect associations compete with the correct associations ; this inhibits the occurrence of the correct responses in a given trial. When a rest interval is provided before you test the gain from a trial, the inhibitions built up during learning die out during the interval and the interference becomes less ; when the test is applied immediately, the diverse incorrect response tendencies exert much greater interference. Better reminiscence for the middle than the end items of a list is the result of the comparatively greater gain from rest to the middle items that are more affected by the inhibitory factors because of their more diverse associations (p. 153). Similarly, spacing of practice is more favourable to the weakening of the wrong response tendencies (p. 168); hence reminiscence effect is less marked in learning by spacing than massing of practice. More responses are correct from trial to trial when items of the list are exposed for longer than for shorter times (p. 162). A longer exposure time helps build stronger adjacent associations that cannot be easily inhibited by the remote and incorrect associations ; hence the larger number of correct responses. Rest after a trial, therefore, brings out greater advantage when shorter exposure is given to an item by weakening the remote incorrect associations. Inter-list similarity makes the learning more difficult because of the greater difficulty in item discrimination which favours the arousal of the wrong response tendencies (p. 164). Rest after practice weakens the incorrect response tendencies. Hence the more marked effect of reminiscence in the learning of a list of similar items. In PA learning we prevent the building up of several associations between items ; the learning is confined to the association between the elements of a pair. Hence the absence of reminiscence effect in PA learning.

Recommended Readings

Geldard, F. A., *Fundamentals of Psychology*, Chapter 12, Wiley, New York, 1962.

McGeoch, J. A., and Irion, A. L., *The Psychology of Learning*, Chapters 10, 12, Longmans Green, New York, 1952.

Munn. N. L., *Introduction to Psychology*, Chapter 11, Oxford and IBH, New Delhi, 1967.

Postman, L., and Egan, J. P., *Experimental Psychology*, Chapter 16, Harper, New York, 1949.

Underwood, B. J., *Experimental Psychology*, Chapter 13, Appleton, New York, 1966.

Woodworth, R. S. and Schlosberg, H., *Experimental Psychology*, Chapters 23, 25, Holt, New York, 1954.

Chapter XI

Reaction Time

Time is used in experiments as an important medium for measuring the dependent variable. We measure the time taken to complete a performance as in mirror tracing experiment (p. 139); we measure the frequency of a particular kind of response within a given time as in the number of shifts in the perception of an ambiguous figure or the number of fluctuations in the perception of a faint stimulus. In conditioning experiments or in experiments on remembering and forgetting, we measure the strength of a response in terms of latency, namely, the time gap between the stimulus and the response. Reaction time too, as a dependent variable, is a measure of the time between the onset of a stimulus and the occurrence of a response. The stimulus used is, generally, a simple one, like colour, sound, touch, taste, etc. The response most often used in reaction time experiments involves the pressing of a telegraphic key.

Different kinds of time measuring devices, called a chronoscope, have been used for measuring RT. We will describe the one most easily accessible, namely, the Vernier chronoscope (Appendix III). In this chronoscope there are two pendulums hanging from the two ends of a metal bar, and there are two keys, one for E and the other for S. Both pendulums are held at an angle so that when released they start swinging to and fro. The pressing of S's key releases one pendulum and that of E releases the other pendulum. S's pendulum is set a little higher than that of E, so that when S's pendulum oscillates at the rate of 77 per minute or .78 second per oscillation, E's pendulum oscillates at the rate of 75 per minute, or .80 second per oscillation. There is thus a difference of .02 sec. per oscillation between the two pendulums. E's key forms an electric circuit with the stimulus, light or sound, so that the moment E presses his key, the stimulus is automatically presented and the pendulum starts oscillating. S is instructed to press his key the moment he observes the stimulus. As S presses his key, his pendulum too starts oscillating. The faster oscillation of S's pendulum lets it catch up after a certain number of oscillations with E's pendulum ; the strings by which the two pendulums are hanging become parallel. E counts the number of oscillations of S's pendulum after which it catches up with E's pendulum. This number multiplied by .02 sec. gives the reaction time. Since the resulting value is the fraction of a second, it is converted into ms (millisecond), which is one-thousandth of a second. Supposing the number of oscillations, in a trial, to catch up with E's pendulum is 8, RT will be 160 ms. This constant multiplier, namely, .02 sec. is called Vernier constant ; it was determined by a mathematician Vernier by name. Since the chronoscope uses the Vernier system for calculating time, it is called Vernier Chronoscope.

The RT is a measure of the time taken by a sequence of processes, namely, those involving the receptor organ, the set of nerves connecting with the sensory centre, the set of nerves connecting the motor centre with the effector, and, finally, the effector organ. Each one takes its own time which add together to give us the measured RT.

Reaction time has been classified as simple, complex, and associative. In simple RT, S is presented with the same stimulus and has to make the same response every time. The mean RT in a certain set of trials provides an estimate of S's RT. When using Vernier Chronoscope, calculate the mean RT by first finding the mean oscillations and then multiplying it by .02 sec. The result should be stated in milliseconds.

In every trial, E first gives a ready signal and then after a pause of 2 sec. presents the stimulus. Since the ready signal puts S in a state of readiness to respond, sometimes he may respond without actually observing the stimulus; his response, thus, becomes premature, and, as a result his RT will be shorter than what it could be had he responded after observing the stimulus. In order to prevent this, one uses catch trials in which the stimulus does not follow the ready signal. If S has a tendency to react even without noticing the stimulus, he will do so also in the catch trial.

S may, then, be specially instructed to respond only when he has noticed the stimulus.

We will see that the length of fore-period, i.e., the time between the ready signal and the presentation of the stimulus also influences the length of RT. An optimal fore-period has been ascertained which ranges from 1 to 2 sec. The interval between the ready signal and the presentation of the stimulus should, therefore, be about 2 sec. which may be determined by mental counting (p. 148). However, S may form a temporal set, after a few beginning trials, i.e., be prepared to respond to the 2 sec. interval and thus press the key without noticing the stimulus. Therefore, off and on, fore-periods of shorter, say 1 sec., and longer, say, 3 sec. duration should also be given. This will prevent the formation of the set.

Simple Reaction Time

In experiments on simple reaction time one may have some such problems as : Simple RT is a function of the type or nature of stimulus, of the strength or intensity of the stimulus, of the length of the fore-period, of the sensory or motor set experimentally induced, of practice, etc. Following is a brief description of some such problems :

1. **Simple RT as a Function of the Type of Stimulus** : Here we are concerned with the difference in RT as related to the different sense organs involved. Experiments using the different sense modalities have shown that the length of RT varies in the order : visual, auditory, touch, taste, smell, the maximum being for visual which has been found to be in the neighbourhood of 200 ms. Individuals, however, differ in the mean length of RT as well as in the dispersion of RT's, as measured by the standard deviation. Since RT is influenced by both practice and fatigue, when comparing the RT for two or more stimuli, it is necessary to use the counter-balancing design (p. 9).

2. **RT as a Function of the Intensity or Strength of the Stimulus** : One has to vary stimulus intensity within the same sense modality, e. g., a faint light and a bright light, a dull sound and a shrill sound, etc. RT will be shorter for the more intense stimulus.

3. **RT as a Function of the Receptor or Affector Preparedness, or, Determination of the Difference between Sensory RT and**

Muscular RT : The ready signal induces of state of readiness both in the receptor organ and the muscle system involved. Special emphasis may, however, be laid on the stimulus or on the motor response while giving the instruction. S may be instructed : " You have to press this key when you see a red light. Be very attentive to the light and press only when you have seen the light. Keep your eyes focussed on the light." The RT will then be treated as sensory. For muscular RT, S may be instructed : "React as quickly as you possibly can. Be always ready to press the key as you notice the light. Be attentive to the pressing of the key." Muscular RT has been reported to be shorter than sensory RT. But since check trials have to be given, the emphasis on the response may lead to premature response ; E's warning to S to avoid this, may tend him to give a balanced emphasis to sensory and motor reactions. If this happens, the difference will be very much minimised.

4. **RT as a Function of Practice :** It has been found that RT decreases with practice upto a certain limit. To ascertain this, one may compare the mean for the first half with that for the second half of a number of trials, or that for the first few and the last few trials. A graphic presentation of RT's for the succession of trials will also bring to light the gradual decrease in RT as a result of practice.

5. **RT as an Indirect Measure of Muscular Fatigue :** It has been noticed that physical fatigue impairs all-round performance. To examine this, measure S's RT for, say, five trials, and then engage him in a continuous motor activity for some time like pulling weight (p. 16) or pressing the dynamometer. Measure S's RT again for another set of five trials. The design to be used is the so-called fore-test-after-test design (p. 11). If the after-test RT is found to be longer than fore-test RT, you come to the conclusion that muscular fatigue has affected S's RT.

6. **RT as a Function of the Length of Fore-Period :** We have mentioned that the fore-period of 1 to 2 sec. is the optimal one; it gives a shorter RT than does a longer or a shorter fore-period. A shorter fore-period does not fully prepare S to react; and a long fore-period lets the state of preparedness fad^ out. To verify this contention, use fore-periods of different lengths, say, 5 sec., 1 sec , 2 sec , 4 sec., and 8 sec. Take, say, twenty trials for each length. Use the counter-balancing design a b c d d c b a. Compute the mean RT for each fore-period separately and also

find the respective standard deviations. Compare the mean values and the variabilities. With a slight modification, you can answer another problem too, namely, the effect of temporal set on RT. Take, say 20 trials using 2 sec. as the fore-period. Take another 20 trials using the same fore-period but interspersed randomly with additional trials. The fore-periods in these trials will vary, say 1, 4, 6 and 8 sec. Take 5 trials for each fore-period, thus, totalling 20 additional trials. In the first case, S is fully prepared to receive the stimulus when the specific time interval has passed after the ready signal; the procedure automatically induces the temporal set in S. When the fore-period changes from trial to trial, the formation of a constant time-set would interfere with the appropriate response set, i. e., the state of readiness to respond. This has to alter from trial to trial according to the length of the fore-period. No time-set will, therefore, be induced in this condition. Use check trials in Condition I, to prevent S from responding to the time interval (p. 232). The formation of the temporal set in the first condition, where the fore-period remains the same throughout, will facilitate the response. As a result, the mean RT for the fore-period of two sec. coming in regular succession will be shorter than the mean RT for the same fore-period interspersed in a random order with fore-periods of other lengths.

7. **R. T. as a Function of Incentive or Reward :** We will note later that knowledge of result provides an incentive to improvement in performance. One may find out the effect of knowledge of result on S's RT. In one condition S's RTs from trial to trial are not disclosed to him; in the other condition S is every time told his RT in the trial. One may use also verbal reward or punishment as the motivating factor. E may praise S for his performance, expressing a pleasant surprise at the speed of S's reaction; he may use persuasions and suggestions that S could react more quickly, showing gestures appreciative of S's speed of response, uttering from time to time words like 'good', 'very good', and so on. In a preceding condition, E remains indifferent to S's performance; keeps on a purely mechanical attitude throughout. To note the effect of verbal punishment, E makes disparaging remarks at S's performance; shows irritation at the tardiness of S's responses ; tells S that he is very slow and sluggish, and so on. In an individual experiment you cannot determine the effect of both positive and negative incentives in the same experiment; you

have to choose between the two. In either case you have to use a control condition of no reward, that is, absence of experimentally heightened or lowered motivation; the control condition should always be used before the experimental condition, to avoid carry-over from the experimental to the control condition. Other details about the procedure have to be the same as described later in the chapter dealing with experiments on motivation.

8. **Reaction Time as a Function of Eye Dominance** : Individuals may differ in the relative sensitivity of the two eyes. In some persons the left eye, in others the right eye, may be dominant. To determine the effect of eye dominance on RT, measure S's RT with one eye closed. In one set of trials, let his left eye, and in other set of trials let his right eye, be open. Compare the mean RT's found for the two conditions. The RT for the dominant eye will be shorter. You may also take a third set of trials with both eyes open. In this case RT is expected to be still shorter. The reason is that with both eyes functioning, the strength of the stimulus is enhanced by the summation of the individual effects of the stimulation of each eye. The increase in the strength of the stimulation results in reducing the length of the RT (p. 232). The problem may be stated as 'the effect of summation of retinal stimulation on the length of reaction time.'

In all the experiments that we have described above, one has to be careful about using check trials off and on, and also the counterbalancing design wherever possible.

Complex Reaction Time

Complex RT has also been classified as (1) disjunctive reaction time and (2) choice reaction time. But it is more desirable to use the two terms interchangeably. In both cases, S expects, from among more than one, either this or that stimulus (disjunctive) to appear on a particular occasion and has, accordingly, to choose (choice) this or that response from among more than one possible responses. Another distinction has been drawn between (1) *b* reaction and (2) *c* reaction ; simple RT is designated as *a* reaction ; *b* reaction involves choosing one key when one stimulus is on and another key when another stimulus is on. Using the Vernier chronoscope (p. 231), you may have a red and a blue light and S may be instructed to press the right key when, say, the red light is on, and to press on left key when the blue light is on. In *c* reaction time, S is instructed to press when, say, the red light is on and not to press when the blue light is on. It is found that *b* reaction time is longer than *c* reaction time. This can be verified by conducting an experiment.

In a modified form of the *b* reaction time, S was presented with different lights, say red and blue, simultaneously, but their relative position changed in a random order from trial to trial. S was asked to press the right key when red appeared to the right of blue, and press the left key when red appeared to the left of blue. In this situation, RT was lengthened. This happened because of the similarity between trials, since both lights appeared in all trials ; the difference was only in their respective positions ; the stimuli were the same. The lengthening of RT was due to the principle of stimulus generalisation which governs the tendency to make the same response to similar stimuli. This tendency interfered with the choice of the appropriate key, and resulted in the increase in RT. The problem dealt with may be stated as the effect of stimulus similarity on RT. You may also use for this purpose visual stimuli having similar hues but differing in saturation, e. g., scarlet and pink. S may be asked to press the right key when, say, scarlet is on and to press the left key when pink is on. As a control, you may use, in another condition, scarlet and green, and compare the RT to scarlet in two conditions.

An experiment on complex RT is reported in Chapter III (pp. 45-50). Complex RT was originally introduced in order to measure the time taken in the mental processes of discrimination and choice. Since complex RT is always longer than simple RT, it was presumed that the difference was due to the time taken in these complex processes. But since there are several other intervening variables, it is now believed that the difference does not give precisely the time taken in the mental operations of discrimination and choice. A measure of complex RT is valuable, however, because in actual life situations we are confronted with a complexity of stimuli and are called upon to choose among a variety of responses the one that is appropriate to each stimulus. From the practical point of view, it is, thus, more useful to know one's complex rather than simple RT.

RT as a Function of the Aesthetic Value of a Stimulus

It has been noted that one reacts more quickly to the stimulus one likes or prefers. An agreeable stimulus evokes a positive reaction—the approaoh reaction ; a disagreeable stimulus evokes a negative, avoidance, reaction. The facilitative or the inhibitive effect of the two modes of reaction influences the reaction time. To examine this hypothesis, E first conducts an experiment, say, on colour preference (Chap.12), using a set of, say, five colours. The result of the experiment enables E to determine S's most preferred and his least preferred colours. E then uses light stimuli of the two colours. In 50 per cent of the trials, the preferred colour is located on the right, and in the remaining 50 per cent of trials on the left. S is required to press the key which is on the same side as a particular light stimulus, i. e., in 50 per cent of trials S presses the right key for the most preferred and the left key for the least preferred stimulus, and in the remaining 50 per cent, he presses the left key for the most and the right for the least preferred stimulus. The two lights are presented in random order from trial to trial. The Mean RT for the two light stimuli are then compared.

RT as a Function of S-R Compatibility

S-R compatibility occurs when the key to be pressed on the presentation of a stimulus is on the same side as the stimulus. Thus, for example, a red light appears on the right and a green on the left. S has to press the right key on the presentation of the red light and the left key on the presentation of the green light. If S is required to press the right key when the green light appears and the left key when the red light appears, we have an instance of S-R incompatibility; the spatial relation between the stimulus and response is different from what usually happens. It has been noted that RT is shorter in the S-R compatibility condition. You can verify this by conducting an experiment.

Associative Reaction Time

The associative reaction time (ART) is a measure of the speed of verbal response to a verbal stimulus. E utters a word, called the Stimulus Word (SW) and S has to utter another word, called the Response Word (RW) that *first comes to his mind*. The time between the stimulus and response gives the association RT. It is so called because S responds on the basis of his associations to the SW. For example, to the word Book, he has several associations like page, paper, print, binding, cover, teacher, school, story, poem, and so on. At a particular moment any one of these associations may be the first to be revived by the SW Book, say, school. The device used for measuring association RT is called the Word Association Test (WAT). The test has been classified as (1) Free and (2) Controlled. In free association test, S gives out any word that first comes to his mind. In the controlled association test a restriction is put on the nature of the association; S is required to give a word that bears a specific relation to the stimulus word. For example, S may be required to respond by giving the opposite of the SW, e.g. high for low, rich for poor, or, a word that stands for a part of the object signified by the SW, e. g., leave for tree, or a word for the while object of which the SW is a part, e. g. forest for tree, army for soldier. There may be still other relation suggested to S like that of coordinates, e. g., milk and bread, or of subordinates and superordinates, e. g., red and colour, furniture and table. The RT for free association is likely to be longer than that for controlled association. You may verify this hypothesis.

It will be noted that in controlled association, the more specific association leads to the formation of a preparatory set in S so that the arousal of the association consistent with the set is facilitated, while other associations are inhibited. Using the controlled association test, one may examine the influence of the set on association RT. S may be given a list of stimulus words. For the first, say, ten words of the list he may be instructed to give opposites, for the next ten, parts, followed by another 10 requiring wholes, and still other calling for synonyms. The mean RT's for each set of 10 words may then be separately computed. In another condition, S may be presented with another list of equally familiar words. But the instruction for the type of association called for changes in a random order from word to word. Mean association RT may then be separately calculated for the words demanding the same kind of relationship. Unlike the first condition, the abrupt change in the instruction from word to word would interfere with the formation of a response set in S which would be manifested in the longer association RT in the second condition. The data may also throw a light on the comparative ease in getting one kind of association rather than another.

The term 'free-association' is used in the context of WAT in a different sense from what Freud meant by the term 'free-association' as a method of psychoanalysis. Free-association as word association test is not strictly free, since here a restriction is imposed upon S; he is required to respond by a word. In the free-association method, there in no restriction. The method encourages the patient to communicate any mental content—a word, a sentence, an incident, a dream, that occurs to him, without any reservation. As a starting point, the analyst selects some element either from the narration, by the patient, of his condition, or of a previous night's dream. He then asks the patient to dwell his thought on that element and give out whatever is suggested to him at the moment. The patient has, further, to think of what he had mentioned, or of some specific content it includes, and then give out what comes to his mind. In this way the analyst pursues a chain of associations, one association leading to another. As a result of his labour, the analyst is rewarded by some association that has a direct relationship to the cause of the patient's trouble—he is able to fish out some deeply repressed mental contents from the patient's unconscious that could not be otherwise easily recovered.

Clinical Use of the Word Association Test

It may be worthwhile to know how the Word Association Test, like the Free-Association Method, has been used for helping mental patients. A list of stimulus words is prepared ; 50 per cent of these are related to sex, social crimes, unpleasant family relationship, experiences of pain, suffering, humiliation, punishment, etc. The presentation of these words ordinarily arouses mental conflict, feelings of guilt, shame, anxiety, failure and frustration. One may have, for example, such words as masturbation, adultery, theft, murder, divorce, disease, death, imprisonment, etc. The remaining 50 per cent are neutral words like chair, water, building, garden, etc. The two kinds of words are mixed up in a random fashion in the total list. You may consult two well-known lists, one prepared by Kent and Rosenoff, and the other by Jung. For taking the test, E utters a word and simultaneously starts a stop watch. S has to utter a word, other than the word given by E, that *first comes to his mind*. E presses the stop watch immediately as S gives the response word. After the test has been completed, E takes S's reproduction by repeating the entire procedure once again, in order to find out whether S gives the same response word and takes about the same time to respond. Every time E gives the SW, he also observes S's objective behaviour which he records. E prepares, in advance, a record sheet having a set of columns headed by (1) SW, (2) RW, (3) RT, (4) Reproduction—subdivied into (*i*) RW and (*ii*) RT, (5) Remark, which includes record of objective observation of S's behaviour. E has to be specially alert to S's repeating the SW, putting a question after it is given, asking E to repeat SW, showing marks of uneasiness like getting fidgety in his seat, nail biting, hair scratching, heaving a sigh, sweating or smiling, making any critical remark about the test or showing any other unusual behaviour. The recorded results are then used for discovering hidden complexes. A complex is a system of ideas, emotions, and tendencies 'centering on an element of strain, failure, dissatisfaction, or sense of guilt'. These complexes are hidden in the unconscious and cannot, therefore, be revealed by directly questioning the patient even if he is fully cooperative. The WAT, like the free-association test, enables one to get a clue about the complex. This is made possible by looking at the details of the WAT data. A careful inspection of the data brings out the complex indicators. The signs of a complex indicator, briefly stated, are length of the RT as compared to S's mean RT, repetition of the SW, asking E to repeat, questioning E before giving the RW, making some remark after giving it, failure to reproduce the RW first given, difference in the RT between the original and the reproduction series, unusualness of RW, e. g., death, or poison to water, expression of excitement, anxiety, or some other unusual behaviour manifested while responding or after responding. The stimulus words accompanied by these unusual features are, thus, identified as complex indicators or key words. The clinician then uses these key words and presents them to S for further elaboration. He may use the free-association method when he asks S to dwell on a key word and narrate his mental contents. These are further used for eliciting other associations, and so on. As a result of his endeavour, the clinician gets at some contents which throw a direct light on the factors that account for the patient's conditions. It may be worthwhile to try the WAT and attempt at the interpretation of your results.

Recommended Readings

Postman, L. and Egan, J. P., *Experimental Psychology*, Chapter 12, Harper, New York, 1949.

Underwood, B. J., *Experimental Psychology*, Chapter 7, Appleton, New York, 1966.

Woodworth, R. S. and Schlosberg, H., *Experimental Psychology*, Chapters 2, 3, Holt, New York, 1954.

54-57/1972 [16]

Chapter XII

Feeling and Emotion

Feeling is a state of pleasantness or unpleasantness accompanying any mental process. In addition, one may conceive also of a netural feeling marked by the absence of either pleasantness or unpleasantness. Emotions are disturbed bodily conditions accompanied by a great variety of conscious states, like anger, fear, disgust, excitement, happiness, sorrow, etc. The aesthetic properties of objects and situations, the fact of their being agreeable or disagreeable, are matters of feeling values. When an object is judged as beautiful or ugly by a person, as having a positive or a negative appeal to him, he is actually expressing his feelings in regard to that object.

The Paired Comparison Method

Experiments on feeling values of stimuli can be done by using a very simple method. The stimulus used may be of any kind, for example, colours, proper names, objects like varieties of fruits, vegetables, geometrical forms, nationalities, etc. Suppose you try to determine your S's preference for a certain number of green fruits, say, orange, apple, banana, guava, plum and peaches. The problem is to find out which fruit your S likes best, which next best, and so on. You have to prepare six 2″ × 3″ cards and write in bold letters, the name of a fruit on a particular card. For the purpose of comparison, present a pair of any two cards to the subject. Since there will be several such pairs, you have first to determine, by using the formula : $\frac{n(n-1)}{2}$, the total number of pairs; here n stands for the total number of stimuli, which in this case is 6. With six stimuli, the number of pairs will be 15. There will, thus, be fifteen judgments that S has to make. Prepare in advance a table defining the order in which the different pairs are to be presented. One such table is given below :

		A	B	C	D	E	F
A	Orange	×	15	10	6	3	1
B	Guava	1	×	14	9	5	2
C	Banana	6	2	×	13	8	4
D	Apple	10	7	3	×	12	7
E	Plum	13	11	8	4	×	11
F	Peaches	15	14	12	9	5	×

The six rows and six columns stand for the six fruits. Each one of the two sets of diagonal cells, the upper right and the lower left ones, formed by the columns and rows, represents a pair. The numbers within the cells give the order in which the pairs are to be presented to S. Thus, for the cells in the lower left half of the table, the order will be AB, BC, CD, and so on. For the cells in the upper right half, the order will be FA, FB, EA, FC, and so on. Cell No. 15, the bottom left cell formed by A (Orange) and F (Peaches), is the last pair to be shown to S in one set of comparisons. The corresponding pair in the second set of comparisons is represented by cell No. 1, the top right cell, and it is the first pair to be presented in this set. The difference will be in respect of the relative position of the two stimuli. In cell No. 15, A (Orange) will be placed to the right of F (Peaches) ; in Cell No. 1, F (Peaches) will be held on the right of A (Orange). You will, thus, note that the cells in the upper right half repeat the same pairing of stimuli, with the difference in the relative position of the members of a pair. This repetition is done to control space Error (p. 65). You can take another cell, No. 11, of the lower left. It represents a presentation in which B (Guava) will be on the right and E (Plum) will be to be its left ; No. 5 of the upper right represents the same pair but this time Plum will be on the right and Guava to its left. You have to use the lower left pairs for the first set of data and, after this is completed, you move on to the upper right pairs.

Having prepared the table for the presentation of the pairs, introduce the respective pairs to S with the instruction : "You may have a liking for fruits ; but you may not like all of them equally ; some you like more, some less. I would present two cards to you, one card bearing the name of one fruit and the other that of another fruit. You have to tell me which one of the two you like more" Present each pair for 2 sec. timed by mental counting.

Write the symbol for the fruit preferred by S in each presentation in the cells of another table similar to that used for presentation of the pairs. Following record will illustrate the point :—

	A Orange	B Guava	C Banana	D Apple	E Plum	F Peaches	F	P
A Orange	×	A	A	A	A	A	5	1.0
B Guava	A	×	C	D	E	F	0	0.0
C Banana	A	C	×	D	C	F	2	0.4
D Apple	A	D	D	×	D	F	3	0.6
E Plum	A	E	E	D	×	F	1	0.2
F Peaches	A	F	F	F	F	×	4	0.8
Frequency	5	0	1	3	2	4	15	3.0
Proportion	1.0	0·0	0.2	0.6	0.4	0.8	3.0	

The treatment of data involves counting the total number of preferences for the different stimuli, separately for each half of the table. You will thus get two sets of total frequencies, one, shown in the above table, at the bottom and the other at the extreme right. The totals are then converted into proportions by dividing each total by n-1, i. e., the number of times a particular stimulus has been compared with the other stimuli. For our example, n-1 will be 5. The two sets of proportions tell you about the consistency of S's judgments. We note that so far as the most and least preferred fruits are concerned, S's judgment remains the same on repetition, and with the altered position of the members of a pair. His most liked fruit is orange and his least liked fruit is guava. The order of S's preference is represented by the histograms on the following page.

The method of Paired Comparison can be used also for determining one's likes and dislikes towards different issues or social groups. You may find your S's preference for different languages, different nationalities, different religions, different political parties, and so on. When so used, it becomes a measure of S's attitude towards the object or the issue. One may use a scale for measuring social attitude, say towards different nationalities, and then also conduct an experiment using the method of paired comparison. One may then note an agreement between the results of the two. If the results tally, i. e., S has a strongly favourable attitude towards the object or issue that he also prefers most, and unfavourable attitude towards what he prefers least, you get an evidence of the validity of your result. You will conclude that most likely your results show your S's real preferences.

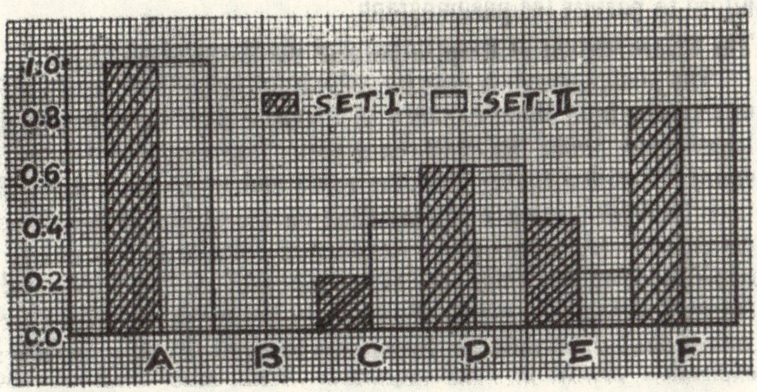

Expressions of Emotion

Emotion is a condition of all round psychophysical disturbance accompanied by a particular variety of conscious state described as fear, anger, disgust, etc. The conscious state in emotion, obviously, cannot be observed by the experimenter. He has to depend upon S's verbal report of the emotional state. Facial expressions and postural changes during the state of emotion have been used as indicators of the kind of emotional state S is experiencing. There is, however, a lot of overlapping between the expressions of the different emotional states, e. g., excitement and anger, and an attempt to classify emotions on the basis of facial expressions has, accordingly, met with failure.

Besides the overt facial expressions and postural changes, there are other bodily changes also that accompany the emotional experience. These cannot be observed without the help of an artificial device. They consist of changes in blood pressure, in the volume of blood supply to the body, in pulse rate, the action of the heart, respiration, etc. Investigations have been made of the relationship between a kind of emotional experience and the covert bodily changes. For the measurement of these bodily changes special instruments have been used, such as the sphygmomanometer for measuring blood pressure, the plythysmograph for measuring change in the volume of blood, the sphygmograph for measuring pulse rate, the electro-cardiograph for measuring changes in the action of the heart, and the pneumograph for measuring change in breathing. We will confine ourselves to the description and use of the last one only, since most psychological laboratories can easily afford to possess the pneumograph.

The Measurement of Respiration and the Respiration Curve

The pneumograph is used for measuring respiration. It consists of a rubber hose about one inch in diameter and about a foot in length held about the chest by a belt. One end of the hose is connected with a rubber tube, the other end of which is attached to a tambour having a marker fixed on the surface of the rubber diaphgram (Appendix III). Respiration consists of two phases: inspiration or breathing in, and expiration or breathing out. Inspiration brings in supply of oxygen to the lungs and expiration pushes out carbon dioxide. Inspiration expands the chest muscles; expiration relaxes it. The expansion of the chest stretches the pneumograph; its volume increases and the air that fills the pneumograph and the rubber tube is sucked in; the diaphgram of the tambour is deflated; the marker attached to the tambour is lowered. The relaxation of the chest restores the pneumograph to its original condition; the air is pushed out and inflates the diaphgram; the marker is raised. The marker is touching a rotating drum and traces a curve on its surface which is very regular under normal condition, as shown below:

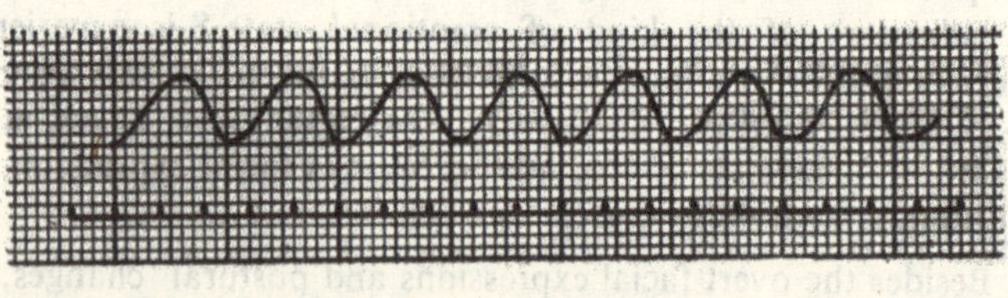

In the above curve the distance from the base of one curve to that of the next is a measure of time and thus gives the index of the rate of breathing. The height of the curve indicates the depth or shallowness of breathing. The visible marks of change in breathing are, thus, the breathing being quick or slow, deep or shallow, and regular or irregular. The speed or rate of breathing is measured by the number of cycles—inspiration and expiration, within a given time, say, one minute. The depth of breathing is measured by the height of the perpendicular dropped from the crest of a wave to its base. Besides these simpler measures, another and a little difficult method involves the calculation of what is called IE ratio or I fraction. The IE ratio is inspiration time divided by expiration time, as shown below :—

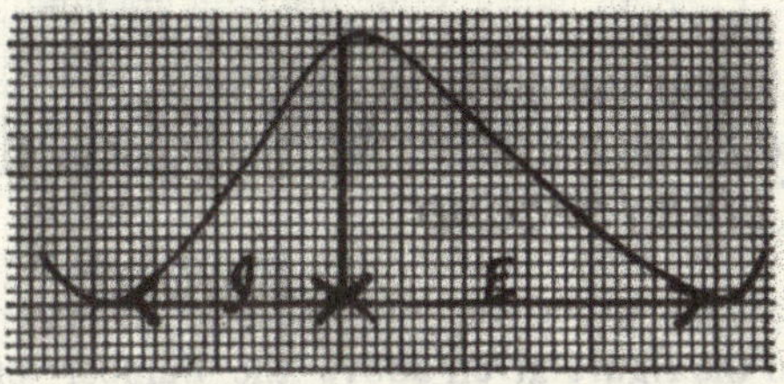

The I fraction is the inspiration time divided by the time taken in both inspiration and expiration. The I fraction is a more convenient measure.

Experiments on Changes in Respiration

1. **Effect of the Arousal of an Emotion on Respiration**: Breathing undergoes visible changes when any emotion is strongly aroused. But it is difficult to arouse any strong emotion experimentally so that one may observe the types of changes that take place, or notice the difference in breathing in different emotional states. One may make an indirect approach to the problem by asking S to narrate some of his very early emotional experiences, like fear, shame, guilt feeling, etc. ; it is presumed that while one is narrating any event in his life that has made a strong impression on him, he will get a revival of the mental conditions that characterised him when that event occurred. E judges each narration for its emotional character and assigns different symbols according to the nature of the emotions. He makes a record of these symbols in the order in which the experiences are narrated by S. While E is narrating the experiences, a pneumographic record of his breathing is also made. E then selects 10 cycles of breathing accompanying each narration and determines the time per cycle on the basis of the time line which is traced below the breathing curve (p. 107). The respiration curves illustrating the changes in breathing when a particular emotion is aroused are shown on the following page.

It will be apparent that more easily measurable changes in respiration are : (1) change in form, i. e., from regular to irregular, (2) change in depth, i. e. breathing becoming shallow or deep as compared to the neutral state, and (3) change in the rate of breathing, that is, breathing becoming more or less rapid as measured by the number of cycles per minute. Measures of IE ratio and I fraction are difficult to apply when the breathing is disturbed and irregular as generally happens in emotional condition.

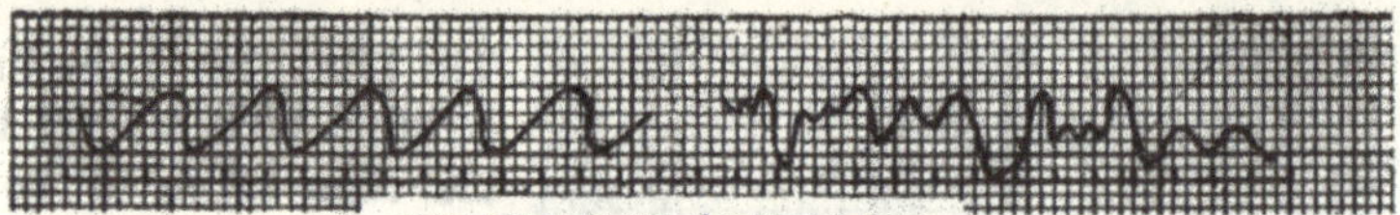

TIME LINE / SECOND

NEUTRAL EMOTIONAL

One may easily find out in the figure given above the number of cycles during the period of breathing in neutral condition and that in emotional condition and then calculate the rate of breathing per minute. One may measure the heights of the curves in the two conditions and calculate the average height in mm. He may conclude on the basis of these facts that respiration was irregular, it alternated in depth and shallowness, it was more rapid—its rate increased, when S was in an emotional state.

2. **Respiration and the Affective State of the Organism :** It has been found that the state of pleasantness or unpleasantness influences the rate of breathing ; breathing has been generally noted to be more rapid in these states, as compared to the condition when S's feeling is neutral. For inducing pleasant feeling E may expose S's nostrils to a fragrant odour, say, the scent of a rose, while S is harnessed to the pneumograph. For inducing unpleasant feeling an offensive odour, say, chlorine, may be used. Since you require only 10 to 15 cycles within each of the three, namely, neutral, pleasantness, unpleasantness conditions, the entire record may be obtained without changing the level at which the tambour is fixed ; the kymograph should be adjusted to move at a very slow speed. With a slow moving drum it is possible to obtain 45 to 50 cycles in one complete rotation. Changing the level at which the marker is touching the smoked paper might affect the shape of the curve and the recorded change in breathing may then be due not only to the change in the feeling state. The cycles of

breathing under each condition are to be marked as such, after the drum has been stopped. The results are to be discussed both qualitatively and quantitatively. The qualitative discussion will be based on the inspection of the changes in the graph, like rate of breathing—rapid or slow, its depth or shallowness, regular, irregular, or suspended breathing, and other visible marks. The quantitative treatment of the data would involve determination of the number of cycles within a time unit, say, one minute, and measuring the height for 10 to 12 cycles in each condition and computing the mean height. In addition, one may also calculate the I fraction by measuring the length from trough to trough and also from the trough of a cycle to the point at which the perpendicular dropped from the crest intersects the line from trough to trough. The ratio of the smaller length to the larger length would then give the I fraction (p. 247). The measure of I fraction for each cycle would then be used for calculating the Mean I fraction for each condition

3. **Respiration and Continued Mental Work** : Let S be engaged in a strenuous mental work, like mathematical calculation, answering problems in in an intelligence test, recapitulating the content of a passage read before the breathing record was taken, and so on. Compare S's breathing record taken in neutral condition, i. e., before he got engaged in the mental work, with the record in the condition of mental work. It will be noted that while he is engaged in mental work the record may show periods of suspended breathing—the stylus remains at the same level; generally the breathing is rapid, irregular and shallow. The I fraction is reduced; in the resting or neutral condition it is generally reported to be .40-.45.

4. **Respiration and Fluctuation of Attention :** An interesting comparison may be made between the cyclic changes in respiration and those in attention. S's respiration record is obtained for the period he is engaged in an experiment on the fluctuation of attention (p. 105). Since inspiration provides for the intake of oxygen which is necessary for the utilization of the energic elements supplied through the blood stream, it may be presumed that the negative phase of attention coincides with the period of expiration when carbon dioxide is breathed out. One may experimentally verify the hypothesis by marking the number of times such coincidence occurs. If the coincidence is noted more often

than that expected according to the rule of chance, the hypothesis may get a support from the findings.

Recommended Readings

Postman, L. and Egan, J. P., *Experimental Psychology*, Chapter 19, Harper, New York, 1949.

Woodworth, R. S. and Schlosberg, H., *Experimental Psychology*, Chapter 7, Holt, New York, 1954.

Chapter XIII

Work and Fatigue

EVERY WORK involves both bodily activities and mental functions. But in some work the bodily or motor activities play a more important part; in others the mental functions have a more important role. In the former, the proficiency of the worker depends upon the capacities of his body, e. g., carrying or pulling a load. In the latter, the efficiency of the worker depends upon the ability to compare, discriminate, judge, reason, etc. The first type of work has accordingly been called motor and the second mental work. In motor work, performance mainly depends upon the involvement of the muscles; in mental work it depends upon the so-called higher mental processes. In between the two we have a type of work which may be called psychomotor work. In such a work the mental aspect is represented by perceptual activities and the motor by activities of the effector organs.

Work and Practice

To understand the concept of work, we may have to distinguish it from practice. Work is that kind of performance which is no more susceptible to improvement by repetition. Practice is a kind of performance which shows improvement by successive repetitions. It is difficult, however, to find any work which is altogether uninfluenced by practice. Only, motor activities of very simple and repetitive type may be presumed to be uneffected by practice. Mental or psychomotor activities, howsoever simple, are never completely unaffected by practice. The distinction between work and practice can be illustrated by comparing the curves of performance that may be plotted for work and practice. The work curve remains at its starting level over a period of time and then gradually falls off that level. Practice curve goes on gradually rising until it reaches a height at which it stays (p. 134). In other words, practice curve shows progressive increment in output or improvement in the quality of performance; work curve shows no such progressive increment. On the other hand, if the work continues without break, the curve shows progressive decrement after a certain time. The following curves illustrate the point :—

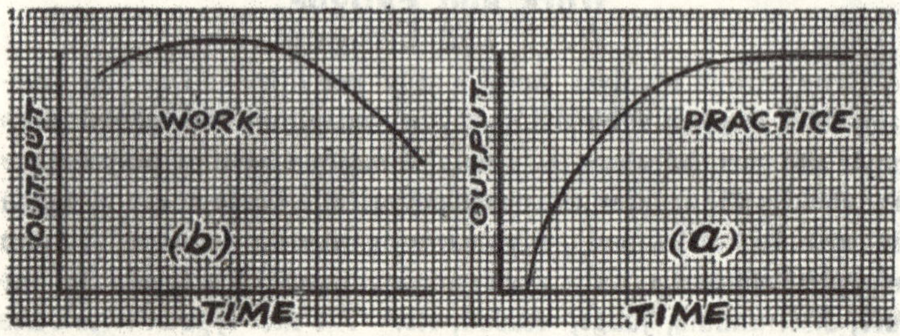

The progressive improvement in performance shown in Fig. (a) marks the effect of practice. The progressive deterioration in performance shown in Fig. (b), after a certain period of work, has been described as the effect of fatigue. Both practice and fatigue effects depend upon the repetition of performance over a period of time. Fatigue effect is marked by deterioration and practice effect by improvement in performance; hence the two are opposed to each other. Since both depend upon performance over a period of time, the two effects may get mixed up, each one counteracting the other. It may be difficult, therefore, to obtain pure practice effect or pure fatigue effect for most types of performance. A distinction can be drawn in terms of the influence of rest on each. While rest dissipates fatigue effect and thus produces recovery from fatigue, rest consolidates practice effect. Performance affected by fatigue, shows considerable improvement after rest; that influenced by practice shows little difference after rest, unless the rest is very short when it produces what we have earlier called reminiscence effect (p. 226). In fact, the improvement observed after rest may be due to the fact, that before rest the effect of practice was depressed on account of the effect of fatigue; with the dissipation of fatigue effect produced by rest, the practice effect appears in its pure form.

Fatigue

Fatigue is a condition of lowered efficiency of the worker as a result of work. It is another name for Hull's concept of reactive inhibition that we have defined earlier (p. 168) as a response produced decrement of performance. IR too, like the concept of fatigue, results from the act of responding and inhibits performance; it too, like fatigue, dissipates with rest.

Fatigue Affects any Continuous Work Objectively, fatigue may be defined in terms of the changes that affect the energic elements supplied to the body. The main sources of energy are blood sugar and oxygen which are supplied to every muscle of the body by the blood stream. The muscles contain a reserve of blood sugar and when they become active this stored provision is made use of. Fresh supply, in order to make up for the loss, is made by the blood. But when the demand exceeds the supply, which happens when a work is ceaselessly continued over a long period, the muscles are deprived of their energy which results in the slowing down of their activity. The impoverishment of the muscles is also due to the reason that fresh supply is blocked by the waste products from the used up blood sugar, particularly, the so-called lactic acid. Rest, or cessation of activity of the fatigued muscles, provides for both restoration of the energic elements and draining out of the waste products to make the supply easier. This is called recovery from fatigue. The deficiency of the energic elements in the muscles is, however, difficult to be directly observed. A more easily accessible objective measure of fatigue, therefore, is the decrement in the output of work, which has been described as industrial fatigue. This is, thus, distinguishable from the less easily observed phenomenon of physiological fatigue.

There is a close relationship between physiological fatigue and industrial fatigue. The former is accompanied, under ordinary conditions, by industrial fatigue. The reverse, however, is not necessarily true; decrement in output may take place even without a physical impairment in the efficiency of the muscles. This happens because of the loss of motivation, the weakening of the urge to apply one's energy to work. This factor is, obviously, purely subjective or psychological and is, thus, related to what has been called subjective or mental fatigue. It is manifested in consciousness by a state of disinterestedness, monotony, or boredom, which is a matter of feeling and can only be reported by the worker from his introspection. This feeling of fatigue may or may not accompany the loss of efficiency. Under certain conditions, one may be working with full zest even though he is at the ebb of his energy.

The feeling of fatigue or boredom accompanies, generally, the more simple, repetitive, routine types of work that offer no challenge to the special skills or capacities of the worker. It may, however, also occur when the worker lacks the skill or capacity to meet the challenge. There is one remarkable difference between physical fatigue and mental fatigue. Rest produces recovery from physical fatigue; it may have no effect on mental fatigue. Mental fatigue is removed by change of work; change of work may have no effect on physical fatigue. This happens because the excessive demand of blood sugar by a certain muscle system, after its own stock is exhausted, causes a general depletion of blood sugar in the blood supply to other muscles also.

We have drawn a distinction between motor work and mental work (p 251). How is the effect of fatigue indicated in these two kinds of work ? In motor work fatigue is shown by progressive decrement in efficiency of the worker which is objectively measured by a gradual fall in the quantity of output or deterioration in its quality. Fatigue does not effect mental work in the like manner. In fact, fatigue is not allowed to accumulate in mental work. A mental work curve plotted for a long period of continued work shows very frequent fluctuations in output throughout ; there are successive ups and downs in the curve. Following is the typical shape of a mental work curve :—

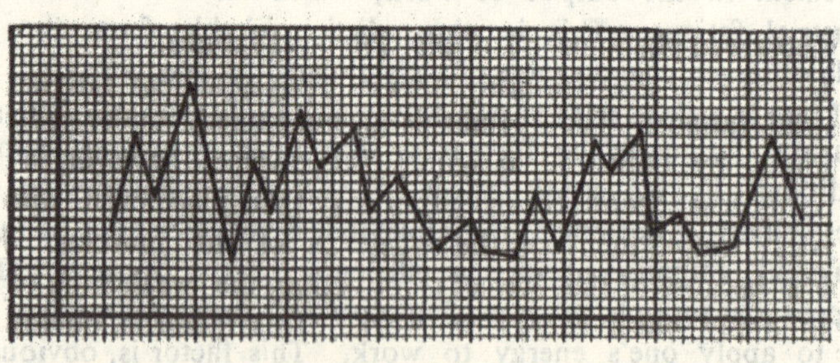

Such fluctuation in output appears because in mental work the worker takes short voluntary rest pauses. The application of energy undergoes rapid oscillations—it does not remain constant. The voluntary rest pauses provide for recovery from fatigue and fatigue is thus prevented from accumulating. Hence there is no marked dimunition in the output of mental work, unless the work period is very long. Having understood the concepts, we will pass on to experiments on work and fatigue.

Fatigue in Motor Work : Ergographic Work : The apparatus very commonly used for measuring fatigue in a highly simple and repetitive muscular activity is the so-called ergograph (Appendix III). It provides for the pulling of a weight attached to a cord by using very restricted muscles of the finger or any member of the body. The extent of each pull is represented by the distance travelled by a stylus touching a smoked paper. S has to pull and release the cord, by which the weight is hanging, at regular intervals over a period of time, till his finger refuses to work any more—it gets frozen, as it were. The vertical lines inscribed on the smoked paper gradually decrease in size till they are reduced to zero height, as shown in the following ergogram :—

You will note in the figure given above that up to the fifteenth pull the height of the graph remained almost constant. Thereafter, you will notice a gradual decline in height which further diminishes till the graph is reduced to a straight line. The point at which the graph shows first decrement in height marks the onset of fatigue which goes on building up until the muscles lose the capacity to respond.

We have noted (p. 252) that rest dissipates fatigue. This hypothesis can be tested by an experiment on the difference in performance between an uninterrupted muscular work and the same work with provision for rest in between. The experiment will be planned by taking two conditions : (1) Continuous or massed performance and (2) Interrupted or distributed work. In order that the experiment be completed within a couple of hours, you should introduce the interrupted work condition first. In this condition, let S make 24 pulls and after every eighth pull allow a rest of 6 sec. Use a 6 kg. weight. S is harnessed to the ergograph and pulls and releases the cord at intervals of one sec. To time S's response, you may use a Metronome (Appendix III) whose pendulum is so set as to swing at intervals of one second, each swing of the pendulum producing a ticking sound. S is instructed to pull at one tick and to release at the next tick. You will note that for 24 pulls, with a rest of 6 sec. after eighth pull, the total work period will be 60 sec. To control the variable of knowledge of result (p. 99), use a screen to hide from S's view the graph traced on the smoked paper. Allow S 10 ms rest and thereafter introduce the condition of continuous work. Let S work for the same total period, i. e., 60 sec., also in this condition. Measure in millimeters the heights of the vertical lines in each condition and calculate the separate mean heights. It has been found that with a weight of 6 kg. complete fatigue is produced after 25 to 30 pulls. It is expected, therefore, that fatigue will set in quite early in the no-rest condition and the total output, i. e., extent of pull, will accordingly be less in this condition, though the total numbers of pulls will be 30, as compared to the distributed work condition where the total number of pulls was decided to be only 24. You will now appreciate why the interrupted work condition was introduced first. Had the uninterrupted work condition come first, fatigue effect would have built up to the extent in 30 pulls that complete recovery from fatigue could be possible in no less than two hours. Obviously, this could be possible only if the total time given to the data collection was more than four hours.

In describing the experiment mentioned above, we suggested a 6 kg weight. Naturally, there will be individual differences in endurance, i. e., the capacity to work at the optimal level for long, between different S's in spite of their having to pull the same weight. It would, therefore, be advisable to decide about the weight on the basis of a few preliminary trials wherein E observes how much effort S has to make while pulling, say, the 6 kg. weight. If he can pull this much weight easily in the beginning, you can decide to use this weight; otherwise, use a lighter weight for him. It should occur to you that weight is a significant independent variable in this experiment. You can have a problem on the relationship between your S's endurance capacity and the weight he is required to pull. You may decide to use three weights, say, 2 kg., 4 kg., and 6 kg., and obtain ergographic data from S for these three weights. You have to be careful about one matter. Use the light weight in the first condition, and let S pull this weight till you mark sufficient drop in the height of the vertical lines, i. e., a clear indication of the onset of fatigue. Allow, thereafter, 10 ms. rest which should be sufficient to bring about complete recovery from fatigue. Then pass on to the next heavier weight which S has to pull the same number of times as the previous one. Allow another 10 ms. rest which is to be followed by pulling of the heaviest weight, namely, 6 kg. All factors, other than weight, should be the same for the three conditions.

Besides weight, there is another significant variable affecting motor fatigue, namely, pace of work. If S has to pull the same weight at a quicker pace, fatigue will set in earlier than if the pace is slow. You may then experimentally examine the relationship between work output and work pace. In one condition, the Metronome is to be set to tick, say, after each second and S is instructed to pull at one tick and release at the next tick. In another condition, the Metronome sounds after, say, every 4 sec. You have to fix a certain duration of work, say, 40 sec., which has to be the same for both conditions. You may decide to use a 4 kg. weight. Take the slow pace condition first so that fatigue effect does not build up to the extent that a long recovery time is needed. Allow , say, 10 ms. rest between the two conditions.

In another problem you may determine the optimal duration of rest for your S. Here too you have to use two or more conditions, in order to manipulate the independent variable, namely, length of rest interval. In this case also do not let your S get completely fatigued. Use the longest rest interval in the first condition which you may introduce when the ergographic record has shown clear sign of the onset of fatigue. Then let S pull the same number of times as he did before the rest interval. In case you notice marked deterioration in output before S has completed the remaining numbers of pulls, stop at this point. Now let S pull the same number of times in the other conditions. Introduce the rest interval at the same point in all conditions. Allow 10 ms. recovery time after each condition. You may have still another related problem, namely, the optimal location of rest interval. Suppose you are using a 6 kg. weight and you have decided to take 24 pulls. Introduce, in one condition, a rest of say, 30 sec. after 10 pulls, in another after 16 pulls, and in still another after 20 pulls. Besides comparing the mean height of the lines in the different conditions, you may also take up an additional treatment of the data, when your independent variable is either the duration or the location of rest interval. Rest produces recovery from fatigue, and a measure of recovery will be the difference between the amount of output immediately before rest and that immediately after rest. The bėst duration, or location, of rest would produce the largest difference between the two. Returning to the location of rest interval, the best location has been found to be the point where fatigue has just set in. The same rest interval introduced after fatigue has sufficiently accumulated will not prove as beneficial.

There may be several other problems related to the efficiency of motor work The report of an experiment on one such problem is given below.

Worker's Attitude towards Work and Performance

Attitude is a system of beliefs, feelings and action tendencies that predispose a person to perceive an object, to act in regard to it and to feel about it in a particular manner. A worker may have an unwholesome attitude towards his employer. He believes him to be lacking in concern for the worker's welfare which makes him feel unhappy or even arouses in him hostile feelings, and prompts him to go slow with his work performance. The latter, naturally, affects his work output. A simple experiment to ascertain the influence of belief on performance can be conducted under the controlled situation of the laboratory using a simple and measurable task. This experiment is an attempt to do this. In other words, it is meant to test the hypothesis : worker's performance depends upon the nature of the belief he holds about the work situation.

Method

Subject : A well built male adult college student.

Apparatus and Material : Ergograph. Metronome. Two wooden cases : 2″ high with a base of 4 cm in diameter and 3″ high with a base of 5 cm in diameter, respectively. Both cases (blocks) were so filled with lead pieces that their total weight was equal, namely 6 kg.

Procedure : S was shown the two blocks lying on the table in front of him. He was then asked to lift them one after the other. This led S to believe that the smaller block was heavier than the larger one. E confirmed this by enquiry from S. S was then harnessed to the ergograph. Data were taken in two conditions, with an interval of 10 ms. in between.

Instruction to S : "You have to insert the first joint of your middle finger in the loop and pull it when you hear one tick and release it when you hear the next tick. As you see, by pulling the loop you are actually raising the heavier block which is hanging at the other end of the string. I have to see with what force and how long you can pull the weight. This is a test of your muscular strength and endurance." Before S got the 'start' signal, he was asked to adjust the movement of his finger to the ticking of the metronome. After 20 pulls of the smaller block (Cond. I), S was allowed 15 ms. rest. He then started pulling the larger block (Cond. II). The instruction was the same for both conditions, only in Condition II S was told "this time you have to pull the lighter weight".

S's Introspection : "I found it easy to pull the weight at first, but gradually my finger got fatigued and I noticed that I was not able to pull as much as before. The first block was smaller in size but I found it to be actually heavier than the larger one, when I lifted them. That is why I could pull the second weight more than the first weight and did not get as much fatigued either."

Result

Fig. 1

Table 1

LENGTH OF PULL IN MM

Pull	Condition I	Condition II	Pull	Condition I	Condition II
1	15	16	11	13	16
2	15	15	12	12	15
3	16	15	13	10	15
4	16	15	14	10	16
5	16	16	15	10	14
6	15	16	16	8	14
7	16	15	17	8	12
8	15	15	18	9	12
9	14	15	19	7	9
10	14	16	20	6	9
Total	152	154		93	132

Table 2

MEANS, DIFFERENCE BETWEEN MEANS, SE DIFF AND t

	Condition I	Condition II
Mean	12.25	14.30
Diff		2.05
SE_{diff}		0.428
t		4.8

Discussion

When S looked at the two blocks lying on the table, the difference in their size produced the size-weight illusion and he thus perceived the larger block, to be heavier than the smaller one. But when he lifted the blocks, one after the other, his visual perception was falsified which produced, as a result of over-correction, the erroneous belief that the smaller block contained more weight than the larger one. This notion influenced his performance as expected ; the Mean for the smaller block is 12.25 mm, which is significantly less than that for the larger block, which is 14 30 mm. and the value of t is 4.8 which is very highly significant (Table 2). S's introspection also supports the result. In the first 10 pulls, the difference in the amount of effort required for pulling the weights is rather small (Fig. 1 and Table 1). But we notice that fatigue effect started appearing earlier for the weight believed by S to be heavier, that is, from the 9th pull, and it also built up faster for this weight so that the difference from pull to pull became increasingly larger in the next 10 pulls. It is presumed that S's belief that the larger weight was lighter kept up his morale a little longer, leading him to make more effort in pulling this weight whice marked the fatigue effect. We might, therefore, conclude that S's attitude towards the task situation influenced his performance quite significantly.

We notice that 15 ms rest in between the two conditions was quite adequate to produce recovery from fatigue since it was not allowed to build up to its maximum limit; S's initial performance in the second condition remains at the level at which he started in the second condition.

Psychomotor Work

It is possible to manipulate the variables of work and rest in the laboratory by using other tasks also like the pursuit rotor, inverted alphabet writing, etc. Though these tasks are not as simple as the ergographic performance, in their case too the effect of practice is not very large, specially when a few preliminary trials have already been given. They can, therefore, be used for experiments on work, rather than only on learning. We are familiar with the pursuit rotor (p. 142). In the inverted alphabet writing, S has to write the alphabets upside down while moving from right to left. When the sheet containing the inverted alphabets is turned, 180 degrees, the letters assume their normal shape and can be easily read. You may use this task in order to determine the effect of rest pauses on performance. Let the total work period, say, 15 min., be divided into 15 1-min. units. S is supplied a blank sheet of ruled foolscap size paper, with serial numbers 1 to 15 written on the right margin, at the head of every third line. After explaining the task to S, E starts the experiment and taps on the table after every one minute, for which he holds the stop watch in his hand. S should turn to the next line each time he gets this signal. S should be told : "This is a test of your capacity to work in an unusual manner. Try to work as fast as you can. Always start from the serial number at the right. I will tap on the table after expiry of every one minute. The moment you hear the tapping stop at the point you have reached and immediately start again from the next serial number." After S has completed the 15-min. period, he is allowed 5 minutes rest and, thereafter, supplied another sheet similarly numbered. He is instructed to write the alphabets as he did with the first sheet. But this time E removes the sheet after 5 minutes work and returns it after a rest of 5 minutes. In this case also S works for 15 minutes but rests for 5 minutes after each 5-min. work. E plots a curve for each 1-min work in each of the two conditions and also calculates the mean number of letters written in each condition; he may test the difference for significance. While discussing the results, E notes the extent of the difference between the last 1-min. unit before and the first 1-min. unit after rest. He, further, explains his findings by using the concepts of reminiscence and reactive inhibition (pp. 226 and 168).

Another interesting experiment may be performed in order to determine whether rest has the same effect on tasks having less and tasks having more dissimilar components. More technically, the problem may be stated as: "Task homogeneity and effect of spacing in psychomotor work." A very simple task, such as repeatedly writing small letters, may be selected. For a more homogeneous task, S may be asked to write only two letters, say, c e, and for the less homogeneous task, let him write six letters like a b f g k m. The entire performance is to be divided into 1-min. units by using the same procedure as suggested for the inverted alphabet writing task (p. 261). S has to perform each type of task under two conditions : (1) Experimental, i. e., S is allowed 1-min. rest after every 2 minutes of work, and (2) control, i. e., S works without rest. Let S work on each task and under each condition for twelve minutes. The total work period will then amount to 12×4 or 48 minutes; adding a total of 12 minutes rest, 1-min. after every 2-min. work in each one of the two experimental conditions, the total work period would finally come to 60 minutes. One may use a counterbalancing design (p. 9) in order to neutralise the effects of practice and boredom, as given below :

6 min.	6 min.	6 min.	6 min.	6 min.	6 min.	6 min.	6 min.
Exp. c e	Cont. c e	Cont. abfgkm	Exp. abfgkm	Exp. abfgkm	Cont. abfgkm	Cont. c e	Exp. c e

It is expected that the gain from rest will be smaller in the six-letter writing task; the response produced inhibition (IR) is likely to be dissipated, not only by the rest following the 2 min. work, but also with the change in the pattern of response. When writing 6 letters, each one requiring a very different pattern of response, as distinguished from writing two letters using very similar response patterns, the IR produced in writing each letter is dissipated during the time S is engaged in writing the other letters. As a result, IR is prevented from accumulating to the extent as in writing only two and very similar letters. The gain from rest, the reminiscence effect, is, therefore, likely to be larger when two letters are repeatedly written. This will be shown in the result by a larger difference between the Experimental and the Control conditions of the more homogeneous task, i. e., ce writing. Another evidence will be a larger difference between the two tasks when performed continuously. The difference between the two tasks should not be as large when performed under the condition of rest, since rest may be superfluous, according to our hypothesis, when the task components are heterogeneous.

Fatigue in Mental Work

We have noted earlier that mental work, unlike motor work, does not show progressive deterioration, unless the work period is very long. We have also noted some special features of the mental work curve (p. 254). You may demonstrate these facts by conducting an experiment on the effect of rest pauses on the efficiency of mental work. You may select a mental task like multiplying one-digit numbers. A sheet containing several columns of one-digit randomly ordered numbers may be used for this purpose. S is asked to multiply each number by the next following and if the product exceeds nine, leave out the tense and multiply the unit number by the next number, till he reaches the end of the column, as shown below ; S should not use paper and pencil for performing the multiplication task. 4, 7, 3, 6, 5, 2—4×7=28, 8×3=24, 4×6=24, 4×5=20, 0×2=0, the final answer. Each column of numbers may be used as a unit of performance. The score may then be the time taken to complete the column. Or, E may signal at the end of each 1-min. work, instructing S to draw a line at the point reached. S works in two conditions. In one condition the performance is uninterrupted. In the other, S is allowed one minute rest after completing each column, or after every one or two minutes of work. In either case, E plots two curves on the same base for the time or the output, as the case may be. S may also be asked to rate himself on a 5-point scale of freshness and tiredness at the end of every unit of work. He just uses one of the following descriptions of his condition:

Very Fresh, Fresh, Undecided, Fatigued

S's rating of his condition is also to be plotted on the same curve. A comparison is made of the Means for the two conditions. In addition, E also calculates the SD's for the two conditions. It is expected that the variability will be larger in the no-rest condition because of S using voluntary rest pauses. As an index of fatigue, E may also find out the difference in the performance between the first half and the second half, or the first quarter and the last quarter of the total work period under both rest and no-rest conditions.

Precision and Steadiness of Motor Work

Experiments have been devised for measuring the precision and steadiness of motor work. Following are descriptions of two such experiments :—

Control and Accuracy of Voluntary Movement : The operation of a machine may involve the problem of display and control. The machine operator should be able to correctly notice a sign (display) and respond to it by making a precise movement (control). The movement may, in some cases, have to be made either in the frontal or the lateral plane. In either case, it may be directed toward or away from the body. A particular kind of movement and in a particular direction may, on the average, be more convenient to make. The designer of the machine may take advantage of this finding and so design the controls in the machine that the operator is required to make the kind of movement that is most convenient. Experiment has been devised to find out which kind of movement can be made most accurately. The apparatus to be used for this purpose is the so-called Tracing Board, (Appendix III). S has to place the tip of a stylus, electrically connected with the Tracing Board, at the opening of the metal strips fixed on the board. He has to draw a line on the glass between the strips, without touching either strip. He should make a continuous movement of the arm from start to finish. The arm should not be resting on the table and should be free from any other kind of support. E should decide about the rate of the movement, say 10 sec., within which the full length of the strips is to be traversed. E should illustrate this rate to S and also let him take one or two preliminary trials. The tracing Board is connected with a time marker, which is touching a rotating drum. Every time the stylus touches a strip, a record is automatically made on the smoked paper (p. 106).

E may take several sets of trials for each kind of movement, say 10 for each, by changing the orientation of the apparatus. He may, thus, determine the difference between frontal and lateral movement, or between outward and inward movement. E may also be interested in determining the difference between the right and the left hand. It is also possible to manipulate the distance between the strips in order to determine the distance at which S makes minimum errors. It has been found that for right handed persons, the right hand is superior to the left hand. Further, movement towards the body is more steady and accurate than that away from the body.

Control of Involuntary Movements : Control of movement involves not only freedom from error while making a voluntary movement. It also implies the control of involuntary movements. A good marksman, for example, has perfect control over such movements. The Steadiness Testor has been devised for measuring the capacity to control involuntary movements (Appendix III). It contains a series of holes in a brass plate which is set at an angle of 45 degrees; the holes vary in the size of their diameter. A metallic needle is electrically connected with the brass plate. S has to hold the tip of the needle, for, say, 15 sec., in each one of the holes in the order of their respective size, starting with the largest one. The needle should be inserted about 6 mm in a hole, in a manner that it does not get into contact with the brass plate. Each time a contact is made, it is recorded by a marker on the smoked drum. S's arm and hand should be free from all support. S is allowed a rest of 30 sec. after each trial. The score will be the total number of errors made in a given series of holes.

E may also repeat the trials in the reverse order, i. e., starting with the smallest hole, and then compare and comment on the scores obtained in the two series. When both series of trials are taken, it may be worthwhile to begin with the series starting with the smallest hole. S's experience of his utter inability to control his involuntary movement may have a disruptive effect on his future performance wihch may take long to wear off. On the other hand, his initial success in the series starting with the largest hole may inspire self-confidence that may keep him steady long enough, in spite of the increasing difficulty of the task. In an individual experiment, however, this assumption may not be supported by the data.

The test of steadiness may also be used as a measure of endurance. Having determined the hole wherein S's errors are the least, E may require him to hold the stylus in it until S loses all control over the involuntary movements. Besides obtaining a record of the errors made within the course of this period, a time line (p. 106), may also be inscribed on the kymograph. The entire period may then be broken up into, say, 10 equal units, and the errors made within each unit of time, may be separately tabulated.

The test of control of movements, voluntary or involuntary may also be used as an indirect measure of fatigue. S may be engaged in a continuous motor activity, for example, performing the ergographic task, or pressing the dynamometer (Appendix III). A comparison may be made between the before and after-tests of the accuracy of movement or steadiness.

Recommended Readings

Underwood, B. J., *Experimental Psychology*, Chapter 8, Appleton, New York, 1966.

Woodworth, R. S. and Schlosberg, H., *Experimental Psychology*, Chapter 25, Holt, New York, 1954.

Chapter XIV

Motivation

Motivation is the process of the arousal of a motive, and a motive is what moves the organism from within. The example of motivational variables are needs, purposes, attitudes, values, aspirations, conflict, frustration, incentives like reward and punishment, praise and blame, and so on. Some of these organismic variables are more or less permanent, for example, needs and values; others are transient, for example, reward and punishment. A motive, even when permanent, is not always active; it remains in a state of quiscence and can be aroused when appropriate changes take place within the organism or in the stimulus situation. We can manipulate a motive by providing for a change in the stimulus situation, or inducing a condition within the organism through a specific instruction to S. In fact, you will note that instruction has a very special use in manipulating a motivational variable.

You will appreciate that experiments on motivation are difficult to perform, because here you are dealing with what is called an intervening variable—one that occurs between the stimulus and the response. The intervening variable cannot be directly observed; it can only be inferred and your inference may at times go wrong. You have, therefore, to make sure whether you have succeeded in manipulating the motivational variable whose effect on S's behaviour you are trying to determine. S's introspection may be of particular value in this respect, though it may not provide an infallible evidence of the operation of a motive.

We will now describe a few experiments on motivation that you can perform in your laboratory. We will begin with a complete report of an experiment on knowledge of result.

Knowledge of Result

Thorndike, the famous learning psychologist, explained all learning, at first, as acquired strength of stimulus response connections. The law of use and disuse accounted for the strengthening or weakening of a connection. Repetition of the learning performance brought the law into play. Later, Thorndike noticed that mere repetition was not enough and had to introduce the law of effect. He came at the discovery of this law while performing the so-called line-drawing experiment. Thorndike marked no improvement in the performance when he withheld from the subjects the knowledge of the amount of error in successive attempts to draw a line equal in length to a target line. But when the knowledge of the result was made available, there was a gradual decrement in the error. Knowledge of result, or the effect of the performance, led the S's to draw a line that closely approximated the target line. In this experiment an attempt was made to verify the finding of Thorndike.

Hypothesis : Knowledge of result functions as an incentive to improvement in performance.

Method

Apparatus and Material : A sheet of foolscap paper, pencil and ruler.

Procedure : The sheet of paper had two vertical lines of dots, parallel to each other and separated by 100 mm. The dots in each line were at a distance of 20 mm. E connected the corresponding dots on the two sides with a ruler which he held in position, and had S place his pencil point on the dot at the left. S was then asked to close his eyes and to draw along the ruler by continuous movement of his pencil till he thought he reached the dot on the right. The experiment was divided into two conditions—A and B. In condition A (WKR), E covered the line drawn by S in order to withhold the knowledge of result. In condition B (KR), S could see his performance before he took the position for drawing the next line blindfolded (KR). The counterbalancing design was used for taking data as shown below :

WKR	KR	KR	WKR
10	10	10	10

Instruction : "Here you see two dots, one on the left, the other on the right. I will place a ruler to connect the two dots. You are to let your pencil point touch the dot on the left and then close your eyes. When I ask you to start, draw a line with your eyes closed along the ruler without halting and stop when you have reached the other dot on the right. You have to keep your eyes closed until I ask you to open your eyes. Do you understand ?"

S drew 20 lines without knowledge of result—every time the line drawn by him was covered before he opened his eyes. He drew 20 lines with knowledge of result—the line drawn by him was not covered when he opened his eyes.

Introspection : "I think I was drawing better when I could see after drawing a line the error I had made. I noticed that I made less and less errors gradually. I presume that I should have made more errors when I could get no chance of looking at the line I had drawn. I had no idea about the extent of error."

Result

Table 1

LENGTH OF LINES IN MM WITH AND WITHOUT KNOWLEDGE OF RESULTS

Trial	WKR	Trial	KR	Trial	KR	Trial	WKR
1	84	11	86	21	98	31	98
2	82	12	90	22	94	32	96
3	88	13	90	23	96	33	96
4	90	14	96	24	96	34	92
5	82	15	94	25	104	35	94
6	84	16	98	26	102	36	92
7	80	17	100	27	98	37	94
8	88	18	102	28	96	38	94
9	92	19	100	29	102	39	88
10	86	20	96	30	98	40	90
Total	856		952		984		934

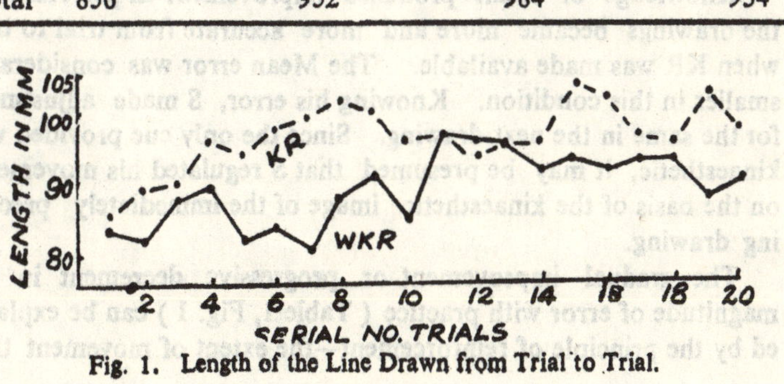

Fig. 1. Length of the Line Drawn from Trial to Trial.

Table 2

MEAN LENGTH, MEAN ERROR, DIFFERENCE IN ERROR BETWEEN WKR AND KR TRIALS

Mean	A WKR	B KR	B KR	A WKR	Total WKR	Total KR
Length	85.6	95.2	98.4	93.4	89.5	96.8
Error	−14.4	−4.8	−1.6	−6.6	−10.5	−3.2
Difference	9.6			5.0	7.3	

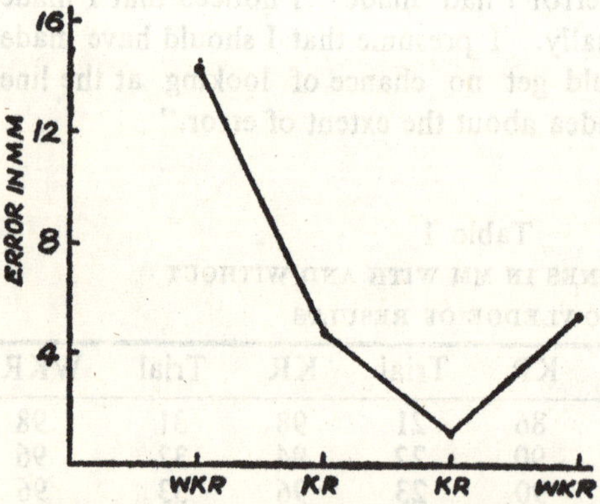

Fig. 2 Mean. Error for the Four Sets of Trials.

The amount of error is 3.2 mm when knowledge of result is provided and it is 10.5 mm when it is withheld, more than three times of the former (Table 2). The amount of error is very large in the first 10 trials, being 14.4mm, and is reduced to 6.6 mm. in the next 10 trials of WKR (Table 2 and Fig. 2). The changes from trial to trial are abrupt in WKR and gradual in KR (Table 1 and Fig. 1).

Discussion

Knowledge of result produced improvement in performance; the drawings became more and more accurate from trial to trial when KR was made available. The Mean error was considerably smaller in this condition. Knowing his error, S made adjustment for the same in the next drawing. Since the only cue provided was kinaesthetic, it may be presumed that S regulated his movements on the basis of the kinaesthetic image of the immediately preceding drawing.

The gradual improvement or progressive decrement in the magnitude of error with practice (Table 1, Fig. 1) can be explained by the principle of reinforcement—the extent of movement that closely approximated the standard length was positively reinforced; that which considerably departed from it was negatively reinforced. Mere repetition was not sufficient to produce any improvement in spite of the fact that S was motivated to draw a line that approximated the target. The errors in the WKR trials show random fluctuations. In the first ten WKR trials, the difference between the first and the tenth trial is of 2 mm. only (Table 1). The difference is 10 mm., on the other hand, between the corresponding KR trials.

We notice a difference of 7.8 mm between the means of the first ten and the next ten WKR trials; we also note a difference of 9.6 mm between the WKR and the KR means for the first ten and of 5 mm for the next ten trials (Table 2). The smaller mean for the next ten WKR trials is, further, due to the earlier trials in this series where the errors are smaller (Table 1). This happened because of the persistence of the habit to draw close to the target which was acquired from practice in the KR condition. The habit, however, gradually declined for want of reinforcement by the knowledge of result and consequently there was increase in the errors in the second half of the next ten WKR trials (Table 1).

We notice a tendency on the part of S to undershoot the line, as negative mean errors have been found for both conditions (Table 2, Fig. 2) The tendency to undershoot, however, is more marked in WKR trials and is minimised in KR trials. In fact, in KR trials we do not only notice some trials producing zero errors, but also overshooting the target. This may be explained as due to the appreciation by S of the direction in which his errors tended; this motivated him to make a correction by further lengthening the line drawn. Thus KR has clearly provided an incentive to S for improving his performance.

Why S showed the tendency to undershoot, rather than overshoot, is not clear from the obtained data. We may presume the influence of a personality variable, namely, the general trait of restraint and caution which leads one to restrict, rather than give unrestrained expression to, his behaviour tendency.

We may conclude that our data support the hypothesis and are consistent with the view that mere repetition is not enough to produce learning.

Effect of Need Tension on Memory

Kurt Lewin developed his theory of need tension according to which the arousal of a need or motive produces a state of tension within the organism ; the tension persists as long as the need is not satisfied. Fulfilment of the need reduces the tension. Lewin and his associates, further, made some deductions from the theory that were stated in the form of hypotheses. One such hypothesis was that interruption of an on-going motivated activity would not let the tension that accompanies the activity subside; the tension would persist even though the activity was stopped for the time being. The effect of the persistence of tension during the period of interruption can be observed in various ways, for example, (1) the tension would sustain the memory of the interrupted task and hence unfinished task would be better remembered when tested than completed tasks; (2) the tension would lead to the tendency to revert to the unfinished task.

Zeigarnik, one of the associates of Lewin, found that the memory for unfinished tasks is better than that for finished tasks; hence the gain in recall of unfinished tasks came to be called Zeigarnik effect, and the ratio obtained by dividing the memory score for unfinished task by that for finished task became known as the Zeigarnik ratio. However, other investigators like Rozensweig, Thelma Alper, etc., found that the Zeigarnik effect was not a consistent phenomenon; sometimes finished tasks were better remembered than unfinished ones. They conceived of two kinds of reactions characterising the attack on a task, namely, (1) ego-defensive, and (2) need persistive. The first happens when the person concerned is ego-involved; the second happens when he is task-involved. A task-oriented S will be concerned with the completion of the task; unfinished task will be better remembered by him because of the persistence of the need to complete the task. But if S's ego is involved in the situation, he will perceive the interruption as his failure to finish the task, as a threat to his ego-value; such task would evidently have an unpleasant association for him. His reaction, while trying to recall the task, would be defensive; the failure of recall would protect the ego against the revival of the threat. According to the Freudian theory of repression, resistence will be imposed on his effort to remember the task. He would be less likely to recall it. Memory for finished and unfinished task will, thus, also provide a measure of ego strength, the capacity to tolerate frustration.

You can conduct an experiment to verify the hypothesis :

unfinished tasks can be better remembered than finished tasks.

Different types of tasks can be used in the experiment. One may have a miscellany of, say, 20 tasks like cancellation, coding, counting backward, sorting coloured beads, etc. E interrupts the performance of half of these several tasks; in the other half S is not interrupted. The interrupted and uninterrupted tasks, however, are introduced in a random sequence. Some investigators have used jumbled sentences—those whose words are disarranged; half of these can be possibly solved, while the other half are impossible of solution as containing an element that does not fit into the sentence. The possible ones are naturally solved and the task is thus completed by S ; the impossible ones are removed after S has worked on them for some time. Each jumbled sentence has a word printed in bold face which is introduced to S as suggesting the central theme of the sentence so that it provides a clue to S for setting the words in a meaningful order. This is really done to focus S's attention on the word. Each sentence is removed from the scene after it has been done with. At the end, E asks S to recall the words in bold face that occurred in each sentence.

The writer has been using a simpler task. E prepares 20 nonsense combinations of two consonants like BK, NC, and so on. Each one is written at the top of a separate cancellation sheet, one combination on one sheet. S is instructed to cancel the letters heading the sheet wherever they occur on the sheet. He is further told that the test is a measure of speed and accuracy of perception of details and that the time is limited ; S should try to do accurately as many as he can within the time limit. In fifty per cent of cases, the sheet is removed after S has reached the end of the sheet ; in the remaining fifty per cent of cases he is interrupted before he reaches the end. The interruption, however, is made long after S has been through the task for the tension to build up ; the sheet is removed only after S has covered the major portion and is near the end of the task. But the interruption is not made always at exactly the same point, for example, E interrupts sometimes when the last, the the last and a quarter, the last and a half, the last two, or the last two and quarter lines are left. The impression is carried to S that time was over and hence E removed the sheet. E holds a stop watch in his hand which he starts and stops to justify the impression. E decides by lot which combinations would go under finished and which under 'unfinished' tasks. The sequence in which the different combinations are presented is also random. After all the sheets have been gone through, E tells S : "You were asked to cancel two letters from each sheet. The different sheets had different combinations of letters to be cancelled. Please tell me what the twenty combinations of letters were." E records S's responses in the order they are made. It is expected that if unfinished tasks are better remembered, they should be the first to be recalled. This could be verified by examining among those correctly recalled how many of the unfinished ones occurred in the first half of correct recalls and how many in the second half. E also finds the ratio of the unfinished to the finished ones correctly remembered. E also takes S's introspection, after he has recorded S's responses, regarding his general reactions to the task and to the performance when he completed and when he could not complete the task. E examines S's introspection for any indication of S's attitude to the interruption, and his main concern while performing the task. This would help E in explaining when his results fail to support the hypothesis.

You will note that in experiments on memory for finished and unfinished tasks, the test is of incidental memory (p. 177). Hence, special care should be taken to conceal the real purpose of the experiment from S. S should take it to be a test of performance, and a measure of speed and accuracy; he should never suspect that his memory for the task would be tested.

The results obtained by the writer's students have invariably supported Zeigarnik's hypothesis, in spite of the comparatively shorter time for which the letters are observed by S in the interrupted tasks. Perhaps, the task being very simple and of a routine nature for college adults, the inability to complete the task may not offer a threat to the ego, as it did not reflect S's weakness in an area that mattered much for him. Hence, the general orientation of the S's remains the same; each one gets task involved.

Effect of Frustration on Performance

Frustration is a condition produced by repeated inability to meet a difficult and stressful situation; it is the reaction to an insurmountable obstacle to the progress of a goal directed activity. It is possible to experimentally induce frustration in S by producing in him the feeling of failure, inadequacy, and ego devaluation, and then examine its effect on S's performance. You can use any task for the purpose. First obtain data on S's performance in a neutral condition. Then, in order to induce frustration present an air of your deep concern with S's output, look intently at his performance, and off and on make critical and disparaging remarks. You may select the solving of anagrams as the task. The anagram is a word whose letters have been disarranged. The solution consists of rearranging the letters so that the combination becomes meaningful, for example, PRSDAE can be rearranged as SPREAD. Prepare two lists of anagrams, each containing, say, ten items. Let the two lists be of equal difficulty value. Each should produce a familiar word. For every word with a certain number of letters in one, there should be a word with the same number of letters in the other list. For every anagram that is soluble according to a particular rule, you should have an anagram in the other list soluble by the same rule. For example, PRSDAE can be solved by making the third letter as the first and setting the last three letters in reverse order ; a comparable anagram will be LOFREW which can be solved as FLOWER by the same rule. Another example will be YUTEAB and YTHORW, each one of which can be solved by reversing the position of the first and the last letters, and making the second two of the four middle letters, to precede the first two. Following are comparable lists of anagrams :

PRSDAE	LOFREW
YUTEAB	YTHORW
PARDI	ORCNW
RBTHGI	OHTSEN
ARDBO	TAYHS
RIYTD	ALKCB
RANWOR	TAMRET
ELDBUN	LEDCAN
ERNIFD	URNOGD
DUTTNSE	CARTEBK

When the two lists have been prepared, arrange the anagrams within each list in a random order. Then decide by tossing a coin which one should be used first. Let each anagram be written on a separate card. Instruct S : "I will give you a card bearing a combination of disarranged letters. You have to rearrange the letters so that they form a meaningful word. For example, EVFI can be made into FIVE by changing the places of the letters. Other similar cards will also be presented, one after the other. Try to solve each card as quickly as you can." E times and records S's performance on each card. While S is solving the anagram, E ostensibly directs his attention away from S. After the first list has been completed, E introduces the second list, allowing a rest of, say, 15 ms between the two conditions, with the following instruction :

"You have done the last problems. They were meant for practice. Now comes the real test. I will give you again another set of similar problems. Only, they are a bit more difficult, but not so for college students. I have tried them on high school boys and they have been able to solve within quite a short time. Naturally, being college students, you will solve them within still shorter time. Here is the first problem." E then watches S's performance intently, looks at the stop watch quite often, and makes such remarks in a stern voice as "you are taking too much time". He then introduces the next anagram and makes similar disparaging remarks off and on "Oh ! you have taken too long". "It's a pity". "I am surprised at you". After S has done three or four anagrams, E says : "You are doing much worse than a school boy—taking so much time in spite of the fact that you have had enough practice. The school boys were given no practice". "I have found them quite easy for college students. What's the matter with you ?" All the time E assumes an air of extreme seriousness, all through gazing at S's performance.

In both conditions, E prepares from his memory a record of S's objective behaviour immediately after S has finished the ten anagrams. E then rearranges the comparable items in the lists putting them in the original sequence. He tabulates the detailed result and then calculates the mean time and SD in seconds. He may also apply a test of significance of difference if it is not apparently quite large. E also prepares two graphs on the same base, using the base line as the serial number of the ten anagrams, and the y-axis as the time in seconds.

Frustration has a motivating effect first ; the individual takes the test as a challenge. But when frustration piles up gradually with the repeated experience of failure, frustration has a disruptive effect on S's performance. The perfomance deteriorates and the individual resorts to an unadaptive behaviour ; he may seek to escape from the situation and be inclined to give up the task ; he may be aggressive to the experimenter or to the task—the aggression will, ordinarily, remain at the verbal level, i.e., he may use some strong expression against the experimenter or criticise the task itself. The overt marks of aggression are biting of nails, scratching one's hair, fidgetting in one's seat, or any other evidence of restlessness. E has to make note of all information he obtains on S's behaviour that is relevant to the diverse effects of frustration. He also examines the progressive changes in S's performance to note the evidence, if any, of frustration tolerance ; may be S's performance improves in the latter part because of this factor. S's introspection may also throw further light on the matter.

Perceptual Defense

Perception is a selective process. The selectivity depends upon the dynamic relationships obtaining within the stimulus field, besides a set of organismic variables like needs, values, etc. (p. 267). One factor which may also be significant in deciding what we do and what we do not clearly perceive at the moment is the mental conflict arousing or ego-threatening character of the stimulus situation. According to the repression theory, our sensory threshold becomes higher when we are confronted with a stimulus that has unpleasant associations for us. The ego defends itself by warding off the possibility of awareness of the threatening stimuli ; the recognition threshold is raised or the perception of the stimuli is blocked. The phenomenon has been described as perceptual defense. The defensive reaction to a threatening stimulus, however, is not universal and we may come across individual differences. Some people are more sensitive to threatening stimuli and perceive them more readily. Thus, besides perceptual defense, we notice what has been described as perceptual vigilance, which implies a condition of increased sensitivity to threatening stimuli.

In order to conduct an experiment on perceptual defense, you may use two kinds of verbal stimuli—threatening or conflict arousing and non-threatening or neutral. The example of the first may be such words as blood, murder, divorce, death, masturbation, pain, hatred, dagger, punishment, prostitute, falsehood, prisoner, starvation, war, tomb, naked, insane, vulture, snake, riot, flood, urine, famine, or similar other words arousing fear, anxiety, shame, or guilt-feeling, e. g., names of private parts of the body, words describing the sex act, etc. In the second set you have such words as garden, field, laughter, honesty, dinner, camel, picture, water, paper, mountain, table, chair, etc. An important control will be to keep the mean number of letters in the two sets the same.

One may measure perceptual defense by determining the mean recognition threshold for the two kinds of stimulus words. This can be done either by determining the minimum intensity of light needed for the clear perception of a word presented in a flash. You need an apparatus for it, the photometer, in order to vary the intensity of light in measurable units. An alternative method is to determine the minimum exposure time needed to recognise the stimulus word. For this purpose, you need a camera-shutter type or a disc tachistoscope (Appendix III). Both provide a measure of exposure time. The two sets of stimulus words, say, ten in each set, are mixed up. Each word is then exposed starting with an exposure time clearly below the recognition threshold. The exposure time is then increased in equal steps till S is able to recognize the word correctly ; you have to follow the procedure for the psychophysical method of limits, using only the ascending series (p. 72). The mean exposure time and SD are then calculated separately for the two types of stimulus words, and, if necessary, the *t* test of significance is also employed.

S's introspection regarding his feelings in respect of the different words is also taken. This is useful because you are manipulating an intervening variable, namely, threatening character of the stimulus word. You have selected the words on the basis of the usual reactions the words elicit. But the usual reactions may not be true of your S. A neutral word like garden, or industry, may have been associated with an anxiety-ridden situation in the life of your S.

To make sure about a word being threat arousing, you may take the word association test (p. 237). Using the various indices, you may select the words that are threatening and those that are neutral for your S.

Your result may show greater sensitiveness—lower mean recognition threshold, to the threatening rather than the neutral words. You may then come to the conclusion that your S is more prone to be vigilant than to be defensive in his reaction. His ego is strong enough to withstand a threatening situation so that he may be able to adjust to the requirements of the situation rather than become unmindful of it or physically withdraw from it. In fact, psychologists have found a relationship between the mode of reactions, defensive or vigilant, to ego-threat and a stable personality characteristic. They, thus, think of two personality types; sensitizors and repressors. The former are more likely to tolerate frustration; they have better memory for finished tasks; and they are more prone to take note of threatening situations. They are, accordingly, also better adjusted.

Level of Aspiration

Most activities of life are directed towards the achievement of a goal one has set for himself. Different individuals, however, set the goal they strive to achieve at different levels. The level at which the goal is set is naturally determined by the expectation of its achievement. By level of aspiration is, thus, meant the expected level of goal achievement within a range of difficulty.

Independent variables like experience of success or failure, social influence, one's self-concept, i. e., the type of person one thinks himself to be, etc., have been explored in experiments on level of aspiration. A few common tendencies have been noted. One keeps his level of aspiration a little above his level of achievement. The experience of success leads to raising and that of failure to lowering one's level of aspiration. The tendency to raise the level after success is, however, stronger than the tendency to lower after failure. Knowledge of the level set by the group to which one belongs also effects one's goal setting behaviour. The study of an individual's goal setting behaviour may, however, present some atypical features. The individual may be unaffected by success or failure. This leads to the classification of the goal setting behaviour as realistic or unrealistic. One person may keep his aspiration persistently high, despite low achievement, and another always low, despite high achievement. Still another person may keep his aspiration sometimes high or sometimes low irrespective of the actual results of his strivings. In setting their aspiration, such persons are non-responsive to their actual achievement. When this happens, the level of aspiration may be more affected by one's self-concept than reality. The incorrigibly optimistic person always over-rates his capacities and aspires for a level of accomplishment that may not be within his reach. The pitiably pessimistic individual always looks at himself through the wrong end of the telescope—minimises his strengths and magnifies his weaknesses. His level of aspiration reflects this down-grading of the self. Such individual differences in the goal setting behaviour have led some people to conceive of the generality of level of aspiration. They think that one's level of aspiration is not specific to the situation in which one may be placed but constitutes a stable characteristic of his personality. Sufficient empirical data have not yet been available to confirm this hypothesis.

Different kinds of tasks have been used in experiments on level of aspiration. In fact, any task that can motivate a person to strive for attaining a certain level of accomplishment may be suitable for the experiment. To arrive at a precise result, the performance on the task should be quantifiable. When E is trying to manipulate success and failure in the task, the task should also be such that the level of attainment remains concealed from S.

We may describe an experiment on "a study of the subject's goal-setting behaviour". One may use the coding task for the purpose. In such a task you may have, for example, a set of numerical symbols each standing for a letter as shown below.

1	2	3	4	5	6	7	8	9	10	11	12
J	P	H	T	C	G	S	K	A	F	L	B

S is presented a sheet bearing a random arrangement of the numbers, as given below, and asked to substitute as many letters in the blank spaces below the number as he can within say, 10 sec.

5	3	8	12	6	4	7	9	11	2	10	1

Fifteen to twenty other similar sheets are presented one after the other. All sheets contain the same numbers from 1 to 12 but their sequence changes from sheet to sheet in a random order. E gives start signal as he presents a sheet which he removes after 10 sec. E uses a stop watch for the purpose. After S has done with the first sheet, he is told the number of letters he could correctly substitute in that trial. He is then asked : "How many letters you are going to substitute in the next trial ?" This becomes S's aspiration which is noted by E. In this manner every time S is told about his achievement and, thereafter, asked to set his goal for the next trial S's achievement and aspiration are recorded from trial to trial. E then finds out the discrepancy between S's achievement in a given trial and his aspiration in the next following trial ; this has been called goal discrepancy. In addition, E also finds the difference between S's aspiration in a trial and his attainment in that trial ; this has been called attainment discrepancy and describes S's success or failure in achieving his goal. Goal discrepancy and attainment discrepancy scores are, thus, found for all trials. Supposing the following data were obtained from a subject :

Table 1

S'S ASPIRATION AND ATTAINMENT FROM TRIAL TO TRIAL AND THE DISCREPANCY SCORES

Trials	Aspiration	Attainment	Discrepancy: Attainment	Discrepancy: Goal
1		5	−1	+2
2	7	6	0	+1
3	7	7	−3	+2
4	9	6	−1	+1
5	7	6	+2	0
6	6	8	−2	+1
7	9	7	+2	0
8	7	9	−4	+3
9	12	8	+1	0
10	8	9	−3	+2
11	11	8	−4	+3
12	11	7	−1	+1
13	8	7		+0
14	7			

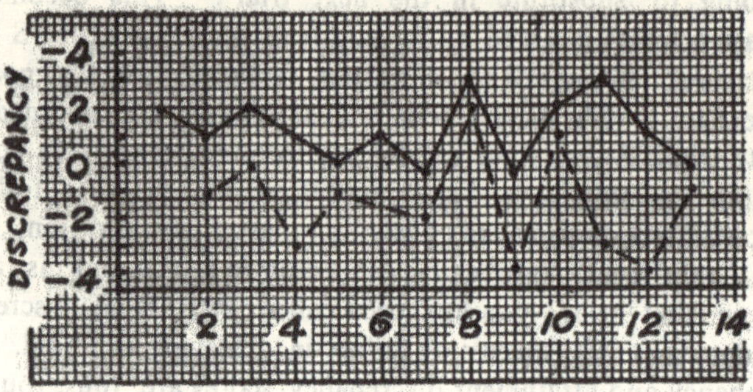

Fig. 1. Serial No. Trials.

Table 2

POSITIVE, NEGATIVE AND ZERO DISCREPANCIES

	Direction		
Discrepancy	+	−	0
Goal	10	0	3
Attainment	3	8	1

We note (Table 2) that out of the total of 12 attainment discrepancy scores 8 are negative—they indicate failure on the part of S to attain his goal ; only two are positive or indicative of success. Further, the range of negative discrepancies is large, namely −4 to −1 while that of positive discrepancies is 1 to 2 (Table 1). The frequencies of the two types of discrepancies are almost in the reverse order, when we consider the goal discrepancy scores—there are 9 positive discrepancies and no negative discrepancy. We may conclude that S is not influenced by the actual experience of goal attainment. Further, he has a tendency to keep his aspiration above his attainment irrespective of previous experience of success or failure (Table 1 and Fig. 1); the curve for goal discrepancy runs higher than that for attainment discrepancy in all trials except one. The data support the general finding that, on the average, there is a tendency to set one's goal above one's attainment.

One may seek to find out the effect of success and failure on S's goal-setting behaviour by reporting to him fictitious attainment scores. For this purpose, time rather than output may be used as the measure. E may hold a stop watch in his hand and measure S's time in completing the coding in each trial; the score unit should be second and not minute, to allow for a wide range of scores. S is asked each time after E reports his attainment : "How many seconds you are going to take next ?" E manipulates success and failure in a random fashion; his reports of S's attainment is 50 per cent of the times higher and 50 per cent of the times lower than his aspiration. The relative frequencies of raising and lowering of the goal consequent upon success and failure, respectively, will be determined and conclusion will be drawn about the general tendency noted in S.

You may intorduce another variable in the situation that may throw a light on S's self-concept as refleced in the tendency to overrate or underrate himself. You put S a question before you report his attainment in a trial. "How may seconds you think you have taken this time ?" and record the answer. You then find, in addition to the other two, another discrepancy score which is the difference between S's judgment on his performance and his actual performance. This has been called judgment discrepancy. More frequent positive or more frequent negative judgment discrepancy would indicate S's tendency to overrate or underrate himself, respectively. A comparison between attainment discrepancy and judgment discrepancy would indicate whether S's judgment on his performance bears any relationship to his experience of success and failure. This would further show whether S does or does not display a tendency for his self-concept to be founded on a realistic appraisal of his past achievements which alone provide an objective evidence of his personal strengths and limitations.

One important point should not be missed. The interpretation of the discrepancy scores will be altered when time rather than output is used as the medium of scoring. Achieving more than what one aspires for will amount to success when the score is in terms of output and failure when it is in terms of time. The raising and lowering of aspiration, as well as overrating or underrating himself, will also be determined differently when time rather than output is used as the score medium. The following points may be taken note of in order to avoid confusion :

I. *Output as Score*

(*a*) Goal discrepancy—attainment in a trial subtracted from aspiration in the next trial.

(*b*) Attainment discrepancy—aspiration in a trial subtracted from attainment in that trial.

(*c*) Judgment discrepancy—attainment in a trial subtracted from judgment in that trial.

II. *Time as Score*

(*a*) Goal discrepancy—aspiration in the next trial subtracted from attainment in the preceding trial.

(*b*) Attainment discrepancy—attainment in a trial subtracted from aspiration in that trial.

(*c*) Judgment discrepancy—judgment in a trial subtracted from attainment in that trial.

When you follow the above rules, a positive discrepancy will have the same meaning irrespective of your using output or time as the score.

You can introduce a social variable also. Take, say, 10 trials in the coding task, using output as score, in the manner described above (p. 283). Then take another 10 trials for which tell S "By the way, I forgot to tell you earlier that I have given the test to several other students in your class, and their average score within the time limit has been 10; some have even completed the entire sheet within the same time limit". After having obtained the two sets of data, treat them separately and make a comparison between them. If the social factor has been brought in to play, S's average aspiration level is expected to be higher in the second set ; the frequency of positive goal discrepancy will be larger, and, perhaps, also the magnitude of the discrepancies ; S may be less responsive to failure as he may be disposed to strive for his group goal.

For all experiments on motivation that we have described, you will notice that your instruction to S does not reveal the real purpose for which the experiment is being conducted. In fact, the purpose is hidden from S. Hence it is necessary that you must use a non-sophisticated subject, i. e., one who has no idea of the problem you are trying to answer by conducting the experiment. It would, therefore, be best to avoid a student of psychology, and if you cannot, select one of a lower standard than yourself, namely, one who is not familiar with the type of experiment. Never exchange the role with your laboratory partner for these experiments.

Recommended Readings

Munn, N. L., *Fundamentals of Psychology*, Chapter 6, Oxford and I.B.H,. New Delhi, 1967.

Underwood, B. J., *Experimental Psychology*, Chapter 8, Appleton, New York, 1966.

Woodworth, R. S. and Schlosberg, H., *Experimental Psychology*, Chapter 22, Holt, New York, 1954.

Chapter XV

Thinking

Thinking is symbolic problem solving. The occasion for thinking arises when one meets a problematic situation for which he has no ready-made solution. He has to find a solution by working on the problem. But the working does not involve overt behaviour, or physical manipulation. In fact, overt behaviour is suspended during the activity of thinking. S deals with the situation by making implicit responses, those that are not visible. These implicit responses are symbolic ; they represent or stand for the objects or parts of the situation that are to be manipulated or for the overt act of manipulation. We find an illustration of the thinking activity in a kind of task that is being frequently used in the study of human problem-solving. It makes use of jumbled or disarranged letters of a word, called anagram (p. 275). S is required to set the letters in order so that the reordering results in a meaningful word, e. g. CKABL can be rearranged as BLACK. S is not permitted to write down the different letters in different orders, in order to get at the correct solution of the anagram ; he has to manipulate them mentally or symbolically, till he arrives at the appropriate solution.

In a simple experiment on problem solving you may be interested in exploring S's mode of attack on the problem, and you may use anagrams for the purpose. You will need, say, 20 five-lettered anagrams, each one convertible into a very familiar word. You may let S have one minute for solving each anagram, after which he is given the correct solution. After S has been through the complete list, you put questions to S in order to find out his method of approach : whether he mentally manipulated the letters by setting them into all possible positions till he got the correct solution, or he just pondered over each anagram and hit the correct solution all on a sudden. The two questions will provide the answer for a trial-and-error approach or the operation of insight. You may further explore whether he used an unsystematic, hit-and -miss method, or made a systematic approach. The results may further consist of the total number of correct solutions made by S converted into percentage. You may also record the actual time taken by S in solving each anagram, where he could do so within the time limit. You may then plot a curve on this basis, using time in seconds—0 to 60 sec., as x-axis, and serial order of the problem as y-axis, and note any improvement made by S as a result of familiarity with the type of problem.

The following is the report of an experiment on another related problem :

Set in Problem Solving

Set is a state of readiness or preparedness to behave in a particular manner in a given situation. In laboratory experiments a desired set can be induced through the medium of the instruction (p. 118). It may, however, be formed automatically when S confronts a succession of tasks that can be tackled in the like manner. S gets prepared to meet a new task by using the procedure that succeeded in performing the preceding tasks. In such a situation one may notice that once the appropriate set has been formed, it has a facilitating effect on S's on-going performance. This is manifested by the ease with which S performs the subsequent tasks—he takes less time, makes fewer errors, gets more strongly involved in the performance, and so on. Set, however, may also hinder the performance of a subsequent task by leading S into a blind alley, i. e., by making him repeat the procedure conforming to the set in spite of its being inappropriate to the task in hand. This has been described as functional fixedness, which might deter the correct handling of the task ; this would not have happened in the absence of the set.

In this experiment an attempt has been made to demonstrate both the facilitative as well as the inhibitory influence of set on problem solving behaviour.

Hypotheses : An appropriate response-induced set would facilitate the responses relevant to the set ; it would inhibit the response inconsistent with the set.

Method

Subject : Male Graduate student.

Apparatus : (1) Stop watch. (2) Forty five-lettered anagrams typed in bold letters each on a 2″×3″ card ; first 15 and last 10, Lists I and III, to be solved according to one rule; the remaining 15, List II, to be solved by another rule.

Procedure : Instruction to S : "I will show you a card having a meaningless combination of letters. You have to rearrange the letters mentally so that they make a meaningful word. There is no time limit. But try to do it as quickly as posible. I will see how soon and how many of these problems you can solve. This is a test of your reasoning ability."

E presented the cards one after the other, and measured S's time in solving each anagram.

S was asked to describe any special difficulty he experienced, or any clue that helped the solution.

Introspection : "The task appeared difficult at first, but after some time I discovered that I could solve each one by the same method. Then it became very easy. But I found later on that the method did not work. At first, I thought that there was something wrong with the problem. But then after some effort, I succeeded in finding the correct word. I tried the other ones ; here, too, the earlier method did not work. Then it occurred to me that perhaps a different method was applied for these problems. I then tried to remember the method by which I had solved one problem and applied it to the next following and it worked. Then it became quite easy. A little after, I again encountered difficulty, but after a few solutions I found that here, too, there was a common method. Having discovered that, the solution became very easy."

Result

Table 1

RAW DATA

(*column heading shows also the correct order*)

List I		List II		List III	
Anagram 35214	Time in seconds	Anagram 53241	Time in seconds	Anagram 35214	Time in seconds
1. CISKT	75	1. TIHRS	80	1. CTWHA	65
2. SUHEO	55	2. EIHTW	72	2. NUSDO	42

Table 1 (*Contd.*)

List I		List II		List III	
Anagram 35214	Time in seconds	Anagram 53241	Time in seconds	Anagram 35214	Time in seconds
3. HGNTI	53	3. NARIT	55	3. GNMOA	20
4. AEWTH	47	4. RVOEC	42	4. HGLTI	15
5. CIBKR	41	5. EROSH	32	5. DATER	12
6. AGSRU	35	6. LMAEC	15	6. WOCDR	10
7. NIDKR	10	7. RVOEL	35	7. EWTRO	8
8. ETWRA	4	8. DARUF	20	8. NURDO	6
9. IUFTR	22	9. EARVB	18	9. MAFER	4
10. PAGER	11	10. KALCB	14	10. TSPEA	3
11. CRFEO	15	11. DAORB	6		
12. UOCDL	10	12. RWOET	10		
13. LBTEA	9	13. TGIHE	8		
14. TOCHL	6	14. DAERB	6		
15. NUWDO	8	15. TAOSR	5		

Table 2

MEAN TIME, SD AND COEFFICIENT OF VARIATION FOR THE THREE SETS OF ANAGRAMS

Set	35214	53241	35214
Mean	26.73	27.20	18.50
SD	21.13	24.20	18.87
CV	82.04	88.97	102.00

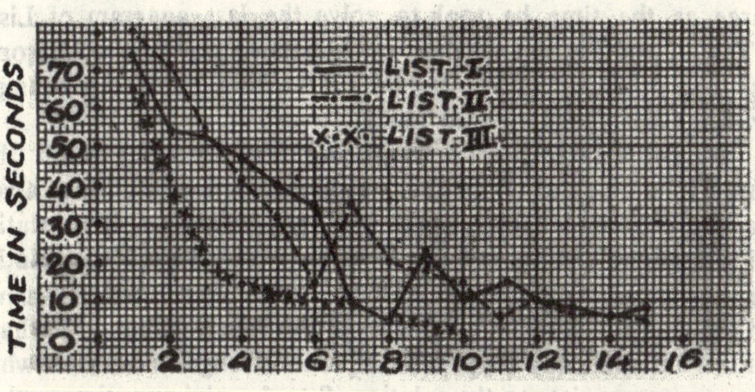

Fig. 1. Serial No. of Problems, List I, List II, List III.

Discussion

The result (Table 1 and Fig. 1) supports our hypothesis. There is gradual decrease in solution time from trial to trial, so that the difference between the time in the first and that in the last trial of List I is 67 sec. ; the first anagram in this List took 75 sec. while the fifteenth only 8 sec. to solve. The decrement in time is more gradual in the beginning ; S did not discover the rule at first, though its implicit influence already started showing itself. There is a steep fall in the curve (Fig. 1) when S reached the seventh anagram. It may be presumed that at this stage S became conscious of the rule. S also admits in his introspection that the solution became easy after he had discovered the rule.

The operation of the same rule induced the set in S to repeat it; this facilitated the process of solution. But the set also hindered the solution of the other list, which called for a different rule. In spite of his familiarity with the task, S took 80 sec. in the solution of the first anagram of List II, more than what he took to solve the first anagram of List I, when he was altogether new to the task. The set produced in solving List I made S repeat the same rule; this was inappropriate to List II. The extinction of the set needed several non-reinforced trials before it was replaced by the set appropriate to List II. Thereafter, the facilitative effect of set could be marked in the solution of List II as well (Fig. 1).

The hampering effect of set again becomes visible when we turn to List III. Though S had already solved fifteen anagrams of List I by following the rule appropriate to List III also, he took 65 sec. to solve the first item of this list, which was eight times as large as the time he took to solve the last anagram of List I (Table 1 and Fig. 1). However, the recovery of the set appropriate to List I was possible after only a few non-reinforced attempts with the rule appropriate to List II.

We notice several other interesting features in our result that throw light on some of the factors influencing the solution of a verbal problem similar to that presented by the anagram. The solution of the seventh anagram of List I, namely, NIDKR made the solution of the immediately following one (ETWRA) much easier, because of the implicit association between DRINK and WATER. Perhaps, DRINK automatically suggested one of its strongest associates which became appropriate to the solution; S took minimum time, only 4 sec. in solving ETWRA. A similar process facilitated the solution of

TOCHL which followed LBTRA (List I) and that of DAORB which followed KALOB (List II). The role of implicit association is similarly demonstrated in the solution of PAGER after IUFTR (List I) and of LMAEC after EROSH (List II). GRAPE is associated with its class name FRUIT, and HORSE with its coordinate CAMEL.

We notice a good example of the mislead from set in the delay in solving the second anagram of List II, after the solution of its first anagram, despite the strong association between SHIRT and WHITE. The ready occurrence of WHITE was prevented because under the influence of set, S automatically applied the rule that had proved successful in solving List I, and being baffled, resorted to the hit-and-miss method.

We also note how set leads to a solution conforming to it by blocking, for the moment, an easier alternative solution. DAERB could be very easily solved as BREAD (List II) by just moving backward. But since this solution did not favour the set, BEARD got a stronger chance to occur despite BREAD being also a still more familiar word. We note a similar case with DAORB whose easier solution would be BROAD, but BOARD a less familiar term was preferred because it conformed to the set. However, BOARD had also a preference because of its strong association with BLACK.

The results support our hypotheses : set both facilitates as well inhibits the solution of a problem.

For determining the role of set in problem solving, you may also adopt a modified procedure. You may let the appropriate set develop while S is working on one list and then introduce another list whose items can be solved not only according to the rule applying to the first list but also by some other rule. We got an example of this in the report of the experiment given above (p. 289); DAERB could be solved both as BREAD and BEARD, the first solution being easier as it required only a movement in the reverse direction. But the operating set led S to apply the rule conforming to the set in preference to the easier alternative. The material to be used for the experiment will consist of : (1) a list of 15 anagrams soluble in accordance with a specific rule, each anagram yielding a single solution; (2) Two lists each of 10 such anagrams that each one can be solved by applying the rule appropriate to the first list, in addition, each one can also be solved in another way. Each item in these lists would, thus, make more than one solution possible ; the other solutions will be in accordance with a rule or rules that would not be the same for all items. Let S first try one of the lists whose items have more than one solution. This should be followed by the list with items having only one solution, and, in accordance with a rule that is applicable to all items. S then works on the other list yielding alternative solutions. Your hypothesis will be that more items will be solved by the rule applicable to the intermediate list from the third than from the first list.

You may have other problems dealing with the facilitative role of extra-experimental associations in problem solving. In one experiment you may prepare a list of anagrams which are soluble according to different rules, but their solutions fall within the same class. This list may be followed by another the items of which, when solved, belong to a different category. Here too while set would facilitate the solution of those anagrams that belong to the same category, it would retard the solution of those that stand for objects of a different category, by giving a false lead. The experiment may also be planned in an alternative manner where your problem will be to determine the role of instructional set in problem solving. In the experiment reported or described above, we have dealt with response induced set and have examined its facilitative effect on solving anagrams. Here we are concerned with the set explicitly aroused in S by E. E prepares three lists. List I contains a succession of items standing for objects of the same class, such as Sheep, Camel, Horse, Donkey, Mouse, Rabbit, Jackal, Zebra, Tiger, Monkey ; each word has its letters disarranged so as to form an anagram. This list is first introduced with the general instruction to solve each item by reordering the letter components. Lists II and III contain the names of, say, countries and fruits, respectively : (1) France, Italy, India, Russia, Nepal ; (2) Orange, Mango, Grape, Banana, and Lemon. These names, too, are converted into anagrams. You will note that the words in all the three lists contain five or six letters, and each word is quite familiar. While introducing List II, E tells S that the anagrams when solved are the names of countries. It is presumed that the difficulty will be minimised in List II where the instructional set is given as compared to List I where S accidentally discovers what he is expected to do. List III like List I is introduced without any explicit instruction. The mislead from the instructional set will retard the solution of this list.

Similar facilitation in solving anagram may be demonstrated in another experiment where the items constitute associative categories i. e., one item suggets another as an implicit associative response to it, e. g., chair and table. Or the items may form a chain of associations, e. g , Water—Drink—Thirst—Hunger—Dinner—Bread—Toast—Butter—White—Black; they are made into anagrams listed in the same order. As a control, there will be another list of 10 items that are apparently unassociated, e. g., Pencil—River—Honest—Garden—Smoke—Broad—Horse—Prison—Letter—Picture. The problem may be stated as : effect of implicit chaining on problem solving.

Concept Formation

A concept is a common response made to diverse objects, events, or situations because they possess some similar characteristics. The response is generally verbal and may be described as a common label attached to objects that belong to the same class. The formation of concepts involves the processes of abstraction and generalisation. Abstraction means isolating the common properties that objects differing otherwise are observed to possess. The common properties are also accorded a common label. The same label is applied to other objects one comes across in future if they possess the qualities associated with the label. This is the process of generalisation. The two processes are generally implicit ; one is not conscious of them while learning a concept. Further, they often go together and it may not be possible to separate one from the other.

Concepts are elements of the thinking process. Thinking is symbolic problem solving (p. 286); while engaged in thinking one is not overtly responding to objects or situations. Instead, one uses the symbolic representations of the objects. Much of these consists of concepts and conceptual processes. To understand the thinking process, it is worthwhile, therefore, to know how concepts are formed and learned.

Diverse kinds of materials have been used in experiments on concept attainment and concept identification. Some have used real objects of different kinds which can be grouped under a limited number of classes on the basis of one or more common characteristics possessed by the members of the group. Others have used drawings of objects that are presented to S one by one for identifying the class to which they belong. Still others have used geometrical blocks, or their pictures, differing in shape, size, height and colour. In order to classify them into different sets, one has to ignore, say their colour and shape, and keep in view either only size, or size and height. Thus all large tall blocks, despite the difference in shape and colour, constitute one class; all small flat ones constitute another class, and so on. Each class is accorded a label which serves as the class name and S has to identify a block by giving its class name. A more convenient device has been to use words instead of objects or drawings. E prepares a list of words, each standing for a separate object or situation. S is required to identify the limited number of categories to be used for classifying them. The following is the plan of an experiment on the attainment of concept, using words. The problem may be stated as "Study of concept formation".

E prepares a list of twenty nouns that are mixed up. The nouns are such that they can be set into five different categories ; each category can be described by a common adjective. The five sets of nouns, together with the adjective describing each set, are stated below:

Small : Ant, Mustard, Pin, Sand
Big : Elephant, Mountain, Ocean, Palm tree
Hard : Gold, Ice, Stone, Iron
Round : Lemon, Ball, Sun, Wheel
Liquid : Milk, Blood, Dew, Water

S is given the instruction : "I will read out to you the name of twenty different objects, one at a time. You have to tell the word that describes each object. After I have read out a name, I will wait for 4 sec. for you to tell me the word that describes it. I will say 'yes' when you will give the correct word, and 'No' when your guess is wrong. You will notice that the objects whose names I give you will be described by using five words only, each word being a common description for four objects. Thus you have to guess the same word for describing four objects. I will tell you the names in a random order so that the names that are described by a common word are not given to you one after the other.

I will go on reading out the names till you have discovered the correct description. Do you understand ?"

E records S's responses on a sheet that bears the list of names in the first column, with other columns for recording the responses.

S is asked to describe in detail the entire process that led him to discover the concepts. His introspection will reveal how he made use of the positive and negative instances in changing the description initially tried by him. Whether he was looking for one description at a time so that only after he had got at one correct adjective and its four correct examples, he switched on to the next one, and so on. Or, he tried to guess all adjectives at a time. Whether he used the hit-and-miss method, or made a systematic approach. These facts may also be explored in the record of S's responses. S's responses may show the tendency for "fixedness", i. e., clinging to a response in the face of its negative instances, or for using the hit-and-miss method by showing a lack of readiness to profit by the information conveyed by E's reaction to S's guess. The introspective data will be used in the discussion.

E tabulates the raw data for the number of correct responses from trial to trial which is also graphically represented. This will throw a light on the gradualness of the process. The raw data would also indicate which concept was easier for S to discover. The writer has noticed that generally 'Liquid' as the common adjective for Water, Milk, Blood, and Dew is not only the first to be discovered, but also it is attained, most often, without any error; it is a dominant associate of each one of the positive instances used in the experiment. On the other hand, 'Small' has been the last to be discovered being a less probable associate to each of the examples given. This type of analysis should lead you to the conclusion that concept attainment is a function of dominance. You may, therefore, state your problem as such, instead of giving it the general form of a 'study of the process of concept attainment'. A tabular presentation of the result, from this point of view, would require separate counts of the frequencies of correct responses in respect of the five different concepts, converted into the Mean frequency per example, and preparation of a histogram on that basis. Following is the result found for a subject :

TABLE NO. AND MEAN CORRECT RESPONSES

Concept	No.	Mean
Small	4	1.00
Big	13	3.25
Hard	17	4.25
Round	10	2.50
Liquid	28	7.00

The method of approach to the problem of concept identification used by a particular S has been technically called strategy. A set of strategies has been isolated, two of which may be mentioned : (1) Successive scanning and conservative focussing, and (2) simultaneous scanning and focus gambling. In successive scanning, S starts with a single hypothesis that he tests in the different instances of the concept which is to be discovered. He abandons the hypothesis when he encounters a negative instance. A particular feature of the instance that illustrates the concept is kept in the focus. It is subsequently replaced by another feature when an instance is met that lacks the first feature. In this manner, by the successive testing of each alternative hypothesis, S comes to identify the correct concept. (2) In simultaneous scanning S starts with more than one hypothesis. He keeps in the focus more than one dimension. Every instance is used for testing all hypotheses. S does not concentrate on a single feature at a time. Whatever positive or negative instance is met with is used for strengthening one and weakening another hypothesis. The first strategy involves a 'slow but sure' attack. The second one may produce a quicker result but its progress is unsystematic.

Following is the complete report of an experiment on concept identification :

Concept Identification as a Function of the Complexity of Dimensions : When several stimuli are associated with the same response because they possess some common features, we get a concept. Concepts are, thus, classes of objects, attributes or relationships among objects. The development of concepts involves the processes of abstraction and generalisation. Studies on concept formation have used different kinds of materials, such as concrete objects, pictures of objects, abstract figures, words. Results of these studies have contributed some knowledge of the ways concepts are learned and recognised. Concepts based on concrete aspects are more easily formed than those involving abstract qualities. Further, increase in complexity of the dimensions underlying a concept makes the task of concept identification more difficult. It has also been noted that the strategies used by subjects in discovering the appropriate concepts differ with individuals.

In this experiment an attempt was made to examine the difference in the identification of concepts using tasks of two different levels of complexity.

Hypothesis : An increase in the number of dimensions along which stimulus items vary, that is in their complexity, will result in greater difficulty in identifying the concepts to which the stimuli belong.

Method

Subject : A graduate male student.

Material : Two packs of 25 cards, each bearing digits, differing in number from card to card within the range of 4 to 9 digits in the first pack, and within the range of 3 to 7 digits in the second pack.

Procedure : The experiment was divided into two parts, Part I and Part II, and was conducted on two different days. In Part I, S was required to classify the 25 cards into five sets on the basis of a single dimension, namely, the location of figure '5' as the first, second, middle, last but one, and last digit; the sets were labelled as AFT, ESN, IMK, OGP, and UBL, respectively, the order of the vowels and the occurrence of the letters F (first), S (second), M (middle), L (last) helped E, without S's knowledge, in identifying the label assigned to a card at the time of its presentation and that of recording S's response. In Part II, S had to classify the cards on the basis of two dimensions : (1) the relative size of the digits on a card; (*a*) largest of all, (*b*) smallest of all; and (2) relative position of the largest or smallest digit, as first, last, or middle; the smallest, however, was categorised only as first or last. The sets were labelled as : LUFT, SINP, JIDL, TAKS, and KELM. Here again, the position of the letters L (largest) and S (smallest) on a card indicated first largest, first smallest, last largest, last smallest, and middle largest, respectively. These indications served the same purpose for E as those in Part I.

Instruction : "Here I have a pack of 25 cards. Each card has some numbers on it. You have to classify the cards into 5 sets.

The sets are named as OGP, IMK, AFT, UBL, ESN. Each name belongs to five cards. No card has more than one name. You have to sort out the cards that have the same name. I will show you a card and also name it. After I have shown each one, I will thoroughly shuffle them, and then again show them one at a time. You have to guess its name from the list of the five names that are here before you. I will wait for 4 sec. and say 'yes' if your guess is correct; otherwise I will tell the correct name. In this manner, you have to guess the name of each card. Remember that each name applies to five cards. I will go on showing the cards, trial after trial. Each time you have to make a guess and each time I will say 'yes' or correct you as the case may be. Do you understand ?"

The list of names was all the time lying on the table in front of S. Each time E thoroughly shuffled the cards before presenting them to S.

The same instruction was given in both parts of the experiment, only the names of the cards were changed.

E recorded S's responses in each trial. After the trials were over S's detailed introspection was taken. He was asked to review the entire process while engaged in identifying the cards. He was given 5 ms, for this purpose. He had to describe the feature or features on the basis of which he ultimately succeeded in classifying the cards; what basis he used at first and what led him to change it ? Whether he found the task easy or difficult ? What was the nature of the difficulty ?, and so on.

Introspection : Part I— "I thought the task to be easy at first. But it was really difficult. Seeing numbers on the card, I first thought that I could sort them out on the basis of the number of digits each one contained or on the basis of their sums, or the occurrence of some common digits. I was not sure. But I found that none of these principles actually worked. I was very much puzzled. I found that gradually my guesses were coming out to be more and more correct. I found that all cards had number 5 and that the position of this number changed. Then I discovered that this number was in the same position in more than one card. I found that it was last in all UBL. Ultimately I discovered that number 5 occurred first, second, in the middle, and at the end in four sets of cards. I could then identify the remaining five cards as OGP."

Part II—"I tried to look for a common number but the principle did not work. I then thought of other alternatives, but none was successful. I felt that the problem was two difficult for me to solve. Then I tried to make blind guesses. Some of my guesses proved to be correct hits. I then concentrated on one-name KELM and tried to find the common features of the cards bearing this name. I discovered that all numbers on this card were odd. But then I found that some cards having other names had also odd numbers. I compared the other odd numbered cards with KELM. I found that the middle number in all KELM was the largest. I then examined some other cards having a common name. I found that all LUFT had the first largest. I then found that all JIDL had the last largest. But I could not get at the others. Then it struck me that now it may be the smallest. I could then name others also."

Result

Table 1

RAW DATA SHOWING NUMBER OF ERRORS PER TRIAL

Trials	No Errors		Trials	No Errors	
	Part I	Part II		Part I	Part II
1	22	22	11	6	16
2	21	23	12	nil	16
3	19	20	13	nil	15
4	17	19	14		12
5	18	18	15		13
6	19	14	16		12
7	15	18	17		12
8	16	18	18		6
9	17	15	19		Nill
10	13	17	20		Nill

Table 2

NO TRIALS

	No. Trials
Part I	11
Part II	19
Diff	8
% Diff.	42.10

Discussion

S took more trials in solving the second problem;the difference was of 8 trials (Table 2); he took 42 per cent more trials. The difference obviously was due to the complexity of the dimensions constituting the concept. The first problem required the abstraction of a concrete element, number 5, whose particular location characterised each set. The second one involved the isolation of an abstract quality, namely, the relative size of the digits on a card, besides their five different locations on the different sets of cards. The result, thus, supports our hypotheses, namely, that the difficulty of concept identification is a function of the complexity of the dimensions characterising a concept.

The introspective data throw light on the strategy used by S. He at first started with several alternative hypotheses that appeared plausible to him. Such strategy has been described as simultaneous scanning. He then changed his strategy and focussed on one feature, namely, the occurrence of 5 in each. He scanned the positive instances of one concept, namely ULB and discovered the common feature characterising them. The strategy that worked in this case has been described as conservative focussing. More or less similar approach is evidenced from S's introspection, to the second problem. The failure of a planned and systematic attack, however, drove him to the hit-and-miss method. This shows S's experience of greater difficulty in solving this problem; one abandons a systematic approach under desperation. S then concentrated on the positive instances of one concept, namely, KELM. He shifted thus, to conservative focussing. Scanning the elements of KELM, he discovered the principle, namely, the relative size and location of an element. It was not very explicit at first and could be generalised only to two concepts. Further scanning made the principle more explicit.

We notice that S started with several alternative hypothesis, but finding none to be successful, his approach became more analytical; instead of starting with a hypothesis and testing it on other instances, he made an inductive approach—scanned the elements of the cards bearing the same name, which led to the discovery of a concept.

We conclude from our results that increase in the number and decrease in the concreteness of the dimension constituting a concept make the identification of the concept more difficult. Further, S may not use a single strategy throughout the process of concept identification. In case one strategy fails, he may resort to another strategy.

Material for Concept Formation

I

First (AFT)	Second (ESN)	Middle (IMK)	Last but one (OGP)	Last (UBL)
.5479	.8574	.37593	.8457	.4875
.58671	.75964	.68574	.93751	.7395
.527824	.958716	.9315731	.436758	.427485
.51728624	.2549871	.8715431	.2796452	.139715
.58976438	.65928736	.213754164	.43769854	.6278245

1. There are 25 cards, 20 cards each containing 4, 5, 6 or 7 digits; 4 cards containing 8 digits; one having 9 digits. This is one very probable mislead—classification according to number of digits.

2. All cards contain two common factors, digits 5 & 7. The presence of 7 in each is a mislead.

II

LUFT	SINP	JIDL	TAKS	KELM
First largest	First smallest	Last largest	Last smallest	Middle largest
634	3586	537	332	898
847	4867	4258	7685	67834
7254	13487	85329	48563	43764
635425	285764	314235	582461	6829153
9535175	2785645	634417	8657942	6237435

Can be divided into 5 sets on ground of number of digits—a mislead.

The above report illustrates the importance of detailed introspection in experiments in the area of thinking. Thinking is concerned with a great variety of implicit responses which obviously cannot be directly observed. They can be known only from the introspection of the subject.

The Mediation Process

We have noticed that concept attainment implies the application of the same category or name to objects that possess one or more common qualities. Symbolically, A possesses quality B; the same quality B is observed in C also; therefore, A and C belong to the same class; the same name may be given to both or the same description will be true of both. It is the mediation of B, the common quality, that leads to the placing of the two different objects A and C within the same class. The entire process, which may be called the mediation process, is represented in the following three-stage learning paradigm :

A—B, B—C, A—C

We are reminded here of the two-stage PA learning transfer paradigm we encountered earlier (p. 191). The above stated paradigm is a similar 3-stage PA learning paradigm. We call it the mediation paradigm since it illustrates the mediation process.

Just as the mediation of the common qualities facilitates concept learning, the mediation of the common term occurring in the first two stages of the mediation paradigm facilitates the third stage learning. Experiments on the role of mediation in learning have used the following types of paradigms :

1. *Chaining* : A-B, B-C, A-C. S learns the A-B, and B-C, lists, one after the other. He is then tested for the learning of A-C list. The hypothesis is made that A-C learning will be easier. When the A-C list is presented to S, A will evoke B, its forward associate in the first list, and C will also evoke B, its backward associate in the second list (p. 193). This would make the learning of the association between A and C easier; the common associate B, the mediation term, will help in holding them together. To ascertain whether A-C learning becomes easier as a mediation effect, one has to use a control paradigm which has no mediating term : A-B, D-C, A-C. The mediation effect would not, therefore, arise, and A-C learning will not be as easy in this case. The paradigm is called chaining because the learning process involves the formation of a chain A—B—C. There is a reverse chaining paradigm also : B-A, C-B, A-C. Here too both A and C evoke their common associate B, the first because of earlier backward and the second because of earlier forward association learning. The control in this case will be : B-A, C-D, A-C.

2. *Equivalence* : Like chaining, which may be forward or reverse, we have stimulus equivalence or response equivalence paradigm. The stimulus equivalence paradigm has the mediation term as the subject of the first two lists, as shown below together with its control.

A-B, A-C, B-C

A-B, D-C, B-C

The response equivalence paradigm uses the mediation term as the response in the acquisition lists, as shown below together with its control.

A-B, C-B, A-C
A-B, D-B, A-C

It has been noted that the third stage learning is easier in the experimental paradigm, whether one uses the chaining or the equivalence paradigm, as compared to the control paradigm. The ease in learning is interpreted in terms of the mediation hypothesis.

It may be difficult in your class room individual experiment to test the mediation hypothesis. You will have to make your subject learn six lists—three experimental and three control. This will be an arduous task and would require much more time than you can afford for any single experiment. But you may use a short cut. You do not let your S experimentally acquire the association of the terms used in the third list with a common term occurring in the first two lists ; you depend upon the existing extra-experimental association of a term used in the first list with a term used in the test list, to provide for the link between this term and another term in the first list. The following will illustrate the point :

A	B	A	C
TFP —	Table	TFP —	Chair

The middle B-C list of the chaining mediation paradigm will

B C

consist of : Table—Chair, the terms of which being too frequent associates need not be learned as such. Rendered in the form of the 3-stage paradigm we have :

(A-B)	(B-C)	(A-C)
TFP-Table	Table-Chair	TFP-Chair

It is possible also to avoid a separate control list. The first list will have two types of response terms, i. e., each response term of (1) will have an implicit association, and that of (2) will have no such association, with a response term of the second list. You can, thus, test the mediation hypothesis using only two PA lists. Following is a report of an experiment where implicit association betweeen words has been used for testing the mediation hypothesis. The introduction portion of the report has been left out as the opening paragraph of this section describes the facts and concepts required for introduction.

Associative Mediation Effect in Verbal Learning

Hypothesis : When two PA learning lists have an identical stimulus term, the learning of the second list will be facilitated if the response words used in the two lists are frequent associates of each other.

Method

Subject : A graduate female student.

Apparatus and Material : (1) Memory Drum. (2) Two lists of CCC trigrams paired with words, each list containing 10 items.

Procedure : The lists had identical stimulus terms. The response terms were such that 5 of these in the first list were frequent associates of 5 of the second list; remaining five response terms of the two lists did not bear such association. The lists are reproduced below :

BKM - GRASS	BKM - CLOCK
XHN - TABLE	XHN - ROAD
DNP - FAN	DNP - RIVER
TFP - WATER	TFP - DRINK
WXR - BALL	WXR - ROUND
BFD - INK	BFD - SAND
GCR - SKY	GCR - STAR
FHK - GOAT	FHK - BREAD
PZN - BOX	PZN - LID
XTB - LOCK	XTB - KEY

The anticipation method of PA learning was used. At first the stimulus and response terms were exposed together for 4 sec. Thereafter, the stimulus term was alone exposed for 2 sec. followed by the exposure of the response term for another 2 sec. A ten second inter-trial and a sixty second inter-list interval were provided. The position of the paired items on the list changed from presentation to presentation.

Instruction : "You will be shown several 3-letter combinations of consonants, called trigram, each one paired with a word. After the entire list has been presented, you will be shown only the trigram for two seconds. You have to remember the word paired with it. You will then be shown the word also. After you have gone through the entire list in this manner, you will be again shown each trigram alone' and thereafter also the word, one by one. Every time you see a trigram, try to recollect its word pair. You have to learn to associate each trigram with its word pair, and when you have succeeded in correctly recalling each word, on seeing the trigram with which it is paired, I will stop showing the list."

Introspection : "I had some difficulty in learning the first list. The words were quite familiar, but it was difficult to remember with which trigram a word was paired. While learning the second list, I noticed that I could learn some words of the list more easily than others. While trying to recall these words, on seeing a trigram, I first got the word from the first list. Only gradually I learned to substitute the new word for it. This did not happen with the other words."

Result

Table 1

NO. TRIALS TO CORRECT ANTICIPATION. NO. CORRECT, NO. INTRUSION, FROM TRIAL TO TRIAL

	List 1	List 2	
Trial	Correct	Correct	Intrusion
1	1	1	4
2	3	3	1
3	7	5	2
4	8	6	2
5	9	6	3
6	10	8	2
7		9	1
8		10	

Table 2

TOTAL AND MEAN CORRECT ANTICIPATIONS OF ASSOCIATED AND UNASSOCIATED RESPONSES OF LIST 1 AND LIST 2

	List 1		List 2	
	Ass.	Unass.	Ass.	Unass.
Total	20	18	34	14
Mean	4	3.6	6.8	2.8
Diff.	.4		4.0	

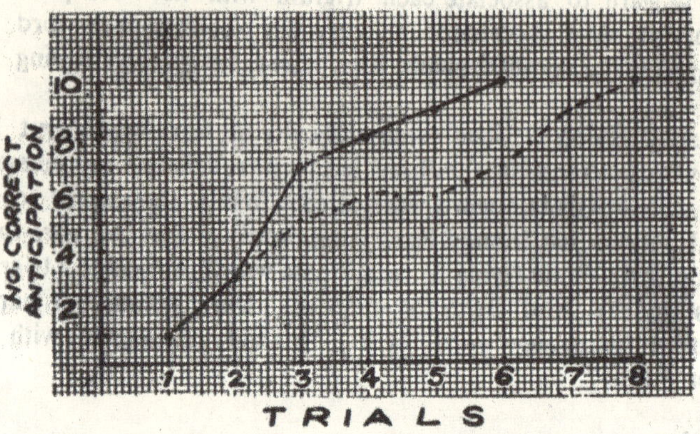

Fig. 1. No. Correct Anticipations from Trial to Trial.

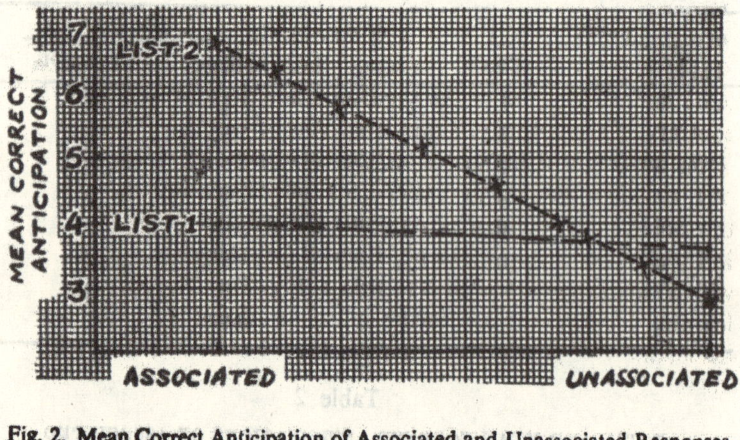

Fig. 2. Mean Correct Anticipation of Associated and Unassociated Responses.

S has taken 6 trials to learn List 1 and 8 to learn List 2 (Table 1, Fig. 1). The number of correct anticipations from trial to trial is larger in List 1 than in List 2 (Table 1, Fig. 1). The total number of correct anticipations of the five associated and five unassociated responses of List 1 and List 2, and their means, are shown in Table 2 and Fig. 2. The Means for the two types of responses in List 1 are 4 and 3.6, and in List 2 they are 6.8 and 2.8, respectively.

Discussion

List 2 learning was more difficult than List 1 learning ; S has taken 6 trials in List 1 and 8 in List 2. The difficulty in learning List 2 was greater on account of the interference caused by the previous learning of List 1. The identical stimulus transfer paradigm of PA learning has been most often found to produce negative transfer. The second list learning requires the unlearning of the first list associations ; S-R_1 connections have to be extinguished before the acquisition of the S-R_2 connections. The interference from the first list learning is evidenced by the large number of intrusions from List 1 (Table 1), and is also supported by S's introspective report.

The negative transfer effect from List 1, learning, however, has been limited only to those five items of List 2 whose response terms are not frequent associates of the corresponding response terms of List 1. The total number of correct anticipations of such responses is only 14, or an average of 2.8 per item, in List 2 ; the total number for List 1 is 18 with an average value of 3.6 per item (Table 2, Fig. 2). The learning of these items of List 2 has been more difficult because of the negative transfer from List 1. On the contrary, the learning of those five items of List 2 whose response terms are frequent associates of the corresponding response terms of List 1, has been much easier ; S's introspection also supports this point. The number of correct anticipations of such responses in List 2 is 34, with a mean per item of 6.8, as against 20 in List 1, with a mean per item of 4 (Table 2, Fig. 2). The facilitation in learning is due to the mediation effect produced by the implicit association in the two lists between the response terms of these items. The already available and easily accessible association provided the intermediate link between the stimulus terms of List 1 and the corresponding response terms of List 2. The learning actually involved three stages ; the middle stage was implicit in the process.

The results supported the mediation hypothesis ; the frequent association of the words attached to the same stimulus terms in the two PA lists had a facilitative effect on the second list learning.

Appendix

Stimulus Terms	TRIALS 1	2	3	4	5	6
BKM	BOX	X	GRASS	GRASS	GRASS	GRASS
XHN	TABLE	TABLE	TABLE	TABLE	TABLE	TABLE
DNP	INK	BOX	INK	GOAT	X	FAN
TFP	X	WATER	WATER	WATER	WATER	WATER
WXR	X	LOCK	BALL	BALL	BALL	BALL
BFD	X	INK	INK	INK	INK	INK
GCR	X	GRASS	SKY	SKY	SKY	SKY
FHK	X	X	X	FAN	GOAT	GOAT
PZN	X	FAN	GOAT	BOX	BOX	BOX
XTB	GOAT	BALL	LOCK	LOCK	LOCK	LOCK

Stimulus Terms	1	2	3	4	5	6	7	8
BKM	X	BREAD	GOAT	LOCK	ROAD	CLOCK	CLOCK	CLOCK
XHN	TABLE	X	CLOCK	BREAD	CLOCK	ROAD	ROAD	ROAD
DNP	LID	X	X	RIVER	RIVER	RIVER	RIVER	RIVER
TFP	RIVER	WATER	DRINK	DRINK	DRINK	DRINK	DRINK	DRINK
WXR	BREAD	ROUND	ROUND	ROUND	ROUND	ROUND	ROUND	ROUND
BFD	X	INK	BREAD	ROAD	X	BREAD	SAND	SAND
GCR	X	STAR	STAR	STAR	STAR	STAR	STAR	STAR
FHK	GOAT	FAN	INK	INK	SAND	ROAD	SAND	BREAD
PZN	RIVER	X	LID	LID	LID	LID	LID	LID
XTB	KEY	KEY	KEY	KEY	KEY	KEY	KEY	KEY

Recommended Readings

Brunner, J. S., Goodman, J. J. and Austin, G. A., *A Study of Thinking*, Chapters 3, 4, Wiley, New York, 1956.

Geldard, F. A., *Fundamentals of Psychology*, Chapter 13, Wiley, New York, 1962.

Munn, N. L., *Introduction to Psychology*, Chapter 12, Oxford and IBH, New Delhi, 1967.

Underwood, B. J., *Experimental Psychology*, Chapter 14, Appleton, New York, 1966.

Woodworth, R. S. and Schlosberg, H., *Experimental Psychology*, Chapters 20, 26, Holt, New York, 1954.

APPENDIX I

Group Experiments

Individual versus Group Experiments

The purpose of this book is to get the student acquainted with the theory and practice of the experimental method in psychology. It was presumed that having fully understood how individual experiments are planned, conducted, and reported, the student will have obtained the necessary grounding for learning to plan and conduct the type of experiments that are reported in standard journals. These reported experiments are based on group data; the experimenter obtains his data from more than one subject. This is necessary for any good experiment in psychology. Psychology deals with human behaviour. Though the general facts of human behaviour are the same for all persons, there are certain peculiarities of individuals that make each person's individual behaviour not identically the same as that of another individual, while both are behaving in the same situation. The results obtained in an individual experiment cannot, therefore, be safely extended to other individuals. Psychology, like other science, however, aims at interpreting and, on that basis, predicting the behaviour, not only of the individual whose behaviour has been observed in the laboratory, but also of other individuals; the results of experiments in psychology have to be generalised to similar cases. The relationship one explores and confirms in an experiment should be an invariable relationship. It is, therefore, necessary that experiments in psychology should be so planned that the results may be justifiably extended to more than one individual. This can be possible only by using more than one subject in an experiment. Hence the special significance of group experiments in psychology.

There are some inherent limitations of individual experiments that can be overcome only in a group experiment. We have noted at several places in this book that some problems cannot be answered in an individual experiment. One very obvious difficulty stems from the 'sequence effect', i. e., effect of the order of placement of two or more conditions of an experiment (p. 8). In a group experiment you may use all possible orders of the conditions and engage some S's in one order, some S's in another order, and so on. For example, in the experiment on reaction time as a function of the type of stimulus you may engage, say, 10 S's using one type of stimulus first and another type next, and 10 S's using the other type first and the first type next. As you will note, in what follows, you may also use separate randomly selected groups for the two types of stimulus, one group for one type only.

There is another difficulty which is no less serious. You have to use separate materials for different conditions of the experiment. For example while comparing massed practice with spaced practice, (p. 166) you have to use different lists for learning in the two conditions. In a group experiment you may use the same list which one group learns by massing, and another by spacing of practice. The identical materials used for the two groups make your result more defensible than when you use different materials presuming that they are comparable. Even while using a single group of S's, you may use each list for massed practice by half of the number of S's and for spaced practice by the remaining half.

Selection of Subjects : Before we take up the methods or designs of group experiments, we should consider how the subjects for such experiments are to be selected. The best methods of selection is random selection. By random selection is meant that those who have not been selected had equal chance of being selected as those who have been selected. The ultimate purpose of any scientific investigation is the ability to generalise from the result of the investigation. The generalisation from the cases observed in the experimental situation to cases not so observed, is possible only if the cases that are observed belong to the population to which the unobserved cases also belong. In other words, the observed cases should constitute a representative sample of the population. A random sample is a representative sample.

To obtain a random sample for his experiment, the experimenter should have an access to the population. This is hardly possible, unless the population is a definite and small population, e. g., the students of a particular college, or the adults residing within a block area, and so on. Even then, the psychologist does not possess that much power as to use every body in his experiment who is caught in the net of his random sample. He can only solicit co-operation by a general invitation issued by some person in authority, or by personal contact of the available section of the population. He can then apply the random method of selection to those who respond to his appeal. Suppose 100 persons have volunteered themselves for an experiment and you actually need 20 subjects for the experiment. You will then randomly select 20 out of 100. For this purpose a crude method will be to arrange the names of the respondents in alphabetical order and pick up every fifth name. Another method is to attach serial numbers 0 to 99 to the names, thereafter, using 100 small sheets of blank paper; one number is written on one sheet. The sheets are then folded and thoroughly shuffled in a basket or bowl. They are picked up from the bowl one by one till one gets 20 pieces. The subjects whose serial numbers appear on the twenty sheets, thus drawn, are selected for the experiment.

A still more refined method is to consult a table of random numbers reproduced in books containing statistical tables. One way to use the table of random numbers is to open any page haphazardly; entering any column one puts one's finger on any number arbitrarily. The last digit of that number will then be used for suggesting the column wherein to seek the numbers that are to be selected. For this purpose, one goes down the column and picks up those numbers that are less than or equal to the total number out of which the selection has to be made. If the total number is 100, select the last two digits from the column till you complete the total number needed.

There may be cases when despite your fervent appeal you may not be able to attract, for making a random selection, more subjects than the number actually needed. Your sample will then be an incidental sample. You may presume even such a sample to represent the characteristics of the population to which it belongs. The subjects that respond to your invitation do so either out of curiosity about experiments in psychology or because of their eagerness to contribute to the promotion of scientific research. If none of these factors is presumed to be correlated with your dependent variable, the sample may be taken to be as good as a random sample, particularly if your experiment has a strong theoretical bias.

Design of Group Experiments

The principal function of any design of experiments, individual or group, is to ensure maximum control in the experiment. Control implies power to (1) manipulate the experimental variable and (2) eliminate, neutralise, or hold constant the extraneous independent variables (p. 6). The stronger the measure of control in the experiment, the greater the confidence with which the result of the experiment can be accepted as an answer to the problem posed in the experiment. The value of a design can, therefore, be assessed in the light of this criterion.

The designs of group experiments can be broadly classified as: A. Identical group design, and B. Multiple groups design. The latter can be further classified as: (1) Randomised groups design, and (2) Matched, or equated groups design.

A. Identical Group Design

The same group is used for two or more conditions of the experiment. The design overcomes many of the limitations of an individual experiment. For example, you can meet the problem caused by the sequence effect (p. 310), or that arising from the doubt regarding the comparability of the materials or task used in different conditions (p. 311). You have to set the conditions of the experiment in different orders for different batches of subjects within the group, or, use in each condition not only one task or one material, but all tasks or all materials, each one assigned to a particular batch of subjects. In the experiment on knowledge of result (p. 268), you may engage, say, 10 subjects in drawing lines without knowledge of results, followed by drawing with knowledge of results, and 10 subjects drawing with knowledge of results and then drawing without knowledge of results.

In the experiment on "Retroactive Inhibition as a function of temporal location of the interpolated task" (p. 223), you have to use three **comparable** tasks for original learning (p. 209) in the three conditions of thee xperiment. Suppose you are engaging twelve subjects in the experiment. You can then distribute the subjects among the different conditions of t e experiment in the following manner :-

	Cond. I		Cond II		Cond. III	
	Learning	Test	Learning	Test	Learning	Test
S1	Task A	Task A	Task B	Task B	Task C	Task C
S2	,,	,,	,,	,,	,,	,,
S3	,,	,,	,,	,,	,,	,,
S4	,,	,,	,,	,,	,,	,,
S5	Task B	Task B	Task C	Task C	Task A	Task A
S6	,,	,,	,,	,,	,,	,,
S7	,,	,,	,,	,,	,,	,,
S8	,,	,,	,,	,,	,,	,,
S9	Task C	Task C	Task A	Task A	Task B	Task B
S10	,,	,,	,,	,,	,,	,,
S11	,,	,,	,,	,,	,,	,,
S12	,,	,,	,,	,,	,,	,,

Similarly in the experiment on 'Memory for finished and unfinished tasks' (p. 272), you may engaae 20 S's and let the order in which the 20 different combinations of consonants be used for cancellation change from subject to subject; so should also the combinations to be interrupted and those to be completed vary from subject to subject.

However, despite your power to control some extraneous variables effectively, as noted above, the identical group design suffers from serious practical difficulties. Even when your experiment requires only two conditions, it would not be desirable to engage the S's in both conditions on the same day. For example in the experiment on intraserial similarity (p. 163) where you use two lists of CCC trigrams, one having similar and the other dissimilar items, your S is very likely to get bored after having been through the learning of the first list. You will have to call him on another day for learning the second list. But he may not turn up again. If your experiment requires the use of more than two conditions, the loss of S's becomes still more serious.

In view of the tremendous difficulties the experimenter faces in getting hold of subjects, because of the exigency of using human material for his experiments, identical subjects design may some time prove highly impracticable. It may, however, sometimes have an advantage over multiple groups design where you will require different subjects for different groups, the total number of S's, thus, becoming as many times the number in the identical group experiment as the number of groups. The experimenter may sometimes encounter difficulty in catching so many subjects in his net. We will also note, while describing the statistical devices used for analysis of group data, that the identical group design entails a less rigorous statistical test of hypothesis (p 320); the value of SE diff. for the same data is reduced when using this design (p. 370).

B. Multiple Groups Design

(1) Randomised Groups : In this design separate groups of S's are used for different conditions. For this purpose, the subjects that are initially selected for the experiment have to be divided into small groups. Say, you have to use one control and two experimental conditions and, therefore, need three groups of subjects. You may decide to have 10 S's in each group. Thus the 30 S's originally selected are to be classified into three groups—one control and two experimental, each containing 10 S's. The assignment of the S's to the groups should be random. An easy method will be to list in one column the names of the thirty S's with serial numbers, from 1 to 30, attached to them. Five numbers are then written in a row against each name, thus—I 0, 1, 2, 3, 4; II 5, 6, 7, 8, 9;...... ....XXX 145, 146, 147, 148, 149. One hundred fifty 2"×1" slips are prepared with numbers from 0–149 written on them, one number on each slip. The slips are folded crosswise and thoroughly shuffled in a bowl (or plastic box). Another sheet contains three columns headed by Group I, Group II, Group III. A slip is then picked up from the bowl, opened and the number read. Under Group I is written the serial number of the S against whose name the number on the slip occurs. The slip is folded and returned to the bowl. The slips are again shuffled and then another slip is drawn. The S in whose row the number on the slip is found is thus identified and placed in Group II. The third draw will give the S for Group III. By repeating the process, all S's will have been distributed between the three groups. If one gets another number from the same row, or the same number over and again, the slip is returned back to the bowl; the S who is identified by numbers in this row has already been placed. The assignment of S's to the three groups may be safely presumed to be random. As a substitute, one may use the table of random numbers (p. 311). In this case, while using a table of random numbers, select the last three digits from the column.

You have to decide next about the assignment of the groups to the conditions, or treatments as they are technically called, since the experimental variable is manipulated in different ways in the different conditions. One group is to be assigned to one treatment. Had there been two groups only, one could achieve this by tossing a coin and deciding in advance that if head turns up, say, Group I, is to function as the control group; failing this Group I would be the Experimental group, and group II becomes control. If there are three groups one may first assign Group I by lot on the basis of three consecutive throws, this time also deciding in advance, say, if head turns up in the first throw Group I is designated as control, if it comes up in the second throw, Group I becomes Exp. I, and if in the third throw it is assigned to Exp. II. Having decided about Group I, one then decides by lot about the two remaining groups. If the number of groups is still larger then the basis of assignment would be as many consecutive throws.

You may encounter a practical difficulty. It may not be possible to prepare in advance the list of the S's who would turn up for the experiment. You have to use each one at the time he comes in response to your invitation. Suppose you need forty subjects, 10 S's to be used for each one of four treatments. Also suppose that your subjects are to be drafted in from among the undergraduate students of a local college. You should have already made a general request to them through the class room teachers, the Principal of the College, or any other agency, to turn up for the experiment within a particular hour on any day suiting each one's convenience. They do likewise turn up on different days, at times in batches of more than one, while you can engage only one and have to fix up other dates for the remaining. Thus, the S's that actually turn up for the experiment will have to be engaged in the order in which they turn up. Let the orders represent the respective subjects. You require forty subjects ; they will have forty ordinal positions—1 to 40. Use Roman numerals for these respective positions (I, II, III......XXXX) and randomly distribute the positions into four groups by the method suggested above (p. 314). After the ordinal positions have been assigned to the groups, randomly assign the groups to the treatments. Now when the actual data collection starts, identify a subject by the order in which he turns up and consult the plan for assignment of the orders to the groups and of the groups to the treatments. Then use him for the treatment to which his ordinal position has been assigned. For example, your problem is to determine the differential transfer effects for the two single-function and one double-function paradigms of transfer in PA learning (p. 191) for which you make use of a control paradigm also, in addition to these three. You could not succeed to prepare in advance a list of subjects for their random distribution in the four groups, and have, therefore, to depend upon whosoever from among those you have invited turns up for the experiment according to his own convenience. You can overcome the difficulty by randomly preparing a plan for the different orders in which the S's turn up, as shown below :

ORDER OF ENGAGEMENT

Treatment	A	B	C	D
Group	2	4	1	3
	IV	II	VI	I
	V	VII	VIII	III
	XI	XIII	IX	X
	XIV	XV	XVI	XII
	XIX	XX	XVII	XXII
	XXI	XXIII	XVIII	XXVI
	XXIV	XXV	XXVIII	XXIX
	XXX	XXVII	XXXI	XXXII
	XXXIV	XXXV	XXXVII	XXXIII
	XXXIX	XXXVI	XXXVIII	XXXX

Suppose a certain S is the fifteenth in order to turn up for the experiment. He falls in Group 4 and receives treatment B.

You will notice how the practical difficulties of the identical group method are overcome when one uses the multiple group method. Each group is engaged only on the day he turns up. The problem about the comparability of the learning lists does not at all exist. The A-B list is common to all paradigms. The C term is also identical except for its position in the lists. The preparation of the lists too is very much simplified on this account.

(2) *Matched Groups and Equated Groups Method* : The randomised groups method has the merit of neutralising the influence of all significant extraneous variables, both known and unknown to the experimenter. The S's are assigned

to the different groups on random basis. The influences of such extraneous independent variables as intelligence, motivation, past experience, socio-economic status, and so on, that might affect the dependent variable, in addition to the influence it has from the experimental variable—the variable that is manipulated in the experiment, are randomly distributed among the S's included in each group. Their total effect, thus, remains constant for all groups. Hence, whatever difference in the dependent variable is observed between the different groups can be justifiably ascribed to the difference in the treatments given to the different groups.

When the experimenter may not be able to identify the significant extraneous variables, the randomised groups method makes him feel confident that their influences on the dependent variable, if any, have been evenly distributed over all groups. Where the significant extraneous variable has already been identified, one may use an alternative method, the so-called matched-groups method. Suppose your problem is to determine the facilitative effect of set on the solution of anagrams (p. 287). Two groups are used, one group solving one list. The groups may be set apart by the randomisation method. Knowing, however, that the ability to solve anagrams is positively correlated with intelligence, and that other variables like relative difficulty, number of components, etc., have been held constant, you may seek to control intelligence only. You obtain the intelligence test scores of the S's. You then locate pairs of subjects, the members of each pair having identical intelligence test score. One member is then randomly assigned to one group and the other to the other group, as shown below:

Group I		Group II	
Subject	Score	Subject	Score
A	85	F	85
B	60	G	60
C	92	H	92
D	72	I	72
E	45	J	45

The advantage from high and the disadvantage from low level of intelligence, so far as their respective influences on S's problem solving behaviour are concerned, are equally counter-balanced in the two groups. Had this not been done, that is, S's were arbitrarily assigned to the two groups, the possibility of more intelligent S's forming one group would have remained undiscovered. The difference found between the groups would then have been wrongly ascribed to the independent variable manipulated in the experiment; at least the difference would be ascribable to both. We will have then come across what has been called confounding, the result of the experiment will be inconclusive.

The equated groups method is similar to the matched group method. In this case, however, the matching is overall. The S's in the two groups may not have common scores between them, but the mean scores and the variance (variance = standard deviation squared) of the two groups should be the same within the limits of chance difference (p. 38). The following is an example of groups equated on the basis of anxiety test scores :

Group I		Group II	
Subject	Score	Subject	Score
A	20	F	6
B	7	G	18
C	13	H	16
D	8	J	9
E	11	K	11
Mean	11.80	Mean	12.00
V(σ^2 8)	12.63	V(σ^2)	12.79

The difference between the means and the variances is too small to exceed chance limits.

After the subjects have been distributed between the two gruops, the assignment of the matched or equated groups to the treatments should be random (p. 314). An important variable in respect of which matching may have to be done in learning experiments is the initial learning ability of the subjects.

You will notice that the randomised groups method is much more convenient and the results obtained by this method inspire greater confidence. For using the matched or equated groups method, you should have a large body of the prospective subjects available for measurement on the extraneous variable that is to be controlled. They have also to be called again in order to be informed as to which ones were selected for the experiment; these are then requested to turn up individually for the experiment; you can hardly depend upon each one of them to turn up. You will then be in a quandry. The method, thus, entails an irrepairable loss of S's among those who volunteer themselves for the experiment; the loss becomes considerable if more than two groups are used and perhaps the method may altogether fail when the matching is to be done on more than one or two variables. The method, thus, makes a demand upon the experimenter which he is seldom qualified to fulfil; he should have perfect control over the population of subjects. Even if this could be possible, one cannot be very confident about the results; the extraneous variables controlled by matching may not be the only one influencing the dependent variable.

It would follow from the above account that the randomised group method is the most convenient and also the results obtained by this method inspire maximum confidence. However, though it is presumed that the random assignment of subjects to groups makes them approximately equal in respect of all significant extraneous variables, in actual practice this claim may not be always substantiated, particularly if the number of S's within a group is small. The matched groups method has an advantage in one respect, namely, one is definite that the variable controlled by matching does not contaminate the variable manipulated in the experiment. Whatever method is used, it is not easy, however, to inspire confidence in the result of an experiment in psychology. The value of replication can never be over-emphasised. The more consistent the results of the replications, the greater the confidence with which they can be accepted.

The Before-After Design

We have come across the before-after design in the earlier Chapters (p. 11). We noticed that the observation of a difference in the dependent variable before and after the introduction of the independent variable supports the hypothesis about the relationship between the dependent and the independent variables. But the doubt still remains, namely that an unanticipated extraneous variable really affected the dependent variable. For example in the experiment on Reaction Time as an indirect measure of fatigue, the before-after design was suggested (p. 233). It was presumed that increase in RT will be due to the generalised muscular fatigue effect produced by the continuous pressing of the dynamometer. One may argue, however, that it was the decline in motivation due to S's engagement in the dull repetitive activity of pressing the telegraphic key in the before RT trials, and not the muscular fatigue, which really affected his RT in the after RT trials. Similarly in experiments on transfer in a sensory-motor task, one may suspect that it is not the intervening practice on another similar task (p. 183) which carries over to the subsequent performance of the first task, but it is familiarily with the first task itself that affects its performance after the second task. There may be another element of doubt. It was not the experimental variable, but an unobserved intervening extraneous variable that really influenced the after-test measure of the dependent variable. The before-after design, thus, introduces a confounding variable (p. 316) which makes the result inconclusive. A control, involving the omission of the intervening pressing of the dynamometer, or practice on a second task, meets these difficulties. The design is shown below :

I Exp.	Test Task 1	Performance Task 2	Test Task 1
II Cont.	Test Task 1		Test Task 1

In an identical group design, half of the S's will be first engaged in the experimental and the other half first engaged in the control condition. In a multiple group design, we will have either randomised or matched groups; one of these will be assigned the control and the other the experimental condition. If the performance in Task 1 before-Task 2 differs from that after-Task 2, in the experimental condition, and no such difference is found in the control condition, one may safely conclude that the intervening independent variable accounts for this difference.

It is, however, quite possible that even in the control condition the subsequent test of Task 1 may not give the same result as that from its earlier test for the reason that earlier engagement in the task also had some effect on its later performance. You may then compare the two conditions in respect of the differences between the two tests. Finding the difference to be significantly larger in the experimental condition, you argue that this was due to the performance of Task 2, your experimental variable. But still the suspicion that an unknown intervening extraneous variable also influenced the dependent variable remains unshaken. To arrive at a more conclusive answer, you introduce another control in the design. The design then assumes the following shape :

Exp. : Yb × Ya y = dependent variable
Cont. I : Yb Ya x = independent variable
Cont. II : × Ya a = after, b = before

The design controls what transpires between the before and after-tests, as well as the effect of prior engagement with the dependent variable. Still greater refinement in the design may be achieved by introducing a third control as shown below :

Exp. : Yb × Ya
Cont. I : Yb Ya
Cont. II : × Yb
Cont. III : Yb

The third control provides for the measure of the dependent variable without its measure on a previous occasion and without the introduction of the experimental variable. The issue about the influence of the suspected extraneous variables can be finally settled : (1) If previous engagement has an effect on the after test, then a comparison of the Experimental and Control II conditions would show a difference in the dependent variable. (2) If an intervening variable affected the dependent variable, then this will bring about a difference between Control I and Control III. By the way, you will appreciate that you can possibly use the design shown above only when you have multiple groups for the experiment, engaging one group in one condition.

Statistical Analysis of Group Data

We have earlier (p. 42) refered to the use of the *t* test for the statistical analysis of individual data. The *t* lest is equally applicable for the same purpose to group data. When we use random groups, we expect no correlation between the performance of the members of one group and those of other groups. But while using identical groups, the performance of a subject is likely to be correlated in the two or more conditions of the experiment. For example while using the same group for finding a difference in the rate of learning of meaningful and nonsense materials, we expect better learners to excel poor learners in both, and, therefore, a significant correlation is likely to be found between the learning score for the two types of materials. We expect similar correlation while using the matched groups design (p. 315). The difference between the subjects in the matched variables within one group will be correlated with the differences in that variable within another group. And if the matched variable influences the dependent variable, the measures of the dependent variable obtained for the two groups will also be correlated.

If there is significant correlation between the measures of the dependent variable in the two conditions, and consequently, their means are correlated, the following formula will be used for the standard error of difference between the means :

$$SE_{diff} = \sqrt{SE^2_{M_1} + SE^2_{M_2} - 2r_{12}\ SE_{M_1}\ SE_{M_2}} \quad \text{......(} i \text{)}$$

When the means are uncorrelated that is r_{12} is eqal to 0, as is expected while using randomised groups, $r_{12}\ SE_{M_1}\ SE_{M_2}$ will also be equal to zero and formula (*i*) will be reduced to formula (*ii*) given below :

$$SE_{diff} = \sqrt{SE^2_{M1}+SE^2_{M2}} \quad \text{......}(ii)$$

Formula (*i*) requires the calculation of r_{12}. This can be avoided by using the following formula :

$$SE_{diff} = \sqrt{\frac{\text{Sum } D^2 - \frac{(\text{Sum } D)^2}{N}}{N(N-1)}}$$

D= difference between score obtained by each S or by matched S's, in the two conditions ..... (*iii*)

N = number within the groups, single or matched

For using formula (*ii*) you have to calculate separately SE_M by the formula : $SE_M = \frac{\sigma}{\sqrt{N-1}}$ (p. 39), for which you have to calculate σ or SD also. When you are not required to find SD, the formula for SE of difference between means will be :

$$\left(\frac{\text{Sum } X^2_1 - \frac{(\text{Sum}X_1)^2}{n_1} + \text{Sum } X^2_2 - \frac{(\text{Sum } X_2)^2}{n_2}}{(n_1-1)\ (n_2-1)}\right)\left(\frac{1}{n_1}+\frac{1}{n_2}\right) \quad \text{.....}(iv)$$

The value of *t* significant at a particular level of confidence decreases with the increase in N, the size of the sample used in the experiment. The table showing the values of *t* significant at different levels of confidence for the increasing size of N is reproduced on p. 323. One has to use N-1 and not N for the respective values of *t* in the table. While using identical groups, or matched groups, N is equal to the number in the group, or the number of pairs constituting the matched groups. With random groups N is equal to the sum of the number of subjects used in all the groups taken together. Supposing there are three random groups each containing 10 subjects, N will be equal to 30 and the values of *t* significant at different levels of confidence (p. 323) have to be looked up for N-3 or 27; each group losing what has been called one degree of freedom. By degree of freedom is meant the freedom to change the values constituting a single set or column of measures. Suppose a group of 10 S's obtains the following scores in learning a list of words :

6, 5, 8, 6, 7, 5, 4, 7, 6, 4

The sum of the scores from which we calculate the mean is 58. With the sum given and nine out of ten scores also given, it is not possible for you to alter the tenth score, without altering the total also; your freedom is restricted. But when more than one scores are missing, these could assume any value without affecting the total. For example, the fourth and fifth scores in the series could be 9 & 4, 10 & 3, 8 & 5, 11 & 2 or 12 & 1, instead of 6 & 7. But once you accept 6 or 7, the other score cannot but be 7 or 6. Thus in a column of measures you lose one degree of freedom. We use formula (iii) in calculating the $SE_{diff.}$ when employing an identical group or matched groups (p. 312, 315). We use the D scores , i. e., the difference between the scores in the two conditions, for the purpose. Hence the loss is of one degree of freedom. But using randomised groups, we treat the scores for each group separately and hence each set of scores loses one degree of freedom, which together add up.

The formulae given above (p. 320) apply when comparing two groups or two sets of measures at a time. If there are more than two groups, or two conditions, one has to find $SE_{diff.}$ between the different combinations of two groups or two conditions, and calculate as many t values. This difficulty can be overcome by using an overall test for comparison between groups, two or more, used in the experiment. This test, called F test, employs the so-called method of analysis of variance. You can consult any standard book on statistical methods to learn the method of analysis of variance.

Factorial Design

The types of experiments we have considered in this book call for the manipulation of a single independent variable. It is possible however to manipulate more than one independent variable in the same experiment, and ascertain the effect of each one on the dependent variable, besides determining their joint effect. The analysis of data will thus yield the **main effects** of the two or more independent variables and their **interaction**. In the experiment on 'Task homogeneity and effect of spacing in psychomotor work' (p. 262), we are actually manipulating two independent variables, namely, (1) task homogeneity and (2) spacing of performance. We planned the experiment in two parts and to counter-balance the effect of sequence we suggested the abcddcba design. A more convenient design that would yield also a more meaningful result would be :

Massed — Homogeneous, Heterogenous

Spaced — Homogeneous, Heterogenous

The design would employ four random groups, randomly assigned to massing and spacing of performance, and randomly assigned homogeneous and heterogenous tasks. For the analysis of the data, one uses the method of analysis of variance, where the analysis results in the partitioning of the main effects of the two independent variables, separately, and of their interaction. You may find significant difference between massing and spacing, also between performance on a homogeneous and that on a heterogenous task; but you may notice the effect of spacing significant when using a homogeneous task and not so when using a heterogenous task, that is, interaction between the two variables; the last result would support your main hypothesis (p. 262) ; this could not be as conclusive without using the factorial design.

You may have even more than two independent variables manipulated in the experiment. There may also be cases when one or two independent variables are manipulated, while still another is assigned. The independent variable that is manipulated has been called active variable; that one which is not manipulated is called assigned variable. For example, you may seek to find the difference in reaction to experimentally induced frustration (p. 275) arising from the difference in level of measured intelligence, or anxiety. The subjects will then be assigned to high intelligence and low intelligence, or high anxiety and low anxiety, groups on the basis of their scores in a test of intelligence or anxiety. Intelligence or anxiety is, thus, not manipulated by the experimenter. The subjects are already characterised by it in different measures. But when you set your subjects into two groups, namely, frustrated and ot frustrated, this happens because you have experimentally manipulated frustration; you have induced frustration by your remarks in one group and you have not done this with the other group.

Utilization of Individual Data Fitted to the Design of a Group Experiment

The student has to depend in a degree course in laboratory experiments, or may be even in the postgraduate course, on individual data. But the instructor can plan a group experiment and obtain data for the experiment on individual basis. After having decided about the problem, he should discuss the same with the different practical batches that he has to meet. Supposing, he decides to plan an experiment on the mediation hypothesis. He uses the following paradigms :

(i)	A-B,	B-C,	A-C
(ii)	A-B,	B-D,	A-C
(iii)	A-B,	D-E,	A-C

He prepares five PA lists and introduces them, fitting the lists in the three paradigms, to each batch he meets, explaining the general hypothesis about mediation (p. 303). He then describes the specific hypothesis that is proposed to be tested, namely, the acquisition of the third test will be least difficult in paradigm (i), and equally difficult in paradigms (ii) and (iii). He then divides the students in each batch into three randomised groups and also randomly assigns the groups to the three paradigms (p. 314), explaining the method used by him. The students that are assigned to a paradigm are then supplied the lists for that paradigm. They are asked to use the usual method of PA learning (p. 155), employing the improvised device for exposure of the items (p. 148). Each one is then asked to obtain data from a single subject outside the laboratory. The data obtained by the students in the different batches are then dictated, classified paradigm wise, by the instructo on the respective days when he meets them next. Each student tabulates the data and plots graphs for the three learning stages of the three paradigms. He compares the learning scores for the respective lists in the the three paradigms, to examine the main hypothesis, as well as to judge on the basis of the scores in the first list whether the assignment of the subjects to the three paradigms was really random. To be random, the A-B learning should involve equal difficulty in each paradigm. Further, the rate of the second stage learning should also be the same in paradigms (i) and (ii) and the learning should presumably be more difficult than the second stage learning in paradigm (iii) because of the transfer effect from first stage learning (p. 193). The student uses the t test for the statistical analysis; he may also use the method of analysis of variance in case he has learned this method. If the result shows that the learning of the A-C list involved the same difficulty in paradigms (i) and (ii), or that A-C learning in paradigm (iii) was more difficult than that in paradigm (ii), the mediation hypothesis would be untenable. An alternative explanation, namely, inter-list interference, becomes more plausible. According to this hypothesis the second stage learning in Paradigms I and II is interfered with because of the competition of response; the B term in the second list evokes by backward association (p. 190) the A term of the first list, which has to be dropped before the acquisition of the association between B and C or D of the second list. The weakening of the A-B association would lessen the interference it would otherwise cause to the acquisition of the A-C association. The rate of the third list learning will, therefore, be the same in paradigms I and II. This is not the case for the learning of the A-C list in paradigm (iii); the strength of the A-B association interferes with the acquisition of the A-C list. Hence the last stage learning becomes more difficult in this paradigm than the last stage learning not only in paradigm (i) but also in paradigm (ii).

It may be worthwhile to introduce the method of group experiments to the students in the manner suggested above. The requirements for the laboratory course may include reports on two or three group experiments on the basis of data pooled from individual experiments.

VALUE OF t SIGNIFICANT AT DIFFERENT LEVELS OF CONFIDENCE FOR VARYING DEGREES OF FREEDOM

df (N-1)	p= .1	.05	.02	.01	.001
1	6.314	12.706	31.821	63.657	636.619
2	2.920	4.303	6,965	9.925	31.598
3	2.353	3.182	4.541	5.841	12.941
4	2.132	2.776	3.747	4.604	8.610
5	2.015	2.571	3.365	4.032	6.859
6	1.943	2.447	3.143	3.707	5.959
7	1.895	2.365	2.998	3.499	5.405
8	1.860	2.306	2.896	3.355	5.041
9	1.833	2.262	2.821	3.250	4.781
10	1.812	2.228	2.764	3.169	4.587
11	1.796	2.201	2.718	3.106	4.437
12	1.782	2.179	2.681	3.055	4.318
13	1.771	2.160	2.650	3.012	4.221
14	1.761	2.145	2.624	2.977	4.140
15	1.753	2.131	2.602	2.947	4.073
16	1.746	2.120	2.583	2.921	4.015
17	1.740	2.110	2.567	2.898	3.965
18	1.734	2.101	2.552	2.878	3,922
19	1.729	2.093	2.539	2.861	3.883
20	1.725	2.086	2.528	2.845	3.850
21	1.721	2.080	2.518	2.831	3.819
22	1.717	2.074	2.508	2.819	3.792
23	1.714	2.069	2.500	2.807	3.767
24	1.711	2,064	2.492	2.797	3.745
25	1.708	2.060	2.485	2.787	3.725
26	1.706	2.056	2.479	2.779	3.707
27	1.703	2.052	2.473	2.771	3.690
28	1.701	2.048	2.467	2.763	3.674
29	1.699	2.045	2.462	2.756	3.659

df (N-1)	p= .1	.05	.02	.01	.001
30	1.697	2.042	2.457	2.750	3.646
40	1.684	2.021	2.423	2.704	3.551
60	1.671	2.000	2.390	2.660	3.460
120	1.658	1.980	2.358	2.617	3.373
200	1.645	1.960	2.326	2.576	3.291

Recommended Readings

Brown, C. W. and Ghiselli, E. E., *Scientific Method in Psychology*, McGraw-Hill, New York, 1955.

McGuigan, F. J., *Experimental Psychology*, Chapters 5, 8, 9, Prentice-Hall, New York, 1969.

Underwood, B. J., *Experimental Psychology*, Chapters 2, 4, Appleton, New York, 1966.

APPENDIX II

List of Experiments Reported and Described or Suggested

CHAPTER IV

Psychophysical Experiments

1. Extent of Muller-Lyer illusion using the method of average error (Reported).
2. Error in the perception of visual length (visual area).
3. Extent of the horizontal-vertical illusion.
4. Effect of knowledge of result on the extent of the Muller-Lyer (horizontal-vertical) illusion.
5. Effect of bisection of the .horizontal line on the magnitude of the horizontal vertical illusion.
6. Error of the visual estimation of size (coin).
7. Two-point threshold .(aesthesiometric index , spatial threshold) by the method of limits (Reported).
8. Error of habituation and expectation as correlates of the attitudes of conservatism and radicalism.
9. Comparison between aesthesiometric indices determined for any two regions on the skin surface.
10. Effect of muscular fatigue on the two-point threshold.
11. DL for hue, using the method of limits.
12. Demonstration of the laws of colour mixing, using the method of limits.
13. RL for auditory acuity.
14. Demonstration of the Gestalt Law of Closure.
15. DL for visual length by using the method of limits (Reported).
16. DL for grey.
17. DL for two-point distance on the skin surface.
18. Span of apprehension, using the method of constant stimuli (Reported).
19. Difference in the span of apprehension for digits and unrelated letters (unrelated letters and words).
20. RL for hue, using the method of constant stimuli.
21. Verification of Weber's law with reference to lifted weights (Reported).
22. DL, using two-category judgments.
23. DL for visual area.

Chapter V

Attention

24. Span of attention as a function of organisation of stimulus materials.
25. Span of apprehension as a function of the heterogeneity of stimulus materials.
26. Span of apprehension as a function of knowledge of result.
27. Auditory distraction and span of visual apprehension (Reported).
28. Distracting effect of noise on the span of apprehension as a function of the complexity of task or materials to which attention is given.
29. Effect of noise on sensory-motor (mental) task.
30. Fluctuation of attention.
31. Respiration and fluctuation of attention.
32. Effect of division of attention on the performance of a psychomotor task.
33. Performing two tasks at a time : a test of the automatisation versus shift hypotheses.

Chapter VI

Perception

34. Rate of alternation in a reversible figure.
35. Rate of alternation in a reversible perspective and retinal adaptation (fatigue, reactive inhibition).
36. Relative dominance of alternating figures in a reversible perspective as a function of angular size (colour, or saturation) of the stimulus pattern.
37. Effect of instructionally induced set on the perception of a reversible figure (Reported).
38. Binocular cues in depth perception.
39. Perception of time : extent and direction of error.
40. Perception of long versus short time.
41. Perception of filled versus unfilled time.
42. Perception of time as a measure of task monotony.

Chapter VII

Sensory-Motor Learning

43. The hand-withdrawal reflex—conditioning and extinction.
44. The eye-lid closure reflex—conditioning and extinction.
45. Mirror-tracing : sensory-motor learning.
46. Learning the maze pattern—sensory-motor learning (Reported).
47. Sensory-motor learning—the punch board maze.
48. The pursuit rotor—acquisition of the tracking behaviour.

Chapter VIII

Verbal Learning

49. Learning of nonsense materials by the method of serial (free) recall.

50. Learning by the method of serial anticipation (prompting and anticipation).

51. Role of reinforcement in verbal learning (serial learning and serial anticipation—a comparison).

52. The bow-shaped serial position curve of verbal learning.

53. The serial position curve : serial anticipation versus free recall (serial recall versus free recall).

54. Serial position effect and learning of related items (cluster effect in verbal learning).

55. Cluster effect as a function of method of learning—free recall versus serial learning (serial anticipation).

56. Organisation level of listed items and rate of learning.

57. Role of reinforcement in paired-associates learning.

58. Learning as a function of meaningfulness of the learning material.

59. Rate of learning as a function of relatedness of the learning material.

60. Rate of learning of related items as a function of the method of learning—free recall versus serial anticipation.

61. Learning as a function of the amount of learning material.

62. Probability of correct recall as a function of presentation time of items in verbal learning.

63. Total time given to the learning task and not the number of trials as crucial element in learning.

64. Rate of learning as a function of intra-serial similarity.

65. Intra-serial similarity and method of learning nonsense syllables (trigrams) — free recall versus serial recall (serial anticipation).

66. Intra-serial inhibition and degree of intra-list similarity in serial learning.

67. Intra-list similarity and paired-associates learning.

68. Rate of learning and massing versus spacing of practice (Reported).

69. Effect of spacing as a function of the difference between the methods of learning.

70. Spacing of practice and paired-associates learning.

71. Differential gain from spacing in learning of meaningful versus nonsense materials.

72. Effect of differential location of rest intervals on the rate of learning.

73. The optimal length of interval in distributed practice.

74. Relative efficacy of part versus whole methods of learning.

75. Incidental versus intentional learning.

76. Active versus passive learning.

77. Verbal conditioning.

CHAPTER IX

Transfer of Training

78. Bilateral transfer in mirror-tracing.
79. Eye to eye transfer in mirror-tracing.
80. Change of orientation of movement and transfer in mirror-tracing.
81. Transfer in mirror-tracing as a function of change of orientation and the hand engaged.
82. Negative transfer in mirror-tracing.
83. Pattern transfer.
84. Habit facilitation in maze learning.
85. Change of orientation and transfer effect in maze learning.
86. Effect of reversal of movement on transfer in maze learning.
87. Habit interference in sensory-motor learning (Reported).
88. Effect of the acquisition of forward association in paired-associates learning on the acquisition of backward association.
89. Paired-associates learning as a function of response familiarity.
90. Negative transfer (habit interference) in verbal learning (Reported).
91. Transfer in paired-associates learning as a function of stimulus generalisation.

CHAPTER X

Remembering and Forgetting

92. Comparison between recall and recognition as tests of retention.
93. Relationship between meaningfulness and retention.
94. Retention and amount of the learned material.
95. Retention and level of learning.
96. Relationship between retention and level of over-learning.
97. Retention and spaced learning.
98. Retention and affective tone of the learning material.
99. Time as a factor in forgetting.
100. Retention as a function of the activity interpolated between learning and retention test (Retroactive inhibition).
101. Retention as a function of the task immediately preceding the learning activity (Proactive inhibition).
102. Retroactive Inhibition as a function of similarity (Reported).
103. Retroactive inhibition and temporal location of the interpolated activity.
104. Spontaneous recovery and amount of retroactive inhibition.
105. Retroactive inhibition as a function of the level of original learning.
106. Retroactive inhibition as a function of the level of interpolated activity.
107. Differential amounts of forgetting in RI and PI.
108. Effect of reminiscence in verbal learning.
109. Reminiscence and massing and spacing of practice.
110. Reminiscence and position of an item in the list.

111. Reminiscence and length of exposure of an item.
112. Reminiscence and intra-list similarity.
113. Reminiscence and paired associates learning.

CHAPTER XI

Reaction Time

114. Reaction time as a function of the type of stimulus.
115. Reaction time as a function of strength or intensity of stimulus.
116. Muscular versus sensory reaction time (RT as a function of effector versus receptor preparedness).
117. Reaction time as a function of practice.
118. Reaction time as an indirect measure of muscular fatigue.
119. Reaction time as a function of the length of fore-period.
120. Effect of temporal set on RT.
121. The role of incentive in reaction time.
122. Reaction time as a function of eye dominance.
123. The effect of summation of retinal stimulation on the length of visual Reaction time.
124. Length of reaction time and choice between a positive and a negative response versus that between positive responses to multiple stimuli.
125. Stimulus similarity and length of reaction time.
126. Length of reaction time and complexity of the stimulus-response situation (complex reaction time) (Reported).
127. Reaction time as a function of the aesthetic value of the stimulus.
128. Reaction time as a function of stimulus-response compatibility.
129. Associative reaction time : controlled versus free word-association test.
130. Influence of set on word reaction time.
131. Word association test as a complex indicator.

CHAPTER XII

Feeling and Emotion

132. Measuring feeling values (attitudes) by the pair-comparison method.
133. Respiratory changes as correlates of emotions.
134. Respiration and affective states of the organism.
135. Respiratory changes in continued mental work.
136. Respiration and fluctuation of attention.

CHAPTER XIII

Work and Fatigue

137. Effect of massing and spacing of performance on the efficiency of motor work.
138. The ergogram as a measure of endurance capacity.

139. Relationship between work output and work pace.
140. Determination of the optimal rest period for physical work.
141. The optimal location of rest period for motor work.
142. Work performance as a function of worker's attitude to work (Reported).
143. Role of rest pauses in the efficiency of psycho-motor work.
144. Task homogeneity and effect of spacing in psycho-motor work.
145. Effect of rest pause on the efficiency of mental work.
146. Control and accuracy of voluntary movement.
147. Control of involuntary movements.
148. Steadiness test as a measure of endurance.
149. Control of movement as an indirect measure of fatigue.

CHAPTER XIV
Motivation

150. Effect of knowledge of result on performance (Reported).
151. Memory for finished and unfinished tasks.
152. Effect of frustration on performance.
153. Perceptual defense.
154. Effect of success and failure on level of aspiration.
155. Study of goal setting behaviour.
156. Self-concept and goal setting behaviour.
157. Group norm and level of aspiration.

CHAPTER XV
Thinking

158. Set in problem solving (Reported).
159. The role of class-set in problem solving.
160. Instructional set versus response-induced set in problem solving.
161. The role of implicit association in problem solving.
162. Associative chaining and problem solution.
163. Concept attainment.
164. Task complexity and concept identification (Reported).
165. Associative mediation effect in verbal learning (Reported).

APPENDIX III

Psychological Apparatus

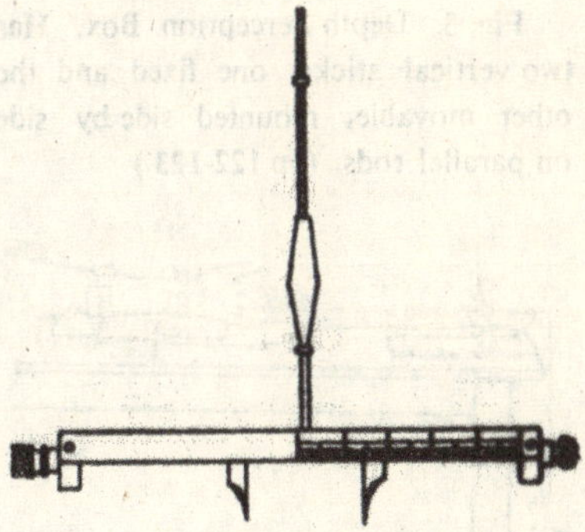

Fig. 1. Aesthesiometer. The distance between the rounded points can be varied for measuring the two-point threshold. (pp. 70 & 81)

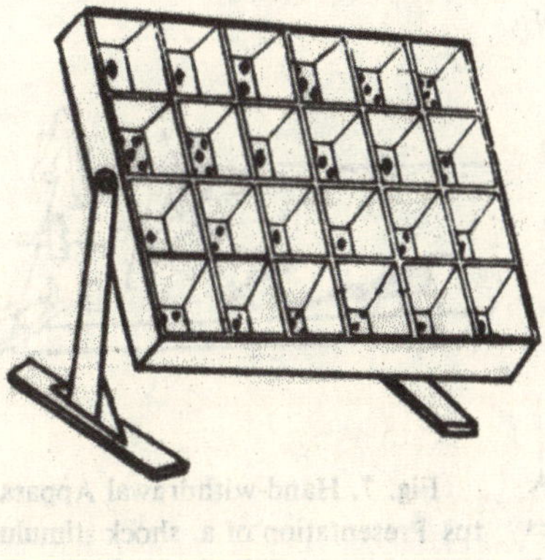

Fig. 2. Card sorting Tray. Each compartment has a playing card pasted on its side wall. (pp. 186-187)

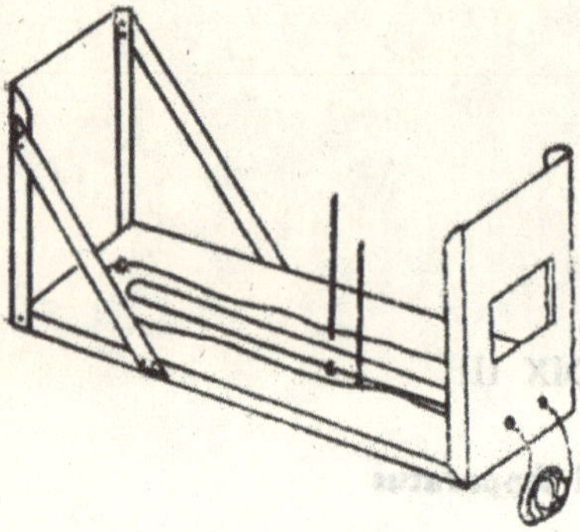

Fig. 3 Depth Perception Box. Has two vertical sticks, one fixed and the other movable, mounted side by side on parallel rods. (pp 122-123)

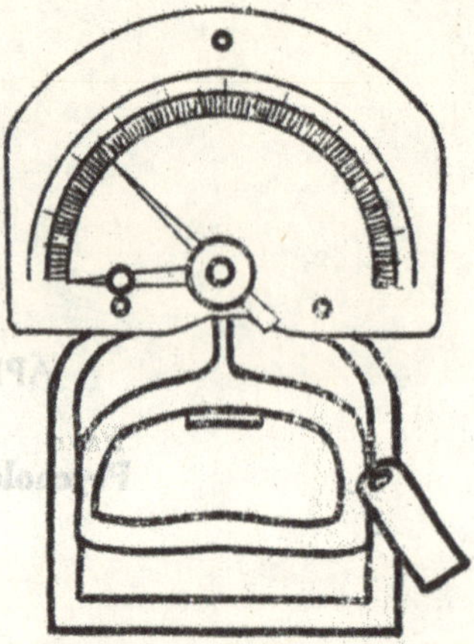

Fig. 6. Hand Dynamometer. Contains a hand grip which when squeezed measures the strength of grip. (pp. 75 & 233)

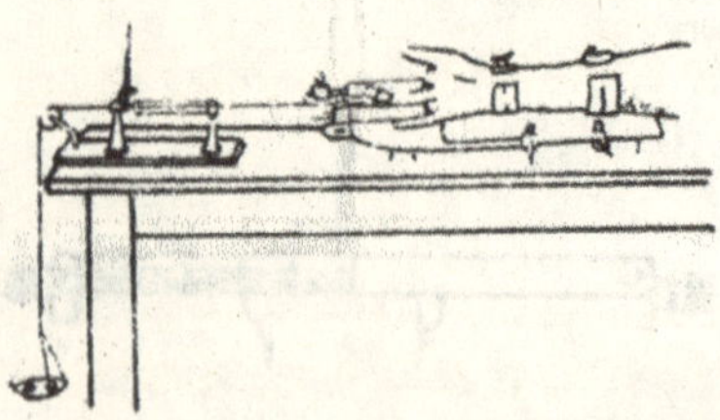

Fig. 4. Ergograph. Subject pulls a weight by moving forward his first finger, inserted in a loop, at regular intervals. (pp 16 & 255)

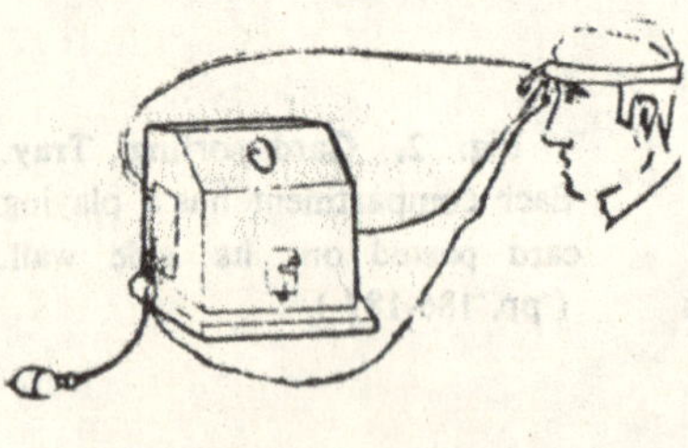

Fig. '5.Eyelid-closure Apparatus. A puff of air is delivered which causes automatic dripping of the subject's eyelid. (p. 138)

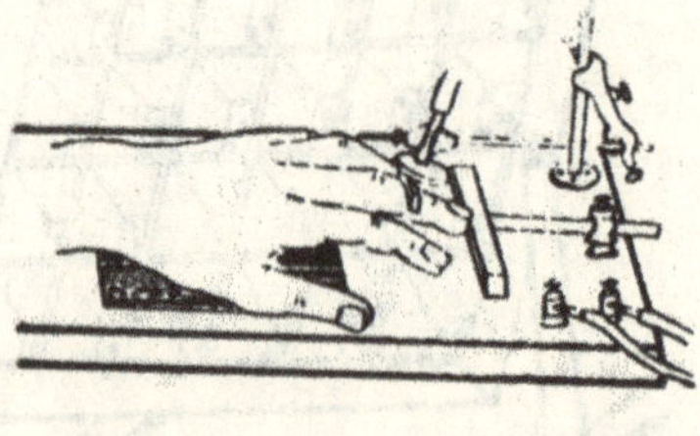

Fig. 7. Hand-withdrawal Apparatus Presentation of a shock stimulus causes automatic withdrawal of subject's hand. (pp 137-138)

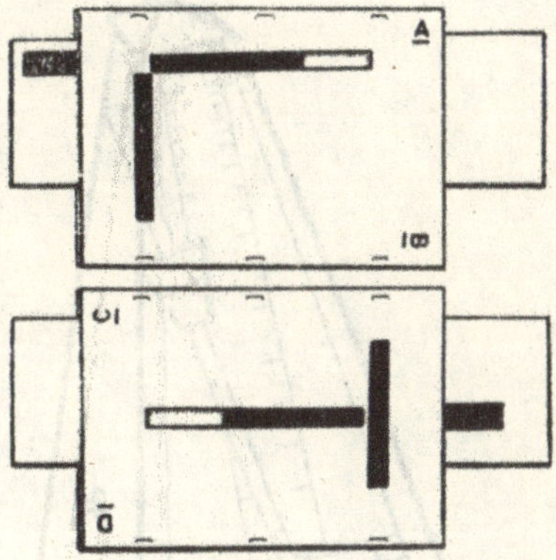

Fig. 8. Horizontal-vertical Illusion Board. The length of the horizontal line can be varied by moving one piece back and forth. (p. 69)

A

B

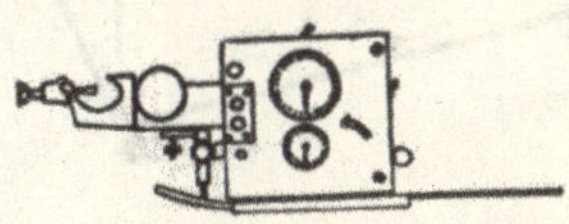

C

Fig. 9. Kymograph : (A) A rotating drum having its surface covered by smoked paper. Its speed of movement can be varied at will. The pointers of the Time-marker (B) and the Chronometer (C) are held in a position to touch the smoked surface. (pp. 26, 106, 118, & 129)

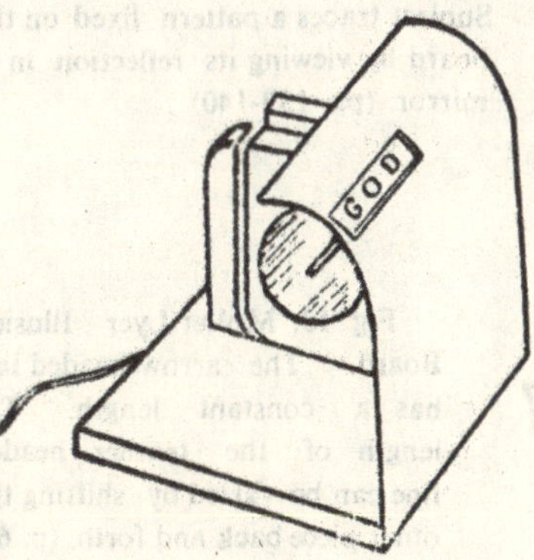

Fig. 10. Memory Drum. The drum moves intermittently, providing a brief exposure to items of a list attached to the surface of the drum. (pp. 26 & 148)

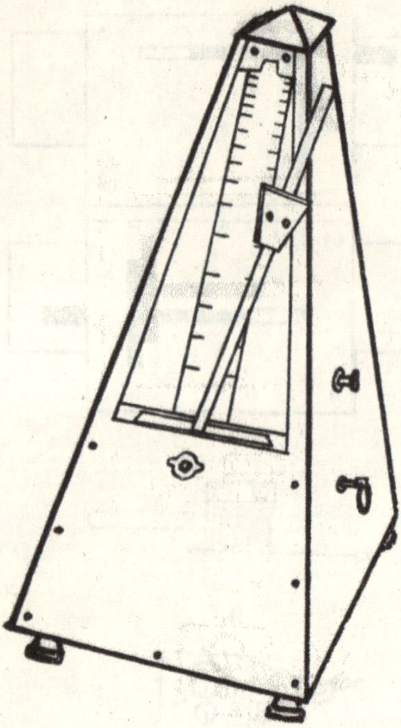

Fig. 11. Metronome. Used for producing ticking sounds at regular intervals which can be varied by shifting a clamp up and down. (pp. 16, 86 & 256)

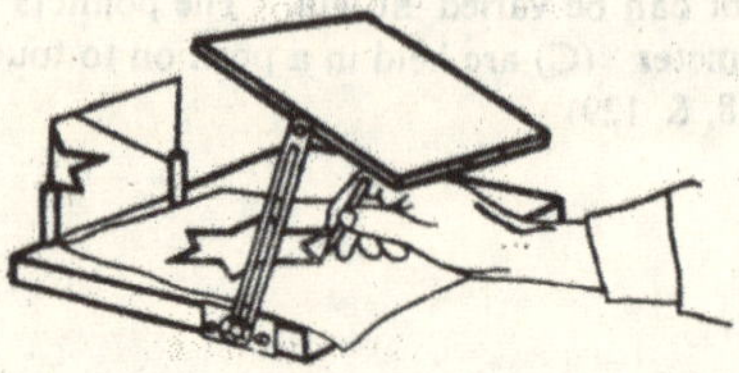

Fig. 12. Mirror-tracing Board. Subject traces a pattern fixed on the board by viewing its reflection in a mirror. (pp. 139-140)

Fig. 13. Muller Lyer Illusion Board. The arrow-headed line has a constant length. The length of the feather headed line can be varied by shifting the otner piece back and forth. (p. 62)

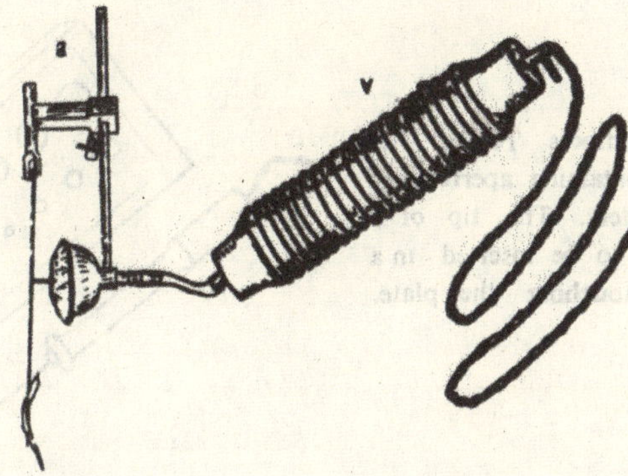

Fig. 14. Pneumograph : (A) A rubber hose held about the chest with a Tambour (B) attached to a rubber tube connected with one end of the hose. (p. 246)

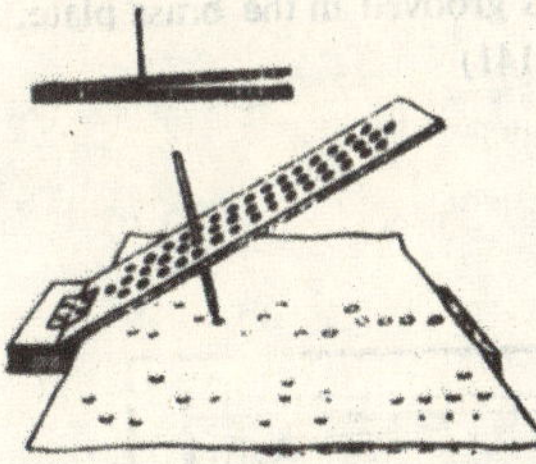

Fig. 15. Punch Board Maze. The lower piece has only one hole in each row corresponding to one of several holes of the row in the upper piece. (pp. 141-142)

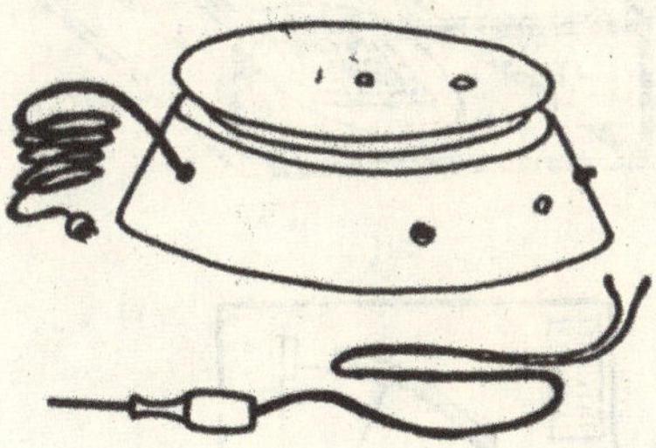

Fig. 16. Pursuit Rotor. The rotating disc has a metal spot near the outer edge. (p. 142)

Fig. 17. Rotator. A disc is mounted on the rotator for high speed rotation, also called colour wheel. (pp. 75, 80 & 106)

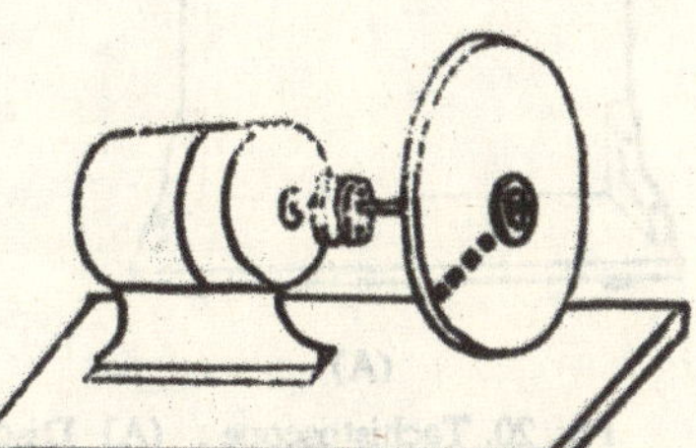

Fig. 18. Steadiness Tester. Has a metal plate containing apertures of various diameters. The tip of a metal stylus has to be inserted in a hole without touching the plate. (p. 265)

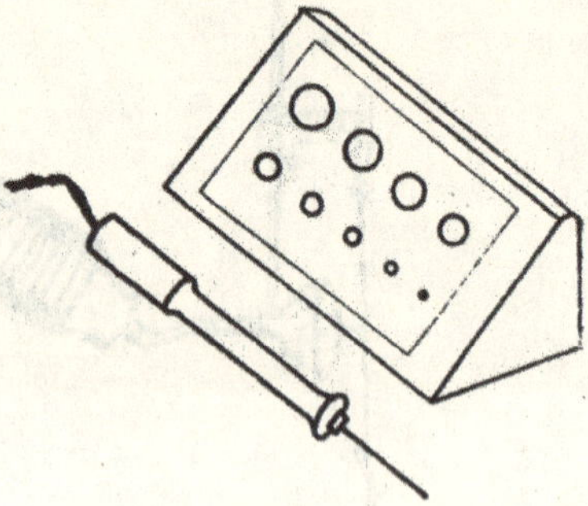

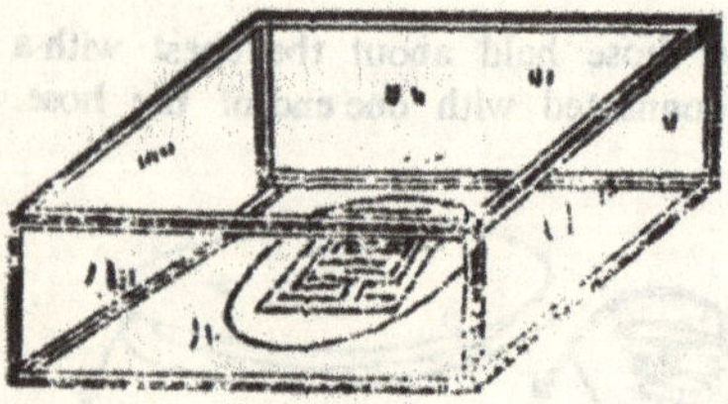

Fig. 19. Stylus Maze. A maze pattern is grooved in the brass plate. (pp. 140-141)

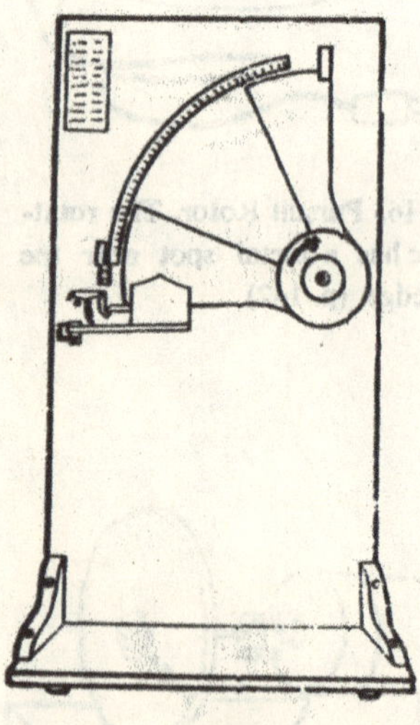

(A)

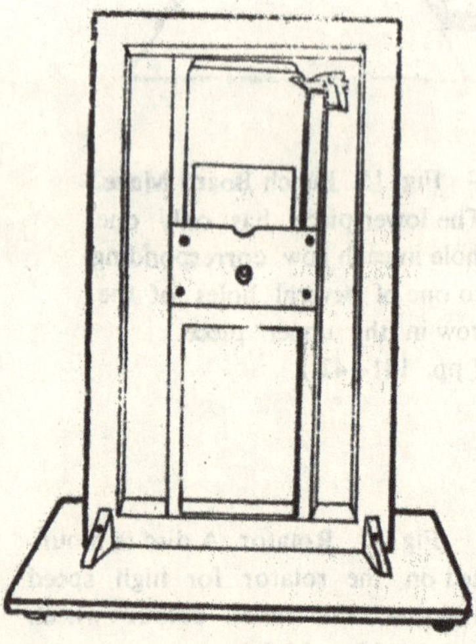

(B)

Fig. 20. Tachistoscope : (A) Disc. (B) Fall. Used for providing brief exposure to a visual stimulus. The disc type also provides for varying the exposure time. (pp. 26, 81 & 101)

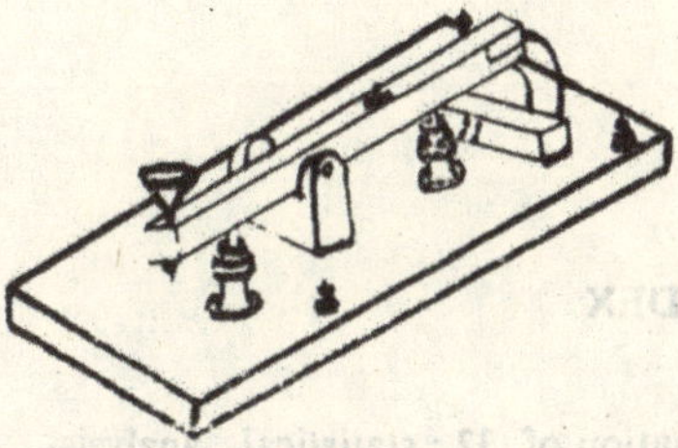

Fig. 21. Telegraphic Key. The pressing and releasing of the key makes and breaks an electric circuit. (pp. 106, 118, 124, 126 & 129)

Fig. 22. Tracing Board. The tip of the stylus has to be moved through the narrow path between the metal strips fixed on the board. (pp. 264-265)

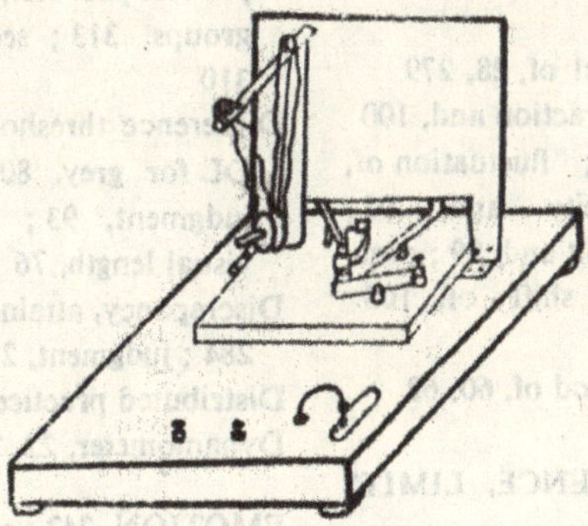

Fig. 23. Vernier Chronoscope. Used for measuring reaction time. (pp. 230-231)

SUBJECT INDEX